KU-209-354

Encounter with God

Every Day for a Year

Edited by Andrew C Clark

Scripture Union, 207–209 Queensway, Bletchley, MK2 2EB, England.
www.scriptureunion.org.uk

Scripture Union is an international Christian charity working with churches in more than 130 countries providing resources to bring the good news about Jesus Christ to children, young people and families – and to encourage them to develop spiritually through the Bible and prayer.

As well as our network of volunteers, staff and associates who run holidays, church-based events and school Christian groups, we produce a wide range of publications and support those who use our resources through training programmes.

Reprinted 2007
ISBN 978 1 85999 670 6

British Library Cataloguing-in-Publication Data
A catalogue record for this book is available from the British Library.

Cover design mhm grax

Printed and bound in China by 1010 Printing International Ltd.

Preface

The Bible can be understood in many ways. It is, of course, the inspired and living Word of God, our primary authority on all questions of faith and Christian lifestyle. It is our mission statement and our vision, our insight into the will of God for us. It is also a collection of writings of vastly different styles written over a period of many hundreds of years. Simply reading the Bible is enough to change people's lives, yet who would say they could not benefit from new insights into its stories, adventures, prayers and prophecies?

Bible reading notes help readers place each book of the Bible in its historical, cultural and biblical context and give guidance on how we may respond to God's Word in our daily lives. Published by Scripture Union every three months, *Encounter with God* offers daily notes on every book of the Bible: our syllabus covers the New Testament in four years and the Old Testament in six.

Encounter with God: every day for a year represents some of the best writing produced for our Bible reading notes over the last four years. Our international team of writers, which includes top scholars, and well-known Bible expositors and pastors, have drawn on their learning and practical experience to trace the story of our redemption.

In Exodus we learn how God delivered his people from bondage in Egypt; chapters 1–39 of Isaiah include prophecies concerning the coming of the promised Messiah; the Gospels of Luke and John portray the life and ministry of Jesus, while Ephesians and Hebrews spell out the significance of his death and resurrection for believers. Other books fill out the picture and give us a taste of the varied literary genres the Bible contains.

We do hope you will encounter God in his Word over the next year in the company of our gifted writers.

Andrew Clark and Venetia Horton

Editors, *Encounter with God*

If you would like to know more about Scripture Union, or would like to subscribe to Encounter with God, *please contact us at www.scriptureunion.org.uk or write to us at 207/209 Queensway, Bletchley, Milton Keynes MK2 2EB.*

Contents

The Writers

Dr T Desmond Alexander is currently Director of Christian Training for the Presbyterian Church in Ireland. He is author of *From Paradise to the Promised Land* (Paternoster); *The Servant King* (IVP), and *The Pentateuch* (Paternoster).

Rt Rev Michael Baughen is the retired Bishop of Chester and a former Rector of All Souls Langham Place. He is the author of a number of books including *The Prayer Principle* and *Your Marriage*.

Rev Merryl Blair is Lecturer in Old Testament studies at Churches of Christ Theological College, Melbourne.

Rev Dr Alastair Campbell was until recently pastor of the Kathmandu International Christian Church. Before that he taught the New Testament at Spurgeon's College in London.

Dr Andrew Clark is commissioning editor of *Encounter with God.* He previously taught in Bible colleges in Hong Kong as an OMF missionary. He is the author of *Parallel Lives*, a study of literary parallels between characters in the book of Acts.

Rev Ian Coffey is a preacher, teacher and writer. He is Senior Minister at Mutley Baptist Church, Plymouth, and also leader of the Spring Harvest leadership team.

Ken Edgecombe is a freelance writer and editor. His latest book, on adolescent faith, is *Will they or won't they?* (SU). He is a former National Director of Scripture Union in New Zealand.

Rev Dr Dick France is an Anglican clergyman and New Testament teacher. Now retired, he is the former principal of Wycliffe Hall, Oxford. He has written a number of books including the Tyndale commentary on Matthew.

Rev John Fieldsend is an Anglican clergyman and a Messianic Jew. He was born in Czechoslovakia. Now retired, he was previously director of the Centre for Biblical and Hebraic Studies.

Rev Paul Goodliff is Baptist Union General Superintendent for the Central region of England. He tutors in pastoral counselling for St John's College Extension Studies, and is author of the book *Care in a confused climate.*

John Grayston is Director of Bible Ministries for Scripture Union in England and Wales. He enjoys skiing.

Richard Harvey lectures at All Nations Christian College. He has an MA in Hebrew and Jewish studies, and was formerly the UK director of Jews for Jesus.

Dr Pauline Hoggarth is International Bible Ministries Co-ordinator for Scripture Union. Her interests include cooking, gardening, cinema, and conversation.

Peter Kimber was until recently Chief Executive and Team Leader of Scripture Union in England and Wales. Now retired in Edinburgh, he enjoys golf.

Whitney Kuniholm is the President of Scripture Union in the USA. He has written a number of books in the area of personal and group Bible study.

Jonathan Lamb is Associate General Secretary of the International Fellowship of Evangelical Students, with special responsibility for Europe. He is a member of the Council of the Evangelical Alliance and the Keswick Convention.

Rev Dennis Lennon was previously Evangelism Adviser to the Anglican Diocese of Sheffield. He is married to Sonja and his books include *Weak enough for God to use* (SU).

Rev Hans Lindholm is pastor of Lötenkryken, Uppsala, and chair of Scripture Union in Sweden. Formerly he was General Secretary of the Swedish IFES-affiliated movement.

Rosemary Linton teaches Christian Spirituality at All Nations Christian College. A native of Northern Ireland, she taught missionaries' children in the Philippines for nine years.

Evelyn Miranda-Feliciano is a best-selling Filipina Christian writer and a lecturer with the Institute for Studies in Asian Church and Culture (ISACC).

Rev Dr Steve Motyer is Lecturer in New Testament and Hermeneutics at London Bible College. He enjoys cycling and gardening and the company of his teenage children, and is the author of several books including *The Bible with Pleasure* (IVP).

Rev Howard Peskett is Vice-Principal at Trinity College, Bristol. Formerly Research Director of OMF, his publications include *Trusting God in Troubled Times* and *Isaiah* (SU *Lifebuilder* guide).

Rev Ross Pilkinton is a former Scripture Union worker in New Zealand. Until recently he lived in Nepal, where he and his wife Marcelle ran a missionary guest house. He also had pastoral responsibilities with the International Nepal Fellowship.

Morris Stuart serves as pastor of the Truth and Liberation Concern Community Church in Melbourne's Outer Eastern suburbs.

Rt Rev John B Taylor is the former Bishop of St Albans, and a writer on the Old Testament. He is also Honorary Assistant Bishop in the Diocese of Ely and the Diocese of Europe.

Grace Thomlinson is involved in Christian resource production and community learning at World Vision, Australia. She has lectured on Christian Ethics and the Old Testament, and shares music ministry with her husband Geoffrey.

Rev Dr Jennifer Turner is Minister of Dianella Church of Christ, Western Australia, lecturer in Pastoral Theology at the Baptist Theological College, and a writer with a special interest in the Bible and small groups.

Rev Dr Rikk Watts is Associate Professor of New Testament at Regent College, Vancouver. An Australian, he is the author of a book on the use of Isaiah in Mark.

Rev Dr Jo Bailey Wells is Lecturer in Old Testament and Biblical Theology at Ridley Hall college in Cambridge. Formerly Dean of Clare College, Cambridge, she is the author of *God's holy people; a theme in biblical theology*. She relaxes by walking her dog with her husband and young daughter.

Robert Willoughby lectures on the New Testament at London Bible College. He is a keen lover of books, music and sport.

From bondage to freedom

Exodus chronicles the key event in the Old Testament, the escape of the slaves from Egypt. Under the leadership of Moses, the Israelites leave their place of bondage and set off for the land of freedom – Canaan. On the way they camp at Mount Sinai, where Moses receives the Law. The covenants and promises God made to Abraham in Genesis are confirmed through Moses. The celebration of the first Passover brings Israel to birth as a *nation*. The Passover sacrifice brings the people of Israel into covenant relationship with God. The Law that will be received on Mount Sinai gives the ground rules for life in the Promised Land – in social, spiritual and personal terms.

The book of Exodus can be divided into three sections: the escape from Egypt, the wanderings in the desert and the receiving of the Law on Mount Sinai. The story has all the thrills of an adventure. The plot twists and turns, as the Pharaoh, Moses and Aaron interact on a knife-edge of tension. The atmosphere is charged with the Israelites' cries to God. Miraculous events accompany their escape.

The name of the book, Exodus (meaning 'going out'), is derived from the Greek version of the Old Testament, the Septuagint. In Jewish tradition the book is called after the Hebrew words that begin the first chapter, *'ve'eleh shemot'* – 'These are the names'. This shows a clear continuation of the story of the patriarchs, which ended in Genesis 49 and 50 with Jacob blessing his sons before dying. The blessing on Judah contains a clear prophecy of the Messiah who would come to restore sovereignty to Israel (Genesis 49:10). Yet Exodus 1 opens with a very different scene – that of oppression and attempted genocide. The promises to the patriarchs are forgotten, as a new king arises who 'knew not Joseph' (AV).

In Jewish life the story of Exodus comes alive each year at Passover. Each year, at a special meal of unleavened bread, bitter herbs and four cups of wine, the story of Passover is recounted, with joy and celebration. The hero of the story is Moses. These early chapters show him in his humanity and weakness, in contrast with God's almighty power and love.

Lessons for us

As Christians we have much to learn from Exodus. Not only did God go to even greater lengths to rescue his people, the church, from slavery to sin, but in Jesus – the Lamb of God who also was sent to die at Passover – one greater than Moses came in weakness and humanity, to reveal the power and love of God.

It is not enough to rely on the witness of previous generations, or on our own early experience of God's love. We need to encounter daily the reality of God. We may face difficulties today in our life, our work, our health or our relationships, but this should not cause us to lose hope. We have in Jesus the strong assurance of God's presence with us, and his ability to bring us through our difficulties. Jewish tradition speaks of the suffering of the slaves, and reminds us that they looked forward to the promises of God that would one day be fulfilled: even the most bitter form of slavery is made sweet with the promise of redemption.

The book of Exodus reveals God in his power, his choosing of Israel and his instructions to them. It shows the need for redemption and forgiveness of sin. It teaches us that God is faithful to his promises, and will provide deliverance from bondage – whether bondage in Egypt or bondage to sin – to those that trust in the 'blood of the Lamb'. As we follow Moses from his birth to his challenge to Pharaoh to let the people go, we see the hand of God in all aspects of the story. We, like Moses, are called to serve a redeeming God.

Richard Harvey

Promise, fulfilment, problem!

Day 1

Moses' long life is filled with Joseph's dying hope: 'God will surely come to your aid'.[1] Spend some time reflecting on this promise.

Exodus 1: 1–22 

The list of those who went to Egypt with Joseph four hundred and thirty years previously (Gen 46:8) is repeated (v 1). Exodus begins with what God has already done, setting the scene for what he has yet to do.

God's promise of descendants to Abraham has been abundantly fulfilled (although notice that it has taken a very long time)[2] – the land of Egypt is literally 'swarming' (verse 7 – the Hebrew *sharatz* usually refers to animals) with them. But this very abundance – the blessing of God – has a negative impact, and the Israelites are now unwelcome guests in Egypt. Can you identify areas in your (or your church's) experience where God's blessings have also brought trouble?

The new Pharaoh subjects the Israelites to forced labour, and then attempts the first recorded genocide of the Jewish people. Male offspring were necessary to continue the line of Abraham, Isaac and Jacob to its culmination in the birth of Jesus the Messiah. Only then would the promise of blessing to all nations be kept.

The midwives did not obey Pharaoh's command. They 'feared God' (v 17), standing in awe of the Almighty and wanting to be in right relationship with him. Their courage is an example to us not to compromise our faith or commit ungodly acts, whatever pressure we may be facing. How easy do you find it to reconcile their actions with instructions given to us in the New Testament about obedience to authorities?[3]

God will intervene to protect his people and keep his promises. The promise of land has yet to be realised. The scene is set for the birth of Moses.

1 Gen 50:24
2 Gen 12:1–3; 15:4–6,13–16
3 Eg Rom 13:1–7; 1 Pet 2:13–17; Acts 4:19; 5:29

How can God's faithfulness be demonstrated in the problems you face today?

Day 2

God's preparations

Looking back, we can see that God has prepared us for the situations we find ourselves in today. Think of examples of this in your own life.

 *Exodus 2:1–10*

Moses is born to parents from the tribe of Levi. He comes from the line that will function as priests before God on behalf of the people. But he is wrenched away from all of that, to experience a very unusual upbringing. Pharaoh's order (1:22) puts his life in danger; Pharaoh's daughter, of all people, rescues him and so guarantees him safety; and his own mother nurses him (and gets paid for it!).

Moses, as his name suggests, has the best of both worlds: in Hebrew, the play on words (v 10) links the name 'Mosheh' with the Hebrew for 'draw out'; the name is also common in Egyptian, meaning 'boy child'. Moses was blessed with a dual identity: a member of the Egyptian royal family, and from the priestly family of Israel. But this blessing must have brought its own tensions – did he sometimes feel cursed, rather than blessed, with a mixed identity?

In Pharaoh's household Moses would have learned the arts of politics and warfare, receiving an education far above his enslaved compatriots.[1] At his mother's knee he must have learned that he was an Israelite, and something of what that meant – putting him in touch with his roots and teaching him about the God of his fathers. From the priestly line, eventually he will exercise a role as prophet,[2] mediator,[3] lawgiver,[4] judge[5] and commander.[6] Moses has been prepared by God for the fulfilment of his plans. No part of our life or experience is ever wasted for God, no matter how unlikely it may seem.

His birth and upbringing uniquely qualify Moses for the task God has for him: to lead his people from slavery to freedom.

1 Acts 7:22
2 Deut 18:15–18
3 Exod 32:31,32
4 Exod 34
5 Exod 18:25,26
6 Num 31:6

God has a special task for each one of us. What is God calling you to today?

Fight, fright, flight

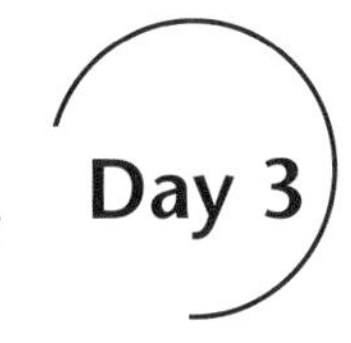

Are you tempted to take matters into your own hands? Or can you wait for God to act?

Exodus 2:11–25 

Moses reacts to the sight of oppression, as we often do, with a feeling of anger. Righteous anger, such as Jesus showed in the Temple, is expressed without breaking God's commandments.[1] But Moses' unrighteous anger boils over into ungodly action.[2] This was no outburst of passion – he stops to look around – but a cold-blooded killing.

The next day he tries to mediate between two Hebrews, but his credibility is in tatters. He flees, and all of God's careful preparation seems to have gone to waste. Whether it was the murder itself, or the fact that it was witnessed, Moses has disqualified himself from leading the Israelites for forty years.

Waiting for God's right time and method is the best way to see results in the situations we face. Here is a case where an act of human aggression leads to forty years' delay. Only after Moses has made a new life for himself as a shepherd and sojourner in a strange land, learning the lessons of survival in the desert, will the call of God finally come.

Moses' flight takes him to Midian. Who is this man, and where is his God? His life is made up of a patchwork of cross-cultural experiences, wandering, fleeing, taking on the customs and cultures of others, living in separation from his people. His wife and father-in-law are not Jewish, but give him a home and a job. His stepmother gave him the riches of Egypt. But only when he meets God will he truly know his destiny. Only in finding God will he find his true self, and exercise the selfless ministry to which God is calling him.

1 Matt 21:12
2 James 1:20

What is your calling in life? Will you wait to let God show you how to handle it?

Day 4

Who am I?

In what kind of circumstances do you feel reluctant or unable to respond to God's call or instruction?

Exodus 3:1–12

It's a curious sight: a bush that does not burn. God uses it to show that he can make himself known to us in any way he chooses, at any time. He is not beyond speaking to us using a bush, a donkey[1] and even a criminal's execution stake.[2]

In this encounter we sense, as with all true manifestations of the divine, both awe and wonder, as sinful man meets with holy God. Moses takes off his shoes and hides his face. There is a right fear of God – not born out of panic, but out of awe and respect. The God who invites us to call him 'Abba' ('Dad') is also the Holy One of Israel. What does it mean for us today to approach God in a holy way?[3]

God cares passionately for his people – as he does for all who suffer.[4] He has seen, he has heard, and he has 'come down' to rescue them (vs 7,8). The parallel with Christ's 'condescension' is apt.[5] The life of Jesus demonstrates the depths of God's sympathy. He feels with us, and enters our human situations.

Moses has every reason to feel insecure at God's call to confront Pharaoh and assume command of the Israelites. Unsure, perhaps, of his own mixed identity, rejected by his people and now living as a stranger in Midian, he has more than one chip on his shoulder. But the very things that he has experienced over the last eighty years now fit him for the task he is to play. With God's help he will overcome his own reluctance, and become the leader required for the mighty act of deliverance.

1 Num 22:30
2 1 Cor 1:18
3 Eg Ps 15; Luke 18:9–14;
4 Ps 72:12–15
5 Phil 2:5–11

So often our 'Who am I?' shows our inability to answer the real question, 'Who is God?' Only in knowing him can we truly know ourselves.

Who are you?

Many search for God, but do not know how to identify him. God identifies himself in his name. He reveals himself through his actions.

Exodus 3:13–22 

Moses shows further reluctance, in addition to his lack of confidence in himself. How will he identify God to the Israelites, and convince them that this truly is the God of the patriarchs come to rescue them? In ancient Egypt the many deities all jostled for attention, and the God of the Israelites did not seem to have done very much for the last four hundred years. It seems that Moses realises the enormity of the task before him, and tries hard to avoid it. Do you recognise this in your own experience?

God, however, will not be tied down to previous understandings or comparisons with Egyptian deities. The name with which God identifies himself can mean 'I am', 'I exist'. Here it is explained as 'I am who I am' or 'I will be what I will be' (v 14). God is a God who acts decisively in space, time and human history, and he will prove himself through the events to come. The name of God, Yahweh (verse 15 – 'LORD' in NIV), whilst difficult to translate, reveals his character, authority and identity. What does it mean for us today to meet God and know his name?

God's rescue of his people will be accomplished with 'a mighty hand' – the working of his supernatural power in overruling the will of Pharaoh (v 19). But to Moses such words are still not enough (4:1). What about us? Are we confident of God's power to save. The Hebrew name of Jesus, 'Y'shua', combines the words for God ('Yah') and rescue ('Hoshea'). In Jesus we meet 'God to the rescue'. God's mighty hand is revealed in Y'shua's death and resurrection. We can trust in him to deliver us from all evil.

In what ways, obvious or subtle, might we find reasons to do the things we want to do, and excuses to put off what God wants us to do?

Day 6

Signs of confirmation

God is patient with Moses' excuses, but his patience has limits. 'Lord, teach me to trust in your calling.'

Exodus 4:1–17

Moses first had doubts about himself; God answers by saying that he will be with Moses (3:12). Then Moses had doubts about God and who he is (3:13); God reveals his name – Yahweh (3:14,15). Now he doubts that the people will believe him (v 1); God gives him signs to use as evidence that God is at work (vs 2–9). It is when Moses returns to doubts about himself (vs 10,13), as though God's reassurances and signs had meant nothing, that God becomes angry with him (v 14). But God is gracious, and says Aaron will help (vs 14–16). What can we learn from this exchange for our own relationship with God? Do we anger God with our excuses or doubts about his nature?

Note that each of the signs that God gives foreshadows events that will follow: the contest with the sorcerers of Pharaoh (vs 2,5; 7:8–12); the plagues (vs 6,7; 9:8–12); the rivers of blood (v 9; 7:14–24). Moses will live through these a second time, and be reminded of his own unbelief and hardness of heart. It will teach him patience to bear with the unbelief of the Israelites, and Pharaoh's hardness of heart.

A simple shepherd's staff given up to God's service becomes an awesome instrument of power (vs 2,17). Moses is given something to strengthen him and reassure him in the part he is to play in God's purposes. Today, we look to Jesus for strength and encouragement in our lives and service, and see the authority of God exercised over all creation. That power is available today to be used in God's service.[1]

1 Eph 1:18–20

Where God calls, he also equips – and where God equips, he also calls! Do you have a sense that God is calling and equipping you for his service?

Moses returns to Egypt

Day 7

Think of ways in which God uses you to help others live for him and do his will.

Exodus 4:18–31 

Moses' journey back to Egypt is not without incident. In a passage that is difficult to understand (vs 24–26), Moses' wife Zipporah saves his life by circumcising their son. It looks as if Moses' failure to perform this rite previously had led to God's displeasure.[1] Circumcision was the sign of the covenant of Abraham, which all male children underwent. Verses 21–23 stress the contrast between the preservation of Israel as the firstborn son of God[2] and the death of the Egyptian firstborn that will follow Pharaoh's hardness of heart. The account of God's displeasure follows directly, and seems related to this contrast. The circumcision was necessary to symbolise that Moses and his family were within the covenant which God had made with Israel, otherwise the same death would result that was to come upon the Egyptians. Circumcision symbolised allegiance to the covenant God. In what ways do we show our allegiance as Christians?

Note that Moses did not send for Aaron: God sent Aaron. As elsewhere in the Bible, the story is presented in such a matter-of-fact way that we can miss the marvel of it. It is God who has prepared Moses and Aaron, and reunited them; it is God, then and now, who brings everything together at the right time.

Our lives are under God's protection, and he gives us the support and counsel of others. As Jethro blesses (v 18) and later advises,[3] Zipporah protects and Aaron speaks on behalf of Moses, we continue to see the making of Moses' leadership. Those called to lead do well to heed the guidance, help and skills of others, recognising that they cannot do everything themselves. It is then that the purposes of God can best be carried out.

1 Gen 17:9–14
2 Hos 11:1
3 Exod 18:1–27

Thank God for, and pray for, those who help you in your journey with God.

Day 8

'You can't make bricks without straw'

***The Israelites believed Moses, and worshipped God.*[1]**
How might Moses have felt then?

Exodus 5:1–21

Moses' direct approach appears to have backfired. Pharaoh's arrogant response paints a picture of a totalitarian regimes determined to stamp out with increased cruelty any attempt at revolt, and is calculated both to increase the workload of the Israelites and to cause division amongst them.

For the Israelites, having to find their own straw or stubble to act as bonding agents in the brick was one extra chore imposed on a people already over-burdened. The cruelty behind Pharaoh's reaction shows the iron grip he wished to maintain on the people. But Pharaoh would find that God's grip – on him and, in a different way, on the Israelites – was stronger. Are there situations today where you feel you are being asked to make bricks without straw? Even in desperate conditions, God can save.

The Israelites show their displeasure to Moses and Aaron. Moses has promised them freedom and God's power – and yet now, as a direct result of their request to worship God, their lives are made harder. How is God working in this? We often ask the same in situations where God's promise or answer seems a long time coming, and the situation worsens instead of getting better.

In the Jewish Passover meal, the straw for the bricks is represented by a sweet sticky mixture made up of chopped apples, nuts and dates. A sweet reminder of a bitter event, because in the light of redemption the pain of the past is forgotten. Pharaoh would not have his way.

1 Gen 4:29–31

How can we hold on to what we know of God's nature and promises in the face of harsh reality?

Man's plea, God's purpose

Moses asked big questions, God gave big answers. Do you dare ask God your questions? And will you accept his reply?

Exodus 5:22 – 6:13 

Moses remonstrates with God. Why did God promise deliverance, when the attempt to leave Egypt only resulted in more oppression? Would it not have been better if the Israelites had stayed as they were, without any hope of release? Now the flickering hopes of the people have been cruelly dashed.

It is right to tell God how we are feeling. As Moses honestly expresses his exasperation, God has more in store for him than he expected. In answering Moses' complaint, God reveals something of his divine nature and purposes, and reaffirms his compassion for his people. He is faithful. He listens to us. He rescues us. He rewards us.

This passage is a high point in the Hebrew Scriptures, and summarises the plot and purpose of the whole Bible. God's name, Yahweh, has been revealed already (3:15). The NIV's 'LORD' barely conveys its uniqueness, mystery and authority. To know someone's name was to know their character and trust in their integrity. This is the name the patriarchs did not know (v 3), yet they trusted in God. Moses should have no doubts.

On the basis of his name, God makes several promises, which in Jewish tradition are symbolised by the four cups of wine drunk at Passover. As each cup is drunk, the promises God makes to Moses are reaffirmed (6:2–8). Each cup has a special name: the Cup of Sanctification ('I will bring you out'), the Cup of Deliverance ('I will free you'), the Cup of Redemption ('I will redeem you') and the Cup of Praise ('I will take you as my people'). If Moses can but trust in these promises, God will do the rest.

Are you ever tempted to argue with God? How does he respond?

A foreshadowing of Christ's work

Exodus can be read at several levels, yet all Christians are agreed, on the authority of the New Testament, that the drama is the greatest Old Testament foreshadowing and anticipation of what in these notes we will call Christ's cosmic exodus by the cross and resurrection. What are they singing in glory at this moment? The book of Revelation calls it 'The song of Moses ... and the song of the Lamb' (Rev 15:2,3), as they praise the Lord of Exodus. The parallels between Moses–Israel and Christ–church are many, profound and compelling throughout our readings. It is as if the Exodus-work of our Lord Jesus had been dramatised and staged thirteen hundred years earlier in a vast open-air theatre in Egypt. No other enactment of God's redeeming purposes for the world shows so vividly the journeying, walking, pilgrimage nature of our faith.

The authority of God's name

The interpretative key to everything that transpires between God, Moses, Pharaoh and Israel in our readings is found earlier at 3:14, when God sends Moses to Pharaoh in the authority of his name, 'I AM WHO I AM'. Indeed, the entire Exodus drama as it unfolds is itself an attempt to explain that name which eludes all explanations. A possible translation is 'I will be present with you'. Moses, hoping perhaps for some sort of plan for the next days, is instead given a name – that is, he is given God! 'Go, and when you get there you will discover that I am already there and will be what I need to be in order to meet you in your need'. It is the name of infinite transcendence and intimate earthly incarnation. Thus all niggardly, rigid small-mindedness in our faith and expectations of God are swept away by the name, replaced by its awe-inspiring vision of the God who with incredible condescension shapes himself to our lives, to 'be present with us' today, and tomorrow, and the next day, and the next.

Dennis Lennon

Learning to act in God's authority

Day 10

God does not send his people out unprepared for spiritual warfare. Moses and Aaron discovered the secret of doing 'impossible' tasks in the power of God. Have we?

Exodus 6:28 – 7:13 

Two men, in their eighties, take on the greatest task in their lives. People who habitually delight to obey God as a way of life, do seem to grow younger in the process.[1] Is that your experience? But first, for Moses, a crash course in spiritual warfare, in the form of snake-handling (now please read 4:1–5). Consider the snake-symbolism operating throughout this episode. The ancient world pictured the forces of primeval chaos as a reptile, a serpent-dragon, which constantly threatened creation. From Eden to Revelation the snake in various forms is forever appearing in human experience.[2] If you must pick up a snake, the only safe way is to grasp it behind its head so that it cannot whip round and bite. Why, then, did God specifically direct Moses to grab his snake by its tail (4:4)? It shows God's total mastery over the powers symbolised by the snake. Thus Moses did with his snake what God in Christ did to the malign 'principalities and powers' on the cross.[3] Now Moses can confront Pharaoh (often, in Scripture, a Satan-figure) and even be 'like God to Pharaoh' (7:1), because he acts in God's authority. In terms of the book of Revelation, we are called to overcome within Christ's overcoming. And when Aaron's snake devoured Pharaoh's snakes (7:8–12), at that moment Moses and Aaron surely exploded with Jewish hilarity (observe the youthfulness of the ageing believer), the laughter of wonder and recognition at God's infinite invention. Exodus laughter, Easter laughter which Christians know so well as Christ's words, 'I have overcome the world'.[4]

1 Isa 40:28–31
2 Isa 27:1
3 Col 2:14,15; Rev 12:7–12
4 John 16:33

Look through the day ahead of you – its demands, opportunities, decisions, people – and bring everything under God's authority. Then go in his peace.

The signs are there to be read

Day 11

God communicates by words, signs and acts. But the acts are never incontrovertible; they only make sense where received by faith. That was Pharaoh's problem. Is it yours?

 *Exodus 7:14 – 8:7*

Although Egypt was reckoned the most polytheistic nation in the ancient world (some eighty deities), Pharaoh was essentially an unbeliever, the archetypal 'free' man: free to mix his myths and manipulate his gods; free to lock his mind and harden his heart against God's revelation; free to bring down upon himself his own damnation. In that sense 'Pharaoh' is alive and well and appears on our TV screens most evenings. It was unwise of him to harden his heart and refuse to listen, in spite of the snake fiasco. In response, the first plague completely turned the tables by posing the counter-question which is fundamental for any individual or society: who creates and sustains life?[1] The population venerated Hopi, the Nile God, for providing their main source of protein, fish. Hopi guaranteed health and fertility. Therefore the Nile turned to blood could mean one thing only: this is Hopi's lifeblood shed by Israel's God, who thereby claims authority over all life. The red Nile is a sign, to the discerning, that the origin and moment-by-moment continuation of our life-energies is the gift of the one Creator-Father.[2] True thanksgiving begins in the moment in which I see my own existence as giftedness. 'The receiver of the gift is himself the first gift received' (Gabriel Marcel).[3] But Pharaoh will have none of it. Unbelief, as ever, scorns the signs and rejects the idea of God's self-revelation through events and words, preferring the alternatives (7:22,23). But faith reads the world as teeming with signs, symbols, parables, riddles of divine action, all connecting and feeding into each other and pointing a way upwards.[4]

1 Acts 17:24–31
2 Luke 12:54–56
3 Philosopher, 1889–1973
4 Job 38–40; Matt 6:25–30

It is possible that in fact we pass through life effectively blind and deaf to God's signs. When did you last see a sign from God and act on it?

Preparation for God's missionary people

Today we see what it means to be God's chosen and called people, who must come out of the world if they are to serve the world.

Exodus 8:8–32 

The second plague was a nightmare for poor Hekht, the deity responsible for regulating the frog population. Thus behind the nuisance and health hazards caused by frogs, gnats and flies (in that heat!), God was at work discrediting the local gods.[1] Therefore we view the plagues not as the work of some destroyer-god on the rampage, but as the Father's love, a severe unremitting love, for people held captive to superstition and idol worship. Be sure of it, God attacks the manacles not the manacled. Consider the catastrophic collapse of political and thought systems in our own lifetime as examples of the same principle. Later, Isaiah will reveal what God really feels about the Egyptians: 'Blessed be Egypt my people'.[2] God chooses and calls a people to bear witness to his purposes in the world. Moses, Aaron, Israel and now the church of Jesus Christ are chosen and called, not to enjoy the privileged status of an elite group but to be the servants of all in God's mission. It is a tough calling being God's elect. We are a missionary people in need of missionary preparation.[3] Hence God says, 'I will make a distinction' (vs 22,23; 9:26). God calls his people to one side, that they might be renewed for service; separate from the world, in order to stand in solidarity with the world. It is of course the mind of the world in its anti-God bias from which we separate.[4] The biblical scholar John Robinson wrote: 'The Christian style of life is marked by an extraordinary combination of detachment and concern. This Christian will care less for the world and at the same time care more for it than the person who is not a Christian. He will not lose his heart to it but he may well lose his life for it'.

1 2 Cor 10:3–5
2 Isa 19:23–25
3 1 Pet 2:9–12
4 Rom 12:1,2; 1 John 2:15–17

We live in the difficult tension between coming out of the world and being sent back into it for service. How does this work out in your own experience?

Day 13

When music-spoiler meets supreme artist

Central to the exodus drama is the mysterious and disturbing idea that God hardens the hearts of some people. Or is there more to it than that?

Exodus 9:1–26

The Lord hardened Pharaoh's heart' (vs 12,16). So was Pharaoh after all simply acting as he was programmed, and then damned for it? Does God treat people like that? There is no such suggestion. Rather, God confirmed and clinched a situation created by Pharaoh himself. We must understand that a neutral, non-aligned relationship with God is not possible. If someone has not said 'Yes' to God it is because they are still saying 'No'.[1] If I am not facing the sun it is because I choose to face away from it. As Jesus said, 'He who is not with me is against me'.[2] Once I have heard a word from God, a neutral position is no longer an option. 'If we are not reconciled to God, we are spoiling the music, we are not just letting the music alone' (Austin Farrar).[3] Thank God, the Holy Spirit is in the world restraining and limiting the effects of our music-spoiling, otherwise we would have long since destroyed ourselves and each other. But the Spirit in his wisdom is sovereignly free to remove his restraining hand and to allow a person to have, in the end, his own way. In Pharaoh's case his hurt pride, his contempt for the Israelites and his cynicism about the plagues as divine 'signs and wonders' were allowed to overwhelm the man and to shut him into himself. In that sense 'the Lord hardened Pharaoh's heart'. But God can work through Pharaoh's resistance as easily as if the man had obeyed, for is God not the supreme Artist, the divine Potter who makes all things serve his design and brings good out of evil?[4]

1 John 3:19–21
2 Matt 12:30
3 Christian philosopher, 1904–68
4 Isa 45:9; 64:8,9; Eph 1:11
5 Rom 1:24

A prayer against hardening the heart: 'Lord, defend me from myself. In your love for me, never give me over to the sinful desires of my heart.[5] Change my heart. Implant in me a passionate eagerness to know and do your good pleasure in everything today. Amen.'

The processes of the primal sin

Day 14

We take a closer look at the psychology of Pharaoh's disastrous pride. It is like probing cancer. 'Search me, O God, and know my heart'.[1]

Exodus 9:27 – 10:6 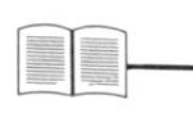

The plagues came on like the countdown to an explosion which will rip open the prison gates for Israel. Pharaoh's personal tragedy was that first, he would not listen to the ticking of the bomb (he hardened his heart, 9:34,35), and then he could not (the Lord hardened his heart, 10:1). All sins are attempts to fill voids, said Simone Weil.[2] What void in himself was Pharaoh attempting to fill by his implacable pride which prompted God's rebuke, 'How long will you refuse to humble yourself before me?' (10:3)? There is, of course, such a thing as a good and innocent pride. It lies in our nature, since we are touched by God's glory as created in his image, to be conscious of our value and to expect that this will be acknowledged. But cast adrift from love and reverence for God, that consciousness degenerates into 'boasting' which is, says Scripture, a distinguishing mark of the fool.[3] Israel will later be schooled in the fundamental wisdom that God 'is your praise'.[4] But in a man like Pharaoh pride, the primal sin, spawns other familiar disorders like arrogance, vanity, anger, contempt for others and pleasure in their humiliation. The psychologist Adler suggests that when pride expresses itself in striving for recognition, power and superiority over others, it is compensating for an inferiority complex! Pride, in its imagined independence from God, generates anxiety since it is a heavy burden to be God and saviour to oneself. And always there is the spectre of one's final negation in death. The irony is that pride's desperate longings for real significance in this world and for real life in the next can indeed be realised, but only through the destruction of our false pride when we come empty handed to God's door (10:3).[5]

1 Ps 139:23
2 Moral philosopher, 1909–43
3 Gen 11:1–9; Ps 53
4 Deut 10:20,21
5 Mark 8:34–38

Reflect on the warning from GK Chesterton: 'Beware the danger of insolence, of being too big for our boots ... Henceforth anything that takes away the gesture of worship stunts and even maims us forever ... If we cannot pray we are gagged; if we cannot kneel we are in irons'.

Total exodus?

Day 15

Pharaoh offers a compromise, a reduced version of exodus. But for Moses the key word is 'total'. Do you, today, face a similar choice in your life of faith?

Exodus 10:7–29

You may want to reflect upon that remarkable little phrase 'not a hoof is to be left behind' (v 26) as a picture of total exodus, a life going out totally to the Lord in grateful love. 'What does it mean to love God? To strain one's soul continually, beyond our powers, towards the will of God, with the goal and desire of giving him honour' (Basil the Great).[1] As Israel comes to birth as a nation, she dare not settle for anything less than a full exodus; she needs it in her DNA. Firstly, because her election and calling is to witness to the unity of life under the one God over all, who is Lord of every inch of existence.[2] Secondly, because her effectiveness as a missionary people among the nations is at stake, and a compromising, accommodating people of God will never challenge the cultures.[3] Thirdly, to be fully available to God for whatever he wills (vs 9–11,24–26). Take a moment to consider how those three exodus-principles translate into our own situation as the church of Jesus Christ. For us, of course, it is an 'exodus' of the heart and mind. But the fundamental question remains: will we allow 'Pharaoh' (the spirit of the age) to dictate the extent of our commitment to the Lord? Indeed, is it already happening to us? Consider how God acted in the plague of darkness to break Pharaoh's hold on Israel. Pharaoh revered Amon-Ra, the Sun-God, the source of all life, as his divine father, styling himself 'Son of the Sun'. Both sun and son were eclipsed in the terrible darkness of God's night, a stunning demonstration of the gospel truth that the Christ-mind can triumph over the Pharaoh-mind in us. 'Sin shall not be your master' – 'live by the Spirit'.[4] Settle for nothing less than a total exodus as you go out to God today. Remember, 'not a hoof...'.

1 AD 330–379
2 Isa 45:18–23
3 Isa 2:1–5
4 Rom 6:14; Gal 5:16–18

If it is true that countless Christians worry more about losing their self-esteem than about losing their souls, then we have indeed sold out to the spirit of the age. Is it true in your experience? How can such subversion occur in the local church?

The mysterious ways of God

Day 16

We see the results of hostility towards God's purposes in a nation, and marvel at Moses' poise in the face of great personal danger. Are you opposing God? Are you calm amidst danger?

Exodus 11:1–10

God's action reaches its climax with the terrible tenth plague. Does God kill children? Here we must think with a Semitic and biblical mind, which saw a spiritual–moral membrane connecting everyone in a community. Even today in contemporary Judaism there is the belief that adultery kills not only the marriage but also 'kills' the children. Similarly the people were implicated in Pharaoh's sin; they existed as a community of disobedience and under a communal judgement. Thus the death of Pharaoh's firstborn (4:22,23) extends to include all firstborn (v 5), in what is a shocking disclosure of the sheer gravity of sin. In the anguish of those Egyptian parents (v 6) we can hear something of the distress of a world groaning under the weight of cumulative sin in which suffering is the fundamental human condition.[1] Yet in the midst of so much danger and chaos Moses acts with courage and conviction in the integrity of his faith: he confronts the despot and dares to warn of the tenth plague. He rests in the paradoxical mystery of God's ways, which can allow Pharaoh genuine freedom to obey or not and then cause the disobedience to serve his plan (v 9).

How much can anyone, even Moses, understand of God's mind in these matters? Moses is aware that he is involved in a drama far beyond the grasp of any of the present actors, happy to play his part without attempting to quiz the author, or change the script, or ask for easier lines to say. It is a daring, wholehearted, essentially carefree attitude. Are you stuck on the absurdity of insisting upon clarity?[2]

1 Job 5:6,7
2 Rom 11:33–36
3 Theologian, 1905–88

Concerning the plague on the firstborn, consider this thought: 'When a composer such as God creates the opera of the world and places in its centre his crucified and risen Son, every fault-finding at his work – ie whether or not he could have done it better – must be reduced to silence' (Hans von Balthasar).[3]

The Passover

Day 17

The two defining moments in the history of redemption are Israel's Passover in Egypt and the cosmic Passover at Calvary. We see how the two events illuminate and interpret each other.

Exodus 12:1–20

God now takes possession of his people to use them in his mission to the nations. To mark the new era, the calendar is radically altered – a new New Year (v 2). So too Christ's appearance relocated history into BC/AD.[1] And the correspondence continues: a flawless lamb (v 5) is killed, whose blood protects the people (vs 7,13) and whose flesh feeds them (v 8).[2] The lamb is to be eaten with urgency, a meal to travel on (v 11). The entire event unfolds within the action of God's justice, his judgement upon the oppressor (v 12), just as the Last Supper–cross–resurrection sequence[3] means that 'the prince of this world now stands condemned'.[4] Not punishment, and never revenge, but a putting right of disorder, the Creator's justice which alone can keep life in this world from moral anarchy. The protecting blood (v 13) is 'a sign for you' that the sacrifice of another life has borne their punishment whereas Egypt, the arrogant, unrepentant jailer, must be her own sacrifice. Yet God commands joy! Celebrate the festival (v 14).[5] The biblical scholar GAF Knight said: 'It is possible for a believing man to thrill in his heart to the joy of fellowship with God even when he is walking through a battlefield, a mental hospital, or a hurricane-devastated area'.

The problems in the world are immense and bewildering, but we do not start from a problem-solving approach. 'Celebrate the festival' is the believer's starting point. Praise begins with what God has done, and brings all life into focus through that lens. In gospel terms, all sin, need and want can now be seen in the light of the cross and resurrection, in which God acts in such a way that the only realistic response is relief, boundless joy and grateful love.[6]

1 Gal 4:4–7
2 John 6:53–59
3 Luke 22:7–20
4 John 16:7–11
5 1 Cor 5:6–8
6 Rev 1:4–18

What, in practice, does it mean to say of our own celebration of the Passover, in Holy Communion, that it is 'to be eaten with urgency, a meal to travel on' (v 11)?

The gift of new life

Israel's destiny was to receive and display God's self-revelation for the sake of all people. Is your church truly letting its light shine?

Exodus 12:21–36

The catastrophic cost of Israel's liberation could mean only one thing: the exodus was for a unique purpose. In Israel, God was forming a people which in grateful love would receive him into every inch of its life, as God's witnessing child among the nations.[1] Her formation, out of a slave mentality, would be intense and often deeply painful when she encountered God as holy, as truth and as love. As when she foolishly misused her Egyptian treasure (vs 35,36), intended for God's service in the future tabernacle (35:4–10), to indulge her old instincts for idolatry in the incident of the golden calf (chapter 32). Yet out of her turbulent journey we have received from Israel a language, an appropriate way in which to think and talk about God, a way of approach and access to him, a worship cleansed from the usual naturalistic and gnostic corruptions.[2] This is Israel's priceless gift to us (along with the Old Testament), without which the gospel would be meaningless. From the beginning, the Passover rite encapsulated for Israel the grounds of her relationship with God. In their new life, in their new land, Israel would strive to keep it alive in the communal memory,[3] yielding their national life to its formative power, constantly recalling that they were once slaves in Egypt. And they must transmit the tradition through each generation via the children (vs 24–28). Before the advent of priests and Temple, Israel's faith was nurtured in the telling and retelling of her story in the home and among the family,[4] a practice quite lost to us under the splintering impact of contemporary life. The poet Kathleen Raine[5] asks why we have allowed it to happen: 'The words: Why did we let them go? Whose are our children, who no longer know "Our Father who art in heaven"? ... disinherited from ancestral wisdom'.

1 Hos 11:1
2 Deut 29:9–18
3 Rom 6:17; 1 Cor 15:3
4 Deut 6:1–9; Judg 2:10,11
5 1908–
6 Author, *The Making of Memory*

'Memory defines who we are and shapes the way we act more closely than any other single aspect of our personhood' (Steven Rose).[6] From today's reading select and memorise a verse until it is yours.

From bondage to freedom – the first steps

We see how important it is for God's people to stay connected to their miraculous origins through memories and signs. How significant are baptism and the Lord's Supper to you?

Exodus 12:37–51

Israel, like the church some thirteen hundred years later, set out on her journey with the rites of her deliverance in place: the Passover meal (vs 21–27) and circumcision as the sign of the covenant (vs 47–49). Our rites define our faith. Therefore Christian baptism and Holy Communion root the believer not in the flux of human ideas and responses, but in those astonishing 'signs and wonders' through which God has for ever changed his relations with the world: Christ's birth, death and resurrection.[1] Rabbinic Judaism believed that the Passover had to be received and internalised by each individual Israelite: 'In every generation a man must so regard himself as if he came forth himself out of bondage' (*The Mishnah*). Christians understand that sort of language. Just as the 'let there be light' of creation is projected into the heart of each believer by the Holy Spirit,[2] so, too, with the Easter Passover. Or do you find yourself holding Calvary at arm's length, unable to hold Jesus in focus? Too easily we can treat the cross like a sort of spiritual cash dispenser in the High Street, which produces the goods without the client requiring to know anything of the process. But we are not the Lord's clients, and simple gratitude requires very much more of us: 'Consider him who endured'.[3] We must come closer, and stay longer, with more focused concentration before the cross. Consider him who carried the dead weight of a forlorn world, lifting it off our shoulders onto his own, making it his own.[4] Consider the price he paid, his plunge into the abyss as he was 'made sin' for us. Consider very carefully his crucifixion.[5] What appalling ingratitude it is to keep him at arm's length. 'What manners! To receive his daily visits not in the living rooms of one's soul but in the kitchen or the hallway!' (Hans von Balthasar).

1 Matt 28:19; 1 Cor 11:23–26
2 2 Cor 4:6
3 Heb 12:3
4 John 19:16–18
5 Matt 27:45,46

If we internalise the Passover, and 'Consider him who endured...', how will that affect the way we consider other people?

Unleavened bread seeks milk and honey

Day 20

We learn more of what it means to travel hopefully. Do you see yourself as a pilgrim?

Exodus 13:1–16 

The destination is 'a land flowing with milk and honey' (v 5), which is more than mere travel brochure puff. In the ancient Near East it was a term for food of the gods, and a picture of a renewed cosmos.[1] But look at the realism: the journey towards 'milk and honey' is accompanied 'year after year' (v 10) by the Feast of Unleavened Bread (vs 3–10). Firstly, because it will constantly remind Israel that the LORD brought them out of Egypt with his mighty hand (vs 3,10). This fact – that we are 'ransomed slaves' – beats like a metronome in the minds of Israel and the church, causing us to remember, as the deepest instinct of our lives, that in everything we belong to the Lord.[2] Each Jewish father is required to re-enact Israel's redemption, to personalise and internalise it in his family. In a symbolic gesture he 'ransoms' and consecrates a representative child (vs 2,12–15). Secondly, leaven was a symbol of corruption, deceit and hypocrisy, therefore unleavened bread speaks of an open, simple sincerity in all our dealings with God and neighbour.[3] (Though Jesus, typically, stood this understanding on its head when he spoke of the positive, life-giving yeast of the kingdom![4]) Thirdly, unleavened bread is obviously incomplete bread, speaking of our flawed and imperfect attempts to build utopia by our own energies. 'This life is not health but healing; not being but becoming; not rest but exercise. We are not yet what we shall be, but we are growing towards it; the process is not yet finished but it is going on; this is not the end, but it is the road. All does not yet gleam in glory, but all is being purified.' You can taste the not-yet-but-getting-there of Luther's words in a mouthful of unleavened bread if eaten with intelligence. We travel hopefully.

1 Eph 1:9,10; Heb 1:11,12
2 1 Cor 6:19,20
3 1 Cor 5:6–8
4 Luke 13:20,21

Take time to meditate upon the significance for your own life of the threefold symbolism of 'unleavenedness'.

Israel on the road

Day 21

Trusting God's guidance means we can stop worrying about his plans.

 *Exodus 13:17 – 14:9*

God does not push his creatures into existence like ducklings into a pond to sink or swim, and to fend for themselves. He has a plan for them ... his plans are all the good that his love can see for us', writes the philosopher Austin Farrar, commenting on the wisdom and foresight of God so wonderfully demonstrated in today's episode. Only God has the big picture, the overview, the author's knowledge of the play from beginning to end. Now Israel needs protection, preparation and a gradual entry into the challenges of her new life.[1] The shortest route from A to B was not in her best interest (13:17,18); an apparently bewildering detour was 14:1–3.[2] We do not need to know God's plan for our lives (if we did we would trust in our knowledge more than we trust in God), but we do need to know the next step.[3] Although it is a plan for eternity, our concerns are with the next five minutes, to discern the 'fiery-cloudy' pillar (13:21,22) which for us will mean the interaction of many things – intuition, prayer, thought, memory, imagination, advice, Scripture, the impact of circumstance and the sense of the Holy Spirit's touch on the tiller.[4] Recall for a moment some of the twists and turns of your own journey which at the time seemed pointless and wasteful and apparently out of touch with God. But now in retrospect, were not some of those experiences life-forming, priceless times, however painful, when you 'learned God' at new levels? A straight road from here to paradise may not give God the time and scope he wants to do things for Israel, or for us. Therefore Israel took Joseph's mummified remains (13:19) as a sign that God keeps his promise[5] – that Israel's present moment is connected to her known past and her unknown future. Joseph is saying, 'Put your faith in God's faithfulness. I don't know what lies ahead ... but I know who holds the future'.

1 Isa 40:11
2 Hos 11:1–4
3 John 21:20–22
4 Prov 3:5,6
5 Gen 50:22–26; Josh 24:32

How are you interpreting the 'interruptions' in your own faith-journey? 'The caterpillar called it the end of the world; God called it a butterfly.'

When the prisoners go free

Salvation is not about words or ideas, but a Saviour strong enough to defeat the tyrant and release the captive. Has he set you free?

Exodus 14:10–31

An appalled Israel realised that in fact nothing had changed. For all the dramas back in Egypt, the coercion by plagues, the tears and finally the letting go, freedom was an illusion while Pharaoh, the jailer, held the prison keys. Only when he is finally overpowered will Israel know real salvation, which is why her exodus-crossing mirrors what happened later at the cross.[1] 'The kingdom of God is not a matter of talk but of power.'[2] In both events God used catastrophic violence against the captors, Pharaoh and Satan, to set his people free.[3] He will finish this business. He lured Pharaoh to this spot at the edge of the sea (vs 1–4) just as later he lured the demonic principalities and powers to the cross for the decisive conflict. Both times the enemy gathered his forces to execute and celebrate the demise of God's servants only to be completely outwitted as they arrogantly overreached themselves and fell headlong into the abyss of God's judgement.[4] The jailer jailed, now all prisoners are free to leave. To go where? The Israelites who traversed the seabed were, Paul writes, 'baptised into Moses',[5] meaning not the amount of moisture applied but that they were joined to their leader and shared his destiny, obeying his astonishing cry, 'Don't be afraid – stand firm – just watch – now move!' (vs 13–15). We could very usefully memorise those four clauses for ourselves, for who knows when we may need them. The trustworthiness of Moses' command could be proved only by trying it out, by going forward beyond reason and understanding to go out of their depth. They could hardly know the miracle-working power of God while they stayed within their own power on the shore. Each step was a debate between what they were and what they might become, but that is the nature of walking by faith; there is no other way, and no other place is secure outside being 'baptised into Christ', sharing in his destiny.[6]

1 Luke 4:18,19
2 1 Cor 4:20
3 Matt 12:25–29
4 Rev 20:1–3
5 1 Cor 10:1–4
6 Rom 6:1–14

'They could hardly know the miracle-working power of God while they stayed within their own power on the shore.' You cannot know unless you let go, and go. Are you a goer or a stayer?

'How can I keep from singing?'

Day 23

Moses' exodus song celebrated a God who fights for the poor and the oppressed. Can you sing it with joy?

Exodus 15:1–21

The first instinct of exodus people is delight. We sing our redemption and we sing our Redeemer (v 2).[1] The fundamental fact about us is that we are saved people. Not righteous or clever or moral or enlightened people, but saved people. We never grow out of or beyond that status; hence in heaven they sing 'the song of Moses ... and the Song of the Lamb'.[2] It is an astonishing song, with its dazzling, unruly imagination (vs 3–12) and wild music (vs 20,21). A dangerous, subversive, revolutionary song of freed slaves which threatens the oppressor. To the poor and downtrodden (in whatever sense) the song speaks of possibility and hope. No wonder Christians in the Third World find in Exodus deliverance, and in Moses' celebration of his exodus evidence that God hates the structures of poverty and injustice.[3] The Latin American theologian Gutierrez writes, 'Good news for the poor is bad news for the rich, and letting my people go is not good news for Pharaoh' (14:5). Compare Mary's song: 'He has brought down rulers from their thrones...'.[4] To all who thirst for another way of living, to be free from the gravitational pull of 'Egypt' with its flat, boring, selfish, safe, 'reasonable' view of life – the prevailing secularism of our culture – the message is that 'the horse and its rider the LORD has hurled into the sea' (vs 1,4,10,19,21). Simone Weil wrote, 'obedience to gravity is the greatest sin';[5] now let the Lord of the exodus teach us how to disobey the forces of gravity as we live within the force field of Christ's resurrection life on the far side of the waters of death. From there, we view and process life through the song's metaphors, symbols, narratives and memories, which are normative and non-negotiable for the people of God. For example: look at today's newspapers through the metaphor, 'The LORD is a warrior' (v 3).

1 Isa 42:10–17
2 Rev 15:2–4
3 Isa 65:20–25; James 2:1–7
4 Luke 1:46–55
5 Moral philosopher, 1909–1943; see 1 John 2:15–17

Moses' song was dangerous, subversive, revolutionary worship. Our worship is mostly domesticated, soothing, safe. How can we get 'exodus' back into our worship?

Can God spread a table in the desert?

We should welcome every situation which drives us back to dependence on the Lord.

Exodus 15:22 – 16:8 

To Canaan via Marah and the Desert of Sin seems an odd route for a liberated people. Apparently our journeying will be as important for us as the arriving. Moses' refrain was 'a three-day journey to worship the LORD' (3:18; 8:27), when in fact the first three days brought them to a crisis at Marah (15:22). Welcome to class one in the desert school of discipleship! First lesson: the Lord is ahead of us, already standing in the midst of our troubles.[1] It would appear that while no one in their right mind would go in search of tribulations, it is possible 'to worship the LORD' in situations of apparent failure and disillusionment, where 'worship' means to discover the Lord afresh at deeper levels.[2] Moses could have acted the medicine man and tried to use homeopathic skills to sweeten the brackish water, but then Israel would have learned nothing except that Moses was some sort of gifted social worker. The point of this episode was to teach Israel a profound life-lesson by helping them to trace the supply back to its source, the gift back to the giver, the healing back to the healer (15:26).[3] It was crucial therefore that the people – that we – should understand that the LORD showed Moses a piece of wood (15:25). The Lord stands behind every means of blessing. So also, a month later, with the next food crisis (16:1–8). The question, 'Can God spread a table in the desert?'[4] can only be answered by God's people experientially, when at their wits' end in a desert.[5] Does this throw light upon some of your own experiences? 'Nothing plays a greater role in God's pedagogical art than the shift from one extreme to the other … this is meant to ensure that we do not settle into any situation but remain pliable, and to make us recognise that true insight does not come from what we have grasped but from ever-greater readiness and deeper obedience' (Hans von Balthasar).

1 Isa 43:1–4
2 Matt 14:22–33
3 Luke 17:11–19
4 Ps 78:19
5 John 6:1–15

Ponder your own recent 'Marah' or 'Desert of Sin' times. Have they led you to a new and deeper dependence upon the Lord?

The thing of the day on its day

Day 25

We are given a spectacular lesson in how to live with God a day at a time.

Exodus 16:9–36

God's love for us is not a gentle sentiment; it is almighty action which will not let us go. Why then does he often seem not to be there? It is the effect of the desert upon our faith. Israel's struggle with her desert (vs 2,3) is a metaphor of our own journey in which the 'desert' is the practical atheism of worldliness.[1] Its dust gets everywhere, into eyes and lungs. Daniel Hardy suggests, 'Our century has seen more concentrated hatred of God than any other ... the denigration of God, the ridiculing of belief in him ... has become a potent force in our civilisation, and it often has the power to paralyse Christian vigour and praise'.[2] To defeat the desert we must take very seriously those strange culinary arrangements with manna and quail. God did not send Israel on her way with freezers filled with a forty years' supply of food. Who needs God when cupboards are full?[3] Instead he broke up his people's long journey into a day at a time and arranged to meet them each day with 'enough for that day' (v 4) or 'gather a day's portion each day' (Jewish Soncino translation) or 'the thing of the day on its day' (GAF Knight). Atheism blurs days and weeks into each other as having no significance other than what we, or chance, can give them. The believer's vision receives each day, each precious, precarious, unrepeatable day as a gift from God's hand; and with it our life and salvation, our calling and work, with all necessary enabling resources to be pleasing to God on this day. People who accept each new day as a gift filled with gifts are above all things thankful people. We see each day coming to us brimming with love, newness, generosity, overflow, prayer, full of possibility. Utterly dependent upon the Father, with empty larders and empty hands we go out to him again today.[4]

1 Ps 73:1–11
2 Author, *Finding the Church*
3 Luke 12:15–21
4 Matt 6:11,25–34

Has the desert-dust of atheism got into your mind? A test: Do you go to God at the start of each day as if your life depended upon it?

Miracles remembered

Day 26

Another crisis, but Moses knows that God works life in the presence of death. Have you learned this lesson?

Exodus 17:1–16 

Amnesia is fatal for God's people travelling the desert. When it strikes, quarrelling and grumbling follow (vs 1–4,7), which is moral and intellectual rebellion against God, doubting his love and criticising his wisdom.[1] Our memories need to be teeming with God's great actions, those events which model and invite faith [2]. Otherwise we are left to the mercy of the present moment (the 'now' which is so precious to our secular culture) and therefore inclined to overrate and absolutise the here and now as the measure of all things. Most serious for 'now' people is the impoverishment of imagination, with disastrous consequence for faith. Faith is fed from imagination working on memory; where those memories are of God's rich love and power, faith becomes restless and filled with creative energy, able to visualise (imagine) fresh possibilities.[3] Such memories are the very opposite to nostalgic hankerings for good times in the past; rather, they supply data for future navigation into the unknown.[4] Spiritual amnesiacs, on the other hand, have nothing to go on, no way of stepping outside the high enclosing walls of the present. They are paralysed by a crisis like the one at Rephidim (v 1). But Moses lived in the presence of God's signs and wonders; they travelled with him in his memory and set the norm for his expectations of God's future actions. He knew enough of God to expect him to be already at work in the impending crisis, standing there before him by the rock at Horeb (v 6). Moses could lead his people through the crisis because he had learned to see the world as a place where God works in ways we can neither initiate nor explain.[5] Miracles remembered will not allow the present to be domesticated. But that conviction never comes to us in our amnesia.

1 Heb 3:7–19
2 Rom 8:31–39
3 John 21:3–14
4 Exod 14:13–18
5 John 2:1–11; Rom 4:17

It has been said that our churches should be 'places of sustained remembering, bearing daily and concrete testimony to the way in which God creates newness out of nothing'. Are we anywhere near that idea?

Day 27 Wisdom from surprising sources

God speaks to us out of his Word and out of his world – we need both in order to discern his will.

 *Exodus 18:1–27*

Our readings in Exodus conclude with the astonishing spectacle of God's great prophet learning divine truths from a pagan priest! But if we are astonished, perhaps it is because our theories of how God speaks in the world are too limited.[1] Moses had no theories. A man who had passed through such deeply creative experiences, who had witnessed so much that was 'counter, original, spare, strange' in God's self-revealing activity (to quote the poet Gerard Manley Hopkins), could see no conflict between God's will revealed through direct communication (33:11) and God's will as it comes to us out of the wisdom of human experience. God speaks both languages.[2] When Jethro suggested a better way in which to administer pastoral care in Israel, Moses at once intuited God's guidance within the advice. Openness with discernment is the key idea here. Jethro was open to his world of experience, and Moses was open to Jethro's wisdom. But then, Moses stood open to the full circle of God's revelatory activity in all its limitless variety, creativity and imaginative range, and in particular its strangeness. We ought to think more than we do about 'strangeness' in our encounters with God.[3] We recall that Moses was the man who encountered God speaking to him out of a burning bush. How long would one need to observe a bush burning before realising that this was no ordinary conflagration, that this bush burned but did not burn out? In other words, Moses possessed curiosity and an enquiring spirit to go with his discerning openness. He was constantly prepared to be surprised by the God of surprises.[4] All creation is transparent to God and available to him as media of his communications, even a mystical Midianite father-in-law!

1 Job 33:14–20
2 Prov 8:1–11
3 Job 38–42
4 Rom 11:33–36

'Openness with discernment'; if God should send a 'Jethro' to speak to you today, could they penetrate your prejudice, your closed-mindedness, your fear of strangeness?

Covenant commitment

God's dealings with the people enter a new stage at this point. After delivering the Israelites from slavery in Egypt, the Lord guides them to Mount Sinai, where he invites the people to enter into a covenant relationship with him.

The ratification of the covenant comes between the story of Israel's divine deliverance out of Egypt and the lengthy report of the construction of the tabernacle. This latter material, which comprises almost all of Exodus 25–40, concludes with the Lord coming to dwell in the heart of the Israelite camp. Exodus 19–24 has to be seen in this broader context; it prepares for the Lord living in close proximity to the people of Israel.

A holy nation

God's dramatic rescue of the Israelites is the first step towards them becoming a holy nation. In Exodus the concept of a 'holy nation' has two main aspects. First, God will take up residence among the people. As the supreme manifestation of holiness, God's presence will have the effect of making the people holy. Secondly, to sustain God's presence in their midst the Israelites must remain pure. While these ideas are developed much more fully in the instructions found within the book of Leviticus, they are reflected in the covenant obligations placed upon the Israelites in Exodus 20–23. In their lives, the Israelites must imitate God. This is set out in terms of how the Israelites must live within a particular historical period and culture. Although this can be off-putting for modern readers who have little familiarity with slaves, goring oxen and the like, the various obligations placed upon the people reflect principles that lie at the very heart of God's nature. While our lifestyle may be far removed from that of the ancient Israelites, Exodus 19–24 reminds us that holy living involves every area of life.

Desmond Alexander

On eagles wings

Day 28

With thanksgiving reflect on how God has guided you on your spiritual journey.

Exodus 19:1–15

While the Psalms often describe God as sheltering his people under his wings,[1] the Lord compares himself in verse 4 to a fully-grown eagle teaching its chick to fly. After pushing the eaglet out of its nest, the adult bird swoops under and carries it aloft, should its untried wings prove inadequate. The picture of the young eagle struggling to fly fits well the experience of the Israelites as they have journeyed from Egypt to Mount Sinai; this also was a time of testing.[2] As God guides you closer to himself, give thanks that he is always there to catch you when your own strength fails.

Having focused on what he has already done for them, God presents the Israelites with a brief but striking description of what he wishes them to become. He invites these fugitive slaves to soar to new heights. They are to become his 'treasured possession' (v 5) – that which a person values more than anything else. They are also to be a 'kingdom of priests and a holy nation' (v 6). God intends the Israelites to fulfil royal and priestly roles in relation to the other nations of the earth. As 'kings' they are to ensure justice for others; as 'priests' they are to provide access to God's presence; as a 'holy nation' they are to reflect in their lives the very nature of the Holy One who will come to dwell in their midst. This wonderful prospect, however, is conditional upon the willingness of the people to obey God fully; the Lord says, 'If you obey me fully … then …'. The record of Israel's history shows they missed the fullness of God's blessing through their disobedience. However, God's promises to Israel are now extended to you and me through Jesus Christ.

1 Ps 63:7; 91:4
2 Exod 15:25,26;16:4

Meditate on 1 Peter 2:9. What does it mean for the church today to be a royal priesthood and a holy nation?

Revealed, and yet concealed

Day 29

Try to imagine yourself standing with the Israelites at Mount Sinai. What emotions do you experience?

Exodus 19:16–25 

The appearance of the LORD on Mount Sinai in the sight of all the Israelites is undoubtedly one of the most dramatic events described in the whole of the Old Testament. Although God reveals himself on other occasions, only here does he come and speak directly to the entire population. Various phenomena are associated with this divine disclosure or theophany. A fanfare announces the arrival, getting louder as God approaches. Here, as elsewhere, the divine presence is denoted by fire which reveals something of the brilliance and purity of God's being. At the same time, a cloud hides God's form from the Israelites.[1] While the Lord desires to establish an intimate relationship with the Israelites, they are prohibited from coming into his immediate presence. Only those who are holy may approach God in safety. It is important for us, therefore, to recall with gratitude that we who 'have been made holy through the sacrifice of the body of Jesus Christ once for all'[2] are sanctified by the indwelling of the Holy Spirit[3] and disciplined by the Father 'that we may share in his holiness'.[4]

A further feature of the theophany is the trembling of the mountain. While this emphasises the all-powerful nature of the LORD, the writer of Hebrews draws an important contrast between Mount Sinai and 'Mount Zion, the heavenly Jerusalem, the city of the living God'.[5] Whereas the quaking of the former is a reminder of the temporary nature of this world, the latter can never be shaken and so will remain for ever. 'Therefore, since we are receiving a kingdom that cannot be shaken, let us be thankful, and so worship God acceptably with reverence and awe, for our "God is a consuming fire".'[6]

1 Deut 4:11,12
2 Heb 10:10
3 1 Cor 6:19
4 Heb 12:10
5 Heb 12:22
6 Heb 12:28

Take time to reflect upon the importance of the command to 'make every effort ... to be holy' (Heb 12:14). How much does seeing the Lord one day mean to you?

God s mission statement for Israel

Put yourself in the place of the Israelites at Mount Sinai and pray for an eagerness to hear what God wants to say to you personally today.

Exodus 20:1–21

An interesting trend of the past decade has been the production of mission statements by all sorts of organisations, both religious and secular. While these may vary in form, they usually convey something of an organisation's purpose or ethos. God's speech in verses 2–17 is a mission statement for the people of Israel. It is a concise summary of what God wants them to be.

These 'ten words', to give them their title in the original Hebrew,[1] have a unique status within the book of Exodus, for they alone were spoken by God directly to the people; at other times Moses acted as a mediator (v 19). The uniqueness of the 'ten words' is also reflected in the fact that they were inscribed on stone tablets by the 'finger of God'.[2]

God's speech highlights ten principles that were meant to shape the behaviour of those standing at Mount Sinai. Although they are sometimes viewed as divine 'laws', the 'ten words' lack the precision necessary for use in a law court. It is wrong to read them simply as laws that distinguish between what is legal and what is illegal. Rather they are a summary of those values which God desires to see reflected in the life of each person committed to serving him. Unfortunately, we tend to reduce the demands of God's mission statement to a minimum. For this reason, Jesus affirms that the statement, 'You shall not kill' (the NIV translation 'murder' is too specific), cannot be restricted to the act of killing; it relates also to hating another individual.[3] Viewed in this way, the 'ten words' are a very radical description of what God wants us to be. They remind us that we should strive towards a perfect love for God and other human beings.[4]

1 Exod 34:28; Deut 4:13; 10:4
2 Exod 31:18
3 Matt 5:21,22
4 Matt 22:37–40

Take two elements of God's mission statement and reflect on how these apply to your own life.

Freed to serve

The gospel liberates us. Reflect on the life-giving freedom that Jesus Christ brings.

Exodus 20:22 – 21:11 

Exodus 20–23 records the conditions of the covenant which God wishes to make with the Israelites. Today's passage, which falls into two parts, introduces these obligations. Verses 22–26 contain two instructions relating to worship:

(a) The Israelites are reminded that God does not manifest his presence through idols of gold or silver; rather he will draw near to bless them when they offer sacrifices to atone for their sin. Unfortunately, as the incident involving the golden calf reveals,[1] the Israelites put 'seeing' God before obeying him.

(b) Although intended also for other occasions, the instructions regarding the building of an altar and the making of sacrifices are immediately relevant for the sealing of the covenant.[2] God leaves the people in no doubt as to how they should worship him.

Verses 1–11 form the opening section of a long list of regulatory principles that conclude in 22:21. Rules concerning the release of slaves are perhaps deliberately placed at the beginning, for they recall the Israelites' own release from slavery in Egypt. By affirming that no one should be enslaved for life against his or her will, these regulations justify God's punishment of Pharaoh and his people. Yet, having set the Israelites free, God now asks them, through the making of the covenant, to submit to his lordship for life. In doing this, they are to imitate the slave who, out of love for his master, renounces his right to go free after seven years. Moreover, implicit in these regulations, especially as regards the female slave-bride, is the idea that even slaves have specific rights which must be met at all times. In becoming their master, God commits himself to caring and providing for the needs of the Israelites.

1 Exod 32:1–8
2 Exod 24:3–8

To what extent is my commitment to obey God based on a true love for him?

An eye for an eye

Day 32

Try to recall an occasion when you have felt that the punishment for a crime was inappropriate. How concerned is God about fairness in day-to-day situations?

 *Exodus 21:12–36*

No human society can survive without laws to regulate behaviour. Laws, however, are much more than a series of dos and don'ts; they enshrine the value system of each society. In these verses God sets out, using selected examples, the values which he wishes to see reflected among his people, Israel. The regulations are given in order of descending importance, beginning with the most serious offences. This is reflected in the punishments; we move from offences that merit death to financial compensation.

At the heart of these regulations is the concept of 'moral symmetry'; the punishment must match the crime. This concept is encapsulated in the well-known expression 'an eye for an eye'. While most people imagine that phrase is meant to be taken literally, such is not the case. In the regulations surrounding verses 23–25, we encounter incidents involving bodily injury, including the loss of an eye. Yet in no case does the punishment involve mutilation of the guilty party.

The punishments concerning the treatment of parents are likely to strike the modern reader as particularly severe. Anyone who curses or attacks, but not necessarily kills, his or her parents, commits a capital offence; such actions are presented here as being on a par with murder. The same scale of values is found in the Ten Commandments, where the requirement to honour parents is placed before the prohibition against killing.[1] How individuals behave within the family will be reflected in their behaviour outside the family. Where respect for parental authority is lacking, there may be no respect for other kinds of authority.[2] Respect for parents is an important ingredient towards creating a society pleasing to God.

1 Exod 20:12,13
2 Deut 21:18–21

Think of practical ways in which it may be possible to demonstrate the high value that God places upon honouring parents.

You shall not steal

Think about an occasion when you have been the victim of theft or financial mismanagement.
What emotions did you feel?

Exodus 22:1–20 

Today's reading continues the list of regulations given by God to the Israelites. Having focused on rules concerning bodily injury, we come in verses 1–17 to offences involving possessions and financial loss. These cover a wide range of situations, revealing something of how people lived three thousand years ago. In spite of the cultural and historical gap between then and now, two important principles are evident in this passage.

First, these regulations emphasise the responsibility which individuals must exercise towards the possessions of others. Anyone causing financial loss, either deliberately or through negligence, must bear the cost. This places an onus upon each of us to consider carefully how we handle the property of others, be they our employer, neighbour or friend. We are all under an obligation to ensure that our actions do not result in financial loss for other people. Slogans like 'buyer beware' have no place in God's kingdom. We should never forget that 'the love of money is a root of all kinds of evil'.[1]

Secondly, these verses highlight the importance of making restitution to those who suffer loss as a result of theft, misappropriation or the negligence of others. At one level, this functions as a deterrent against taking or destroying what belongs to others. More importantly, it compensates the victim for the wrong done against him or her. Theft causes emotional scars that need to be healed. By making the guilty party compensate the victim directly (and not the state), God's heart is glimpsed in these regulations as they seek to reconcile the parties involved.

1 1 Tim 6:10

Read Luke 19:1–9 and reflect on the transformation that occurred in the life of Zacchaeus when he encountered Jesus. Is there someone to whom you ought to make similar restitution?

Day 34

Religion that is pure and faultless

Today's passage highlights some important practical principles for serving God. Before reading it, reflect upon what you would consider to be your priorities.

Exodus 22:21 – 23:9

This passage forms a distinctive section within God's statement of the covenant obligations being set before the Israelites. Verses 22:21 and 23:9, which are intentionally similar in wording, frame this passage, setting it apart from what comes before and after. No longer do we have regulations with prescribed punishments, as in 21:1 – 22:20. Even God recognises the limitations of trying to legislate for holy behaviour. Here he exhorts the people to act in ways that cannot be enforced by law. God's moral standards are high; he requires us to go beyond merely keeping to the letter of the law.[1]

To be a holy nation, the Israelites must adopt a caring attitude towards the weakest members of their society. Attention is drawn to those who are especially open to exploitation: widows, orphans, resident foreigners and the poor. In telling the Israelites to care for those who are vulnerable, God reminds them of their own experiences in Egypt. Compassion must also be shown to those who hate us (vs 4,5). Jesus' command in Luke 6:35 echoes God's instructions to the Israelites. Through being compassionate the Israelites reflect God's holy nature (v 27).

The Israelites are also commanded to be impartial in their treatment of others. God relates this primarily to the Israelites' legal system, which, lacking professional lawyers and judges, depended heavily upon the trustworthiness of all involved. Favouritism was not to be shown to either the poor or the rich. No one was to be swayed from telling the truth by public opinion or bribery. Consider the different ways in which you may be influenced to be less than truthful.

1 Compare Mic 6:8

Read James 1:27. To what extent is your religion 'pure and faultless'? Are there any practical steps that you can take to help a widow or an orphan?

Holy days and holidays

Day 35

Reflect briefly on the quality and quantity of the time that you set aside for worshipping God.

Exodus 23:10–19 

After exhorting the Israelites to be holy in their treatment of other people, God stresses that their commitment to him should influence their use of time. Verses 10–19 form a carefully composed unit, that falls into two parts, centred around verse 13. Each half is further subdivided by the repetition of the numbers six (vs 10,12) and three (vs 14,17) respectively.

The first half of today's reading concerns the Sabbath. Later it is described as the sign of the covenant being established between the LORD and the Israelites.[1] For this reason, disregarding the Sabbath was equivalent to rejecting God; anyone who broke the Sabbath was severely punished.[2] Symbolising God's rescue of the Israelites from toil and bondage in Egypt, the seventh day and the seventh year were to be occasions of rest from labour.[3] These times were also intended for the good of others, particularly the poor, slaves and resident foreigners – even animals, both domestic and wild, benefited. Is rest part of your weekly routine?

The second half of our reading focuses on three pilgrimage feasts which the Israelites were to celebrate annually. These were intended to remind the people of God's role in providing for their prosperity within the land; for this reason they were not to appear before him empty-handed. The Feast of Unleavened Bread recalled the Passover and Israel's rescue from Egypt. The Feasts of Harvest and Ingathering celebrated different phases of the harvest which extended over several months. Although the Israelites possessed no land when God spoke to them at Sinai, these instructions offered hope for the future.

1 Exod 31:13–17
2 Num 15:32–36
3 Exod 13:3–10

God gives to the Israelites a routine of living that was designed to enhance their relationship with him. Are there any ways in which your routine can be changed to improve your relationship with God?

You cannot serve God and

Day 36

Prepare for today's reading by remembering several specific things that God has done for you in the past.

Exodus 23:20–33

These verses form the concluding part of God's speech to the Israelites at Mount Sinai. In terms of both content and style this section differs from those that have gone before. These verses are marked by a much more personal tone (note the frequent use of 'I' and 'you') as God exhorts the Israelites to remain loyal to the covenant being established.

God's remarks underline the reciprocal nature of the covenant being made at Mount Sinai. With God's help the future comfort and prosperity of the Israelites is secure, and they will be divinely enabled to overcome all their enemies. Blessing, however, depends upon the willingness of the Israelites to obey God. While the Bible never presents obedience as a prerequisite for entering into a personal relationship with God, no one can truly claim to love God and not obey him.[1]

By entering into the covenant at Mount Sinai, the Israelites pledge their exclusive allegiance to the LORD. After doing so, they must not make a treaty or covenant (the Hebrew word *berit* can be translated as either 'covenant' or 'treaty') with any of the inhabitants of Canaan. This would inevitably lead the people of Israel to adopt the religious beliefs and practices of those already living in the land. As Christians we must always be careful that our actions do not lead us to compromise our loyalty to God. As regards our allegiance to him it must be 'either God or …', not 'both God and …'. We must also be on our guard that we do not make loyalty to God an excuse for sinful intransigence in our dealings with others.

1 John 14:15

Reflect on those areas of your life where the pressure to compromise your sole allegiance to God is greatest. Pray for wisdom in order to know how best to handle these situations.

In the Lord s presence

Day 37

Try to imagine what it must be like to enter God's presence and behold him in all his radiance and splendour.

Exodus 24:1–18 

After receiving some final, personal instructions, Moses returns to the people and reports all that the LORD has just said. On hearing the detailed obligations of the covenant, the Israelites express their willingness to obey. Moses then records the LORD's words in writing. It only remains for the covenant to be formally ratified.

The building of the altar and the offering of sacrifices reflect the instructions given in Exodus 20:24. For a second time Moses reminds the people of their duties under the covenant about to be established. When the people express their acceptance of these obligations, Moses seals the covenant by sprinkling them with sacrificial blood. This cleanses the people of their sin, and assures them of God's forgiveness. These activities, which foreshadow the making of the new covenant through the blood of Christ, are an important reminder as to why the cross is central to our salvation.[1]

With the sealing of the covenant the Israelites enter into a special relationship with the LORD. In recognition of this, Moses and the seventy elders ascend Mount Sinai; previously God had prohibited the people from coming up the mountain. Their journey comes to a climax when they see God. Although they witness God's glorious nature, no attempt is made here to give a full description; rather we are only told briefly about the splendour of the ground upon which God was standing. No harm comes to those involved. On the contrary, they feast in God's presence. When Christians partake in the Lord's Supper, they also commune with God and anticipate a greater day of feasting in Christ's presence.[2]

1 Heb 9:11–22
2 Matt 26:26–29; 8:11

Read Matthew 26:26–29 and meditate on the words '... until that day when I drink it anew with you in my Father's kingdom'.

A spiritual gospel

Clement of Alexandria, an early Christian writer, aware that John's Gospel was different from the other three, described it as 'a spiritual gospel'. This may not be quite fair to Matthew, Mark and Luke, who can hardly be described as 'unspiritual', but it is easy to see what he meant. From its very first verse John's account of Jesus raises our sights above this world. It is not that John's Jesus is less than fully human – he becomes tired and thirsty, he knows anxiety and grief, companionship and betrayal, he lives a robustly physical life and he dies a graphically physical death. But, for all that, we are left in no doubt that the real truth about Jesus is not so much about a first-century Palestinian preacher as about the Son of God on earth, the 'Word made flesh'.

John tells fewer stories, but often at greater length, because he tells each story not for its own sake but to introduce us to the profound truths about Jesus which are illustrated. Thus the few miracles he records are referred to as 'signs', and sometimes a discourse following the story teases out some of the theological implications. John writes in simple language, with a fresh and arresting style, and yet the thoughts he conveys are very profound. Familiar themes such as light and darkness, water, life and death are filled with new meaning and take us to the heart of people's relationships with God. Sometimes characters in the stories misunderstand Jesus' words (in this section notably Nicodemus in chapter 3 and the Samaritan woman in chapter 4), and their puzzlement is a challenge to us to penetrate below the surface meaning. Often there is an element of ambiguity or double entendre, so that it is possible to understand what is being said at more than one level: see for instance the language about the Son of Man being 'lifted up'. John's language may be simple, but understanding it is not easy!

The Gospel opens, not with an account of Jesus' human birth and background, but with a prologue (1:1–18) which takes us to the heart of who Jesus is and why he came. Here is no gradual uncovering of the truth but a sublime declaration of how God has become human, so that we may see what is invisible. A Gospel which begins like that is clearly going to make huge demands on its readers.

A lot of space is devoted to debates between Jesus and the Jews. Some modern readers find this language difficult. But it may be worth bearing in mind that the same Greek word means 'Jew' and 'Judean' (ie inhabitant of the southern part of Israel), and that while Jesus was a Jew he was not a Judean. This is the language of a Galilean visitor, engaged in dialogue with Judeans in their capital, Jerusalem.

Testimony to Jesus

In the four opening chapters we are vividly introduced to one of John's main themes, that of witness, as one person after another is brought to testify, sometimes despite themselves, to who Jesus really is and to the new life he offers. In this way John begins to build his case, which will develop through his very personal selection of stories and sayings until he reaches his intended goal: 'These are written that you may believe that Jesus is the Christ, the Son of God, and that by believing you may have life in his name' (20:31).

John 21:24 tells us that the source of this searching account of Jesus is 'the disciple whom Jesus loved', one of his closest companions on earth. Tradition has always identified this 'beloved disciple' as John, the son of Zebedee (who is curiously never mentioned by name in this Gospel), and while scholars have never been able to agree about just how much John may have contributed to the writing of the book, most would accept that it is his uniquely personal memory of Jesus which undergirds it and gives it its very distinctive character.

Dick France

Day 38

God became human

This is holy ground: prepare to be humbled and amazed by what God has done.

John 1:1–14

There is nothing else like these verses in Scripture, or in all literature. Only John refers to Jesus as 'the Word'. But his opening phrase 'In the beginning' gives us the clue, for when God first created the heavens and the earth, it was by his Word: 'God said …'.[1] Since then he had spoken by the prophets. But never before had that powerful Word entered directly into our human condition: the Word 'became flesh'. That is what happened at Bethlehem, and the world has never been the same again.

So the baby of Bethlehem is, quite simply, God. John is daringly explicit in verse 1; 'the Word was God'. That same God who created the universe lay helpless in a manger. And because he did, light and life have come into the world.

But this is too strong meat for human consumption, and the world which he made did not want to recognise its creator. And so it has always been. Jesus divides people. There are the many who do not want to know, and remain in darkness, and there are the few who through this amazing act of divine humility are able to become children of God through faith. This is no ordinary human choice, it comes from God, who alone can give the 'new birth' which Jesus will demand in chapter 3.

For them the light has shone. In a rare first-person comment (v 14),[2] John reflects on the privilege of having 'seen his glory', of seeing in the confines of a human life the very 'grace and truth' which are the defining characteristics of God himself.[3]

1 Gen 1:3
2 Compare 1 John 1:1–3
3 Eg Exod 34:6,7

Have you grasped the enormity of what the Christian faith is claiming about Jesus? How will you help others to grasp it too?

The first witness

What do others learn about Jesus through me? 'Lord, teach me how to be a signpost pointing to you.'

John 1:15–28 

The prologue is not yet finished: verses 16–18 draw out further aspects of what happened at Bethlehem. One was the dawning of the age of grace, taking the place of the Law given through Moses. This grace comes to us in Jesus Christ, and there is no limit to it.

In verse 18 John attempts to express the inexpressible, to the consternation of translators! God is invisible, but in the coming of Jesus he has become visible. And yet this visible person is himself God. In the most likely Greek text, John says literally, 'No one has ever seen God; the only God who is in the Father's bosom has revealed him'. No wonder the footnotes proliferate! But if human logic cannot cope with divine grace, that does not make it any less true. Framing these extraordinary verses is the first of the witnesses John will call to testify to who Jesus is. John the Baptist, great man that he was, refused any glory for himself. He had, he claimed, no status of his own beyond that of a 'voice' – but what a voice! According to Isaiah 40:3 he was to herald the coming of God's promised salvation.

Even John's famous demand for people to be baptised was not an end in itself, but served to prepare people for the one who was to follow him. And who was that one? When John quoted Isaiah 40:3, 'Make straight the way for the LORD' he implied much more than that another prophet was to take over from him.

Jesus later said that John was 'Elijah'.[1] He had greater significance than he dared to claim for himself. But Elijah was expected only as the forerunner for the 'great and dreadful day of the LORD'.[2]

1 Matt 11:14
2 Mal 4:5,6

How can we make sure that our testimony, like John's, directs people's attention to Jesus and not to us?

Jesus' first followers

Day 40

What first led you to follow Jesus? Thank him again today.

 *John 1:29–39*

We continue with the testimony of John the Baptist, not now in the indefinite language of verses 26 and 27, but about a specific man who was walking there by the Jordan. So Jesus comes into the story with no explanation of his human origins, as one of the crowd who had come to John's baptism.

John again insists that Jesus is his superior. In this Gospel there is no account of Jesus' own baptism. It is not his baptism which is important, but what was then revealed by the coming of the Spirit upon him. John's outward baptism in water was to give way to something more real and fundamental, baptism with the Holy Spirit, and that could be given only by one who was himself anointed with the Spirit. John sees more in Jesus than that. He is the Son of God, a title with far-reaching implications which will be explored throughout this Gospel. And he is the Lamb of God who takes away the world's sin (v 29). John's Gospel does not say much about why Jesus had to die, but this one phrase says it all. It is the language of Old Testament sacrifice,[1] of the innocent victim whose death brought life to someone else.

The two men who were following John the Baptist were Andrew and perhaps John himself. They took his testimony to heart, and followed where he directed them. However, the key to their new allegiance was not only in what John said, but in meeting Jesus. It would be fascinating to know what passed between the three men in the house (v 39). It changed their lives. Many others have met with Jesus in less literal ways, and have never been the same again.

1 Exod 12:1–13; Lev 14:10–32; Isa 53:7,8

Son of God; Baptiser with the Holy Spirit; Lamb of God who takes away the sin of the world – how far do these phrases sum up your experience of Jesus?

Three more disciples

'He brought him to Jesus' (v 42). Are you bringing people to Jesus too? Pray that today's reading may inspire you.

John 1:40–51 

Probably the most important thing Andrew ever did was to bring his brother to Jesus. His testimony ('We have found the Messiah') together with Jesus' own welcome, produced the future leader of the Christian movement. Andrew is the patron saint of personal evangelists. Philip was won by a more direct approach from Jesus himself (v 43). We do not know what 'conditioning' if any preceded the summons to 'Follow me'. Nathanael, like Peter, was drawn in by another's testimony, this time not a brother but a Galilean friend. His initial scepticism when he heard of a Messiah from the obscure little village of Nazareth (he himself came from Cana, just over the hill!) was overcome not by argument but by the simple invitation to 'Come and see' (as in v 39).

The dialogue which follows when Jesus meets Nathanael leaves us guessing. What was it that Jesus had seen under the fig tree which so impressed Nathanael that he suddenly acclaimed this hill-villager as 'Son of God' and 'King of Israel'? (v 49).

It is a secret between the two of them, but perhaps verse 51 offers us a clue. There Jesus pictures himself, the Son of Man, as like Jacob's ladder,[1] the means of communication between heaven and earth. In alluding to Jacob's dream, he may be picking up the theme of his earlier comment about a 'true Israelite, in whom is nothing false' (v 47). 'Israel' (wrestler with God) was Jacob's other name,[2] while his original name 'Jacob' meant a usurper or cheat.[3] But in Nathanael (who had perhaps been meditating on the Jacob story under the fig tree?) Jesus found an Israelite worthy of the name, a man to be trusted.

1 Gen 28:12
2 Gen 32:27,28
3 Gen 25:26; 27:36

Think about the different ways people are brought to Jesus. Are there people you know who could be brought as Simon and Nathanael were?

Water into wine

Day 42

Pray that in this story you may 'see his glory' as the first disciples did.

 *John 2:1–11*

Here is a story which can be read on different levels. At the simplest level, it shows us a Jesus who joined in the fun of a village wedding, and added to the festivities with his own special (and extraordinarily lavish) contribution of wine. Jesus could sometimes be stern and forbidding, but here we see the jovial Jesus who earned a reputation as a 'glutton and a drinker'.[1] Jesus is no killjoy; still less a teetotaller!

The 'glory' Jesus revealed by this 'sign' was more than simply enjoying a feast. Here was a situation which was beyond human resources. His mother's instinctive appeal to Jesus to help shows an awareness of his special powers, and in the event her faith was amply justified. When his disciples 'put their faith in him' (v 11) it was not just as a provider of food and drink, but as the powerful Son of God who could be relied on to solve far more serious problems than a mere social embarrassment.

Surely there is still more to this event. Why the odd emphasis on the six huge water jars used for Jewish ceremonial washing? Is this a hint that we should read this story, like many others in John, as a pointer to the real nature of Jesus' mission? Just as John will later show how Jesus comes into the religious festivals of Jerusalem and brings something more lasting to those who believe in him, so here the water of Jewish ritual gives way to the rich wine of the new life which Jesus offers.[2] And the new is better than the old (v 10). As he puts it later, 'I have come that they may have life, and have it to the full' (10:10).

1 Matt 11:19
2 Mark 2:22

Which of these images of Jesus do you need most: the fun-loving Jesus, the problem-solving Jesus, or the giver of new and abundant life?

A demonstration in the Temple

Day 43

Pray that more of the 'zeal for God's house' shown by Jesus may characterise you too.

John 2:12–25 

Here we see a sterner Jesus, and one who was not afraid to provoke opposition. The Temple in Jerusalem was not only the centre of worship, but also the focus of Israel's national existence and pride. At Passover time it was crowded and busy. Jesus' action takes place in the large outer court of the Gentiles (not in the Temple building itself), where the traders' stalls were established with the approval of the priests. So his violent protest was a strike not only against the traders themselves but against the Temple establishment. No wonder they wanted to know his authority for such an outrageous act!

His reply (v 19) is typical of the ambiguity we find in John. Naturally, they took his words literally (and it was his alleged threat to destroy and rebuild the Temple which was brought against him at his trial and on the cross),[1] but John explains that there was another level to it.

Yet the two are not unconnected, for throughout Jesus' teaching and the rest of the New Testament there is a developing theme of the replacement of the literal Temple. It has outlived its usefulness and must soon be destroyed[2] and replaced with a new temple 'not made with hands'.[3] 'Something greater than the temple is here',[4] he said, and the apostles speak of a new temple made up of 'living stones': 'we are God's temple'.[5]

When Jesus died the curtain of the Temple was torn apart, and with his resurrection we have opened to us a new way of coming to God. This dynamic new theology lies behind Jesus' cryptic words, and later his disciples would come to see what it was all about.

1 Matt 26:59–61
2 Mark 13:2
3 Mark 14:58, NRSV
4 Matt 12:6
5 1 Pet 2:5

Are we also in danger of keeping the old system going when God is calling us to a new way of worshipping him?

New birth – new life

Day 44

Here are the very foundations of being a Christian. Pray that you may grasp them clearly.

 *John 3:1–21*

Jesus' discussion with Nicodemus leads so naturally into a statement of the essential gospel that it is hard to say when direct speech ends and John's comment takes over.

Put yourself in Nicodemus's place, a respected but cautious religious leader. Is it any wonder Jesus' bombshell in verse 3 left him floundering? His lame objections in verses 4 and 9 reveal a mind unable yet to see beyond 'earthly things'. Jesus is speaking of something radically new and different, new birth through the Spirit of God. Only he, who has come down from heaven, can open the way to heavenly life.

But he comes not only to reveal truth, but also to bring new life. Like the mysterious bronze snake in the desert,[1] it is as he is lifted up (in death on the cross) that he can offer new life. It is as he is 'given' (v 16) that he can save others from eternal death.

The Israelites needed only to look at the snake to escape death. So also the way to find life through Jesus when he is 'lifted up' is to believe in him. This key word, which we have already met in 1:12, recurs in verses 15, 16 and 18 as the divider between those who live and those who die eternally. God's love which aims to save the world depends on a response of faith. Without it, condemnation remains a terrible reality.

As we saw in the prologue (1:4–11), Jesus has brought light into the world, but not everyone welcomes the light. They have too much to hide.

1 Num 21:4–9

This passage has spoken of new birth by the Spirit, of believing in Jesus, and of coming to the light. Think about how this total view of salvation can best be expressed to people today.

The one who comes from above

Day 45

Pray that John's unselfish testimony to Jesus may be a model for your own.

John 3:22–36 

To the outsider it must have seemed as if Jesus was setting up as a rival to John the Baptist, leading his own baptising movement, and attracting more people than his predecessor (see 4:1,2). And John's followers expect their leader to resent the newcomer (v 26). For John, however, it is not a matter of human prestige, but of what is 'given from heaven', and his comments about Jesus in 1:26,27,29–34 have already shown us that he was well aware of his own status as merely the forerunner. So he is content to stand aside and let Jesus take the limelight. Jesus is the bridegroom; John is only the best man. To see Jesus' ministry develop is John's greatest joy. 'He must become greater while I become less' (v 30).

After verse 30 the text again runs on without a clear break from the words of John the Baptist into the comments of the Gospel writer. In verse 31 'the one who is from the earth' refers to John. There is a quantum difference between him, as a human preacher, and Jesus, the Son of God. To listen to Jesus is to hear not just an opinion but divine truth.

So this Galilean stranger who has suddenly appeared among John's followers by the Jordan is revealed by John's testimony as sharing the authority of God himself, and related to God as son is to father. And if the Son has such divine authority, everything depends on how we respond to him. To believe in him is life; to turn against him is to incur God's ultimate displeasure.

We are left in no doubt of the seriousness of the choice with which Jesus confronts us. This is not a choice between rival religious teachers: it is a matter of life and death.

If it is true that Jesus 'speaks the words of God' how should we respond to his teaching?

Living water

Day 46

Do you ever feel spiritually thirsty? What do you do about it?

 *John 4:1–15*

The story of the Samaritan woman is one of John's longest accounts of Jesus meeting with an individual. It will take up three of our notes. Yet she is a person of no importance, a very ordinary and probably rather disreputable member of a tribe despised by Jews, and a woman in a male-dominated society.

For Jesus to speak with such a person at all is remarkable, and would no doubt have raised eyebrows in Jewish society (v 27). Even more remarkable is the way he takes her seriously, deals with her questions, probes her needs, and in the end wins not only her but her whole village to recognise him as the Messiah.

Yet he begins the conversation not with her need but with his own, with the simple request for a drink. It is enough to catch her interest, especially coming from a lone Jewish man. But the conversation quickly turns round, and soon it is Jesus who is offering the gift, and the woman who is asking for it.

In the Middle East water is not only a necessity but the essential basis for living. On a hot day the thought of 'living' (which to the woman would mean 'running') water conjures up a vision of all that is delightful. Of course Jesus meant it as a symbol for spiritual resources but the woman, like Nicodemus before her, cannot yet see beyond the literal level.

The water Jesus offers does not need to be drawn, because it is 'in them'. In place of a religion of externals, he offers internal spiritual resources which are infinitely renewable.[1] This is not 'running water', but the water of life, life in all its fullness.

1 Jer 31:33,34

What can we learn from Jesus' approach to this woman for our own attempts to communicate spiritual truth?

Spirit and truth

Day 47

Are we the kind of worshippers the Father seeks?

John 4:16–30 

Rather than trying to overcome the woman's misunderstanding of what he meant by 'living water', Jesus changes tack, and raises a subject which directly exposes her need. In asking her to bring her husband Jesus was surely aware that he was touching on a sensitive issue, and his awareness of her personal circumstances clearly made a deep impression (see v 29).

However, she is understandably reluctant to pursue the issue, and abruptly changes the subject. A man of such supernatural knowledge must be able to answer the question which has kept Jews and Samaritans apart for centuries. 'This mountain' is Mount Gerizim, which overlooks Jacob's Well near Nablus. The Samaritans had their own temple there until it was destroyed by the Jewish King Hyrcanus in 129 BC, and they continued to worship on the mountain after that (as they still do today).

Jesus will not be drawn into ecclesiastical politics. Even if the Jews are 'right' (v 22), the point is no longer relevant, because a new way of worship is to take the place of a physical temple or holy site.[1] It is not the place that matters, but the God who is worshipped.

We probably shouldn't find anything in verse 24 to surprise us, but we need to constantly refocus our hearts to maintain our perspective on worshipping God. To this obscure, anonymous woman, Jesus reveals himself more explicitly than to anyone else in the Gospel stories (v 26). No wonder she was impressed!

1 See the note on John 2:12–25

In what ways are we tempted to focus on buildings and places rather than worship of God? Today how can we make sure that 'spirit and truth' remain the focus of our worship?

The harvest of eternal life

Day 48

Pray for a true sense of priorities in God's service.

 *John 4:31–42*

Just as the woman failed to understand the spiritual level at which Jesus talked about water, so the disciples also think he is talking about literal food. But the 'food' he talks about is doing God's work.

The specific 'work' in which he is engaged is harvesting, and in this context, he probably has in mind the gathering of believers from even a Samaritan village. He used the same picture of harvest for the work of preaching the good news when he sent the disciples out to share his mission.[1]

Perhaps this was winter time, four months before the spring harvest, but verse 35 may simply be a common saying, pointing out that there is a proper interval between sowing and reaping. But the laws of agriculture do not apply to spiritual harvesting, and the seed which Jesus has just sown in his talk with the woman is already about to bear fruit, as the villagers approach (v 30). So sometimes sower and reaper rejoice together, as God's miraculous harvest sprouts to sudden ripeness. More often there is a time of waiting, and the disciples have the privilege of coming at the end of that time. Those who have already sown (v 38) are probably the prophets, up to the time of John the Baptist, but now is the time for Jesus and his disciples to reap the harvest.

And so in verse 39 we return to the Samaritans, and this unlikely harvest is brought in. Jesus' willingness, as a Jew, to stay two days in a Samaritan village was a clear pointer to the way the gospel was to break down the barriers of society and to welcome the most unlikely recruits into God's people. Jesus is the Saviour not just of the Jews, but of 'the world'.

1 Matt 9:37,38; Luke 10:1–3

Are there new areas where God is calling you to harvest (or to sow)?

The second sign

Do you find it easy to 'take Jesus at his word' (see verse 50)?

John 4:43–54

This second 'sign' recorded by John, like the first which also took place in Cana (2:1–11), is closely linked with faith. The man's acceptance of Jesus' assurance, when there was no evidence for it, was a singular example of faith, and the response of the whole household to the miracle was to believe.

The story is similar in some ways to that of the healing of the centurion's servant,[1] but the setting, the personnel and the details of the story are different. These two stories, together with that of the Syro-Phoenician woman's daughter,[2] are the only recorded examples of Jesus healing from a distance. John's careful recording of the time and circumstances underlines the remarkable nature of the cure, and the supernatural authority of the man who could so confidently declare it. Here then, it would seem, is a firm basis for faith.

Yet verse 48 sounds a note which recurs in John's Gospel, that it would be better to believe without such tangible proof (20:29), and that a faith based only on 'signs and wonders' can be inadequate (2:23 – 25; 6:26–29).

The same ambiguity about miracle-based faith underlies the curious comments of the evangelist in verses 43–45. In returning from Samaritan territory to Galilee Jesus was going back to 'his own country', and the people of Galilee were willing to welcome him as a miracle-worker on the basis of what he had done in Jerusalem. Yet verse 44 reminds us that such adulation might be only skin-deep, that more would be required to persuade his own people to recognise their 'prophet' for who he really was, as the Samaritans had done.

1 Luke 7:1–10
2 Mark 7:24–3

What are the dangers in promoting 'signs and wonders' as a basis for faith in Jesus?

Identity and mission

The primary attack on the Christian faith today surrounds our convictions concerning the uniqueness of Christ. In a world peopled by Buddhists, Muslims and Hindus, can we really proclaim Jesus Christ as the only way? In this milieu of increased religious pluralism and heightened intolerance towards universal and absolute claims we need to return to the authoritative words of Jesus himself, and in John chapters 5 and 6 he couldn't be more direct. First, John develops the theme of *Jesus' identity*. In 5:12 the religious authorities question the formerly paralysed man about the identity of his healer: 'Who is this fellow?' Then there is the extended debate concerning Jesus' relationship with God the Father. In chapter 6, after the miracle of the loaves and fish, the people pose another question of identity: 'Surely this is the Prophet who is to come into the world' (6:14). And at the end of our section Peter confesses that Jesus is the Holy One of God (6:69).

Second, John explains *Jesus' mission*. Frequently making references to Old Testament themes such as the Passover, the exodus, and the manna in the wilderness, Jesus teaches that he is sent by God to achieve the Father's purposes and to give his life for others. Much of chapter 6 is devoted to an extended treatment of what it will mean to benefit from Christ's work.

Sharing the good news

Both themes – *identity* and *mission* – are important aspects of our Christian proclamation. The church today must reflect creatively on how to communicate these truths. These chapters will provide us with important clues not only concerning the substance of the gospel but also how we can communicate it. The personal encounters of Jesus with those in need, and the graphic images he uses to describe spiritual satisfaction, may help us bridge some gaps when it comes to sharing the good news with others.

Jonathan Lamb

Do you want to get well?

Day 50

This passage reminds us of the danger of religious legalism. Pray for humility and responsiveness as you come to read it.

John 5:1–15 

There is something ugly about formal religion. It offers rules not solutions, condemnation not liberation. The contrast between legalism and the life-giving ministry of Jesus is seen today. First, the story tells us about the man's helplessness. For thirty-eight years he had been paralysed – 'withered' (AV) is a graphic description of an empty and hopeless life. Many of us can identify with this: living in the shadow of past failure, or an emotional or spiritual life crippled by past disappointment. Jesus' question is pertinent: 'Do you want to get well?' (v 6).

Secondly, the story tells us about Jesus' compassion and authority. He acts entirely out of grace. He requires nothing of the man, whose response seems self-centred, even ungrateful (vs 7,15). With an authoritative word (v 8), Jesus heals him. This points not only to Jesus' mercy to those in need now but also to his ultimate authority on the last day (verses 28 and 29 use the same verb for 'get up').

Thirdly, the story tells us about religious legalism. Religion blinds people. Instead of recognising the miraculous or rejoicing in a radically transformed life, the Jewish authorities were concerned about technicalities. They demonstrated the cold, unbending attitude of religion that has lost sight of the true purpose of God's Law. We should take note of the lessons in this passage ourselves. We can miss Jesus' blessing in our lives and churches, because we are not ready to face the implications ('Do you want to get well?') or because we are dominated by law not grace. We can slip into a mode of thinking which is more concerned about religious rules than about the life-changing ministry of the living Lord Jesus.

Pray that the Lord will liberate you from anything in the past which paralyses you.

Who do you say that I am?

Day 51

Pray for a deeper understanding of Jesus' uniqueness and a fresh encounter with him today.

John 5:16–30

There is no doubt that one of the major challenges to Christian faith today focuses around the question of Jesus' unique identity (v 17). This section of the Gospel tackles the theme head on. No wonder Jesus' words led to Jewish hostility, for now it was not simply a matter of Jesus breaking Sabbath regulations (v 16) but of his outrageous claim in calling God his Father (v 18).

First, Jesus is engaged in his Father's work (v 17). He does not cease his gracious work on the Sabbath, and Jesus' own acts of mercy simply reflect what his Father does.

Secondly, Jesus and the Father express a perfect interdependence (vs 19,20). He is describing a uniquely close relationship of love, dependence and communication. And thirdly, like his Father, Jesus is empowered to grant eternal life (vs 21,24).

Fourthly, Jesus has been entrusted by his Father to judge all people (vs 22, 25–29). The Old Testament indicated that judgement belonged to God,[1] and Jesus' claim to have authority to judge further reinforced both his authority and Jewish hostility. He makes it clear that people's reactions to him will determine their destiny (vs 21–25). And finally, Jesus does not leave us the option of acknowledging him as simply a great moral teacher. He must be honoured and worshipped as God himself (v 23). In a world which is uncomfortable with absolute claims, we Christians can easily go soft on our commitment to Jesus, the unique Son of God. This remarkable passage equips us and motivates us anew to proclaim him as the universal Lord.

1 Deut 32:35–43

Are we sometimes in danger of becoming over-familiar with the Lord Jesus in our language and attitudes, bearing in mind what we have seen in today's passage of his universal lordship as Son of God?

Evidence that demands a verdict

Day 52

Today's passage calls for some heart searching. Pray for an openness to the Holy Spirit as you read about formal religion and true faith.

John 5:31–47 

Cult leaders claiming divine authority are just as much a mark of the twenty-first century as of the first. Jesus implies that gullible people accept anyone coming in their own name (v 43). Jesus presents the case for his claim to unique Sonship.

First, Jesus' claims are supported by *John the Baptist*. He came to bear witness to the light (1:6–8) to the truth of Jesus himself (vs 33–35). Then Jesus' claims are supported by *his works*. All that Jesus did was the fulfilment of the work that the Father had given him to do (v 36).[1]

Finally, Jesus' claims are supported by *the Scriptures*. Here Jesus plays an ace card. For the Jewish authorities, Moses and the Law were held in high regard. These very Scriptures, Jesus affirms, bear witness to his uniqueness (v 39).[2] For all the Jewish authorities' diligent study (v 39), theirs was a theoretical knowledge (vs 46,47). They knew every detail of what Moses had recorded, but they had missed the heart of Old Testament teaching. Moses himself had become their accuser (v 45)!

They also suffered from distorted motivation (v 44). They were more interested in their own religious club and the affirmation of their own colleagues than the praise of the One who matters most of all. And finally they had a rebellious spirit: 'you refuse to come to me' (vs 40,43). Believing in Jesus is not a matter of intellectual argument. Ultimately it is a matter of the will.

This section encourages us with the truth about Christ, but also provokes us to evaluate our own response to him.

1 Luke 7:18–22
2 Luke 24:27

Are there areas in your spiritual life which need to change if you are to avoid the fatal errors of the religious leaders in this passage?

A little goes a long way

Day 53

Do we sufficiently bear in mind the need to carry out God's work in God's way?

John 6:1–15

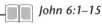

The Passover Feast (v 4) was the festival celebrating the deliverance from Egypt, when Moses led the people out of slavery. John had recorded that Moses wrote about Jesus (5:46), the true Deliverer. The incidents which follow highlight Jesus' ability to rescue those in need. Had the disciples learned to trust Jesus in every situation? Jesus uses the situation to test them (v 6), just as God tested his people in the wilderness.

First, there is Philip's secular perspective (v 7). His response to the need of the crowds is governed by the market place. 'We don't have the money'. There are many times when instead of trusting the Lord our Provider, we draw our own conclusions. I have frequently been challenged by believers in post-communist countries who have very few resources compared to Western Christians, and as a consequence have developed a more daring faith. Then we read of Andrew's narrow horizons (vs 8,9). He finds the boy with the meagre packed lunch but can't see how such limited means can meet such extensive need. We can be just as half-hearted as Andrew, belittling the very gifts God has given. Next John records Jesus' lavish provision – everyone had enough to eat (v 12), and there was a substantial amount left over (v 13).

Finally, John records the crowd's hasty judgement. They saw in Jesus a fulfilment of the Old Testament promise of a prophet to succeed Moses.[1] But in the heady atmosphere of the nationalistic Passover Festival, they mistakenly saw him as the military king whom they could manipulate (v 15). We too can be guilty of trying to shape Jesus to fit our aspirations, rather than bowing to his authority.

1 Deut 18:15

How can we encourage one another in the church to depend more fully on God's resources?

The 'I' of the storm

Day 54

Moments of vulnerability are moments of opportunity for God's blessing.

John 6:16–24 

It was no coincidence that, after being buoyed up by the miracle of loaves and fish and doubtless enjoying the crowd's adulation, the disciples now faced a humbling experience which would teach them fresh dependency on Jesus. He knew what lay ahead that night, and the importance of the further revelation of his identity for the disciples.

Jesus allows them to confront their need and vulnerability. The disciples were not novices, they were skilled fishermen who knew the lake. But John gives enough clues to reveal the mood: it was dark; Jesus was not with them; they were struggling with strong winds and a rough sea. It can sometimes feel like this in our own discipleship. Despite our experience or abilities, we're not making progress; the mood is dark and sometimes despairing; and often it seems that the Lord sends us on this journey to teach us something significant about himself.

Jesus then assures them of his presence. In response to their terror at seeing someone walking on the water, Jesus says: 'It is I; don't be afraid' (v 20). These words confirmed his true identity. 'I am – don't be afraid' calls to mind the great 'I AM' statement the Lord made to Moses.[1] There are many times in the turbulence of our own lives when we need to hear Jesus speak these words to us.

The text implies still more. After the revelation of his identity and presence John records, 'then they were willing to take him into the boat' (v 21). Allowing Jesus to step into the turmoil of their lives led to a probable further miracle: 'immediately the boat reached the shore where they were heading' (v 21).[2]

1 Exod 3:14
2 Ps 107:23–30

Pray for those who are facing a storm in their lives or some sustained opposition in their Christian service.

Day 55

Bread of heaven

'Feed me till I want no more.'[1]

John 6:25–42

There are always people seeking Jesus for the wrong reason. Their agenda may be political, looking for a military leader (6:15), or for personal, physical and material benefit (6:26). Jesus seeks to help people move beyond the surface issues, beyond the material, to recognise that spiritual life and satisfaction can only be found in the bread from heaven, Jesus himself.

Jesus has the Father's approval (v 27). People do not engage in the work God requires through attempting to earn salvation, but simply by believing in him (v 29). Nothing can be earned; it can only be received by faith in Jesus.

Jesus is the Father's provision (vs 32,33). The crowd wanted proof (vs 30,31) but manna, like the multiplied loaves on the hillside, perished. The true bread from heaven comes from God, and gives life to the world.

Jesus is the fulfilment of the Father's will (vs 37–40). He underlines again his dependence on the Father who sent him (v 38) and his commitment to the Father's purposes (v 39). Our task is to believe (v 29), to come (v 35), and to eat (v 51).

Some of those who heard Jesus that day were like their predecessors in the wilderness: they grumbled (v 41). They saw only a carpenter's son and not the Lord of life (v 42). But for those who believe, there is the experience of the full reality of Christ's life, the deep satisfaction that he alone can give, and the absolute certainty of a secure destiny (v 42). Every fragment will be gathered up in the basket (v 39)!

1 William Williams, 1716–1791

We often experience spiritual dryness. How does this passage encourage us towards a more dynamic spiritual life?

Food for life

'If you want to understand the Christian message, you must start with the wounds of Christ'.[1]

John 6:43–59

Much of John's Gospel is devoted to the cross. In chapter 6 Jesus is already speaking of his mission as he turns to the central gospel themes of his death and our salvation.

Jesus states that the living bread is his flesh which he gives for the life of the world (v 51) and builds a contrast with manna in the wilderness. Those who ate it were sustained temporarily, but eventually they died (v 49); eating the living bread results in eternal life. Manna was provided for a restricted group for a limited time; the living bread is for 'the life of the world'.

Although these verses remind us of Communion ('this is my body, given for you'),[2] they point first to Jesus' substitutionary death for all who believe, for all who 'eat' this bread. We should never lose sight of the profound wonder of Jesus' self-giving for us.

There is an essential need for all men and women to receive all that his sacrificial death achieved; to accept fully, to imbibe, to rely wholeheartedly on him. This specially involves receiving his Word (v 63; 5:24). Jesus is calling us to give ourselves completely to him, just as he has given himself for us.

Eating Jesus' flesh and drinking his blood brings us into union with him (v 56). Anticipating his teaching about the vine and the branches, John describes how we participate in God's life as we believe in Jesus.

There is a simplicity about this section which underlines Paul's conviction: 'for me to live is Christ'.[3] There is no hope outside of him. His death on the cross is the foundation of our union with him and of our eternal destiny. It is the answer to the world's deepest needs.

1 Martin Luther, 1483–1546
2 Luke 22:19; 1 Cor 11:24
3 Phil 1:21

In what ways can we nurture our spiritual life through Jesus' words?

True discipleship

Day 57

What are the main sources of satisfaction and fulfilment in your life?

John 6:60–71

This is one of the sad moments in John's account. 'From this time many of his disciples turned back and no longer followed him' (v 66). Many people are scandalised by the idea that Jesus is the unique Son of God, or that eternal life comes only through the foolishness of Jesus on the cross. It is precisely because of this difficulty that Jesus summarises the entire discourse of this chapter in one verse: 'The Spirit gives life' (v 63). Christian faith and discipleship arise only as we are enabled by God's Spirit to respond to the words of Jesus (vs 63,65).

Some in the crowd were only interested in a Messiah who would fulfil their own political agenda. But to worship the material rather than the spiritual is the sin of idolatry. The mission of Father, Son and Spirit is to enable us to participate in the spiritual life of God himself. As some of Jesus' followers turned away, he asked the twelve if they were about to do the same. And in characteristic forthrightness and with inspired faith, Peter declared two truths which are relevant to every age (68,69).

First, there is nowhere else to go, no other genuine source of life, no other reality. 'To whom shall we go? You have the words of eternal life' (v 68). Secondly, Jesus is the Holy One of God, the Messiah, the true Deliverer. Peter had come to see the true identity and mission of the Lord Jesus. He realised that there was nowhere else – no one else – in the universe where eternal life could be found, but in the Bread of Life.

When we are tempted to seek satisfaction from other sources or decide to follow other paths, Peter's response is one that we should ponder: 'Lord, to whom shall we go? You have the words of eternal life'.

Spend a while today renewing your commitment to follow Christ wholeheartedly.

A hardening of attitudes

In spite of Jesus repeating the exodus miracles – feeding the crowds and exercising authority over the sea – the crowds reject his claims. After a series of increasingly tense exchanges, attitudes also harden and the people take up stones against him. That this occurs during Tabernacles, the greatest and most joyful of all the feasts, celebrating God's past provision and future promises, only heightens the sense of irony and pathos. What has caused such a rift? One reason given by Jesus is the superficiality of Israel's assessment of him: they judge by mere appearances (7:24). People have certain expectations about how God should act. However, as Jesus makes clear, their understanding is tragically inadequate. Holding rigidly to their traditions they attribute Jesus' works to Satan, and seek to kill him (7:32).

Blinded to our need

Jesus reveals that only through him will Israel fulfil her calling. Just as long ago Yahweh showed mercy to idolatrous Israel, providing water (7:37,38) and light (8:12) for her in the first exodus, so too does Jesus (1:14,17.) He demonstrates his compassion for the woman caught in adultery (7:53 – 8:11). But even many of those who believe in him cannot accept that they also need this kind of liberation (8:32–33).

Above all, it is a question of Jesus' identity (8:58). He simply speaks the truth, neither defensively nor arrogantly, and leaves his justification with the Father (8:54). The Father acted, not only through the signs he continues to perform, culminating in the raising of Lazarus, but also by resurrecting Jesus.

We too have our expectations, our grids, our approved credentials, our pedigrees and traditions. Is it possible that we too might be blinded by them to the true character of God and run the risk of attributing his merciful works to the evil one?

Rikk Watts

How are we being heard?

Day 58

Ask God to grant you wisdom that you might know his ways.

 *John 7:1–13*

Jesus' support is waning (6:66). His brothers urge him to go public to bolster his following by impressing them with more mighty deeds. And what better setting than Tabernacles, Israel's most popular feast?

It is extraordinary to see how much Jesus cares about how he is heard. He does not bulldoze on regardless. While not altering his essential content to make things more palatable, he takes account of his hearers' perceptions and the prevailing political climate. God takes us and our context seriously. Knowing our cultural blindspots and wanting us to understand, he responds accordingly.

Sadly, often followers of Jesus have lacked this caring flexibility. 'God is with us,' we say, so full steam ahead – whether steadfastly pressing on because we have always done it this way or pandering to novelty and fashion for the sake of attracting whatever attention we can get. It might seem courageous, even spiritual, but if it ignores how those around us interpret our actions, it can easily be counterproductive.

Now, it is not as if Jesus avoids conflict. He has his mission. As the one who fulfils Tabernacles he cannot but attend and he goes up 'secretly', planning his actions carefully, choosing the right moment so as to avoid possible misunderstanding. His time as a public figure will come soon enough. However, it will be consistent with his message and shaped so that we might hear. When this true bearer of the Father's image, this faithful Son, this truly human one is finally made manifest to public gaze, his kingship and the Father's heart will be revealed in the glory of the cross.

Thank God, whose compassion extends to taking us so seriously that he cares about how we hear him. Think about ways in which you, by following this example, can help your neighbour see Jesus.

So where did you get your degree?

Reflect on those moments when God has spoken to you in the most unlikely ways and through the most unlikely people.

John 7:14–24 

Having arrived secretly, Jesus now acts publicly. However, what Israel needs is not more signs but understanding, so he teaches in the Temple. This too creates a problem. Only qualified rabbis are authorised to instruct here. What are his credentials and who is his teacher? This is still an issue today. Professionally-trained theologians sometimes sniff at home-grown preachers who may then respond with equal and feisty conceit. Both are mistaken. As Jesus declares, the issue is not formal credentials but intent. Education, denominational heritage, race, and gender, all pale beside the question, 'Is this from the Father?' (v 16).

Jesus says that those who really want to obey God will recognise what teaching comes from him. Could it be that we are often at loggerheads as, focusing on our own glory (v 18), and because of the absence of what our particular circle considers appropriate credentials, we fail to see that God is speaking?[1] This is why Jesus' opponents, although appealing to Moses, do not in fact obey him (v 19) and end up criticising Jesus' healing on the Sabbath (5:1–11). They set circumcision over against Sabbath because they think primarily in terms of rules. But circumcision and Sabbath concern the same thing: the entering of people into covenant rest with the Father. And that is precisely what Jesus does in restoring the lame man (v 23). Indeed, what better day than the Sabbath which both remembers and anticipates God's past and future deliverance of his people? If they really desired God's will they would realise that people matter more than formal adherence to rules. Sabbath, after all, was made for people, not people for Sabbath.[2]

1 2 Cor 10:7–11
2 Mark 2:27

Praise God for his abundant and merciful love for us and pray that we will reflect his priorities in our dealings with one another.

Day 60

Watch out for preconceived ideas!

'For my thoughts are not your thoughts, neither are your ways my ways.'[1] Think on how this has been true in your life.

John 7:25–36

Convinced the Messiah's origins would be shrouded in mystery, the people of Jerusalem are sceptical (v 27). They know where 'this man' is from. Ironically, of course, they do not; they do not realise that this 'man' is the Father's Son. Why? Because, as we have seen, their focus on tradition and rules (good though they may be) instead of on showing mercy, blinds them to what God is really like (v 28b).

Before we criticise, we might admit that this can happen to us too. Powerful additional traditions and expectations slowly evolve, perhaps our personal experience unduly colours our biblical interpretation, and soon we have our own grids to discern if something is from God. We somehow lose sight of what matters: being full of grace and truth – in that order (1:14). Sooner or later God works in a way that does not fit our grid. We reject it because 'we know'.

The Pharisees, secure in their superior 'knowing', attempt to remove the disruption. There is no need, says Jesus. He will soon be gone, but warns that having been rejected now he will not be found later. For others, although their grid did not particularly associate the Messiah with mighty signs, they sense that God is in this: compassion is evident, the lame walk. Yes, they were not our expectations, but then would they be so inappropriate to the Messiah? They do not fully understand, but they are prepared to let their preconceptions go. They believe. Time and again it is such people, humble and open to the truth that there is more mystery and mercy to God than we often realise, who carry the kingdom forward.

1 Isa 55:8

Praise God that he does not limit his merciful redemption to our small horizons. Pray that he might give us hearts as generous and people-focused as his.

The river of life

'As the deer pants for streams of water, so my soul pants for you, O God.'[1]

John 7:37–52

One rabbi declared that 'he who has not seen the joy of the water-drawing has never seen joy'. All, whether rich, poor, friend, or stranger were welcomed, and more sacrifices were offered at Tabernacles than at any other time. Israel not only celebrated God's harvest provision but both recalled the exodus and anticipated her restoration and the gathering of the nations to Jerusalem.[2] On this highest day of this greatest feast, priests drew water from Siloam ('sent one' 9:7); to pour upon the altar. It symbolised intercession for rain, recalled the provision of water from the rock in the wilderness (which some believed now resided under the altar),[3] and foreshadowed the eschatological rivers of salvation which would one day flow from the Temple,[4] itself seen as the navel where heaven joined earth.

It is here Jesus declared, 'If anyone thirst, let him come to me! Out of his stomach will flow rivers of living water!' (see also 4:10,20–24). The implications are staggering: Jesus, himself the life-giving smitten rock sent down from heaven, and all those who believed in him, would become the new dwelling of God's presence from which the Spirit would flow to restore creation. In spite of all we possess, our hearts long for something more. Jesus has quenched the deepest thirst of millions for a meaningful, lasting, loving relationship. With joy they have drawn water from the wells of salvation.

The call to love God and neighbour resulted in schools, hospitals, democratic institutions, and the passion to treat all people with dignity and respect. It led William Wilberforce to combat slavery. It has reconciled races and nations, bringing them joyfully into God's presence. No wonder tyrants fear him. Is he not indeed the true water of life?

1 Ps 42:1
2 Zech 14:9,16–18
3 Num 20:2–11
4 Ezek 47:1–12; Zech 14:8,10

Thank God for his great gift, and pray that not only may your life be filled with the Spirit, it may also become a source of life to others.

We beheld his glory

Day 62

'Give thanks to the LORD, for he is good;
his love endures forever.'[1]

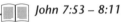

 *John 7:53 – 8:11*

Adultery is a soul-destroyingly painful situation to live through. It causes great hurt and shatters lives. Worse still, many offenders feel utterly isolated and abandoned by the church. This desperate woman (where is the man?) is dragged in. Apparently set during Tabernacles, the contrast between remembering God's merciful provision and the leaders' harsh demand is stark. What will Jesus do? Intriguingly, his questioners must have understood something of Jesus' concerns: the 'rules versus people' tension is clear.

Jesus writes on the ground, twice, with his finger. Was he doodling? Was it incriminating evidence against the woman's accusers? There is one other place in Scripture where something similar happens. God himself wrote the tablets of the Law twice because the first set was broken due to Israel's golden calf idolatry.[2] The woman's accusers 'know' the Law requires death. But what the Law actually says is that in her first exodus Israel became an adulteress,[3] and God showed mercy. Through writing on the ground twice, Jesus implies the question, why not also in this second exodus?

Biblically, adultery applies to all kinds of idolatries: greed, selfishness, and so on. All cause great harm. Yet God is rich in mercy. Breaking faith with one's spouse is a grave offence. It is easy, especially if our own marriages are insecure, to stand with those who 'know' the Law requires, if not stoning, then censure, rejection and isolation. Or we can hear Jesus and by repeating his utterly undeserved words of mercy – 'I don't condemn you ... go, stop sinning' – we too can become channels of the life-giving, restoring water of the Spirit. Or perhaps you stand with the woman. Remember, Jesus' words are for ever. Let yourself hear them.

1 Ps 118:1
2 Exod 32:1–20; 34:1–4
3 Exod 34:6,7

Kneel in awe of God's mercy, and pray that he might grant you to be a channel of such grace to others.

The fullness of the Spirit

Day 63

'He will not falter or be discouraged till he establishes justice on earth. In his law the islands will put their hope.'[1]

John 8:12–30 

The metaphor of light is frequently applied to God, and Israel's calling to be a blessing to the nations imaged her Father who caused light to shine in darkness.[2] Isaiah's Servant, Israel, was to be 'a light to the nations'[3] and restored Jerusalem was to attract them to the brightness of her shining.[4] Zechariah links this with Tabernacles,[5] which may explain why on the night before the water-drawing all of Jerusalem was illuminated by four massive seventy-five feet tall candelabras in the Temple. It is here, having supplanted the Temple as the source of living water, that Jesus reinforces his claim: 'I am the light of the world.' He is the fullness of the Father and of Israel's calling. In him the blind will see and (idolatrous?) nations find life (9:41). Yahweh's true Son establishes Yahweh's justice, and it is full of mercy and forgiveness. Israel should know this because that is what she experienced in the exodus and many times after. But somewhere along the line something got terribly lost. She no longer knew the Father.

One of the great tragedies of the church is that we so often accept the gnostic division between spiritual and physical. We focus on one or the other. But the truly Spirit-filled person should be concerned about justice, just as any Christian who seeks justice should be concerned about Jesus and his Spirit. This should hardly surprise us. God created us, body and spirit, to live in a physical world. We are not to love only God or our neighbour. Truly charismatic Christians love God with all their hearts, and should love their neighbour too.

1 Isa 42:4
2 Gen 12:3
3 Isa 42:6
4 Isa 60:3
5 Zech 14:7,16

Praise God for his concern for the real lives of real people and pray that you too might reflect his concern for all those who bear his image.

Whom do we have as Father?

Day 64

'One of you says "I follow Paul", another "I follow Apollos" … Was Paul crucified for you?'[1] Meditate on the sin of party spirit.

John 8:31–47

The tension between Jesus and Israel is growing. We know his enemies have been plotting against him (see 5:18). But now Jesus has some tough words for those who believed.

A Jew's identity was inextricably linked to his Abrahamic lineage; it made him special, second to none. Jesus calls this privilege into question. Why? Because Abraham cannot save them from their slavery to sin, a slavery they share with the rest of humanity. How quickly belief turns to hostility when the nerve of righteous superiority is touched! Here we are confronted with one of the uncomfortable things about Jesus: the absolute nature of his claims. He is quite clear that the Jews are in bondage and he is the only way to freedom. These believers are offended. But Jesus insists it is action, not bloodline, that determines parentage.

For many centuries the church has been divided by denominational loyalties. Divisions were sometimes so serious that any coming together between opposing sides was violent. Our loyalties to our founding fathers run deep. But, and without singling out any one group, we might need to ask whether we are first Anglican (or Baptist, etc) and second Christian. I have often wondered why it is that we happily admit that other Christian groups belong to the body of Christ, but insist that unless they jump through our hoops they cannot be members of our denomination. I am not against denominations per se, but can they encourage an in-crowd mentality and a feeling of superiority? Perhaps it would do us all good to remember the 'bottom line': everyone, regardless of pedigree, needs the Son to set them free. For the rest let great grace be evident.

1 1 Cor 1:12,13

Praise God for the centrality of Jesus among believers and ask him for more grace over other matters that could so easily divide.

The way of the resurrection

Day 65

'Those who honour me I will honour'.[1]

John 8:48–59 

Matters come to a head, and as Jesus claimed all along, the Jews seek to kill him (v 50). Abrahamic descent is not the issue; Israel can be God's son[2] only insofar as the nation follows Jesus, the only begotten Son who alone reflects the Father's glory (1:14,18). The Jews revile these claims as demonic. Centuries of Christian faith make it hard to taste the original acrid offence: how can these claims possibly be true of God? Jesus' response is instructive. Those concerned with their own honour defend it. Not he. It is the Father he honours; and his honour rests with the Father. David too had to learn that Messianic kingship was not about fighting his own battles, but the Lord's.[3] The temptation is not far from all of us. Our name is besmirched, our gravitas trifled with – archers appear behind the slits of our eyes.

The staggering thing about Jesus' claims is that they are borne not of overweening arrogance, but the truth. I too would join Jesus' critics in denouncing his insanity, were it not for one thing – the Father indeed glorified him. Through his Word the lame walked, the blind saw, and finally the dead lived.[4] We need to be struck again by the wonder of this; for who else can stand before the grave and call its captive out of freedom?

Our world is as fixed on status as it was in Jesus' day. It is easy to strike back, to demand satisfaction. But the only satisfaction that lasts and is truly worthy of the name is that given by the Father to those who are willing to lay down their honour to be his agents.

1 1 Sam 2:30
2 Exod 4:22
3 1 Sam 25:26–28
4 John 11:43,44

Praise God that he sent us his Son, and pray that we too might seek the Father's honour, even when our own is under attack.

The dangers of Bible study

Reading the gospels we unconsciously find ourselves on Jesus' side in his confrontations with his opponents. This is unfortunate. We shall derive more benefit if we identify ourselves with the Pharisees. After all, they were the evangelicals of their day. They took Scripture seriously. They were rightly concerned to evaluate any teaching which might lead people astray. They were doctrinally sound, as Jesus acknowledged. So what went wrong?

It was essentially a problem with words. The Pharisees argued, defined and refined but gradually they lost sight of the reality behind the words. By defining, for example, what constituted work on the Sabbath, they lost sight of the purpose of the Sabbath. Though they searched the Scriptures diligently they could not recognise the reality of which the Scriptures spoke – namely Jesus. They became blind.

Recognising God at work

Reading the gospels we naturally have a certain smugness because we understand who Jesus is. But the Pharisees had no such privilege. They were faced with an itinerant preacher with no credentials other than his actions and his words. He was not, apparently, 'one of us': he didn't 'use our kind of language' or 'move in our circles'.

The problem is, how do we recognise God's voice when we hear it or his actions when we see them? If we cannot perceive his purposes we condemn ourselves to be trapped in our traditions, unable to 'see' him or act in faith when he speaks. In John 10 Jesus speaks as a shepherd whose flock will recognise his voice and follow him. Seeing and responding are crucial concepts in these chapters. There are no prizes for merely hearing and discussing. Christian discipleship is a process by which we think and live ourselves into the life of Jesus: it grows gradually out of daily obedience to his Word and prayerful listening to his voice.

Peter Kimber

None so blind

Bring to God afresh any ongoing suffering or disability you may be experiencing, and ask him to show his glory through it.

John 9:1–12 

A blind beggar prompts the disciples to ask a profound question about the consequences of sin, but Jesus has little appetite for philosophical questions. If the disciples had known the Book of Job rather better they might have been prepared for Jesus' rather brusque reply. God has his purposes in allowing suffering in his world and the reasons are his alone.[1] Punishment is something we all understand. We can understand how the sins of parents can afflict their children, but it seems terrible that the blind man's affliction was allowed 'so that the work of God might be done'. What was 'the work of God' which Jesus came to do? Surely 'to free prisoners, open blind eyes, and liberate the oppressed'.[2] In this instance we can see how the man's blindness worked for the glory of God, but is that true of suffering in general?

Here is another great 'I am' statement (v 5).[3] This incident had a unique importance as a sign about the nature of Jesus. It is about spiritual and physical blindness, with the latter a visual illustration of the former. Spiritual blindness is as innate as this man's physical darkness, and only Jesus can illuminate it. In that sense we are all blind from birth. Time and again the gospel writers grappled with the mystery that their contemporaries were so blind to the person and divinity of Jesus.[4] It was plain to them that Jesus was God's Son: why could others not see it? Isaiah recognised that this blindness was recurrent throughout Israel's history.[5]

The disturbing thing is that it was religious people, studious, committed, scrupulous people who were blind while irreligious people seemed able to see who Jesus was without much difficulty.

1 Rom 8:17–25
2 Luke 4:18
3 Also 8:12
4 John 12:38
5 Isa 53:1; 6:9

Does it worry you that religious people can be blind to the uniqueness of Jesus? What does this teach us?

Day 67

Made good but gone wrong

God's good laws easily degenerate into legalism. 'Lord, save me from such a mindset.'

John 9:13–23

Why did Jesus so often provoke confrontation by healing on the Sabbath? Since he did only those things which the Father showed him, there was nothing accidental about these incidents.[1] Jesus chose his battlegrounds with care and Sabbath observance had obviously degenerated to the point where it distorted the divine intention. A benevolent commandment had become a symbol of sick religion.

But be sympathetic towards the Pharisees: they were the evangelicals of their day. Their devotion to the Law had noble and painful origins in the nation's history but it is in the nature of fallen humanity that we miss the mark, like a bent arrow. There is an in-built tendency towards legalism in all religion and they had become victims of that trend.

Verse 16 perfectly states the Pharisees' dilemma. If you break the Law you must by that very fact be a sinner, but how can God endorse the work of a sinner by performing a miracle? They hoped to find some demonic characteristics about Jesus' healing which could resolve the problem,[2] but the disarming simplicity of the blind man's testimony did not let them off the hook. Either God was at work or Jesus was a sinner. Perhaps the healing was a confidence trick, so the parents were interrogated. But there was no escape.

What does this incident say to us? Contemporary healing events often pose similar problems because they may not occur within our own theological community. Are they genuine or did the patient simply experience a temporary remission from cancer or whatever? Could healings even be evidence of demonic activity? Those who experience such healing usually have no more doubt than the man in this incident.

1 Luke 13:14
2 Matt 12:24

Are you conscious of religious customs which actually obstruct the work of God's kingdom?

One thing I know

When church traditions seem to be at odds with your experience of God, why not ask him for a clearer understanding of his nature?

John 9:24–34 

Why does God make life so difficult? In the passage there are two opposing positions. The Pharisees knew about the Law of Moses: don't break the Sabbath. Anyone who does should be stoned to death.[1] The whole weight of tradition and Scripture supported the Pharisees. How could they seriously place against that the actions of a nobody from nowhere – except that the 'nobody' had performed a unique miracle.

There is a very uncomfortable principle here which the church has had to face many times in its history. How should we evaluate new developments? Wherein lies the difference between a dangerous heretic and God's prophetic messenger? Was Martin Luther the voice of God to a corrupt church or a dangerous schismatic? Was Martin Luther King the voice of conscience to the segregationist churches of America or just a populist demagogue? How are we to judge?

Jesus' answer on this and similar occasions was to question people's understanding of God's character. Is God more likely to heal people than to hurt them? If we care for our animals enough to rescue the injured, isn't it intrinsically likely that God would treat us similarly?[2] Again, for what purpose did God give the Law? Was it to harm people or to help them; to give them rest or to impose unreasonable bondage? Expressed in that way, was the healing of a blind man something that God might endorse?

The answer seems pretty obvious, but there is a terrible power in peer pressure. The Pharisees felt safer in the crowd. Tradition is the glue which holds society – and particularly religious societies – together, isn't it? Here as elsewhere the sturdy testimony of the blind man counts for far more than theoretical objections.

1 Exod 31:14
2 Matt 12:11

How would you complete the sentence, 'One thing I know; once ... but now ... (v 25)'?

Much more than a miracle

Day 69

When we 'see' who Jesus is, we spontaneously worship him. Let's begin by doing so.

John 9:35–41

Jesus' miracles were never ends in themselves, particularly as John recounted them. They were always signs pointing to something more significant, so why did Jesus perform this healing sign?

The implications of this event are disturbing. Here are men devoted to the service and worship of God yet this story implies that they are spiritually blind. They cannot 'see' what is God's work and what is not. They cannot differentiate between the outward forms and the inward reality of worship, so all their disciplined study seems to have been counter-productive. They could not 'see' who Jesus was. Jesus acknowledged what was praiseworthy in the Pharisees but he deplored their practices.[1] Now he reveals himself overtly to a blind beggar much as he revealed himself to an immoral Samaritan woman. Isn't it terribly unfair that God appears not to reward the diligent student of theology and reveals himself to people who don't even seek him? Instead he actively seeks them. He has time for the poor and the despised.

There is an old chorus which goes, 'He did not come to judge the world; he did not come to blame; he did not only come to seek, it was to save he came'. While Jesus did not enter this world to judge it, John is very clear that his very presence and actions bring about judgement. People either want to enter the light of the glory of God, or they want to hide from it;[2] they either want spiritual sight or they want to stay blind. Yet paradoxically it is those who pride themselves on their spiritual insight who are most in danger of blindness. The Pharisees deeply resented Jesus' implied criticism of them – but they wouldn't do anything about it. Only the 'blind' man worshipped Jesus.

1 Matt 23:2
2 John 3:18

Is there any Pharisaical blindness in us? Jesus' purpose is to heal spiritual blindness where he is allowed to do so.

A hunger for God

Day 70

We won't hear God speaking if we don't listen. Take time to be still in God's presence.

John 10:1–10 

There was an old widow in northern Scotland who had only five sheep. It was the time when greedy landlords were driving out their tenant farmers to replace them with more economical sheep rearing. But the old widow would not be driven out. At the next shearing time the landlord ordered his shepherds to gather up her sheep with his, so that she would at last be without a livelihood. The shepherds did so and when the widow complained, the landlord said, 'Well, if you can find your five sheep among the thousands in the fields you can have them back'. The widow walked calmly down to the field and cried, 'Anna, Beth, Morag, Shona, Catriona – come away home,' and her five sheep obediently walked back to her cottage. They knew her voice.

Jesus makes the unequivocal claim to be the Shepherd of God's people and the evidence is that those whose hearts hunger after God will recognise his voice. They are a self-identifying group. Recognising the authenticity of Jesus is therefore not simply a rational or emotional affair; rather it is a hunger for reality – for God himself rather than for words about him. 'How blest are those who know their need of God; the kingdom of Heaven is theirs.'[1] The desire for God is like homesickness: nothing else will satisfy it.

Jesus offers a means of evaluating false prophets or ideologies. Does the heart leap in response to his voice? When we listen to God's word being proclaimed or when we meet someone whose face and life portray a close walk with God, does something in us cry, 'Yes, that is it: that is what I am looking for'. More searchingly, do people respond like that when they enter our churches or when they meet us?

1 Matt 5:3, NEB

'My sheep listen to my voice and they follow me' (v 37). Have you heard Jesus' voice recently?

One Shepherd; one flock

Day 71

'I lay down my life for the sheep' (v 15). Take time to meditate on this reassurance of Jesus' love for you.

John 10:11–21

This is a very searching passage for all Christian leaders, for it implies that the genuine shepherd has a degree of commitment to his flock that may cost him his life. Anything less than that suggests some measure of self-serving: am I in Christian service to satisfy my need for fulfilment, or is my primary concern for the well-being of the flock? Looking back over Israel's history Jesus sees a long line of 'wolves' who have in one way or another plundered the flock. By contrast his genuineness is shown by his utter self-giving. 'Who is equal to such a task?' as Paul asked.[1]

Verse 14 is extraordinary: we are known in the same way as God the Father and God the Son know each other, yet John throws in this statement almost as an aside. Contemporary Western culture is obsessed with asking: 'Who am I?' We don't even know our real selves, let alone anyone else. To be fully known and still be loved is almost beyond belief. Jesus gives that unqualified assurance that he knows and loves his sheep to the point of death. As we enter into the enormity of that it must surely erode our deepest insecurities.

Jesus' statement that he has sheep from other folds than Israel is the ground of our hope as Gentiles. Is there a wider implication than that for verse 16? We Christians like to define very closely the boundaries of God's people, usually restricted to those who think as we do, but God probably says to all of us, 'I have other sheep that are not of (your particular) fold'. Membership of a 'true' church is usually defined in doctrinal terms. But Jesus' definition is, 'My sheep hear my voice and they follow me'.

1 2 Cor 2:16

'There shall be one flock and one Shepherd' (v 16). Thank God for the unity of God's people in Jesus.

Words and deeds

Ask God's help to see beyond the words of Scripture to the reality of which they speak.

John 10:22–42 

If Jesus' words in yesterday's passage were those of a madman (v 20), what was the source of his power? His opponents wanted to conclude that his miracles were either fraudulent or demonic, but Jesus would not let them off the hook: they were done 'in my Father's name' so that was not an option. You can't invoke God's name in your prayers and have them answered by the devil. The critics could not see beyond the words of Jesus; they could not read the deeds for what they meant.

Jesus had implied unmistakably that he was God's Son and provoked outrage. 'All right,' says Jesus, in effect; 'if you want to be literal, how about Psalm 82:6? If God is content to call the rulers of the nations "gods" why stone me for saying "I am God's Son"?' Jesus knew his Scriptures better than his opponents and turned their literalism against them.

Words are important, not for themselves but for what they communicate about reality. Jesus' opponents knew the Scriptures but could not see the one of whom they spoke. Jesus was adamant that 'the Father is in me and I am in the Father'. Later he makes the far more extraordinary statement, speaking of his relationship with his disciples, 'I in them and you in me'.[1] This is the level of intimacy and unity that Jesus offers his disciples, and before it we can only bow in humility and incredulity. How can it be?

As we look at the life of Jesus we see in his every word and deed the love of the Father. But he is 'in us as God was in him'! Did ever a handful of monosyllables contain such an unimaginable burden of meaning?

1 John 17:23

Take time to enjoy the extraordinary relationship you have with God through Jesus.

Discovering Jesus

John wrote his Gospel with the express purpose that his readers might personally discover Jesus for themselves (20:31). What do we learn about him here?

The first theme that John emphasises is Jesus' clear sense of God's purpose being worked out through his life. He was a *man with a mission*, and, as our readings show, that mission was moving towards its climax.

Secondly, Jesus *lived in obedience to God's will*. He wasn't swayed by popular opinion and was even willing to be misunderstood by those closest to him. What mattered most was doing what God required. This is poignantly summed up by Jesus' statement: 'Now my heart is troubled, and what shall I say? "Father save me from this hour"? No, it was for this very reason I came to this hour. Father, glorify your name!' (12:27–28).

Thirdly, Jesus *knew that there was a cost to all this*. The grain of wheat had to die in order to bear fruit (12:24) and the way of salvation was the road of the cross (12:32–33).

Journeying with Jesus

One is haunted by a memorable phrase from John's pen. 'Whoever claims to live in him must walk as Jesus did' (1 John 2:6). Lifelong learning has become a buzz term in educational circles. But it has lain at the heart of Christian discipleship since Jesus first issued the call, 'Follow me'. Disciples do not remove their 'L-plates' this side of heaven.

So as we journey with Jesus over the next few days, let's do it with a commitment to learn something new about following God's purpose for our lives with glad obedience and a willingness to pay whatever it costs. After all, as Jesus promised, 'Whoever serves me must follow me: and where I am, my servant also will be. My Father will honour the one who serves me' (12:26).

Ian Coffey

When God delays

Ask God for patience and insight for some of those inexplicable situations you may face.

John 11:1–16 

Sometimes it's hard to be a believing believer. God seems unconcerned about our need and deaf to our prayers. Why won't he act?

Three close friends of Jesus faced this struggle. They had done everything by the book. Martha, Mary and Lazarus had opened their home to Jesus as an oasis of calm, serving him with devotion and developing a close relationship of trust. John points out twice that these were special friends (vs 3,5).[1]

So why didn't Jesus act instantly when a serious illness struck Lazarus? Is this any way to treat your friends? Didn't they deserve better? A clue is found in his comment that God had a greater purpose that was being worked out (v 4).[2]

We know the end of the story already, that resurrection life would touch this family and their tears would be turned into laughter. But on the day Lazarus died, Jesus was not there and the sisters were left alone with their pain and their questions. The disciples couldn't understand Jesus' actions either. Why was he returning to an area where his life had been threatened (v 8) – a decision that would put their lives at risk as well (v 16)?

Jesus lived by God's direction and urges us to do the same (v 9). We don't have all the answers as to what God is up to and the walk of faith is not meant to be a neat little parcel with no room for questions or doubt. Often we are so caught up with the immediate problem we are unable to see God's greater purpose being worked out. We are called to trust – especially when we can't work out what God is doing.[3]

The Puritan William Gurnall captured it brilliantly when he wrote, 'We live by faith, and faith lives by exercise'.

1 Compare Luke 10:38–42
2 Rom 8:28–30
3 Ps 37:1–7

'Father, in those situations where I cannot understand you – teach me to trust. Amen.'

Day 74

'Blessed are those who mourn'

'Test the physician before you open yourself to him. Determine whether he can be ill with one who is ill, weep with one who weeps'.[1] Jesus passes the test!

John 11:17–27

By the time Jesus arrived at Bethany the funeral was over but the official mourning continued, with many visitors offering comfort to the sisters who had lost their brother (v 19). There may be some significance in the comment that Martha went to meet Jesus while Mary stayed at home (v 20). Was Mary overcome with grief – or perhaps feeling too angry at Jesus' delay in responding to them at their time of great need?

The thing that stands out from Martha's encounter with Jesus is her trust in him. Even her question about Jesus not arriving in time to heal Lazarus is mixed with a powerful statement of faith (vs 21–22). Her honest conversation with Jesus prompts two remarkable comments.

First, Jesus makes one of his great 'I am' statements (v 25) – one of seven that John records in his Gospel as Jesus claims to be the unique Son of God.[2] Secondly, Martha herself comes out with a statement that ranks alongside any of the great confessions of faith recorded in Scripture (v 27). In these moments of grief and confusion we find revelation and faith – side by side.

Perhaps this gives us a clue as to the special blessing promised to those who mourn (see Matt 5:4). In our darkest moments, as we reach out to God we can learn more about his character and purpose.[3] Suffering can lead us to a more intimate relationship with him.[4] In turn, this can feed our faith and take us to new and deeper levels of trust. The dark night of the soul can lead us through to a new dawn of faith.

1 Origen, c185–254
2 See also 6:35; 8:12; 10:9,11; 14:6; 15:1
3 2 Cor 1:3–7
4 Job 42:5

How about a call or a letter to someone recently bereaved to assure them they are not forgotten by God – or you? Spend a few moments lifting them in prayer and asking what you can do to help.

The Lord of life

Hear Jesus' words: 'Do not be afraid. I am the First and the Last. I am the Living One; I was dead, and behold I am alive for ever and ever! And I hold the keys of death and Hades'.[1]

John 11:28–44

Jesus often acts in ways we cannot understand. Mary is as honest as her sister in echoing Martha's question as to why he had delayed responding to their cry for help (vs 21,32). Yet even in her doubt there is a note of faith.

Even the mourners were wondering why Jesus had failed to perform a miracle to keep Lazarus alive. John goes out of his way to explain the deep impact Lazarus' death had on Jesus. Three times he refers to the profound emotional response he witnessed, including the memorable phrase, 'Jesus wept' (v 35).

Why was Jesus so deeply troubled? (The verb in the original Greek *embrimaomai* actually indicates a strong sense of anger). After all, if he was about to raise his friend to life and bring unspeakable joy to a broken-hearted family – why weep? Perhaps part of the answer lies in Isaiah's prophetic remark that the Messiah would be, 'a man of sorrows and familiar with suffering'.[2] Jesus was entering into the grief and helplessness we all share in the face of death. Here at a friend's grave he identifies with the awful, ultimate consequences of human rebellion, knowing that within a matter of days he would undertake the 'great reversal' through his sacrificial death on the cross. In anticipation of his own defeat of death's power, Jesus releases Lazarus from its grip with a mighty word of command (v 43).[3] He is the Lord of Life![4]

1 Rev 1:17–18
2 Isa 53:1–12
3 Col 1:15–20
4 Matt 28:16–20

Reflect on these words of the Baptist preacher CH Spurgeon (1834–92): 'I have a great need for Christ; I have a great Christ for my need'.

Belief and unbelief

Day 76

'Heavenly Father, clear my mind now of noise and distraction that I may hear your voice speaking through Scripture. Amen.'

 *John 11:45–57*

Today's reading paints a sharp picture of the contrast between belief and unbelief. Look at the different reactions revealed in the passage.[1] Some who had seen Lazarus brought back to life were now convinced that Jesus' claims were true and put their faith in him (v 45). Others (for whatever motives) ran off to tell the religious authorities, who called an emergency meeting. They knew they had a crisis on their hands and, although they could not deny the truth of the miracles (v 47), they feared the loss of their own powerbase (v 48).[2] Self-interest obscured their vision and hardened their hearts. John records an (unconscious) prophecy given by the High Priest. Caiaphas, at one level, was making a statement about ridding themselves of a troublemaker. But at a deeper level, he was prophesying that Jesus of Nazareth was about to die as the sin-bearer for people of all nations (vs 51,52).

It is curious how the raising of Lazarus became a defining moment. For some it opened a doorway to faith. But for others (who were meant to be 'experts' on God) it caused them to shut the door and draw the bolts of prejudice and fear firmly shut. They began to plot how to take Jesus' life (vs 53,57) so he slips from public view until his appointed hour (v 54). Our reading underlines the truth that it is impossible to look at Jesus and remain neutral about him. His challenging claims continue to divide people into two groups: those who choose to open their hearts and others who choose to harden them.[3]

1 2 Cor 4:1–6
2 Prov 1:7
3 John 1:10–14

Can you think of some people in your own circle of friends who are not yet followers of Jesus Christ? Spend a few moments praying for them by name and asking God that their hearts and minds would be open to the truth about his Son.

Costly service

In what ways do you serve God? Take a moment to think about some of the things you do – and the way in which you are doing them.

John 12:1–11 

This rather special party – called to celebrate Lazarus' new start in life – offers insights into the right ways and wrong ways of serving God. Mary reveals the sort of worship and service that delights God's heart (vs 2–3).[1] It was motivated by love (nothing else could explain such a selfless, humbling act). It was costly (even if Judas was guilty of exaggerating, the perfume was expensive!). Her actions laid her open to criticism (but then real love is always willing to pay that price). And what she did left a lasting impression. Decades later John could still recall the powerful aroma of the perfume (v 3). And two thousand years later the memory of her extravagant gesture lingers on.[2]

Judas, on the other hand, is a prime example of how not to serve God (vs 4–6). On the surface he appeared to be trustworthy and even held the post as treasurer for the disciples – but inwardly his motives were selfish. (See verse 6 – where John pulls no punches in calling him a thief.) He appeared to be serving the Lord, while all the time he was serving himself. His critical spirit showed he looked for good reasons for thinking bad things (v 5). And as his story tragically unfolds, Judas shows how wrong actions can ultimately lead to disaster (see Luke 22:1–6; Matt 27:3–5). He was sowing the seeds that would produce a terrible harvest.

Mary and Judas provide a challenging contrast of right and wrong motives when it comes to Christian service. Which of the two gives the closest description of the way we serve?[3]

1 Col 3:17
2 1 Cor 13: 1–13
3 Ps 100:1–5

Consider this checklist of questions about our service for God. What are we doing? Why are we doing it? How are we doing it? Who are we doing it for?

Day 78

Hindsight

Make time to be still before God and give over to him some of those things that have occupied your time this week. Ask him for the ability to view your circumstances from his perspective.

John 12:12–19

John is an honest writer. Even though he was present on this occasion when Jesus rode into Jerusalem, seated on a donkey and receiving the acclaim of the large crowd, John freely admits that it wasn't until much later that he and his fellow disciples realised the significance of what had taken place (v 16).

This event marked what we now call Palm Sunday and the start of the week that would lead Jesus to the cross and beyond to the empty tomb. With hindsight, John could see the enormous significance of what was being played out in the Easter event. The cries of the crowd were echoes of Old Testament passages[1] and the strange sight of a King on a donkey, a direct fulfilment of Zechariah's prophecy five hundred years earlier.[2] These things only became clear to John and the other disciples *after* Jesus had risen from the dead. How they must have read and re-read the Scriptures and gasped in amazement as they began to understand the significance of the events they had seen unfold before their eyes.[3]

At one level John had seen Jesus emerge into view, enter Jerusalem for the Feast of Passover and receive public applause. But, looking back, John saw God at work at a deeper level. Here was Jesus, God's long awaited Passover Lamb, in the final stages of the road to Calvary where the greatest rescue act in human history would be accomplished.

1 See Ps 118:25,26
2 See Zech 9:9
3 Luke 24:25–27, 44–49

'Father, teach me to understand your greater purpose and to grasp the deeper significance of events. May I have wisdom to understand your ways. Amen.'

The cost of following

Day 79

Something to consider today: 'The greatness of a man's power is the measure of his surrender.'[1]

John 12:20–26 

Jesus didn't meet every request or answer every question that was put to him. Today's reading highlights one such incident. Some Greek visitors attending Jerusalem for the Jewish Feast of Passover were keen to meet Jesus and discover for themselves what he was teaching (v 21). Philip and Andrew relay the request to Jesus, but the surprising result is that it appears the Greek visitors didn't get their interview. This is not rudeness on Jesus' part, but a signal that a crucial moment in his mission had arrived, 'The hour has come for the Son of Man to be glorified' (v 23).

John makes a great emphasis in his Gospel about Jesus following God's clock – and now its hands were moving to the significant hour for which he had come to earth.[2] Instead of meeting new people, Jesus spells out the cost of his mission (v 24). Like a seed that falls into the ground, dies and multiplies, so his death will produce a rich crop of people rescued by God's grace. He reveals a single-minded focus on this task.

He links his obedience to God's plan to the willingness of those who follow him to go the same way.[3] Anyone who claims to follow him, must walk his path.[4] That involves laying down selfish independence and surrendering to God's will (vs 25–26). Jesus lived at the heart of God's timetable and so must all who claim to follow him. And that is the place of safety and of honour in God's eyes (v 26). Perhaps – like Jesus – that may mean disappointing others and refusing to meet their expectations, in order to obey God and live under his smile of approval.[5]

1 William Booth, 1829–1912
2 John 13:1
3 Heb 12:1–22
4 1 John 2:6
5 Phil 3:7–11

Many Christians pay a high price for following Christ. Perhaps you could remember some of them in your prayers today?

Day 80

Living in the light

'Lord Jesus Christ, Light of the World, illumine my path today.'

 *John 12:27–36*

The awareness that his 'hour' was fast approaching must have stirred mixed emotions for our Lord. This was a time of deep disturbance at the core of his being that we can hardly imagine. Notice that Jesus does not pray that he will be able to escape all he faces, but rather that God the Father will receive glory through his obedience (vs 27–28). There is a lesson here for us. How often do we pray, 'Lord, get me out of this!' rather than 'Lord, be glorified in this situation'?

God's voice of approval is heard by the incredulous crowd, although not many were clear what the noise was (v 29). As Jesus anticipates the cross and Satan's crashing defeat, he speaks about being 'lifted up', and that through this means people will be drawn to him. John (again with the benefit of hindsight) understood this had a deeper meaning (v 33). Even today the message of Jesus' death on the cross still draws people to the love and forgiveness of God.

Jesus answers the questioning crowd's challenge with a word picture (vs 34–35). The world is a dark place and Jesus – the Light of the World – has come. People have a clear choice. They can believe in the light, walk by its glow and trust its power. Or they can stay stumbling around in the dark. The promise that Jesus offered then he offers now; those who live by the light can become children of that light.[1]

I find it hard to live as a child of the light sometimes.[2] Perhaps by focusing more on glorifying God and lifting up Jesus, that light would shine through me more clearly?

1 John 8:12–30
2 Matt 5:13–16
3 1 John 1:5–10

How can I let the light of Christ shine through me today? What is God calling me to say or do (or not say or do) that will make his light more visible?[3]

Walking in the light

Day 81

'Lord Jesus, please soften my heart; warm it with your love.'

John 12:37–50 

Today's reading underlines some very different responses to Jesus, his miracles, teaching and claims. John records that some flatly refused to believe (vs 37–41). No amount of miracles would persuade them because 'there are none so blind as those who will not see'. John explains their stubborn refusal with Isaiah's prophetic insights into the coming of the Messiah. He describes what is sometimes referred to as 'penal blindness'. One consequence of sin is blindness to truth, and the more you harden your heart, the harder your heart becomes.

Then there were those who secretly believed (vs 42–43), but they were more afraid of what people would think and the costly implications of 'coming out' as followers of Jesus. John drops a large hint that some of the influential religious hierarchy were in this category – but fear of men was a bigger motivation for them than love for God.

Jesus himself mentions a third group – those who believe but never follow through (v 47). He warns that it is possible to be devoted hearers of God's Word without being practitioners.[1] We've probably all heard stories about people who could recite texts from the Bible but didn't have the first clue about putting them into practice. And they have done great damage to the cause of Christ. It is possible for any of us to come out with the right words, but not to live our lives accordingly.

As Jesus points out, his words are spoken on the authority of God the Father (vs 45,49). He is the one who will judge those who refuse to believe (v 48). It is by coming to the light and walking in obedience to that light, that we can find eternal life (vs 46,50).[2]

1 James 1:22–25
2 Ps 27:1–14

Refusing to believe, secretly believing and believing but not following through all amount to the same thing – unbelief. Do you agree?

Jesus and his friends

The Gospel of John can be divided into two main sections, 'the Book of Signs' (chapters 1–12) and 'the Book of Glory' (chapters 13–21). We are now going to study the opening of this second part, which takes us up to the death and resurrection of Jesus. We are invited to the evening before the Passover feast. The following day, when the paschal lambs were to be slaughtered in the Temple, Jesus would die on the cross as the Lamb of God.

The narrative brings us close to Jesus himself, who spent the last night before his death with his friends. The atmosphere is heavy with emotion and the disciples' unanswered questions. Jesus shows his strong affection for his fearful disciples; he does most of the talking, but he also listens to them as they express their misunderstandings and confusion. Six of the twelve are mentioned by name, but Judas Iscariot manages to play an important role without opening his mouth.

On an occasion like this, one would expect a retrospective mood but Jesus is looking forward to his imminent death and to what will follow. He is talking of his departure, but also of his invisible return and his renewed presence through the Holy Spirit. We have here some of Jesus' most fundamental sayings on the nature of the church.

There are numerous allusions to the Lord's Supper throughout John's Gospel, so it seems odd that he is the only evangelist not to record any explicit reference to the meal on this last evening. But John's emphasis is always to record words and actions of our Lord which are not included in the other Gospels, presupposing that the basic facts are already known. So instead we have Jesus washing his disciples' feet and the parable of the vine and the branches. As you read, look out for illuminating contrasts such as leaving – coming, love – hatred, Spirit – world, fear – trust, guilt – righteousness, grief – joy.

Hans Lindholm

Washed by Jesus

Be prepared to come with your dirty feet to be served by Jesus.

John 13:1–17

Uppsala: it was Maundy Thursday and we decided that we would wash each other's feet. A few chairs had been put out at the front of the church, and I was ready with a bowl of water and a towel. One or two people had already agreed to come forward, but we also decided to make an open invitation. Soon all the chairs were occupied by both adults and children. I still owe some people a foot-wash!

Jerusalem: it was due to bad management. No one had organised a slave to wash the guests' feet. None of the guests felt called, so the Master himself got up from the meal ...

No wonder Peter reacted. His concern for his Lord was impulsive and outspoken as usual. At first he would not accept his Lord's embarrassing offer; then he went almost too far in his wish to be completely united with Jesus. Are we willing to be served by Jesus? Or do we refuse his help because of some false humility, which is in reality, pride?

To have one's feet washed by Jesus is to receive 'the full extent of his love' (v 1), to 'have ... part with' Jesus (v 8), to become clean (v 10) and to have an example to follow (v 15).

Just as the foot-washing has a deeper meaning, so the phrase 'had a bath' (v 10) is used in various forms and settings in the New Testament to signify baptism.[1] But even the disciple who has already been cleansed in his unity with Christ will constantly need to ask for forgiveness as he is 'soiled' by his daily pilgrimage.

1 See 1 Cor 6:11; Eph 5:26; Titus 3:5; Heb 10:22

How should the foot-washing love of Jesus change our attitudes to one another? Think of one practical way you can serve another believer today.

Day 83

Who is the traitor?

A searching prayer: 'Surely not I, Lord?'[1]

 *John 13:18–30*

Judas is an intriguing character. We are touched by his tragic fate, the fruit of his own choices as well as the inevitable fulfilment of the Scriptures. What kind of a person was he? What were his motives?

He was a respected disciple, entrusted with the money. The others were astonished when Jesus said that one of them was going to betray him. It is not easy to spot a 'Judas' in a group of disciples: even Peter and the 'disciple whom Jesus loved' (probably a code name for John) had to find out by asking the Lord. The name 'Judas' should not be used to condemn others; rather it is a painful reminder for ourselves: who has never betrayed Jesus?

Jesus alone knows the traitor, as we saw yesterday (vs 2,10–11) and hear again today in his words (vs 18, 21). Dipping a piece of bread in a dish came to signify the identification of a traitor, but traditionally it is a host's sign of lasting friendship. In a final attempt to reach Judas's heart, Jesus offered him forgiveness and fellowship. When Judas refused his offer – accepting the bread but not the fellowship – Satan entered into him.

The chain of events leading to the death of Jesus is a shabby story. The Greek word for 'betray' can also be rendered 'hand over' or 'give up'. It is used when the Jewish leaders leave Jesus in the hands of Pilate,[2] and when Pilate sends him to be crucified.[3] So much more astonishing then, that the same word is also used when God gives up his Son into the hands of sinners.[4] Sinful history is transformed into Good News.

1 Matt 26:22,25
2 John 19:11
3 John 19:16
4 Rom 8:32

Examine your relationship with Jesus: do you have a pure and honest heart or do you feel like someone who has betrayed their Master?

The unexpected way to glory

Day 84

What would it involve to glorify God in such a way that all glory will be his?

John 13:31–38 

Yesterday we ended in the dark night of betrayal (v 30) and today we start in glory. These are two sides of the same event: the death of Jesus. Betrayal and the cross look like defeat, but in the very moment that Judas went to the high priests, Jesus' glorification had begun. He had come for this very purpose.[1]

The Greek word for 'glory' concerns the relationship between what somebody is and how he is considered. To give glory to God is to recognise who he is. 'Now is the Son of Man glorified', that is, through the cross he is shown to be the Saviour of the world. 'God is glorified in him': through the cross God is revealed as love beyond understanding. Peter was eager to follow his Master, so he wanted to know where he was going. Once, I thought songs of praise were the best way to glorify Jesus. But Peter saw much deeper, wanting to obey him and lay down his life for him.

Still, how was Peter to handle his own denial of Jesus? Would the glory be lost for ever?[2] Jesus, of course, knew that Peter would let him down (v 38). So how was Peter going to follow Jesus when he had not been able to do so on the very evening when he expressed his wholehearted devotion (v 37)?

The answer, of course, is the cross which changed everything for Peter, for me and for all sinners. To glorify Jesus is to confess one's dependence upon him. Once I have done that, then, at last, Jesus can be for me what he has always been: the Saviour – even though this may ultimately lead to death for his glory.[3]

1 John 12:23–28
2 Rom 3:23
3 John 21:19

Only those who place all their dependence and glory in Jesus can truly love. Show true love to your fellow disciples without secretly despising them!

Day 85

Reasons for trust

What makes your heart troubled? Bring your worries to the Lord again today.

 *John 14:1–14*

Jesus is a sensitive listener to our worries and questions. His invitation to trust in God and in himself gives us good reason for such confidence. The first image is of his Father's house with its many rooms. I had a taste of heaven at a retreat centre with single rooms where my name was on the door and a fresh flower on the table.

Jesus was a carpenter by trade,[1] a craftsman with unique skills. He had to leave his disciples to prepare a place for them – and for us – in the Father's house. The second image is of the way. Thomas wanted to know where Jesus was going, just as Peter had done a moment before (see 13:36). But Jesus had already spoken about the final goal, so he pointed to himself as the only 'way'.

A group was being led through the jungle. When somebody expressed worries because no path could be seen, the guide stopped and pointed to himself: 'I am the way'. In all his 'I am' words, Jesus identifies with God's holy name[2] and also proclaims his uniqueness. There are no other 'ways' or 'truths' or 'lives' like his: Jesus – the name above all names.

The third image is Jesus himself. Philip was sure: Jesus could not mean that they had actually seen the Father, which every Jew knew was impossible.[3] But Philip (like many people today, perhaps) wanted to see God – either as unquestionable proof or out of a deep longing for him, a longing which has been with us since the creation. Jesus is the human face of God. He is the God who shows what man is, and the man who shows what God is.

1 Mark 6:3
2 Exod 3:14
3 Exod 33:20

Invite somebody who has a troubled heart to claim their place in the Father's house; to follow Jesus' way; to see Jesus as the human face of God.

On the wavelength of the Spirit

Day 86

Are Christians today more aware of the absence or the presence of Jesus? Pray that you will really know he is with you today.

John 14:15–31 

I remember hearing a morning devotion on Swedish radio many years ago which used the image of a man on his way to be interviewed at a TV studio. The man told his friend: 'Now I will enter a secret room from where I can transmit my thoughts to millions of homes simultaneously'.

Jesus went to his Father, who is in a secret 'room' at the centre of the universe. From there the Spirit of truth is sent out. We all have to have some sort of receiver in order to see or hear the person in the studio: in this passage Jesus points to his commands and our obedience to them as the 'receiver' we all need. When we read his Word with humble, receptive hearts we can hear him speaking to us.

The Greek word for 'obey' also implies 'watch', 'keep', 'preserve' and 'maintain'. We are to uphold the teachings of Jesus, because they are as precious as gold. This would probably answer Judas' question (v 22). The world may be interested in supernatural manifestations, but is it willing to obey the commands of Jesus? Without his Word there is no promise of the Spirit.

Our televisions must be perfectly tuned for a good picture and clear sound. Throughout this passage Jesus talks about love as being the 'wavelength' of the Spirit. But this is more than a TV broadcast: the Holy Spirit carries the presence of Jesus and his Father into the hearts of ordinary Bible readers (vs 21,23). Let us open the Word and be willing to receive the love of Jesus and to love him in return.

When the Spirit makes the words of Jesus become flesh in us, others get to know him. Maybe you have read something in your Bible recently which you would like to share with somebody else?

Day 87

The true vine and its branches

Pray that the two key words of today's meditation, 'remain' and 'fruit', may become a reality in your life.

John 15:1–17

Israel is described as a 'choice' vine[1] – a vine which God delivered out of bondage and planted in the promised land.[2] Now Jesus claims to be the true vine, that is, the true Israel (not a 'new' vine). Throughout this passage we are urged to 'remain' or 'stay' in Christ. It is easy for an activist like me to forget that we can do nothing apart from him. Our 'remaining' in Jesus is made concrete in two ways. First, his Word is the unifying fibre of the vine, so we are to live in the Word and to allow the Word to live in us.

Secondly, the life-giving sap of the vine is his unceasing love. So we are to remain in Christ (v 4), in his Word (v 7) and in his love (vs 9–10). It is impossible to remain in Christ without his Word, and the main function of the Word is to convey his love.

A living branch of the vine can do nothing but bear fruit, which is the whole idea of the vine as well as the single objective of the caring gardener. That is why branches without fruit are cut off, while those bearing fruit are pruned (or 'cleansed'). Every branch has some experience of the sharp knife of the gardener.

Jesus gives one command: 'Love each other as I have loved you' (v 12). The lasting fruit is love: to honestly share what we are and to receive others as they are. The constant temptation for Christians is to pretend to be better than we are and to try to control and correct others. Bearing fruit is not our choice, but an appointment and a promise given by Jesus (v 16).

1 Jer 2:21
2 Ps 80:8–19

How can your church become a place of true love?

'They hated me without reason'

Day 88

How can Christians build a healthy, biblical relationship with the world?

John 15:18 – 16:4 

In Sweden one hundred years ago there was a clear division between the church and the world. This division was emphasised by different styles of clothing and by churchgoers' attitudes towards such activities as theatre-going, the cinema and dancing. If the picture then was perhaps too black and white, even tending to encourage 'Pharisaic' attitudes, today it seems blurred: it is sometimes hard to perceive any difference between the attitudes of the secular world and those of churchgoers.

Perhaps the words at the beginning of this passage, 'If the world hates you ...' (15:18) and the warning in 16:2 indicate that the intensity of conflict between the church and the world will vary at different times and in different places. We do know that the 20th century saw more martyrs and persecuted disciples than any other century in the history of the church.

Our task is to be faithful to the Lord, not to provoke hatred from the world or to provide reasons for hatred against us (15:25).1 But have we been faithful? Has Jesus spoken to people through us (15:22)? Has he worked among them through our actions (15:24)? If not, the guilt is ours.

Perhaps an attitude of indifference is the Western equivalent of hatred? Because of this, the enemy has often succeeded in watering down the gospel message. The emphasis of this passage is, of course, on bringing comfort to the suffering and persecuted children of God (16:4). Jesus has a message for all his disciples who are misunderstood, scared and lonely: 'There is nothing wrong with you. You have been hated without reason, just as Jesus and his Father who are perfect are hated. The world hates you, because you do not belong to the world, but are servants of the suffering Lord'. You are sharing the burden and mystery of his cross.

In what way does the world trouble you? If you feel no pain, are you living the gospel?

The hard work of the Spirit

Day 89

Many people today are searching for their own brand of spirituality. Pray that your search will match the aims of the Holy Spirit.

John 16:5–16

The Spirit is shy. Like a good manager, he does not want to shine himself, but would rather promote Jesus (vs 13–14). In this passage, it is as if the world is a court of law: Jesus has been accused, and in a few hours he will be killed as an evil-doer. But after he has been taken away, the Counsellor will come and plead his cause. (We can also see this happening in Acts, which could be called 'Acts of the Spirit'.) God rejected the verdict of the Sanhedrin and of Pilate. They sentenced Jesus to death, but God sentenced him to life. Hence the contrasting 'But God ...'[1] and the inevitable choice between obeying God or obeying men.[2] In raising Jesus from the dead, God demonstrated to the world the righteousness of Jesus and the sinfulness of his accusers.

Now imagine that my heart is a court: if Jesus is on one side and I am on the other, who is righteous and who the sinful one? The Counsellor is also known as 'the Spirit of truth' (v 13), so his judgement is trustworthy. When he comes to me, my perspectives are changed and a new honesty makes me a humbler person.

Our sin is that we often choose not to believe in Jesus, though we usually believe in ourselves. Righteousness is made available because Jesus has healed what was broken: like a good repair-man, he only left when the job was done. Judgement in this context is a great liberation, condemning the evil one and not human beings. This is an ongoing process in the believer's life. We go through the same process over and over again, and gradually, the Spirit creates a mind of humility, righteousness and victory.

Note the beautiful relationships within the Trinity (vs 13–15). Everything that belongs to the Father is given to Jesus, and the Spirit is communicating it to us.

1 Acts 2:24; 3:15
2 Acts 5:29–30

What truth has the Spirit been communicating to you recently, and should you share it with someone else?

A serious game of hide-and-seek

Day 90

Sometimes we have the painful experience of losing sight of Jesus. 'Lord, teach me to look for you until I find you again.'

John 16:17–33 

How precious is Jesus to us? I am afraid we often take him for granted. His first disciples heard some strange words about 'in a little while', but they did not understand. Yet, within a few hours their Master would be taken away from them. They were to taste a loss and grief as painful as their subsequent joy was wonderful (vs 20, 22).

I suspect that my experience of periods when Jesus was invisible to me is universal among believers. He may be hidden behind so many real things and unreal emotions, but the pain is real enough. The image of a woman in labour (v 21) is often used to express the anguish of God's people[1] and as a description of the last days.[2] I will never forget the smile of relief on the tormented face of my wife when our first child was successfully born!

Jesus had to disappear for 'a little while' to become the Saviour of the world. Maybe my superficial faith has to be broken down to make my dependence upon him essential – so that I know he is my Saviour. Finding the living Lord again has given me a resurrected faith and a great joy.[3]

In verse 28 Jesus gave a summary of his mission, not very different in style from the rest of the text. But suddenly the disciples grasped the meaning of his words and commented that at last he spoke: 'clearly and without figures of speech' (v 29). Probably it was their own state of mind that had changed.

1 Jer 13:21; 6:24; Micah 4:9–10
2 Matt 24:8; 1 Thess 5:3
3 Song 3:1–4

Are you ashamed to go to church when your faith seems weak, or do you really need your fellow believers in times of despair?

His task fulfilled

Day 91

Give praise to your heavenly Father for sending Jesus to bring us eternal life!

 *John 17:1–12*

Finally, the hour had come (v 1),[1] the very reason for which Jesus had been sent into the world. A major theme of John's Gospel is the relationship between the Father and the Son: the Father sent his Son to carry out a very special task, and now the Son is about to accomplish his work and return to the Father with his 'final report'.

The cross is the place of glory (vs 1,4–5,10) because the source of eternal life can only be found in the death of Jesus. There have been many spiritual leaders, but Jesus alone has the power to give eternal life – life in all its fullness – to ordinary mortals. This unique life-giving power flows wherever there is an honest and open relationship with God.

We may have many ideas about what God is like, but we cannot have any actual knowledge of him unless he chooses to reveal himself to us. That is why Jesus came to make God and his name known to us. But knowledge of God cannot be revealed in a merely academic way; it is based on the mysterious relationship between our glorious God and sinful man. Hence the need for Jesus, his cross and his word.

The disciples were not the only ones to worry about the future. Jesus had been with them and protected them so that none except Judas had been lost. Now Jesus himself felt that they would face many dangers after he had left them, so he committed them into the power of God's name.[2] Jesus is explicitly praying for those given to him and not for the world (v 9), not because we should not pray for the world but to focus this particular prayer on his friends.

1 John 2:4; 12:27; Matt 26:18
2 Rev 7:2–4; 14:1

What is your mission in life? Maybe your Father in heaven would appreciate a situation report?

A prayer through time and space

Can you identify those who are the focus of Jesus' intercession? Are you among them?[1]

John 17:13–26

Here is a paradox: the disciples of Jesus 'are not of the world' and therefore 'the world has hated them' (v 14). But Jesus does not want to 'take them out of the world' (v 15) – on the contrary he has 'sent them into the world' (v 18). In short, we are to live in the world but we should not be part of the world. Maybe the worst mistake the church has made is to be too much of the world yet too little in the world. Jesus is not impressed by closed Christian sub-cultures and cliques, but rather by ordinary people, who – in the turmoil of modern society – are protected 'from the evil one' by his ownership of them. Their survival depends on his sacrifice and his Word – and so they are 'truly sanctified' (v 19) and become natural witnesses to God's unceasing love (v 23).

Some have stated that there is no place for the church in John's Gospel, but here we see Jesus praying for the future generations who will be brought to faith by the message of the apostles (v 20). Jesus is praying for us!

His main objective is unity – between himself and his Father, between God and his church, but also between believers. It is not by accident that Christian unity is emphasised in every epistle of the New Testament. There is no more effective obstacle to the progress of the gospel than conflicts between believers. With such a church it takes the continuous work and presence of Jesus to make God known to the world (vs 25–26). Note the longing of Jesus to be with us and to show us his glory throughout all time and space (v 24; compare v 5)!

1 Heb 7:25

How would the love of God reach the people around you if you were not part of their world?

Be shocked, be changed!

The Passion stories have frequently been tamed by repetition and distance from the actual events. If only we could take a living step back in time to that Passover season it would fundamentally change our perspective. For the next fourteen days we shall read about failure, forgiveness, intrigue, duplicity, and the forging of unlikely alliances in order to get rid of Jesus. Sacrifice triumphed over power, grace overcame failure, and a costly life of discipleship was eventually embraced as they all responded to Jesus' call to follow him.

Let me ask you to do three things as you study this portion of the Gospel. First, read with imagination. Go back to that Passover season. Go to the olive grove at night. Walk along the Via Dolorosa to Calvary. Imagine the women and men gathered there, the scoffing of the crowd, the ribaldry of the soldiers, the agony of Jesus. Imagine the surprise when he enters the room where the disciples were waiting in fear.

Secondly, experience the emotions. Allow the weight of the events to penetrate your being: betrayal, denial, miscarriage of justice, violence, treachery, a mother's grief, the disappointment of the disciples, forgiveness, delight at his resurrection. All of these events evoke powerful and life-changing emotions.

Thirdly, think laterally, and make some sacrificial decisions! Allow this timeless narrative of the passion and resurrection to change your ambitions and goals. There are some challenging principles here about the nature of God's kingdom and its values; about the cosmic significance of the death of Jesus; about the natural inclination of powers and principalities to be opposed to Jesus, the Lord of Glory. How tame has this shocking story become to you and your church? What kind of discipleship is an appropriate response to this incomparable sacrifice? Like Peter, will you accept the invitation, 'Follow me'?

Morris Stuart

Courage defeats betrayal

Day 93

'We shall match their power to hate with our power to love.'[1]

John 18:1–14 

His action was deliberate, callous. The olive grove in the Kidron Valley was a place of retreat for Jesus and his disciples. Yet the traitor chose this place of sacred memory for his final betrayal. The power of the bribe outweighed everything.

Whenever self-interest takes over our hearts, we can lose all scruples, and, whether for money, status or some other personal indulgence, betray our best friend to our worst enemy. From the time Jesus resolutely set out for Jerusalem,[2] he was determined to drink the cup the Father had given him. At the first mock trial he would tell the judge: 'You would have no power over me if it were not given to you from above'.[3] Here in the olive grove he shows the traitor, his 'captors' and his disciples that he is the master of his own destiny: he presents himself to be arrested. 'Who is it you want?'... 'I am he'.[4] With these simple words he defeated them. 'They drew back and fell to the ground'!

Subterfuge, swords and military might were no match for his authoritative honesty. And it has always been so. The earliest Christian martyrs laughed at the lions. While being burned at the stake, they praised their Lord in defiance of flames. In Alabama, civil rights campaigners knelt and prayed in the streets in the face of rubber bullets and water cannon. On a hillside in Crossroads Township in South Africa, women, defenceless against *sjamboks* and police dogs, sang '*Akanamandla!* Satan's had it! He has no power!'

Such pilgrims prove that they can match the adversary's power to hate with their power to love. We are challenged to do the same, and so demonstrate that sacrifice can triumph over power.

1 Martin Luther King, 1929–68
2 Luke 9:51
3 John 19:11
4 Compare Exod 3:14; John 8:58
5 Francis of Assisi, 1182–1226

'For, it is in dying that we are born to eternal life.'[5] What powers can you defeat in this way today?

He chose denial

Day 94

Direct questions demand truthful answers! 'Lord, save me from the shame that comes from cowardice.'

 *John 18:15–27*

You are not one of his disciples, are you?' The proposition was put to him three times. There was something about Peter that gave him away. Yet he chose denial. We cannot easily deny our history, our reputation and our passion. Somehow they will 'out' to praise or damn us. Personal habits become personal history. Personal history shapes our personality, which defines us. No matter how many times Peter had said, 'No I am not', the question would have persisted. Someone would have recalled an event which proved Peter's loyalty to Jesus: 'Didn't I see you with him in the olive grove?' It was there, in defence of Jesus, he had impetuously cut off the High Priest's servant's ear, yet here at his house Peter denied any involvement.

Contrast this with Jesus. As he stood before the High Priest, facing interrogation and violence, he was resolute, not simply because he was God, but particularly because he chose the harder way: '... if I spoke the truth, why did you strike me? Why question me? Ask those who heard me ... I have spoken openly to the world' (vs 20,21,23). Here is someone who was fearless and secure even in the face of certain death, and we are called to be the same. This is easy to say and hard to do, as Peter discovered.

Discipleship is costly, and the road to perfection is cluttered with many, many failures. These we must embrace: the possibility of failure, betrayal and denial. We are capable of all this and more. But as we shall see before this story is over, there is life after failure, and grace to restore us after we have done the unspeakable. 'Oh, the depth of the riches of the wisdom and knowledge of God! How unsearchable his judgements, and his paths beyond tracing out! ... To him be glory forever!'[1]

1 Rom 11:33,36

The cross before me, the world behind me – no turning back!

Kangaroo court

Day 95

'Lord, open my eyes and heart to you.
Let me feel your loving presence.'

John 18:28–40 

As is the way of kangaroo courts, everyone wanted to have clean hands. The rules had to be followed. The answers to questions had to be legally correct. The Jews wanted to celebrate Passover properly. They would not enter the Roman governor's palace. Pilate wanted to be politically prudent and legally correct: 'Take him away yourselves, and judge him by your own law'. These legal and ritual niceties cloaked the reality that this was the most critical miscarriage of justice in human history, and the precursor to its most heinous crime: the murder of God among us!

This trial was not just about legality. It was about morality and the clash of kingdoms. The prisoner was indeed ruler of a kingdom. Its values were and are altogether different from those of the kingdom that was conducting his trial. In his kingdom, suffering is preferred over violence, morality over legality, truth over power, and faithfulness over success. He was such a threat, that his adversaries (the Jewish religious hierarchy, the common people, the leader of a rebellion and the Roman state), once sworn enemies of each other, united in an unlikely coalition to destroy him. Their eyes were blinded to the truth, for, '... had they known (who he was) they would not have crucified the Lord of glory'.[1]

We need to open our eyes again to see our Lord, Jesus of Nazareth, as he truly was, and what threat he posed to his society. We have spiritualised him out of all recognition. Our romance with the culture of success, our avoidance of sacrifice, and our preference for comfort and security, all align us far closer with those in this story who were preoccupied with matters of ceremonial ritual uncleanness and correct legal speech.

1 1 Cor 2:8
2 John 8:32

'You will know the truth and the truth will set you free'.[2]

Crucifixion is a grubby business

Day 96

'Bearing shame and scoffing rude, in my place condemned he stood'.[1]

John 19:1–16a

Pilate found no reason to charge him with any offence, yet he had him flogged. He tried to absolve himself of any moral responsibility, but the power of the mob and his sensitivity to his political position led him to act against the truth that he knew. In the end, political expediency won the day. He handed the prisoner over to be crucified, resorting to the coward's defence: 'I was only following orders'!

What this grubby affair tells us is that Jesus' crucifixion did not take place in a social and political vacuum. Instead there was a volatile intersection of fundamentally opposing interests: the Roman state, the Jewish religious hierarchy and the Jewish insurrectionists. This was the historical context in which the Son of God loved me and gave himself for me. It was a time of danger, deviousness, violence and volatility. The literary beauty of the record may camouflage the ugliness of the passion, but there can be no doubt that, had we been there, the scene would have struck us as ugly indeed.

As it was for Jesus, so it is for us. The context in which our faith is to be lived out is that same violent, volatile, devious and dangerous world. Yet, as we observe many of our worshipping communities today – especially in the West – we cannot help but conclude that danger, deviousness, violence and volatility represent an unwelcome, unexpected and ill-fitting context in which to live out our Christian discipleship.

We may prefer peace and happiness. Yet Luke defines for us the meaning of true happiness: poverty, hunger, weeping, exclusion, insult, rejection and slander.[2] His sentiments would be totally out of place in many of our worshipping communities today!

1 Philipp Bliss, 1838–76
2 Luke 6:20–22
3 Luke 6:23

'Rejoice in that day and leap for joy, because great is your reward in heaven'.[3]

Jesus of Nazareth, King of the Jews

Day 97

'We may not know, we cannot tell what pains he had to bear. But we believe it was for us, he hung and suffered there.'

John 19:16b–30 

They removed all of his clothing. They divided these final possessions equally, and gambled for the seamless undergarment. The literary record seems so detached, but its plain meaning is that our Saviour was left to hang as a common Roman criminal: naked, exposed to the elements, and to the eyes of his adversaries, his friends and his grieving mother.

For hours he hung there, his body racked with pain, drenched with his sweat and soiled by his own body fluids and waste. This was no pristine crucifix, no ornament for holy veneration. It was an ugly sight, matched in gravity only by his extreme aloneness: 'My God, my God, why have you forsaken me?'[1]

'It was for us he hung and suffered there'. This is a vision that should bring us to tears and inspire in us gratitude, and obedience. His death also had a larger purpose. He died to reclaim and reconcile that same dangerous, devious, volatile and violent world whose representatives, incited by principalities and powers, crucified him. By that cross, he 'disarmed the powers and authorities, he made a public spectacle of them, triumphing over them ...'.[2] There, he also '... reconciled to himself all things, whether things on earth or things in heaven, by making peace through his blood, shed on the cross'.[3]

This is an incomparable sacrifice, and a death of cosmic significance, and we, his disciples, are the undeserving beneficiaries. Now we have work to do, not simply grace to enjoy! God's intention is that '... through the church, the manifold wisdom of God should be made known to rulers and authorities in the heavenly realms ...'.[4] We have seen our Lord bring about reconciliation through his personal sacrifice. We must follow in his footsteps.

1 Mark 15:34
2 Col 2:15
3 Col 1: 20
4 Eph 3:10

'God so loved the world that he gave ...' What can I give today?

The task is complete

Day 98

'There was no other good enough to pay the price of sin. He only could unlock the gate of heaven and let us in.'

John 19:31–42

He sucked the wine vinegar from the sponge, uttered his final words, and took his last breath. Jesus of Nazareth was dead. After piercing his body with a spear, the soldiers removed it from the cross. It was the end of a day's work for the Empire. It was the dawn of a new day for all humanity. A new way was opened to God, to reality and peace. The most despicable crime was the cradle for the most generous act of grace by a loving heavenly Father.

The secret disciples, Joseph and Nicodemus, now become our heroes. In the wake of the humiliation of the trial, the Via Dolorosa and the crucifixion, they give the most dignified gift to Jesus: a proper burial. They obtained the cloths and spices and wrapped the body themselves, then laid it in an unused garden tomb. This was an unheralded task and, as it turned out, one for secret disciples.

They may not have had the courage to walk openly with him in the hostile streets of Jerusalem. No one knew of their secret but unwavering devotion, yet when their moment arrived, they did not shrink from their duty. We may never know who Jesus' disciples are. Some keep us company. Others remain silent, watch from the sidelines, and come visiting at night. But when they do their duty, in response to the Spirit's prompting, they can put to shame even the most brazen disciples. We need to accept those who do not neatly fit into our accepted categories on the basis of their confession, and allow them space for their fruit to confirm the validity of their faith.

'Lord, help me to play my part, without looking at the failure or gifts of others.'

Night nurtures gloom; dawn brings, hope

Day 99

The light of Christ shines in the darkness. The darkness has never overcome it.

John 20:1–9 

It had been a terrible weekend. After three years or so, the most momentous events of their lives had climaxed in the most public humiliation imaginable. Their teacher was dead; executed as a common criminal. The new dawn would never break. The kingdom which he promised would never come. The body in the garden tomb was proof of that! They now faced a future without purpose or hope.

Confused and bewildered, they retreated to share their disillusionment and lick their wounds. My guess is that they did not sleep much that weekend, racked with grief and disappointment as they were. Perhaps, as we might often do towards the end of a sleepless night, Mary Magdalene traded restlessness for activity: 'If I cannot sleep, then at least I can do something useful!' So out into the dark before dawn she went, making her way to the tomb.

The body was gone – shock! The cloths were undisturbed – amazing! Hope began to rise again, at least for John – after his race to the tomb (vs 4,8). Sometimes, just when we *feel*, no, when we actually *see* our hopes dashed and our dreams sealed in a tomb, some Mary of Magdala comes running, and breaks our cycle of self-pity with news of undreamed-of possibilities. And faith begins to grow again.

Friday night was awful. Saturday night was a gloomy eternity, but Sunday saw a new dawn. And the messenger was as unlikely as she was unexpected. Mary was of doubtful reputation. Mary was a woman. Yet she was the first to break the news. God trusted the unacceptable and the unlikely with the unexpected. Peter and the other disciple listened, ran and believed. Will you accept good news from unlikely lips?

'Lord open my eyes to see your glory, my ears to hear your Word, and my heart to receive new life.'

I have seen the Lord

Day 100

'Only God himself can let the bucket down to the depths in us'.[1]

 *John 20:10–18*

He called her by name. She instantly recognised him. Rabboni was not dead. He was alive and now presented himself to her, and spoke her name in that dear, familiar way. The narrative is simply written, without affectation or intention to persuade the sceptic. Mary's grief and bewilderment are clearly shown. Her interpretation of the body's disappearance is not surprising: 'They have taken my Lord away ... and I don't know where they have put him' (v 13). This story does not read like a piece of contrived religious propaganda. There is a 'take it or leave it' simplicity to it which challenges us to exercise a faith which does not deny reason, but goes beyond it.

Faith is the consequence of a journey through doubt, grief, bewilderment and disappointment. It is not a cheap substitute for these. We are not expected to disengage our minds, or forget our emotions and our struggles in order to have faith. If we process ours as honestly as Mary did hers, we will share her testimony: 'I have seen the Lord!' (v 18).

Often, when we find it difficult to 'see the Lord', we tend to assume that it is because our intellect and the rest of our (sinful) humanity are in the way. We repress doubts, questions, and real emotions, taking refuge in a 'blissful' relationship with Jesus. But it is a mistake to 'just forget about yourself and concentrate on him and worship him,' as the song suggests. This path can never be sustained. Life happens!

Embrace disappointments. Express your fears. Face your doubts. Ask questions relentlessly! Relate to God on the basis of rugged reality, and I guarantee you will hear him call your name and your response will be as instant as Mary's.

1 CS Lewis, 1898–1963

'Lord, I pray that my relationship with you will always be based on reality.'

Seeing is believing

Day 101

Just when things appear to be at their most hopeless, the presence of Jesus transforms everything. 'Lord, make it so today!'

John 20:19–23 

The scene was one of utter bewilderment and fear. The doors were locked. At least one of the two disciples who had raced to the tomb believed something! Mary was consumed with joy, which was threatening to be infectious. She had seen the Lord. He had spoken to her. But she was Mary Magdalene, and, in this context, common sense had to prevail. Whose word could be trusted?

And then he came and stood among them and, in that inimitable voice, spoke to them: 'Peace be with you!' (v 19). He showed them the incontrovertible evidence: the wounds in his hands and his side. Thus the matter was settled. Even if they never saw him again, they would never again doubt that he had conquered death and was now alive. Then, together with his word of peace, he bestowed on them his perpetual presence, the Holy Spirit, who would be their comforter, their teacher, their guide into all truth and the One who would bring conviction in their future work in a hostile world.[1]

Imagine the emotions as they recalled his final teaching session and his prayer for them before his arrest. Their grief was being turned to joy. The narrative has abbreviated the moment considerably. I suspect, and it is only my conjecture, that Jesus took time, perhaps approached each one in turn, allowing for astonishment to overcome despair and doubt. Imagine the incredible release of tension as the noise filled the room, until again he said: 'Peace be with you!' (v 21).[2]

There was no condemnation for betrayal, or doubt, or ignorance, only the strongest affirmation expressed in a commission to carry on his work: 'As the Father has sent me, I am sending you'. What an amazing Saviour we worship as Lord!

1 John 16:8–11
2 See also John 17

'Lord, you are too wonderful! Your grace is all I need.'

Thomas the doubter

Day 102

God would rather deal with an honest sinner than with a hypocritical saint! 'Lord, help me to be completely honest when I speak to you.'

John 20:24–31

Thomas is my hero. He does not subscribe to the idea that, in order to have true faith, you have to put your brain in your pocket! Jesus appears to him, not as a concession to a less than godly disciple, but as a matter of respect for him. He would face Thomas as he did the others, in the same locked room while they were all together. He would utter the same word of peace, and would invite him to examine the same incontrovertible evidence. It was enough. Thomas saw and believed.

The resurrection narratives are transparently honest, focusing on the doubts, scepticism and fallible humanity of the disciples. After three years of sharing Jesus' life, there were still things which they never really understood, and issues with which they were not comfortable. I am certain that part of the intention of the author was to illustrate the process of journeying from these realities to a life of faith firmly rooted and grounded in the resurrected Christ. These narratives are meant to stimulate and encourage belief, so that we may have life in Christ.

God meets us where we are, and that is usually a place of need, of failure, doubt or discouragement. God does not expect us to make a pretence of joy when the truth is that we are discouraged. We are not expected to affect happiness when in truth we are sad, certainty when in fact we are racked with doubt and disappointment. We need to end the conspiracy of hypocrisy, so prevalent in our churches, which often 'forces' us to pretend that we are something other than what we truly are.

1 Alexander Whyte, 1836–1921

'The perseverance of the saints: the falling down and getting up, falling down and getting up, all the way to heaven.'[1]

Faith and fishing

Day 103

'Ask me not where I live or what I like to eat ... Ask me what I am living for and what I think is keeping me from living fully for that.'[1]

John 21:1–6 

Amazing! Why did they go fishing? Was it because they had spent over a week in seclusion and food supplies were getting low? Or could it be that, after the two appearances, they were beginning to doubt again? When would they be certain enough not to require a steady diet of appearances to sustain their faith?

Elijah was the same. On Mount Carmel he witnessed a major victory. He had experienced God dramatically in earthquake, wind and fire. Yet his memory failed. Discouragement got the better of him, and in spite of all the evidence, he chose to continue in doubt, so much so, that he could not conceive of God speaking to him through a different medium: the still small voice.[2]

We can often be the same. Like the disciples, we like to be sustained by a constant diet of appearances, without which we may descend into discouragement and doubt, and take to our fishing trawlers again. But the fallback option will not necessarily guarantee our success. The disciples were skilled at their trade. The Sea of Tiberias was well known to them. In the midst of their uncertainty and confusion, it should have been a secure occupation, guaranteed of success. Yet they trawled all night and caught nothing.

A simple question from Jesus can often bring us back on track: 'Friends, haven't you any fish?' 'Folks, hasn't it worked? How about doing it my way? Throw your net on the right side of the boat'. And surprise, surprise! We find ourselves unable to cope with the generous answer to our problem. Jesus' answer to his disciples was overwhelming and utterly convincing. From then on they should need no more appearances, nor should we!

1 Thomas Merton, 1915–68
2 1 Kings 19:3,4,11–13
3 Heb 11:1

'Now faith is being sure of what we hope for and certain of what we do not see.'[3]

Breakfast on the beach

Day 104

'Lord, you prepare a feast for us, and say, "Come and eat with me".'

John 21:7–14

The first time he came to them, they were terrified and bewildered. The doors were locked. On that occasion they all needed evidence. The second time he came, the doors were still locked, but this time Thomas needed evidence, and the rest, affirmation of their trustworthiness as reliable witnesses. And now, the third time it was different. They already had the evidence, and the affirmation. The 'secret' needed a more ordinary setting to reinforce its credibility.

It is one thing to claim to have seen a resurrected human in a secret hideout. It is another thing when he appears to you and your mates on a popular beach early in the morning when all the other fishing trawlers are coming back into port. This appearance was in full public gaze! And there was more. He was calling out instructions to them from the shore, as if they didn't know what they were doing. He had a fire lit, and fish already cooking, and bread, and a welcome: 'Come and have breakfast'. This narrative is so disarmingly transparent and simple. It beggars belief to think it was in any way a contrived piece of religious propaganda intended to convince anyone about anything. It is simply the retelling of an early-morning incident.

The more significant meaning is in the elements, especially the bread and the fish and his characteristic action as he took the bread and broke it and gave it to them, and likewise the fish. Memories rush in, of a little boy with five barley loaves and two small fish, and of five thousand men plus women and children on a Galilean hillside; of an upper room after Jesus washed their feet; of his last supper. No wonder they never asked who he was. They knew it was the Lord.

'Lord, help me to recognise your actions when dealing with me, so that I may know again and afresh.'

Do you love me?

'Lord, you know all things; you know that I love you. What is your message for me today?'

John 21:15–19 

Do you love me?' is perhaps the simplest and most searching question that can be asked of anyone. They had exchanged no words since the denial. It was nagging away at Peter. Maybe he was waiting for a rebuke. He knew he deserved it. Carefully he prepared his defence, repeating in his mind what he would say when the Judge of all the earth confronted him. But in the end there was no accusation, simply a question about motives: 'Do you love me?' If that was settled, nothing else need be said. This weak man, Peter, would still have the capacity to 'feed my lambs'; 'take care of my sheep'; 'feed my sheep'.

It was while we were still sinners that Christ died for us.[1] Peter was probably not fully aware at the time of the extent of God's generosity. When we do something wrong, as we are filled with remorse, the evil one whispers condemnation to us: 'Look what you did!' But God whispers the question: 'Why did you do it?'

Yes, Peter failed miserably. He regretted it bitterly, but he loved the Lord. That is why he was hurt when the question was asked for a third time. But it was only because the Lord wanted to reinforce his forgiveness of Peter, and make it quite clear to him that there was life after failure, grace after denial; 'Feed my sheep ... Follow me!'

Very often, as far as God is concerned, the only thing standing between ourselves and continued fellowship with him is our inability to face our failure, and the astonishing requirement that we have to be able to forgive ourselves, even though God has already done so! We simply need to be able to answer that most searching question with a simple confession: 'Yes, Lord, you know that I love you'.

1 Rom 5:8

'Lord, your forgiveness alone is all I need. Restore me and help me press on with the new task you are giving me.'

No turning back

Day 106

'No one who takes hold of the plough and looks back is fit for service in the kingdom of God.'[1]

 *John 21:20–25*

Looking back is hazardous. When we take our eyes off Jesus, we lose our perspective, and sometimes our way. Jesus' call to us is simple and direct: 'Follow me!' This is the challenge of discipleship in the gospel story: 'take up your cross daily and follow me' ... 'unless a man renounces all that he has he cannot be my disciple' ... 'follow me and I will make you fishers of men.'[2] The call to us is personal, sharp, unique.

Peter and the disciple whom Jesus loved (John, presumably) had a close personal relationship. During the three years they spent with Jesus, their lives were closely linked. They were both present at some of the key moments in the story of Jesus: the transfiguration, the struggle in Gethsemane, the trial at the High Priest's house, the discovery of the empty tomb and the undisturbed cloths – to mention but a few. It was therefore quite reasonable for Peter to assume that their future assignments would also be linked, hence the question, 'Lord, what about him?'

Our business with God, however, is unique and personal. God's call on my life cannot be duplicated. What I am called upon to do, only I can do. No, this does not mean that I am indispensable, and that without my efforts God would be thwarted. But what it does mean is this: in the broad scope of things, my place in the work of the kingdom is unique and irreplaceable. So, when Jesus says: 'Come, follow me!' I must fix my eyes on him, and follow him whatever the assignment, and whatever the cost.

1 Luke 9:62
2 Mark 1:17

I am a child of God. I am unique. I am not a copy. I am an original. I am responsible.

Faith in times of trouble

Day 107

'How sweet the name of Jesus sounds in a believer's ear; it soothes his sorrows, heals his wounds, and drives away his fear.'[1]

Psalms 42,43 

These two psalms clearly belong together, as can be seen by the shared refrain (42:5,11; 43:5). John Stott helpfully gives them the title 'The causes and cure of spiritual depression'. All of us have times in our lives when for one reason or another we feel low, and alienated from God. Here are lessons we can learn to help us in such times.

In each stanza we find that the author first of all *expresses his feelings* vigorously. He feels parched, cut off from God's presence (42:1–3); overwhelmed, drowning in the flood of chaotic events (42:7); and misjudged by those who laugh at him and oppress him (43:1,2). He 'tells it as it is' and we need to learn to do the same in our prayers. It hurts him deeply when people mockingly ask him, 'Where is your God?' (42:3,10). It really does seem as if God has forgotten him (42:9), and he is not afraid to say so.

At the same time we find that in each stanza the author somehow *expresses his faith*. He recalls the joy he has experienced in leading worship (42:4), with the implied hope that such times may yet return. He acknowledges to God that it is '*your* waves and breakers that have swept over me' (42:7), recognising that he is not in the grip of chaos. He longs that God would send forth his light and his truth to guide him (43:3), as God led his people by the pillar of cloud and the pillar of fire by night during the exodus.[2] Trust expressed even when we are 'in the dark'[3] is of great value.

Finally, in each stanza the author talks to himself, he *makes himself think*. As the commentator John Goldingay puts it, 'the psalmist exhorts himself to let his awareness of the past and his hope for the future determine his attitude to the present'.[4] If you are feeling discouraged and sad today, here is a way to defeat the blues and overcome the enemy.

Often when we are depressed the last thing we want is for someone to exhort us. But to exhort ourselves may be just what we need. Pray for someone you know who is depressed (yourself?), that light may dawn for them.

1 John Newton, 1725–1807
2 Exod 13:21
3 Isa 50:10
4 *Songs from a Strange Land*, IVP

You alone are worthy

Day 108

Give thanks to God for his great love. Remind yourself that love is the reason he will always listen to your praise and thanksgiving.

Psalm 44

One of the great ways to cheer ourselves up each day is to remember what we had to face the day before! The writer of this psalm mentions two things from the past: the way God helped his people by crushing their enemies (vs 1–8), and the way God humbled his people (vs 9–26). It's a game of two halves. The writer approves of the first half and is humbled by the second. He cannot see what it is in the people's conduct which has brought about the change (vs 17,18,20,21).

We can be encouraged by this. The sufferings we face are not all because of our sins,[1] and our triumphs are not all because we are worthy of credit. We are often tempted to think they are, but Shakespeare gave wise words to Hamlet: 'Use every man after his desert and who shall 'scape whipping?'. Let us become neither smug nor unduly worried about the circumstances we face.

Then where is God? If he is not punishing or rewarding as simply as we sometimes think, what is he doing? He is working out his plans which may involve us in ways we never thought of. Look at verse 22 again. I have a friend whose husband was lost in an accident. Two years later she asked, with frightening honesty, 'If God is not involved in ordinary cause-and-effect circumstances, then where do we look for him?' We cannot easily answer except in the ways that Job's comforters answered him, and they were worse than useless. Perhaps we have to read again the last verse of this psalm: 'Please, God, help us for your love's sake. Enable us to trust even when we don't understand'.

1 Job 42:7–9

Consider what it means to your life today that God is love, and his character is unchanging.

Wedding march

Day 109

Ask God to deliver you from being impressed by pretentious displays of status, and to lift your heart to worship him.

Psalm 45 

This psalm is a wedding song. It addresses the groom in its first half and the bride in its second. It talks of splendour and magnificence, which are symbolised by beauty (v 11), rank (v 9) and wealth (v 8).

But the beauty, rank and wealth are only the symbols of the occasion, not the essence of it. To find that we have to look for character, not image. Character is within, and in its absence the external trappings would not only be empty, but a positive reproach.

Fortunately, the character is here too (v 2). This is a king who, even on his wedding day, can be reminded that there is work to do for truth, and that he is the man to do it. Warriors for righteousness have not always been famous for sensitivity. This one, though, is touched by grace (v 2) and linked with humility (v 4), characteristics that can only be gifts from God (v 6), and which, much later in Israel's history, are applied to Jesus himself.[1]

When we talk of Jesus and a wedding we may wonder about the bride, and remember what the New Testament says about the church, the bride of Christ, and the marriage supper of the Lamb.[2] Our Lord is a warrior for truth, righteousness and humility, and he is preparing a bride of equal status. We, the church, are that bride, and he will surround it with splendour unimaginable. The reward for fighting wickedness is an anointing with the 'oil of joy' (v 7). Let us, then, be willing partners in the forging of our characters.

1 Heb 1:8–9
2 Eph 5:25–32; Rev 19:6–9

Ask God to help you to accept whatever he needs to do with you today, and to be willing to let him work through you to the benefit of others.

He will be exalted in the earth

Day 110

The creator of the Alps and the Himalayas also made the buttercup and the marigold. Mountains fall at his command – yet he waits for us to turn to him in repentance and love.

Psalm 46

This life is full of troubles. Wherever we are, whatever we do, we can never know ourselves to be secure against the ravages of storm, accident, bereavement or simple worry. The threat of tragedy and loss are the life experience of us all.

This psalmist isn't any different. Verses 2 and 3 are not a picture of casual damage. They are cataclysmic. How does the writer react? By claiming closeness to God: mightier far than anything in the world he has made; the refuge of his people. So good is he that, at his word, the raging waters of verse 3 give way to a river scene suggesting the kingdom of heaven.[1]

Verse 6 is a powerful reminder of the inevitability of war[2] which we see and read about daily in the news, but even though we may not be able to see it or recognise it, calm is restored at God's command. The writer of this psalm knew whom to praise for the peace he saw and for the ultimate justice we still wait to see. Although we view God at present from a world still subject to sin and suffering, decay and death, we need to take heart from the promise that he has not abandoned us, and there will come a day when justice and peace will be brought to all of creation by the one who holds the world in his hands. This is our God. No storm too great for him,[3] no dictator too strong. Even though we may wake already worried about the day ahead, we have this promise, that our God reigns.

1 Rev 22:1–5
2 Matt 24:6–7
3 Mark 4:35–41

'The Lord Almighty ... is our fortress' (v 7). What is the problem or the fear uppermost in your mind today? Dare to ask God to help you see your problems through his eyes.

Hail, King of the earth

Day 111

Spend some time worshipping the One who is Lord of lords and King of kings.

Psalm 47 

There have been many rulers in the history of the world. The best of them have done great things for their people. The worst of them have done, and are still doing, unspeakable things to their nations. If we could have one wish for the twenty-first century, perhaps it would be that prime ministers and presidents might be courageous enough to make a stand for what is just and true, however unpopular.

One thing of which we can be sure, however, is that there is One who is superior to every earthly ruler and will remain so for ever. He is, of course, superior in might and power, but he also far surpasses all others because he is beyond moral reproach. That 'the great King over all the earth' has chosen not to eliminate tyranny by force is not a sign of weakness nor of complacency. It is the evidence that he wants us all to gain the benefits that can only come from choosing to do what is right.

He has intervened in the past (v 3). He will do so again in the future.[1] Who can say exactly what he is doing now? One thing is sure: we are either among those he will one day rescue from the wrongdoers, or we are among the wrongdoers, and he will give his verdict in justice and in love.

This is our God, supreme above all governments, the most absolute and benevolent ruler the world will ever see, recipient of the accolades of the universe, standing astride the heavens, and ready to receive our praise. 'Clap your hands … he is greatly exalted' (vs 1,9).

1 Rev 7:17

It is not always easy to give thanks joyfully, but this is the response God's love demands of us. Pray that God will give you a joyful and thankful heart.

Security from the storm

Day 112

Think of a time when a storm raged in your life and give thanks to God for his protection.

Psalm 48

The psalm opens with a statement of the greatness of God and we are invited into Jerusalem, the holy city, as a sanctuary from every sort of danger. The psalmist gives thanks for what God has done for his people. Specifically, he has brought about the rout of the enemies of Jerusalem, just as if they were ships blown ashore in a storm.

I once visited the town of Fort Dauphin, in southern Madagascar. It has a large, sweeping bay, and, right in the middle, is a half-sunken ship. Around the perimeter of the bay are three more rusting hulks. I asked one of the local people to tell me what had happened. 'Storm,' he said. 'About five years ago. They blew ashore'. I could only begin to imagine the force of the storm that took out half a fleet in a single day. Fort Dauphin is a windy place anyway, so I suppose the sailors are careful, but this one beat them. Some force. The relics remain.

That's the picture of verse 7. Memorials to a mighty force, that of a God who protects his people. What is an appropriate response?

The only appropriate response is faith. God is great, he has moved before, he can be relied upon again. The Jewish nation has suffered extremely, and some of them have given up looking to God. But, really, where else can they look? Where can we? There is no better place, person or creed for us to look to. The God of history, who rides the heavens: he is our God.

Think of some of the 'memorials' to events in your past and give thanks to God for the weathered storms of yesterday. Ask for increased faith for those of today and tomorrow.

We're all in this together

Day 113

Give thanks to God for the sacrifice of Jesus, and the great love with which he regards us.

Psalm 49 

I do not expect to get to know a reigning monarch on first-name terms, nor do I expect to spend time with most of the people written about in the newspapers and glossy magazines. But all of us, whether we are rich and famous or come from one of the poorest parts of the world, we are all going to die.

The circumstances may be different in each case, and none of us knows the time, but no one can avoid that last appointment which was made for us on the day of our birth. The wise, the stupid, the rich and the destitute are all finally equal in this one thing.[1] We shall leave behind alike our mansions or squalor, our fame or misfortune. We shall take only our character.

But just as surely as no one else can buy us out (vs 7–8), God stands ready with a ransom sufficient for the whole lot of us. This writer is sure (v 15) that he will rise from the grave. But there is one thing we should know: God can hardly be expected to search out my grave if I have not introduced myself to him before I get there. He only comes by invitation.

So let's not be too impressed by riches or fame (v 16), even when they are ours – especially when they are ours. We can't all have them, and that alone should give us a clue as to their real worth. Rather, we should value understanding and wisdom (v 20), which is available to all.

The fear of the Lord is the beginning of wisdom.[2] It is wise to prepare for possible problems, and more than foolhardy not to prepare for the inevitable ones. Nothing is more inevitable than death.

1 Eccl 9:2
2 Job 28:28; Prov 1:7; 9:10; Ps 111:10

Perhaps you keep a diary. Looking back over the years, can you see how God is slowly shaping you?

Day 114

The God of all the earth

Praise God because, needing nothing, he chooses to desire our worship.

Psalm 50

Once more, mankind needs reminding that God is the only God.[1] He has no need of sacrifices or burnt offerings 'for every animal of the forest is mine and the cattle on a thousand hills' (v 10).

To his own people God says, 'You can bring me nothing that is not mine already, but call on me and I will deliver you' (vs 7–15). Perhaps this was the psalm that inspired John Milton's poem *On His Blindness* – 'God doth not need either man's works or his own gifts'. There is nothing that God's people can bring him to increase his wealth or buy his favour.

As for the wicked, they had better abandon any form of religious observance (v 16), lest they add hypocrisy to their list of sins. The wicked are those who incline more naturally towards self-indulgence than towards God and the details of self-indulgence are listed here as theft, adultery, deceit, slander and disloyalty, but these are only examples. Saddest of all, perhaps, is that when God did not judge their evil on the spot, they accepted this as licence to add to it.

The fact is, we all belong in the 'ungodly' half of this psalm. We all incline toward the evil of self-indulgence, and should be beyond the pale of God's recognition. All our religious observances should cause God to recoil from our hypocrisy.

Yet the good news is that it is not so. We cannot buy God's favour, yet any thank-offering we might clumsily, unworthily or utterly ineptly seek to make, as long as it comes from some wish to seek God and not to enhance our own reputation, will 'prepare the way so that I may show him the salvation of God' (v 23).

1 Job 38:4

We cannot buy our way into the kingdom, but there is One who has paid the price.

Cleanse me, O God

Day 115

Give thanks to God, because the sinner can turn from his wickedness and live.

Psalm 51 

It is important to remember the background of this famous psalm, as these are the words of a man who is deeply conscious of his sin. This is David after his adulterous affair with Bathsheba and the murder of her husband.[1] Small wonder that he was desperate for God to show his mercy (vs 1,2,7–9).

But he didn't have to react this way; he could have resorted to self-justification ('soldiers do get killed'); or tried to transfer the blame (Bathsheba shouldn't have flaunted herself'); he might simply have denied it. These ploys have been used since the time of Adam. The Sunday papers will probably carry examples – you have done it yourself. So have I.

David's great virtue is not that he is sinless, but that he wants to put things right. And then he expects to sing God's praises (v 12) to the benefit of others (v 13) and the glory of God (v 19). But only then.

Some friends told me of how their son, aged eleven, stole some money and bought some toys. Sadly, he found he could only use them when his bedroom door was shut; he had to keep them in a secret place and he was in constant dread of being discovered. When he was finally – and inevitably – caught, his shame was surpassed only by his relief.

We all want to praise God openly, and see our neighbours respond to our witness. Perhaps we have some cleaning up to do first. The release of joy will be worth the discomfort and embarrassment of confession.

1 2 Sam 11

'Lord, wash me according to your great compassion, and take pleasure in the clumsy offerings of this sinful heart.'

Day 116

Lies, damned lies and appearances

There is only one sort of love worth trusting in: God's unfailing love. 'I will praise you for ever' (v 9).

Psalm 52

It is possible to be admired without being admirable. It seems that simply because they are famous, we hang on the words of the personalities of the moment, and if these people are misguided, or wicked even, their words are actually harmful because they invite approval. Tolstoy once said: 'It is amazing how complete is the delusion that beauty is goodness'. He could have added 'or that fame is wisdom'.

The writer of this psalm knew that this was not true. The 'mighty man' of verse 1 is challenged with not only being evil but of boasting about it. No matter how accustomed his public was to hearing this boasting, he remains a disgrace in the eyes of God. So do today's so-called heroes whose actions reveal their greedy, spiteful, or selfish motivation. So do I if I do not constantly examine myself in the light of God's judgement.

One of the things God hates is deceit. The lies mentioned in verse 3 will bring about the destruction predicted in verse 5. Liars are evil. The great wealth that many of them accumulate does not give them permission to be different from the rest of us (v 7).

I read a magazine article once about Meryl Streep. Having told me she is a woman of great acting talent, which I knew, it went on to say that she chooses her film roles partly on the basis of whether the film would make a positive or negative contribution to the world. This is a much greater basis for admiration than the great talent, and way greater than the fame which has resulted from her talent. Ms Streep says she wants to use her talent as an influence for good in the world. Could we in all honesty say the same?

How can you use your special talents to benefit the world? Ask God to show you the plan he has for you.

Only a fool denies God

Day 117

If perfect love casts out fear, ask the God of love today to help you to know the peace of which he is the prince.

Psalm 53 

I remember my father chuckling years ago about some self-confessed atheist whom someone had called 'worse than a fool'. When the man demanded to know why he was so abused, the reply was, 'Because the Bible states that a fool says in his heart there is no God, but you've gone and blurted it right out'!

We live in a world of fools where God is denied and his name is blasphemed. I have been asked in formal interviews whether my faith might make me a work-place embarrassment. One might have thought that a declared allegiance to the ways of truth and love would be an asset!

Those who have 'liberated' themselves from godly obligations are not, however, consequently free. Apart from being corrupt and vile, as the psalmist suggests (v 1), they remain fearful when they don't have to be (v 5) and can fall victim to superstition and the occult. Shades of New Age spirituality, where superstitions as old as primitive man dictate allegiance to all kinds of crystals, charms and fetishes and freedom is sought in nature or drugs.

Given the prevalence of this lifestyle, especially in the West, we can become dulled to the reality of what we are seeing, even lured into acceptance of it. 'Spirituality' without God cannot be just another way of searching for God. The devil has few new tricks, but a host of disguises.

'Oh that salvation would come out of Zion' (v 6). It is still only God who can restore the fortunes of his people. True, he may use avenues that we may find diverse and obscure. We should not be too hidebound in our expectations or reactions. But let us also be discerning and not be deceived by the nonsense offered by a godless world looking desperately for peace.

Give thanks to God for the salvation he has accomplished. Jesus reigns, now and for ever. Pray for some individuals you know that they may seek God and learn to call him Lord.

Save me – now!

Day 118

How can we be confident that, when we need him, God hears our urgent requests? Thank him that nothing is beyond his knowledge or caring.

Psalm 54

When David wrote this psalm, he was hiding from Saul who was trying to kill him.[1] His call to God is not an academic nicety nor a general acknowledgement of a known truth. This was a direct call for help in a specific situation.

This prayer is one among many that tell us about the dealings David has been having with God, in which he has learnt things and has followed different instructions according to the circumstances. The psalm arises, therefore, from his relationship with the Lord. This is no sudden discovery of God because things have got a bit difficult.

He explains the situation (v 3), although God must know it already. Why does God want us to talk to him, when there is nothing we can say that he does not know better than we do? It can only be because he wants us to deepen our relationship with him by laying our needs before him.

David names God as his help (v 4), making his reliance specific, tells how he feels (v 5) and makes clear his intentions (vs 6–7). I don't think this is a bargain with God – 'If you get me out of here, I'll offer a sacrifice'. Rather, I think it is a statement of intention: 'You are great, and I will offer a sacrifice'. He plans to bring a freewill offering, not to pay a bribe or a debt.

So, what do we learn from this urgent prayer? That God wants to hear our requests; that we are free to ask for what we need; that we ought to let God know how we feel; that we should be ready to praise God freely and, central to it all: it is because of the nature of God that we have hope (v 1).

1 1 Sam 23:14–29

Praise God for his goodness, for his greatness, and for wanting us to talk with him. Do your prayers in time of need come in the context of an ongoing relationship?

On the wings of a dove I'll fly away

Day 119

Is God your refuge and strength? Reiterate your trust in him as you come into his presence.

Psalm 55 

This is another psalm inspired by the need of its writer. Troubled by his thoughts, by the enemy, by fear, and above all by the betrayal of a friend, his response is to say, 'Cast your cares on the Lord' (v 22).

This is good counsel, though it is easier said than done. What is it to throw our troubles on the Lord's shoulders?

We shall need to begin with the understanding that God knows and cares about our individual circumstances, although we have to learn that he is concerned with our greatest good, and this does not always match our idea of it! If we are surrounded by enemies we are most likely to wish with all our hearts that they would go away, but God may need us to meet them in battle and know the confidence that comes only through victory. He may even need us to learn humility through losing some battles.

If our enemies are around us and we have asked God to deal with them, yet they still seem to flourish, then it will be faith which declares that God is still in control and will one day bring about justice for all. If he has not done so yet, then he must have his reasons.

I read recently of a Christian in Sierra Leone who, having witnessed at firsthand some of the atrocities of the war in that suffering country, said, 'I realise that the only security we have is God'.[1] There is no guarantee that Christians will be protected from danger, though they may be. But we have the promise of God himself that we shall one day be raised in fullness and newness of life. The challenge is to live in the present with the final hope held clear.

1 IFES *'Special Report'*, 1999

In the fear, the cancer, the storms and the heartbreaks of this world, our God is real, and his power is as great as his love. Why not reaffirm today the last words of this psalm: 'I trust you'?

The tabernacle

The Israelites are eager to move on to the Promised Land, but how can they go forward without the assurance of God's presence? As with our own spiritual lives, the 'mountain top experiences' had to be followed by the daily rhythm of worship and prayer, to ensure that faith grew.

In chapters 25–31, and again with variations in chapter 35, God provides Moses with instructions to build a large tent-like structure that the Israelites are to take with them on their journey. Instructions are also given for the accompanying furniture and equipment, and the installation of its attendants, the priests. Just as the order of creation (Gen 1:1 – 2:3) is given in seven stages, so the instructions for the tabernacle are communicated in a series of seven sections, (Exod 25:1; 30:11, 17, 24, 34; 31:1, 12). What is this tent? The word in Hebrew – *mishkan* (Exod 25:9) – means 'dwelling place'. The root word *shakan* applies to anyone who lives nearby. In modern Hebrew your neighbours are *sh'kenim*. Yet such an ordinary word comes to express the very presence of God in all his holiness, majesty and power. For the *mishkan* is also called a *mikdash* – a place of holiness. God can be found everywhere, yet for the Israelites this was a special reminder of his presence with them. When the *Shekinah* of God, the 'glory of the Lord', came upon the tabernacle, this was not an easy moment or relaxed occasion. Rather every worshipper present was brought to an awareness of God's awesome holiness, and realised their own need of forgiveness and cleansing.

The tabernacle reminded the Israelites of the presence of God in their midst, protecting them, correcting them, judging them, forgiving them. If a crime was committed, if impurity occurred from contact with death or disease, if instruction and judgement was needed, the 'tent of meeting', another name for the tabernacle (Exod 33:7), was where such matters were resolved.

Richard Harvey

God s gift

Day 120

What has God given you? What can you give him?

Exodus 25:1–40 

God instructs Moses to invite the people to bring gifts for the construction of the tabernacle. A list of valuable items follows, including precious stones and what are probably dolphin (sea–cow) skins (v 5). The list divides into seven categories of metals, dyed materials, fabrics, timber, oils, spices and gems. This perfect number and combination shows each item has a part to play as the skilled craftsmen combine them to make 'something beautiful for God'. More important than the value of each item is the giver's motive, and the gift's purpose.

The Hebrew word *terumah*, which begins this section (v 2), is not the usual word for 'gift' or offering. It refers to a specially consecrated donation, something that is set aside by its owner for a particular and holy use. Nothing less than the best will do, and the giver's willingness to give is emphasised (v 2). The purpose of the gift is then revealed (v 8). God himself will 'dwell among them' (v 8), and he himself will give the plans for the construction of his own personal residence.

What follows are the details for the construction of a movable palace. Included in this chapter are the details for the ark of the covenant, the atonement cover, the cherubim, the table for shewbread, the menorah, the lampstand, all of which are referred to in the letter to the Hebrews.[1] Only in Christ can the sacrificial system of the Old Testament be truly understood, but the features described here are those that are necessary to provide a king with food, light and comfort, whilst restricting access to him through a system of inner, outer and private quarters. In Christ we are given 'private access' to God, and we can invite him to live in us.

1 Heb 8–10

Make a list of the gifts and talents that you can use in the Lord's service.

Day 121

How can I come before God today?

What areas in your life are open to God today?

Exodus 26:1–37

The floor plan of the tabernacle resembled a fenced rectangle, 150 feet long and 30 feet wide.[1] In the middle of this area was a covered inner rectangle 30 feet long and 15 feet wide. At the front were the altar for sacrifices and the laver, a large bronze basin used to wash away the blood of the sacrifices. The inner rectangle was made of a collapsible wooden frame covered with four layers of curtains. It contained two sections separated by a curtain, the Holy Place and the smaller Holy of Holies. Inside the Holy of Holies was the ark, with the mercy seat on top covered by the cherubim. Inside the Holy Place were the table for the 'Bread of the Presence', the lampstand and the altar for incense.

The symmetrical patterns and proportions found in the design of the tabernacle show God's concern, as in his work of creation, for order, harmony and right relations. The tabernacle is to be a place for the offering of sacrifices to God, so that right relationships between a holy God and sinful humanity can be restored. The curtain separating the Holy of Holies and the Holy Place, is called *parokhet* in Hebrew (v 31), which comes from the word meaning 'to bar the way', and prevented access. In later Jewish tradition this curtain now covers the holiest place in the synagogue, where the scrolls of the Law are kept. If it is no longer used, it cannot be destroyed, but must be stored away. The *parokhet* represented the necessary barrier between God and humanity. For our protection the holiness of God is veiled. Only one who came as God in man could destroy the barrier of sin.[2]

1 1 Kings 6
2 Matt 12:6; Luke 23:45; Heb 10:20

Wherever you may be, find some time today to meet with God.

Why sacrifice?

Lord, give me deeper understanding of the meaning and purpose of sacrifice.

Exodus 27:1–21 

Altars were the places where sacrificial animals were brought, killed and boiled or roasted by fire. The altar was a seven foot square construction, four feet high with sides of seven feet, with bronze horns at each corner.[1] They came to symbolise a place of refuge[2] and a place where forgiveness could be found.

The significance of the altar often escapes us. We need to understand what it means in the Hebrew Bible, in order to have a real appreciation of the ministry of Jesus in the New Testament. Without sacrifice true worship of God could not take place. Prayer and sacrifice were the two indispensable aspects of Israelite religion and worship. Abraham and Isaac had set up altars,[3] Moses asked Pharaoh for permission to go into the desert to offer sacrifices.[4] With the making of the tabernacle there would be one altar only where sacrifices could be offered.

The joy that is expressed by pilgrims coming to Jerusalem for the three annual festivals of Passover, the Feast of Weeks and the Feast of Tabernacles is in part because they were bringing offerings to sacrifice to the Lord. If a promise had been broken, a crime committed or an injustice caused, repentant sacrifice would put it right. Holiness for the ancient Israelites was not just linked to moral sin, but also to other ritual and physical defilements, like leprosy and contact with a corpse. All these needed sacrifice and prayer. For the Israelites then, like us today, there could be no assurance of God's acceptance and forgiveness without the shedding of blood.[5] For Israel, the blood was shed at the altar day by day. For us, the unique sacrifice of Jesus is sufficient for every day of our lives.

1 Ps 118:27
2 1 Kings 1:50
3 Gen 22:9; 26:25
4 Exod 3:18 – 17:15
5 Lev 17:11

'Thank you, Lord Jesus, for your sacrifice of yourself on the altar of the cross.'

A perfect High Priest?

Day 123

How is what we are reflected in what we wear?

 *Exodus 28:1–43*

Eight articles of clothing are described for Aaron the High Priest (vs 4,36–38,42,43). His appearance must have been striking. Ben Sira (190 BC) describes him as 'like the morning star appearing between the clouds, like the moon on a festival day'. The High Priest's clothing distinguished him from the other priests and the ordinary Israelites. This was not for self-glorification but to point to the ministry he was called to perform.

The prominent use of gold and purple, colours of royalty and wealth, pointed to privilege and blessing (vs 6,13). The stones (v 9) engraved with the names of the tribes of Israel reminded the High Priest that he was to represent the entire community. With God's help, he had executive decision-making powers that significantly affected the lives of others. The priests administered justice, taught God's Laws and discerned his will as they served the people. But the descendants of Aaron did not always live up to their priestly function, and at the time of Jesus the priesthood was a corrupt political institution sold to the highest bidder. Only a High Priest greater than Aaron could restore the priesthood to God's original intention.[1]

Aaron's robe was decorated with gold bells and pomegranates (v 34). These were not just ornamental but had an important function. Once a year he alone could enter the Holy of Holies, on the Day of Atonement. Would his sacrifice for the sins of Israel be accepted, or would God judge their sin as they deserved? The noise of the bells and pomegranates as he moved told the Israelites that he was still alive, and had not been struck dead.

1 Heb 7:26 – 8:6

What 'priestly role' are you called to play today? How does Jesus help?

Called, equipped and ready to serve

Day 124

How has God been preparing you to serve him?

Exodus 29:1–46 

The institution of the priesthood, like the practice of circumcision and the keeping of the Sabbath, was one of the hallmarks of God's covenant with Israel. Only through the coming of Jesus as the 'Great High Priest' would the institution of the priesthood be changed, so that the church would become the 'priestly nation' by which the world might see and know the character of God.[1]

This section speaks of the elaborate procedures by which Aaron and his sons were installed as priests to serve the Israelites before their God. The whole process took seven days, and would have been accompanied by much prayer and preparation. The animal sacrifices, cereal offerings, washing of the body, dressing in special robes and anointing with perfume all pointed to the important nature of the priesthood, and the holy nature of the work the priests were called to do.

The use of blood is significant in this chapter. Blood represents the life that has been offered up to God.[2] It is applied to the horns and base of the altar (v 12), then sprinkled over it (v 16). Then it is applied to the ears, thumbs and toes of Aaron and his sons (v 20). All that they hear and do, and wherever they go, must be consecrated, set apart in the service of God. Finally, the clothes they wear are dedicated to the Lord's service (v 21).

Our understanding of consecration may not be as visual as this, but we too are called by God to a 'priestly role', are cleansed and consecrated by the shed blood of Jesus and 'washed ... in the blood of the Lamb'.[3]

1 1 Pet 2:5
2 Lev 17:11
3 Rev 7:14

Read again the summary of this section (vs 42–46) and apply it to your own life, meditating on how Jesus meets with you today.

Going up in smoke!

Day 125

What are the most precious things in your life?

 *Exodus 30:1–38*

The five items in this section, the altar for incense, the half-shekel levy, the bronze laver, anointing oil and the ingredients for the incense complete the instructions for the tabernacle. Although they come as an appendix to the main instructions, they are by no means an afterthought! The materials required for them were anticipated in the list of donations previously given.[1] Without them the tabernacle could not be used for the regular worship for which it was designed.

The incense was a sweet-smelling mixture which, when put on the fire of the 'altar of incense' gave off a delicious savour that took away the smell of the animal sacrifices and produced thick clouds of smoke. The burning incense is often compared with the praises and prayers of God's people, a fragrance which pleases God himself.[2] The incense must be made and used according to the precise directions given otherwise it is invalid (v 9). Incense used correctly reminded the Israelites of the presence of God in their midst. Just as a pillar of cloud and a pillar of smoke accompanied them as they travelled through the wilderness, so the cloud of incense that was seen throughout the camp as sacrifices were offered assured the Israelites of God's presence and acceptance.[3]

Incense was a rare and expensive commodity. The incense for use in the tabernacle was not to be used for ordinary purposes (v 37), and incense offered to other gods was a terrible sin.[4] Incense rightly offered speaks of true worship. We are called to offer that which is precious and costly. Our prayers must come from sincere hearts and minds, offered to God in a spirit of openness to his will. Not just our prayers, but all of our lives, must be a fragrant offering to him.[5]

1 Exod 25:3–6
2 Ps 141:2
3 Lev 16:2,13; Exod 13:21
4 Jer 1:16
5 2 Cor 2:14–16

How can you make your life more of a fragrant offering to God today?

Now enjoy a rest!

Have there been times in your life recently where 'business' has replaced godliness?

Exodus 31:1–18 

The seventh unit of tabernacle instructions focuses on rest. The Sabbath as an institution was unknown in the ancient world, and is fast becoming a rarity today. Yet here is the key to the life of a believer, the rhythm that God himself laid down in his work of creation (v 17).

Just as the tabernacle was a building that made a particular space holy, so the Sabbath makes a particular time holy. In observance of the Sabbath the Israelites remembered God's works of creation and redemption[1] – even God 'refreshes himself' (v 17; compare 23:12).

It is not easy for us in our busy lives to remember and apply this principle, but Jesus the Lord of the Sabbath reinforced it by healing on the Sabbath.[2] The construction of the tabernacle was a most holy task requiring all the dedication, craftsmanship and valuable materials the Israelites could offer. But even more valuable than what they did for God by this service was what God had done for them. He had redeemed them from slavery in Egypt to be his people. By resting after the work of construction was done and honouring the Sabbath-day principle, the Israelites were reminded that they were slaves no more.

The sign of the Sabbath (v 13) was to show that something of God's cosmic plan was intimately linked with his relationship to his people Israel. They didn't deserve it because of any of their own qualities as a people; rather it was a proof of God's covenant commitment to them, for which they were to be eternally grateful. The God who is Creator of space, time and nature, had given his promise to be with his people. In Jesus this 'Sabbath rest' is open to all, not just for one day in seven, but for all time.[3]

1 Deut 5: 12,13
2 Matt 12:8; Luke 13:10–17
3 Heb 4:1–11

Are you taking time to enjoy the Sabbath?

God's requirements

The early chapters of Exodus (1–31) tell the story of how the nation of Israel takes shape despite severe opposition in Egypt; its escape from slavery to freedom under the leadership of Moses; and the formalisation of its new identity through a covenant relationship with the Lord, Yahweh.

The next few chapters, and the subsequent books of Leviticus, Numbers and Deuteronomy aren't inconsequential to this story of beginnings. They show us more of what God required of his special people in their relationships with him, with each other and with the surrounding nations. Much of what they contain belongs to an ancient world, with an agricultural context and a ritualistic religious expression. But some awareness of their content helps us better to understand the Old Testament books containing the later history of Israel. They also provide background to the ministry of Jesus and some practices of the early church, especially its Jewish members. A serious look at them will provide principles for spiritual and social life that give guidance to aspects of contemporary Christian living.

True worship

In chapters 32–40 the people of Israel are facing a mixture of excitement, turmoil, despair and awe. Moses, their trusted leader, has been called to meet Yahweh upon the mountain to receive his teaching. We pick up the story when the people have been waiting for many days for Moses to return from the mountain to retake the reins of leadership. But he hasn't come! Over these next days we will discover their response and his reaction. We will observe Moses in his deepening relationship with Yahweh. And, most importantly, we will gain glimpses of what it means to worship the living God who calls us, over three millennia later, to be his people. Study of these chapters might be enhanced by making rough sketches of the sacred objects described and using a Bible commentary to clarify details.

Grace Thomlinson

No substitute for the true God

Day 127

Remember a time when you were kept waiting. How did you feel?

Exodus 32:1–24 

Shortly before this episode, the Israelites had gathered around Mount Sinai with Moses. Now they congregate there again, this time around Aaron, whom Moses has authorised to decide difficult issues in his absence.[1] And they have a difficult issue – Moses seems to have disappeared! Many days before he had climbed the mountain to receive the tablets of the Law from God, and has not returned. Surely something must have happened to him. After all, they know it is a fearful thing to get too close to the living God.[2] They can wait no longer. They want a new, safer god to help them continue on their journey and so enlist Aaron's help.

Aaron's choice of god probably reflects common ancient usage of the calf as a symbol of divinity.[3] The strangest jump in logic is that this handmade golden calf could be designated the god Yahweh who had brought Israel out of Egypt! And their mixture of religious ritual with social revelry is a dangerous way to celebrate.

Aaron doesn't seem to think there is anything really disturbing about the incident. He passes the buck to the people and even to the calf![4] God has a different estimate of the seriousness of this idolatrous incident, which breaks specific commandments so recently given.[5] He is ready to destroy these people and begin a new line through Moses – until Moses intervenes, pleading that the people be spared, to maintain the reputation of God's gracious power among those who had witnessed the exodus. But when he sees for himself what is really going on in the camp, his righteous anger leads to the destruction of both tangible objects of the event – the tablets and the calf. He understands and models for the people that worship of the true God cannot be compromised.

1 Exod 24:14
2 Exod 19:16–25
3 1 Kings 12:25–33
4 Gen 3:12,13
5 Exod 20:2–4

When faced with a spiritual crisis, how do you respond?

No compromise with a holy God

Day 128

Have you ever had to stand up for God in a difficult circumstance? What motivated you?

Exodus 32:25 – 33:6

The Bible often records occasions when people are asked to make a deliberate choice to stand up for God and his ways. Sometimes there is a broad community response; sometimes just a few feel able to answer the call.[1] The Levites who respond to Moses become committed to much more than they bargained for! They become God's instrument for punishing the disobedient and unrepentant. But their obedience sets them on the right course for future ministry.[2]

Why does God take the sin of the golden calf so seriously? He commands this genocide, refuses Moses' intercession, threatens to delete the memory of his chosen people, punishes them with a plague and threatens further destruction and desertion.

What kind of God is this? He seems heartless and fickle, far from the loving and merciful God we prefer. There is no easy answer to this dilemma, one that recurs in many events of the Old Testament,[3] but several things can be said here.

First, God is always consistent within himself and will not compromise his character. His love and mercy are counterbalanced by his holiness and justice. He not only reaches out to create covenant relationship, he longs to create community where his character is the yardstick. As he shines his holy light on his people, unholy darkness must be dispelled.[4]

Secondly, God's people must live on God's terms and be prepared for his discipline when they don't – and that may be unpleasant.[5] The Israelites have blatantly broken key commandments and they have to learn at this early stage that they cannot get away with it.[6]

1 Josh 24:19–24
2 Num 3:5–10
3 Josh 7:20–26
4 1 John 1:5–7
5 Heb 12:4–11
6 Acts 5:1–11

Reflect on the holiness of God. What dark areas in your life should you open to his light?

Practising the presence of God

Day 129

Prepare yourself to come into the presence of God. What do you expect from this encounter?

Exodus 33:7–17 

What a long way Moses has come since we were first introduced to him as the one called to lead his people out of Egypt.[1] At that time he was quite unsure about the identity of the God Yahweh who demonstrated his presence at the burning bush, and was full of excuses about his own inability to fulfil his calling. In the intervening period he has faced many challenges that have thrown him back on the mercies and power of God, and Yahweh is now his friend.

It seems Moses and Yahweh habitually had an intimate and honest relationship – they would meet in a special tent away from the hubbub of general life. The people could only watch with reverence the outward signs of these encounters – maybe because of their fear of personally meeting with God; maybe because of the recent ruptures in their covenant relationship with him. Sadly, many people today – even in the church – are only wistful observers of the worship of others, standing at a distance and never really experiencing the reality of the presence of God for themselves.

Interestingly, Moses still needs reassurance of support for what lies ahead in his responsibility to lead the people to the promised land. Feelings of personal inadequacy can reappear even for those closely in touch with God.[2] Here Moses may wonder if he can continue to trust his key support person, Aaron. Perhaps he is expecting his young aide Joshua to take over the role. But Yahweh has even greater plans – his own presence will lead the nation to their place of rest. Moses seems to recognise that this is both essential and adequate for the mission.

1 Exod 3
2 Jer 15:15–21; Luke 7:18–23

How strong is your sense of the importance and adequacy of the presence of God in both big and small issues in your daily life?

Seeing the glory of God

Day130

If God were to reveal his glory to you, what would you expect to experience?

 *Exodus 33:18 – 34:9*

Moses has a deep hunger for a growing relationship with Yahweh. Assured of his guiding presence, he now asks to see his glorious presence. He has already seen 'theophanies' (visible representations of God) in the burning bush, upon Sinai and in the cloud and fire, but he senses God's true glory is beyond all these. God warns him that there are limits to what is possible for human beings to experience, but accommodates his request in an appropriate way. What happens physically between Moses and God as they meet in the cleft of a rock high up on Sinai is beyond our understanding, but the spiritual dimensions of the encounter are clearer.

The glory that is revealed to Moses is not God's bodily splendour but that of his moral being. Goodness, mercy, compassion, graciousness, patience, love, faithfulness, forgiveness and judgement are the components of his character ('name') – note the parallels between these and the fruit of the Spirit that we as Christians are called to cultivate.[1]

Moses' immediate response is submission and worship. By now he has experienced so much more of this glorious God than when he fearfully enquired concerning his name at their first encounter,[2] but it is definitely a new awareness of the full glory of Yahweh that causes him to bow to the ground. A vision of the glory of God often has this effect.[3] However, it may also be the warning of punishment for guilt, even to future generations, that prompts his reaction. For Moses, in keeping with his role as intermediary for his people, immediately confesses their sin and asks for God's forgiveness, ownership and protection. Seeing the glory of God has moral implications.[4]

1 Gal 5:22,23
2 Exod 3:6,13–15
3 Matt 17:1–8; Rev 4:1–11
4 Isa 6:5–7
5 John 1:14

'We have seen his glory, the glory of the One and Only, who came from the Father, full of grace and truth.'[5]

The conditions of worship

Day 131

What are you prepared to commit yourself to in order to have an ongoing relationship with God?

Exodus 34:10–28 

Finally, after lots of 'toing and froing', Yahweh responds positively to Moses' plea for national forgiveness and restoration. Israel will indeed be a special people, living in a covenant relationship with an awesome God. However, certain conditions need to be met for the relationship to be maintained. Such stipulations were always part of typical covenants of the day. Two are detailed here.

The first cautions the Israelites about their relations with other nations. They are not to make alliances of any kind with those who do not worship Yahweh, as their religious practices will seduce Israel away from the one who jealously protects his covenant relationship with them. God promises he will drive out the potentially ensnaring population, but Israel has to do its part as well – by removing all items of pagan worship. Sadly, their history shows the results of their failure to obey.[1] Christians, for similar reasons, are discouraged from forming significant alliances with unbelievers.[2]

The second encourages cyclical celebrations of feasts, when the actions of God in deliverance and provision are to be remembered. Sacrifices of the firstborn and first fruits, along with the keeping of the Sabbath, will perpetually maintain the covenant commitment between Yahweh and his people. This commitment is formalised in the Decalogue – the ten summary laws of the covenant.[3]

Christians sometimes want to see obedience to the laws of God as belonging only to the Old Testament. It is true that we live in a world where some of the biblical detail has no direct application (vs 25,26). But putting God before all other allegiances,[4] and regularly remembering key events of our faith,[5] must never be neglected by those who claim to follow Jesus.

1 Judg 2:10–15; Jer 7:16–19
2 2 Cor 6:14 – 7:1
3 Exod 20:1–17
4 Matt 6:33
5 1 Cor 11:23–26
6 John 15:10

'If you obey my commands, you will remain in my love… .'[6]

The results of worship

Day 132

Have you ever seen a person with a 'radiant' face? What was the context and how did you respond to them?

 *Exodus 34:29–35*

We sometimes speak of a bride being 'radiant' – the happiness of love and commitment bursts out through her eyes and her smile. However, there seems to be something quite different about the glowing skin of Moses' face. It didn't come from human emotion, but rather from his supernatural encounter with the glory of God. This radiance is immediately visible to those who greet him as he descends the mountain with the new tablets in his hand, but strangely he is unaware of it himself.

Sometimes the face of a Christian friend communicates a similar unconscious radiance of the presence of God. Such warmth can provoke a resonating inner glow in us, as we catch something of the wonder of intimacy with God. But sometimes it causes us embarrassment or coyness, especially at times when our own walk with God is not as close as it might be. Moses' friends react even more strongly. They are afraid to come close to him at first, probably fearing they are getting dangerously close to Yahweh's awesome presence.[1] Moses needs to reassure them, and institutes a practice of wearing a face covering unless speaking to or from Yahweh.

Moses' visibly radiant face communicates at least two important things in this context. It demonstrates that he is repeatedly in intimate communion with God.[2] It also reaffirms his leadership under God, which has been seriously questioned during the golden calf incident. The resulting conviction that Moses is truly being given words by God for the people provides a turning point in their obedience. Can people tell when you have been in God's presence?[3]

1 Exod 20:18–21
2 Exod 19:9
3 2 Cor 3:7–18
4 2 Cor 3:18

'We, who with unveiled faces all reflect the Lord's glory, are being transformed into his likeness with ever increasing glory.'[4]

The offerings of worship

Day 133

What are the most precious things you could offer to God as an act of worship?

Exodus 35:1–29 

Prior to a recent family wedding the young couple circulated a list of items – including colours and sizes – that would be useful in their new home. After the big event they no doubt checked their presents against their 'wish list' to see how well their needs had been met by the gifts of their friends. Those friends also hoped they had purchased appropriately!

During his second visit up the mountain,[1] Moses had received a list[2] of Yahweh's instructions for the tent of meeting ('tabernacle') and its fittings – including colours and sizes. It is now time to invite the people to give generously in order that the furnishings might be prepared. Materials of many kinds are needed – precious metals and stones, dyed fabrics and skins, wood and oils.

Amazingly, offerings of every kind arrive in abundance from all sectors of the community. They come from the people's own possessions, carried with them out of Egypt, and are given willingly as people's hearts are moved to contribute to this sanctuary for the presence of God. Special mention is made of women who not only donate precious jewellery but also their handicraft skills.

This giving means much more than our present-giving. It is not just to create a beautiful place of worship; it is an offering to the Lord. It is part of a larger offering of time and life, as symbolised by the faithful setting aside of one day in seven for the Lord. Keeping this day of rest includes not lighting indoor fires to cook food.[3] People are to be free from regular routines in order to focus on the God who has created and delivered them.[4] Do we also have willing, thankful and generous spirits?

1 Exod 24:12–18
2 Exod 25–31
3 Exod 16:21–26
4 Exod 20:11; Deut 5:15
5 Frances Ridley Havergal, 1838–79

'Take my life and let it be consecrated, Lord, to thee.'[5]

The gifts of worship

Day 134

For what kinds of ministry do we need to be filled with the Spirit of God?

Exodus 35:30 – 36:7

Bezalel is a skilled trades person with an important job – constructing the new sanctuary. His role is threefold: to design the detailed implementation of God's instructions; to have practical involvement in various kinds of crafts; and to teach others how to do the work. He and his partner Oholiab are the figureheads of a great team of willing construction workers, bringing the gifts of their skills to be used for this special purpose. Each morning they are joined by others bringing gifts of their resources, until the offerings are so abundant that they interrupt the work and Moses has to call a halt to their contributions so the work can proceed!

Two interesting features emerge from this story. The first relates to the gifting for the task. When the people bring their natural gifts to God's service, these are enhanced by their willing obedience to God's call. While artistic gifts are not specified among the New Testament's 'spiritual gifts',[1] God includes them among the diversity of skills which he uses for his glory. There is no task for God that is too insignificant for empowerment by the Holy Spirit – and no task that doesn't need it!

The second relates to the resource giving. How often do we see such a superabundance of generosity for the sake of the kingdom of God? Most Christian ventures do not have to keep turning people back from giving as Moses had to! Maybe we are too selfish with our possessions. Maybe we do not place sufficient value on the cause. Jesus commended the motives and generosity of the woman who poured her precious perfume on him[2] and the one who donated her last coins.[3]

1 Rom 12:6–8; 1 Cor 12:7–11, 28–31; Eph 4:11; 1 Pet 4:10,11
2 Mark 14:1–9
3 Mark 12:41–44

Do you need more generosity or more reliance on the Holy Spirit – or both – in the ministry God has called you to?

The environment of worship

Close your eyes and imagine you are in the place where you usually worship with God's people. What do you see? What does it mean to you?

Exodus 36:8–38 

We are now given a lengthy account of the work required to build the tabernacle. The amount of detail in the next few chapters is far more than most of us would include in a report on any new house we might be building and furnishing. In this chapter alone, fourteen verses describe curtains, covers and fastenings, and seventeen explain supporting frames, crossbars and posts! Apparently there are some key specifications missing that make it impossible to reproduce accurately the complete construction. However, we can admire the overall design, so simple in its concept and so practical in its portability. We can appreciate the skills needed to produce such colourful and expensive fabric, with its fine embroidery and other finishing touches. We can praise the precision processes required to craft wood and metal so beautifully.

But why such a detailed account? This is no ordinary building – this is to become the house of God. No detail mentioned is unimportant – not just because of its practical function, but also because of its symbolic value to worship. The curtains and covers were to shape the tabernacle, and the spaces they protected were to house the sacred furniture. The decorative cherubim symbolically guarded the sanctuary.[1] The materials used were the finest and rarest available, and the colours came from most precious and costly dyes, for only the best was worthy of Yahweh. The small components that allowed the tent and its furnishings to be easily packed up and moved on reminded the people that they were pilgrims, ready to be on the move towards their promised land.[2]

1 Gen 3:24; 2 Chron 3:7,10,14
2 Num 4:1–33; 10:11–36

What would you like your worship environment to say to you about God?

The symbols of worship

Day 136

Do you have a pencil ready for some sketching? Ask God to give you skill, and make this exercise meaningful as you draw some of the objects in the tabernacle.

 *Exodus 37:1–29*

A photographer often takes a view of the big scene and then gradually zooms in to smaller objects of key significance. Something like that happens here. We've been shown the broad sweep of the tabernacle; now the focus moves to its various furnishings. Each golden piece is set apart purely for sacred use and is highly symbolic of some aspect of worship.

The first mentioned, the ark of acacia wood overlaid with gold, is given a special place at the centre of worship. It is here that the presence of God will dwell. The tablets of Law placed inside will be guarded by the cherubim adorning its cover. Moses will come here to meet with God[1] and here the High Priest will make atonement for the people – a foreshadowing of Jesus Christ, who many centuries later became both atoning sacrifice and great High Priest.[2]

The table and the utensils that will hold sacred food and drink are to remind the people that Yahweh is the one who gives them sustenance. The lampstand represents the light of Yahweh, and its almond tree decoration his watchfulness over them. The altar of incense is to disperse its fragrance – created by the painstaking skill of a perfumer – as a symbol both of the ever-present God and the prayers of his people.[3]

Our table is the one around which we meet for communion, taking the food and drink that is symbolic of the spiritual benefits we enjoy because of Christ's death.[4] Jesus is the light who calls us to walk in his light and to let it shine before others.[5] He is God's fragrant offering who calls us to spread his fragrance wherever we are.[6]

1 Exod 25:22
2 Rom 3:25; Heb 9:7,11–12; 10:10–12
3 Rev 8:3,4
4 1 Cor 11:23–26
5 Matt 5:14–16
6 2 Cor 2:14

Do others see the living Christ through the symbols and realities of your corporate and personal worship?

The oversight of worship

Day 137

Prayerfully prepare to enter the presence of God in worship.

Exodus 38:1–31 

The close-up views continue with descriptions of two more furnishings, both made of bronze in keeping with their eventual location in the courtyard. The altar of burnt offering, along with its utensils, will be situated at the entrance of the tabernacle, where sacrifices of various animals and grains will be made for a range of purposes.[1] The mirror-finished basin will hold water for the priests' ritual washings.[2]

The scene then changes to the exterior of the tabernacle where its large surrounding courtyard is to be fenced by fine linen curtains supported by posts with bronze bases and silver fastenings – less expensive fabric was used outside the holy place. Only the entrance curtain will hint at the splendour to be found closer to the presence of God.

The crafting of the sanctuary components now complete, we marvel at the skill and diligence of Bezalel and Oholiab in their oversight of these essential preparatory tasks for the worship of God's people. Another overseer, Aaron's son Ithamar is given credit for keeping tally of the resources used in the tabernacle. The total amount of precious metals seems quite large for a people wandering in the desert. However it doesn't seem out of keeping with the opulence of Egypt from which they had obtained resources when they left.[3] More important than its value is the generosity of the people in making such a large amount available for the service of Yahweh, and the great care with which it is utilised. This logistics task, and the giving it represents, is not as visible as the fine craftsmanship, but its behind-the-scenes contribution is just as essential in the creation of an environment where people could focus on God.

1 Exod 40:29; Lev 6:9–13
2 Exod 30:17–21; 40:30–32
3 Exod 12:35–36

Pray for God's people around the world who will soon gather to worship, especially those who prepare to serve and lead them in both obvious and unnoticed ways.

The garments of worship

Day 138

'I delight greatly in the Lord; my soul rejoices in my God.'[1]

 *Exodus 39:1–43*

Monarchs and civic leaders often wear special garments at important events, symbolically representing their high office. In many church traditions those in ordained leadership also wear special clothing when serving in public. Some are simply styled, others more elaborate.

The high-priestly model designed for Aaron described here is definitely at the elaborate end of the spectrum! Its fabric was woven from the same expensive yarns as the curtains, with the addition of fine gold strands. The colourful main garment, the ephod, completely covered a plain blue robe worn underneath except for a hem decorated alternately with golden bells (which indicated movement in and out of the sanctuary) and embroidered pomegranates (representing God's provision). Special ornaments overlaid the ephod, which was worn only for ministry in the sanctuary. Precious stones engraved with the names of the sons of Israel were placed on its shoulder pieces and breastpiece, symbolic of bringing the whole of Israel into God's presence. A turban completed the outfit, with the inscription on its flower-like brooch summarising the purpose both of the clothing and the person who wore it – 'Holy to the Lord'. All of the priestly family had simpler linen tunics, headwear and underwear, with the colour-embroidered sash an indication of their special office. At their ordination, Aaron and his sons had to wash before dressing, then they and their garments were anointed and consecrated.[2] We may not wear special clothing for worship, but we have the same need for cleansing and consecration before embarking on service for God.[3]

With the garments ready, the whole preparatory work is now complete and ready for Moses to inspect. He finds all is in line with the instructions the Lord had given him.[4]

1 Isa 61:10a
2 Exod 29; 40:12–15; Lev 8
3 Heb 10:22–24
4 Gen 2:1–3
5 Isa 61:10b

'For he has clothed me with garments of salvation and arrayed me in a robe of righteousness.'[5] Thank God again for your complete acceptance in Christ.

The completeness of worship

Day 139

'Come, let us bow down in worship.'[1] *'Ascribe to the LORD the glory due to his name.'*[2]

Exodus 40:10–38 

The stage is set for a great drama. The backdrop is about to be erected. The stage manager is in place, and the key actors are ready to dress for their parts. The divine participant is waiting in the wings. At last the presence of the Lord will dwell among his people!

It has been about a year since the exodus. Moses is given instructions directly from God and he makes sure that they are carried out exactly. The tabernacle itself takes shape, and its various furnishings are located, moving outward from the inner sanctuary to the outer courtyard. Three sets of curtains are hung, ready to shield the ark and the entrances to the tabernacle and the courtyard from interference or distraction. The whole process is almost like watching the now familiar pieces of a large jigsaw being put together into a meaningful picture.

Each component is consecrated with oil and set apart for worship. Aaron and his sons are likewise consecrated to a hereditary role of priesthood. The stone tablets of the Law are placed inside the ark for the perpetual guidance of God's people and each vessel is commissioned for its specific purpose.

But the picture is not yet complete! It is missing the central piece until the presence of Yahweh fills his new earthly dwelling as the focus of worship.[3] He comes in the cloud that will symbolise his presence and his guidance for years to come. Moses, not yet invited to meet his Lord in this inner sanctuary, can only witness his glory from outside.

Over a millennium later, another cry of 'It is finished' reverses the process. The curtain protecting the holy place was torn from top to bottom, allowing direct access to God for all who would seek him.[4]

1 Ps 95:6
2 Ps 96:8
3 Ps 96
4 John 19:30; Matt 27:50–51; Heb 10:19–23
5 Heb 10:22

'Let us draw near to God with a sincere heart in full assurance of faith.'[5] Rejoice in your welcome!

A message of encouragement

What a treat we have in store! I must say at the outset, however, that Hebrews is quite a demanding read, as well as being one of the most encouraging texts of the New Testament.

Encouraging: that is the author's own description of his purpose (13:22). We do not know who the author was, but the most likely candidates are Apollos (see Acts 18:24) or Barnabas, who as a Levite (Acts 4:36) would have been interested in thinking about Jesus' ministry in priestly terms.

Whoever he was, why did he want to 'encourage' these 'Hebrews'? Clearly, the author was deeply concerned about them. They were 'messianic' Jews (or converted Gentile proselytes), who, it seems, were thinking of reverting back to Judaism, abandoning the 'messianic' part of their faith. I believe that we must imagine Jews like those described in Acts 21:20. They are still full members of their synagogues, but they have also been meeting on the first day of the week to celebrate the resurrection of Jesus the Christ in whose name they were baptised. But relations with the synagogue have been very difficult in the past (10:32–34), and persecution for their faith is still a real threat (12:3–4). Some have given up the Sunday gatherings (10:25), and the author discerns a real danger that they may renounce their baptism into Christ altogether, or simply slip away from it by default. Hence the warnings and encouragements to meet frequently, not to neglect or retreat from the implications of their faith, and to persevere in their commitment.

Arguments to counter

We can imagine some of the arguments which might have inclined these Jewish believers to give up their belief in Jesus as Messiah: 'We believe in God's covenant with Abraham, and his special relationship with Israel, don't we? And we believe, don't we, that we received purification from our sins when we repented as Jews? So we wouldn't be losing all that if we just went back to being "ordinary" Jews!'

These arguments set the agenda for this passionate letter! The author disagrees very strongly with this viewpoint, which, incidentally, is very similar to that still held today by those who believe that the Jews have their own separate, but equally valid, covenant with God. By powerful scriptural argument, the author seeks to convince these 'Hebrews' that, if they revert to Judaism, they will not have what they had before because Jesus has made an absolutely decisive difference.

Structure of the epistle

Perhaps to emphasise the importance of his vital message of the efficacy of the blood of Christ alone to cleanse us, the author has actually constructed the letter in such a way as to place this message at the heart of a series of truths about Jesus. The first two chapters speak of Jesus, God's final Word incarnate among us. 3:1 – 4:13 speaks of Jesus, God's answer to hardness of heart, while 4:14 – 10:39 explains that Jesus is our faithful and merciful High Priest, able to save completely.

The long central section could be described as having been written in a concentric pattern, as shown in the list below (A,B,C,B,A) and, interestingly, the middle part (C) also has a concentric pattern, focused around 9:11–14. This vital paragraph, therefore, literally sits at the heart of the message.

- (A) 4:14 – 6:12: Opening exhortation and warning
- (B) 6:13 – 7:28: Jesus, the Melchizedek priest who truly saves
- (C) 8:1 – 9:28: Jesus, the Mediator of the new covenant
- (B) 10:1–18: Jesus, the Priest who truly sanctifies
- (A) 10:19–39: Concluding exhortation and warning.

The book concludes with lessons on how the Old Testament truly encourages us to believe (11:1 – 12:3) and discipline, worship and practical living on the threshold of heaven (12:4 – 13:25).

Steve Motyer

Day 140

The last word

Remember the last time you looked at a starry night sky. Remind yourself of what you know about the size of the universe.

Hebrews 1:1–14

Hebrews opens with a terrific flourish. Verses 1–4 may have been an early Christian hymn, but even if not, they are certainly worth singing now! Every word counts as the author introduces us to Jesus as (maybe) his readers had never thought of him before. He is not mentioned by name until 2:9, so here we meet him through his great titles: 'Son' (v 2), 'heir' (v 5), 'Lord' (v 10), and even 'God' (v 8). It is perhaps significant that he is not called 'Christ' here, although verse 9 refers to his 'anointing'. It could be that, by concentrating on Jesus as their 'Christ' or 'Messiah', the first Jewish readers had missed out on a fully rounded understanding of who he is.

So we must be careful not to miss out either! Focus first on verses 1–4:

- The contrast between Old Testament Scripture and God's new speech 'by his Son' (vs 1–2). God has not just spoken again, but has spoken finally, replacing diversity and incompleteness (v 1) with fullness and exactness (v 2). The Son encompasses the whole world and all its history – all space and time – by 'his powerful Word' (v 3).
- The special relationship between God and his Son (v 3). The light source, and the light emitted – can we imagine a closer relationship despite the distinction that exists between them?
- The inclusion of 'purification for sins' within his work of creating and sustaining the world (v 3).
- His total uniqueness (v 4), greater than all 'angels' (and for the first readers, this would also mean greater than all other gods).
- The quotations that follow, mainly from the Psalms, were probably meant to stimulate worship, as well as amplify the truths expressed in verses 1–4.

Do you truly believe this about Jesus? Now follow God's instruction to the angels (v 6), and use verses 5–13 as the basis of your own worship of Jesus the Son of God.

The true human being

Day 141

Jot down a short answer to a difficult question: what would you give as the dictionary definition of 'human being'?

Hebrews 2:1–9 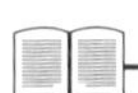

Jews believed that the Law was revealed to Moses through angels (a belief based on Deuteronomy 33:2).[1] But now God has spoken directly, through his Son. This contrast leads the author into his first 'warning' (vs 1–4): the Law prescribed punishments for transgressors[2] so how much more dreadful will it be for those who 'ignore' the 'great salvation' revealed by the Lord himself?

Having issued this warning, the author launches into his explanation as to why it is vital to hold on to Jesus Christ (v 5 begins in the original with 'for ...'). His first reason is that Jesus is God's chief human being; so if we lose touch with him, we will miss out on God's glorious plan for humanity.

This is an unusual perspective on Jesus, and it is fascinating that the author puts it first. He develops the theme by quoting Psalm 8:4–6 (vs 6–8). This is a creation psalm, describing the relationship between humanity and the world, but it only makes sense if we apply it to Jesus. It is simply not true that human beings are 'crowned with glory and honour' and reign with 'everything under their feet'. Many people live in terrible degradation, and all of us are inescapably subject to our circumstances. But 'we see Jesus ... crowned with glory' (v 9) because of his death for us and so, ultimately, we too will be 'brought to glory' (v 10).

1 See also Acts 7:53; Gal 3:19

2 For example Num 15:32–36

Thank God for Jesus, your 'grown-up Brother', and ask that your humanity may begin to reflect his. Are there any particular ways in which you need to become like him?

Being family

Day 142

Write 'trials and temptations' at the top of a sheet of paper, and then make a list of yours. Be honest.

 *Hebrews 2:10–18*

This passage contains two further reasons why we must not 'ignore' Jesus.[1] Chapter 2 actually lays a foundation for the whole letter: all its themes reappear later.

First, because he is family with us (vs 10–13). Families are single units. This is taken for granted in non-Western societies, but it is not so obvious in the West, where the family has been reduced to 'nuclear' size, and tends to function as a loose collection of individuals. Western readers need to think in a different way in order to grasp what is being said here about Jesus. It is he, actually, who 'brings many sons to glory' (v 10). He and they are 'of the same family' (v 11), and this means going through the same experiences, particularly being 'made perfect through suffering' en route to salvation. He is both our elder brother (vs 11–12) and our father alongside God (vs 10,13). So how could we break the bonds of family with him?

Secondly, because he shares flesh and blood with us (v 14). This answers the unspoken question, 'how is he family with us'? The answer is: 'in the most wonderfully literal way possible, by fully sharing our human "flesh", so that he might save us from the death (and the fear of it) which plagues humanity'. As in poetry, the very meaning of these verses in the Greek is reflected in the way they are written with a repeated pattern: he has become like us (vs 14a,17a) ... so that we are released from death (vs 14b–15,17b) ... because he longs to help us (vs 16,18). The incarnation of Jesus means a family bond with the human race – specifically with 'the seed of Abraham' (v 16), the 'people' for whose sins he makes atonement (v 17). Those people can claim him as brother. What a privilege! And so whatever temptations and trials we bear ('tempted' in verse 18 means both), we can bring them to him, knowing that he is 'able to help'.

1 Heb 2:3

Now put verse 18 into practice, and ask the Lord for his help with the sufferings you listed. It's why he came!

Don't give up!

'Hardness of heart' is a spiritual disease, according to the Scriptures. List its symptoms.

Hebrews 3:1–19

'Fix your thoughts on Jesus' (v 1). In a way, this is the central message of Hebrews. We meet the same command to 'consider him' in 12:3, on the other side of the long argument through which the author tells us how to think rightly about him. If only we thought about Jesus more – seeking to understand him, to imitate him, and to follow him – our worries and problems would fade.

In addition to Psalm 95:7–11, quoted in verses 7–11, we need to have two passages from Numbers in mind as we read this chapter: Numbers 12:1,8 (quoted in v 5) and Numbers 14.[1]

The first passage concerns Moses, who is portrayed by the Lord himself as greater than any other prophet because he does not receive God's Word through dreams or visions, but through face-to-face encounter. But Jesus is greater still: just as the son and heir to an estate is greater than a servant on it (vs 5–6).

The 'Hebrews' believe that it will not make much difference if they renounce their allegiance to the Son but maintain loyalty to the servant, Moses. What sense will that make?

The second passage concerns the Israelites' rebellion, which denied them entry to the Promised Land. The author is very afraid that his 'Hebrews' are about to make the same mistake with the same terrible result: death, banishment, alienation from God. He fears that sin may deceive them into hardness and unbelief (vs 12–14).

That leads us to the main quotation from Psalm 95 on which we will focus tomorrow. The author reads it as a present challenge, addressed to us now by the Holy Spirit (v 7), telling us that hard hearts never hear the voice of God.

1 Num 14:29 is quoted in verse 17

What medicine would the author of Hebrews prescribe to cure 'hardness of heart'? Take some, if you see any symptoms in yourself.

Under the searchlight

Day 144

You are caught in the beam of a searchlight so bright it reveals everything about you – your secrets, thoughts and fears. How do you feel?

 *Hebrews 4:1–13*

When the Holy Spirit takes God's Word and applies it to our hearts, it probes our actions and motives, exposing what displeases God and leaving it bare before him for judgement. What a bleak picture this is (vs 12,13)! How can we 'give an account' which will in any way excuse what God's Word reveals in our hearts? We cannot. But the point is – we are not meant to stay in verses 12–13: we move on to verses 14–16!

The author gives an example of how the Holy Spirit works with an example from his own reading of the Scriptures (v 7). The Spirit's 'today' in Psalm 95 was also 'today' to the Hebrews, just as it is for us: we will hear God speak 'today' as well, but not if we harden our hearts.

On this basis, the author then draws a parallel between us and the people to whom the Psalm refers, the exodus generation who heard God's voice through Moses but failed to enter the Promised Land under Joshua. He develops an argument about them that runs like this: God swore that, because of their rebellion, they would not enter his 'rest'. Never mind, then, that Joshua claimed to give them 'rest' from their enemies.[1] God must have meant another kind of rest, which they did not enter.

Genesis 2:2 tells us that that rest was God's own personal Sabbath-rest after creation. The Hebrews should have entered that kind of intimate fellowship with God, but God barred them. So if God promised it[2] and they did not enter it, the promise must remain to be fulfilled (v 9), and we must make sure we do not miss the opportunity! So the Scriptures probe our hearts too: is there faith within (vs 2–3)? Zeal to enter God's 'rest' (v 11)? Or slackness, disobedience, hardness?

1 Josh 22:4; compare Deut 25:19; 1 Kings 8:56
2 For example Josh 1:13

Look ahead to 4:14–16 and bring to 'the throne of grace' the feelings and fears you experienced under the imaginary searchlight.

Our great high priest

Day 145

Apply to yourself the three descriptions: 'ignorant', 'going astray' and 'subject to weakness'. Are they true of you, if you're honest?

Hebrews 4:14 – 5:10 

This passage opens the main, central section of the letter (4:14 – 10:39), which focuses on Jesus as our High Priest. And – as so often in the New Testament letters – the opening paragraph of a section gives a 'nutshell' presentation of what is to follow. Notice here *what our 'great high priest' means for us* (4:14–16). In three words, he means sympathy because he fully shares our trials and temptations; confidence because he gives us full access to God, and grace because he will never reject our prayers for mercy and help!

What it means to be a high priest (5:1–4). Here is a summary of what priesthood meant for Aaron and his sons: being human (v 1a); representing others before God (v 1b); offering sacrifices for sin (v 1c); having special care for the ignorant and weak (v 2a), and being appointed by God (v 4). But in Aaron's case there was a fatal flaw – he needed his own ministry as much as anyone. How could he represent himself before God, and deal with his own ignorance and sin? So we need another high priest.

For Jesus to become high priest (5:5–10) meant receiving the special commission from God summarised by Psalms 2:7 and 110:4 (vs 5–6), and then going through a process of ordination far greater than Aaron's (vs 7–10). The author reflects Jesus' experience in Gethsemane[1] in his description of the agony of faith with which Jesus faced death for us, 'learned obedience', and became a high priest who truly is 'the source of eternal salvation for all who obey him' (v 9).

This is a scriptural passage to prize! Every theme here will be developed in the chapters which follow. Jesus' attaining 'perfection' (5:8–9) does not imply previous imperfection (far from it – see 4:15), but rather his wonderful humanity: he grows, like us, into full 'humanness', in fellowship with God.

1 For example Mark 14:32–42

Apply to yourself whichever verse in today's passage most speaks to you, and turn it into heartfelt prayer.

The horror of rejecting Jesus

Day 146

Prepare by reflecting on 'let us hold firmly to the faith we profess' (4:14). What can you do to make your Christian commitment public?

 *Hebrews 5:11 – 6:8*

Today we read the first really severe warning passage. The author is deeply concerned that the 'Hebrews' have not grown as they should, and that they cannot absorb 'mature' teaching about the Messiah (vs 11–14). Then he tells them that, nonetheless, he is going to give them mature teaching (6:1–3), because if they should abandon their Christian commitment, there will be no way back to God again (6:4–6). So it is absolutely vital that they should 'go on to maturity' (6:1).

The author apparently teaches that we can lose our salvation. So what are we to make of passages that seem to contradict this?[1] And what does 'fall away' mean (6:6)? How *serious* does a sin have to be, before it counts as 'falling away'?

Remember those to whom this letter was addressed: they are Jewish Christians, still members of the synagogue, tempted to abandon Jesus as their Messiah, and to revert to 'simple' synagogue faith. Doubtless they thought they would still have all the synagogue-blessings they had before their baptism as Christians (6:1–2) – fundamentals of the Jewish faith which they lightly 'Christianised' when they were baptised.

But no! If you commit yourself to 'membership' with those who regard Jesus as a rightly-crucified blasphemer, then repentance will not work for you, we are told here. The door to fellowship with God is not open to those who re-crucify his Son.

The 'falling away' is thus very serious indeed: it amounts to joining the enemies of Jesus. Note that the author does *not* say that those who fall away cannot later repent and return to Jesus, merely that, as Jews, they cannot find effective repentance before God.

1 For example Rom 8:31–39; John 10:27–30

The 'Hebrews' shrank from being persecuted for their faith. Pray for the persecuted church today, that the Lord will keep all such believers from 'falling away'.

Safe for evermore

Day 147

Think of a commitment which you simply can't imagine breaking. Reaffirm your pledge to keep it, 'the Lord being my helper'.

Hebrews 6:9–20 

Two difficult questions are raised by Hebrews 6: can we lose our salvation?[1] – and if 'Yes', then can we ever be sure of salvation? And is it impossible for those who 'fall away' to return to the faith they rejected?[2]

We thought about verse 2 yesterday. But what about verse 1? Verse 8 says that, like scrub ground, those who reject Jesus will end up 'burned'. Today's passage, in contrast, ends with a wonderful statement of assurance of salvation (vs 16–20). The 'two unchangeable things' (v 18) are God's Word and God's oath, which together mean absolute security for those who hope in Jesus as 'an anchor for the soul, firm and secure' (v 19). Think of all the storms of life – all imaginable temptations and trials – battering at you but completely failing to shift you from your mooring in Jesus!

This is exactly what Paul says in Romans 8:31–39. So there can't be a contradiction between that passage and this. But perhaps there's a contradiction within this chapter, between verses 4–6, and verses 18–20? Surely not! The answer appears when we think about Abraham, (v 13). The oath in verse 14 occurs in the story of the (near) sacrifice of Isaac. Abraham's faith was certainly battered as he walked towards Mount Moriah with his son.[3] But he held on to God, trusting in his truth and goodness. Salvation depends on the relationship between us and the Saviour. If we renounce the Saviour, how can we be saved? But the more we grow into union with him, then – like a couple celebrating their golden wedding – the less thinkable it is that we should ever reject him!

1 Compare Heb 10:26–31
2 Gen 22:1–19
3 Compare Heb 11:17–19

Pray for those you know, whose relationship with the Saviour is weak. Can you encourage them in any way?

Old covenant Christians?

The 'Hebrews' were a contradiction in terms: 'old covenant Christians' who were drawing back from the boundless generosity and the openness of the gospel of grace. Does that sound too remote from our own circumstances to merit our concern? Not a bit. In responding to their spiritual confusions the author revisits the absolute bedrock of Christian faith and hope, and in terms which have a special power. At first elusive and difficult because of their Jewishness, and their concern with the minutiae of Jewish worship, our four chapters will open up fresh dimensions in our relationship with God. They will also, if we are attentive, extend and enrich our repertoire of words and images by which we may grasp the meaning of salvation.

Moving beyond the Law

The writer takes his readers on a tour their traditions, making a running comparison between the old and the new covenants. His point is that the old covenant could not deliver because it was superficial and transitory. Its priests aged and died, its sin-sacrifices were at best only symbolic and could not possibly atone for the guilt of human beings. The old covenant instructed and demanded obedience to the Law but could not lift a finger to help sinful worshippers keep the Law. Its rituals could not reach the conscience and the heart of the individual.

Our everlasting Mediator

At the centre of his new creation, his new covenant, God places his Son. Christ is the one who replaces all the paraphernalia of the old system with his own body. He makes the covenant 'work' by his own sin-bearing death and keeps it flooded with life and energy by his own risen life as our everlasting Mediator of the covenant. Look out for the breathtaking way he enfolds all that we are in our weakness, with all that he is as the True Man.

Dennis Lennon

Deep connections

Day 148

God desires that we should be hopeful, joyful, confident people, through faith rooted deep in Christ's eternal priesthood. 'Lord, make me like this!'

Hebrews 7:1–10 

Awaiting execution in a Nazi cell, Dietrich Bonhoeffer wrote to a friend, 'Keep a ground-base of joy alive in you'.[1] Bonhoeffer's joy is rooted in an eternal source which is beyond the reach and authority of earth-bound processes of decay, even in a prison cell.[2] How fascinating and significant, then, that at the start of Abraham's story as the father of God's people (which is our story) he should encounter a sign of hope and joy: enter Melchizedek.[3] His name and title are loaded with Christ-symbolism (vs 1,2). But priestly kings were not unknown;[4] even they came and went in the stream of life. How could any of them, or any of our present-day 'ways of salvation', inspire hope and joy when they themselves, however impressive, end in death? But our writer, arguing in the rabbinical manner from the silence of the Genesis text, has Melchizedek prefigure Christ, eighteen hundred years later, appearing out of eternity (v 3).

Jesus is in a class of one. He transcends every message whose illusions are rendered worthless by the inescapable finality of death. He is himself, as risen Son of God, the inexhaustible wellspring of hope and joy.[5] He is no longer time-bound as we are; yet he is not outside time, but always sharing our human condition in ways wonderfully suggested by Melchizedek who ministered in God's name to the battle-weary Abraham with the Christ-gifts of blessing, wine and bread. Thus Jesus ceaselessly comes to us from out of his eternity (he is King) to refresh our lives with his life (he is Priest) according to his omnipotent sympathy (he is our Kingly-priest). Simply allow yourself to receive his gift of hope and joy.

1 1 Pet 1:3–7
2 Rom 8:28–39
3 Gen 14:17–20
4 Josh 10:1
5 John 4:10,13

To 'keep a ground-base of joy alive in you' is about connecting deep into Christ. Take this moment to examine your spiritual sources.

The enfolding

Day 149

Remember that Christ has pledged to enfold your life in his. Allow him to save you in every aspect of your existence, 'completely' (v 25).

Hebrews 7:11–28

A converted thief in Tokyo first saw the Ten Commandments on the wall of a church. He read 'You shall not steal' not as a grim warning (old covenant) but as a marvellous promise (new covenant). An externalised word and ritual, administered by weak mediators (vs 23,27),[1] can never master 'the fury and the mire of human veins'.[2] A covenant is only as strong as its mediator. Only the Melchizedek-Christ, in 'the power of an indestructible life' (vs 15–17,24–28) can energise and maintain the breathtaking new covenant relationship (v 22).[3] As our mediating high-priest he is continuously, moment by moment, saving us by adding all that he is to all that we are.[4] Here is the profound Hebrew understanding of mediator and people as 'the One for the many – the many in the One'.[5] Do you despair of ever believing, obeying, loving, serving God as you know you should? Allow Jesus to take your unbelief into his belief, your disobedience into his obedience, your 'un-love' into his total love. That is to say, allow him to enfold you 'completely' (v 25). Similarly with prayer and worship. Christ does not even leave us to pray directly to the Father, at the mercy of our moods, confusions and feebleness, but by the Holy Spirit our prayers enter Christ's prayer and participate in his. Raised by the merit and power of his prayer, our voice inextricably mingled with his, Christ offers prayer and worship to the Father which is both his and ours. We, the many, pray together with the One, alone.[6]

1 Gal 3:23–25
2 *Byzantium*, WB Yeats
3 1 Tim 2:5,6
4 Matt 26:26–28
5 Ex 28:29,30
6 1 Cor 1:30,31

Christ by his life and sacrifice 'once for all' (v 27) has already done everything necessary for us to 'draw near to God' (v 19) through him. Allow yourself to receive this incredible gift. We really are saved 'completely' by faith, not by works.

New covenant life

Day 150

Old covenant attitudes may still lurk around our Christian life casting a shadow over our relationship with God and inhibiting joy. Come into the freedom of new covenant life.

Hebrews 8:1–13 

It never was an entirely happy marriage. God and Israel had exchanged vows at Sinai but the relationship could not survive her relentless spiritual promiscuity.[1] The fact is that, regardless of what the law demands, our instinct is to pursue what we most desire, for we are driven by what most gives pleasure, and we become what we most love.

God's new covenant is therefore directed at healing our sin-enchanted desires and loves by the explosive dynamic of his Word which the Holy Spirit will 'put ... write' in hearts and minds (v 10). As the Spirit brings the Word into our inner life, receive it deep and hold it there, ponder it as you turn it over and over responding in prayer and praise.[2] The Word is felt in the heart, under the root of our thought, received into the textures of the mind, held in the memory,[3] oxygenating our inner world, implanting new love and desires in place of the old sin-enchanted motivations; the Spirit's voice is discerned as that mysterious 'soft, barely audible sound of almost breathing' of Elijah's experience.[4]

The outcome is a startling, authentic, growing individuality (v 11). The church is not another collective, but a community of individuals who are constantly becoming themselves, through the Holy Spirit's work in them. 'It is not in a mirror that a man recognises himself truly; it is in the call that comes to him and in the promise that he received' says the Old Testament commentator Hans Wolff. This is new covenant spirituality.

1 Jer 3:1–5
2 James 1:21
3 Ps 119:97–104
4 1 Kings 19:11–13

Out of today's reading and reflection, are you aware of any particular word, an emphasis, a picture, a call or a promise which the Holy Spirit desires to 'put ... write' in your heart? Drop all else and take hold of it.

Healing the centre

Day 151

There is a shape, a geometry, to the spiritual life and at its centre is a conscience seeking access to God. Come to him now.

Hebrews 9:1–10

The greatest personal blessing? A clear conscience at ease in the holy presence of God. The conscience ('con-science', a co-knowledge) has direct awareness of God's Law, and direct knowledge of our actions; it compares the two and passes sentence.[1] We all know about the 'pangs' of conscience, its 'nagging' and its 'demands'. The poet John Donne said that man is the only creature who 'works on himself with inborn strings'. Knowledge cannot help us here; paradoxically the more sensitive the conscience (because informed by God's truth) the more it torments![2] But it can also be desensitised, even 'cauterised', by persistent sinful habits of mind, and we are then in terrible danger of losing the ability to feel shame.[3] The conscience is not a dispassionate observer of what goes on in 'the foul rag and bone shop of the heart',[4] it is itself infected by those disorders.[5]

The guilt and pollution of 'acts that lead to death' (v 14) encrust the conscience as a weight and defilement: then expect those 'inborn stings' of alienation, the loss of inner peace and spiritual confidence, a fear of the light. Access into God's holy presence is barred by the worshipper's own conscience. How deep and thoroughgoing is Christ's 'new order' (v 10, literally 'new putting right')! By his blood he 'clears the conscience' (v 9) of its inward bondage to spiritual failure.[6] He releases and revivifies it to be a co-witness with the Holy Spirit within as we walk in the light, emancipated at the very centre of our being 'to serve the living God' (v 14). By the renewing of our conscience the Lord restores to us an essential part of our inner navigational system, not functioning independently of the Holy Spirit, but available to him.

1 Rom 2:14,15
2 Rom 7:7–11
3 1 Tim 4:2
4 *Circus Animals*, WB Yeats
5 Mark 7:17–23
6 1 John 1:5–7
7 Rom 9:1

'I speak the truth in Christ ... my conscience confirms it in the Holy Spirit'.[7] Keep the conscience lively by regular self-examination, confession and repentance.

We have access

Day 152

In today's reading we ponder the gift behind all other gifts: access into God's presence through the exchanged life. Praise him!

Hebrews 9:11–28 

The story of the man who took bath after bath in the same stagnant water is enough to make the flesh creep. We have a horror of contact with filth, disease, contamination and death. God abhors the uncleanness of sin.[1] It taints and defiles; it outrages his holy love for his creation. We are so much at home with sin that we have no idea of what sin is, therefore we need to go back to school in the old tabernacle with its rich drama about spiritual uncleanness debarring access to God (vs 18–22).[2] In our innate unwillingness to face up to the problem and because of our vanity, we are prone to attempt reformation, some spiritual–moral smartening up of our appearance before God, but that is as futile as pouring eau de cologne onto an open sewer.

To the tabernacle again, and its mysterious ritual of cleansing through 'exchanged life' in which sin is lifted, symbolically, off the guilty and transferred onto a 'perfect' victim in a vicarious and atoning death. 'Everything ... is cleansed with blood' (vs 22,23), the worshipper is forgiven, cleansed and sanctified for access into 'the Most Holy Place' (v 8). So much for the symbolic figure; the reality in Jesus Christ is too extraordinary to comprehend; it jams all thought and blows the fuses of imagination. For Christ is both the mediating High Priest who on behalf of his people takes the atoning blood and opens the way of access to God, and the One whose blood is offered! (vs 11–15,23–28). He 'became', on the cross, that hideous and abhorred and most appalling thing, the polluting sin of the world.[3] With Paul we add 'for me'.[4]

1 2 Cor 6:15 – 7:1
2 Lev 5:2,3; 7:19–21
3 2 Cor 5:21
4 Gal 2:20

God, in his essence, is love and self-surrender. Look back to Christ's sacrifice, but also forward to his coming in glory 'to bring salvation to those who are waiting for him' (v 28). What a day that will be!

Here I am

Day 153

Imagine a universe where God is fobbed off with third-rate worship. Then consider why the Son of God took a body.

Hebrews 10:1–10

The spirituality of the new covenant claims every inch of existence.[1] It is concerned with the total reaction of the whole person to the whole of life, since we are created to love and glorify God. 'God is no trainer of souls bent on attaining extravagant record performances. He is a lover who wants nothing but great love and who accepts with a smile anything such a love invents to offer' (Hans von Balthasar). Yes, but which of us loves God like that? A glance into our own hearts suggests our love and adoration are in need of redemption.[2] So we try harder, change the music, attend courses, seek out new styles, only to sink back into ourselves exhausted by our efforts.

Listen: Christ is our Saviour 'completely' (7:25). If because of our weakness we are unable to honour the Father with love and worship worthy of him, Christ will save us even in this. Therefore 'a body you prepared for me' (v 5), in which Jesus lives in full self-surrender 'to do your will, O God' (v 7), for the Father's sake, and for ours, because he gathers up our stutterings, our splutterings and mumblings and bumblings into his perfect obedience, praise and prayer.[3] In an incredible act of solidarity he extends his own holiness to include all of us.[4] 'We have been made holy' through his self-offering. Our status before the Father is that we stand sanctified within Christ's sanctification (v 10). We serve the Father, not in order to be accepted, but because we are already accepted in Christ. 'We have been made holy through the sacrifice of the body of Jesus Christ once for all' (v 10).

1 Rom 12:1,2
2 Job 1:6–11
3 Col 3:1–4
4 1 Cor 1:30

'It is the heart that is not yet sure of its God which is afraid to laugh in his presence' (George MacDonald, 1824–1905).

Therefore let us

Day 154

The new covenant creates a radical and practical realignment of our relations to God, to others, and to ourselves.

Hebrews 10:11–25 

The logic of the new covenant builds to 'therefore ...' (v 19). Huge consequences follow. First, 'let us draw near to God' (v 22). It is now safe to do so. Christ has cleared the spiritual minefields between ourselves and God. Go in. He has replaced every barrier to the presence of God with his own cross-scarred body (v 20).[1] Practise the presence of God with an assurance which grows and strengthens, becoming 'full', as you daily prove the promises by faith (v 22). 'Draw near' is both a once-for-ever step (into your status before God) and a life process (into expanding delight in him).[2] Also 'let us hold unswervingly to the hope we profess' (v 23).[3]

'Spiritual ambiguity' is all the rage at the present time; it appears as a stylish, post-modern, sexy, personal fashion statement suggesting open-mindedness and sophistication when in fact it may be little more than a self-flattering cover-up for loss of nerve. But meditation in Scripture and prayer will allow the spring-steel of Christ's unswerving commitment to you to strengthen the spine of your commitment to him. Yet we will neither 'draw near' nor 'hold unswervingly' by going solo, therefore 'let us ... encourage one another' (v 25).[4] God has given us to one another. The mature Christian, says the author George MacDonald, 'does not take his joy from himself. He feels joy in himself, but it comes to him from others, not from himself – from God first, and from somebody, anybody, everybody next ... his consciousness of himself is the reflex from those about him, not the result of his own turning in of his regard upon himself'.

1 Luke 23:44,45
2 Ps 36:7–9
3 Rom 8:31–39
4 Gal 5:26 – 6:2

God – what keeps you from 'drawing near'? Hope – are you holding on unswervingly? Others – are you an encourager?

Day 155

On the plateau

Our readings in Hebrews conclude with a call to wholehearted discipleship for the long haul. 'By perseverance the snail reached the ark'.[1]

Hebrews 10:26–39

Like the reappearance of a former lover, the old ways may at any time reassert their fascinations for us, but particularly when we hit the midlife plateau and there is still a long, long, way to go.[2] After a brilliant start (vs 32–34) these Christians were running out of steam, tempted to reconnect with the old rituals (vs 26,35). Our discipleship will be decided not by the sprint through the foothills, but in how well we manage the long haul across the plateau (vs 35,39; 12:1–3)[3] with the stamina and strategies of the long-distance runner.[4]

And should we fall back into compromise with the world, God is faithful, he cares enough to bring us under the discipline of his severe love (vs 27–31; 12:5–7). 'For to say a man might disobey and be none the worse would be to say that *no* may be *yes* and light sometimes darkness' (George MacDonald). Are we infected with the modern dread of making and keeping a life-binding vow? The sting is in the word 'binding'. 'I've moved on! I've become another person, open to new ideas, I cannot be shackled by old promises'. The sadness for that person, says GK Chesterton, is that 'he is wandering in a hungry search for a certain exhilaration which he can only have when he has the courage to cease wandering' (v 39). Give yourself wholly to God, then bolt the back doors, leave yourself no way out, blow up your bridges and burn your boats, accept no calls from the 'old rituals'.[5] Congratulations. Open the champagne.

1 CH Spurgeon, 1834–92
2 Num 32:117
3 Gal 3:1–5; 5:7
4 Matt 10:22
5 1 Pet 1:13

Discipleship is a journey into life in all its fullness: the total reaction of the whole person to the whole of life. Are you stuck somewhere on the plateau?

Running the race

In chapter 11 we look at many of the saints gone before. Early in my ministry I had to do two Bible expositions on Moses. The key fact that has been with me ever since is that Moses did not have 'a great faith in God' but 'faith in a great God'. That is the key to so much in chapter 11. Then in chapter 12 we are expected to strip off, put on our spiritual running kit and run the race before us. We may not live an out-of-the ordinary life but we are expected to be faithful (3:2) and achieve 'what is pleasing to him' (13:21).

The purpose of discipline

Like the heroes of chapter 11 we need to see more of God. It seems that often we have in our minds a false image of God formed rather than the full reality. This would account for misunderstanding the purpose of discipline in 12:4–13. If we still hanker for a God who saves us from all trouble, discipline seems wrong.

Matters of morality

Misunderstanding of God's ways can also occur over matters of morality, such as in the important marriage verse in 13:4. Today it seems that even keen Christians can ignore their conscience when it comes to an immoral lifestyle. Is that because they have not seen God as judge (12:4) but rather as a God of love, regardless of one's actions? Even concepts of leadership can go astray if Jesus Christ is not our model (12:7–8). Personal sacrifice for the faith has been a mark of many Christians across the centuries. Yet there is also much more comfort-Christianity: happy to give money, to keep a clean life, to do good sometimes, to go to church on Sundays if convenient, and to avoid trouble by not witnessing. This attitude is hit hard in 12:11–14, a precursor of the later call to 'go to him outside the camp, bearing the disgrace he bore' (13:13).

Michael Baughen

Day 156

Matching up to God s faith-measure

Pray for the courage to apply these verses honestly and openly to your life of faith, and be ready to respond.

Hebrews 11:1–7

Mention 'certainty' as a Christian and some people get hot under the collar. They do not think faith can be certain and accuse us of personal inadequacy in wanting it. God says the opposite! In verse 1 it is clearly stated that he intends us to have deep certainty. It comes the more we trust the Word of God (v 3). How else can we have a creation world view? As we do, we find it powerfully true and relevant. So our certainty grows. Yet it also comes (v 6) from a strong belief in the true God and a heart earnestly seeking him. Many say they believe in God and expect his handouts but that's all they want of him. Real faith bows in adoration and obedience and is matched by a longing to know him more and more. The closer we come to him the more our certainty increases.

Abel and Enoch showed a certainty of faith by deep devotion. Abel expressed it by bringing the best of his flock to God compared with the 'anything will do' attitude of Cain.[1] It is the heart that counts to God. How does he see our offerings of money, time and talents? Enoch 'walked with God'.[2] No great exploit of faith is recorded. That's so encouraging to all who live devotedly for their Lord where they are. Enoch was unlikely to be on a human honours board but he is up at the top of God's!

Noah really did have to take God at his word and had to do so in a hostile unbelieving environment. What courage! What an encouragement! Like millions since throughout the world from workplace to prison camps he stood firm on the certainty of God and his word.

1 Gen 4:3–7
2 Gen 5:22–23

Ask yourself today: is my life lived with such genuine faith that I am pleasing to God? Then ask God with no holds barred: what more do you require of me?

God is working his purpose in your life

Day 157

Ask the Lord to help you stand back from your present circumstances and to see his 'big picture'.

Hebrews 11:8–22 

We marvel at Abraham's faith, exchanging the security of urban living for a nomadic life in tents and a journey with no specified destination, except that it would be into a foreign land where he would be a stranger. So many Christians have faced a similar call. We can think of a hundred excuses – schooling, our house, children so settled, relatives, climate, language – so how did Abraham do it? Primarily because he knew God was calling him (v 8) and that is really the only question to settle. Once we accept that, then, like Abraham, we must obey and go (v 8). Then we need to trust God and his purpose in whatever the future holds. This assurance can only come out of the devotional closeness that we saw yesterday. In James, Abraham is described as 'God's friend'.[1] There was real closeness.

He also trusted the promises of God that he was going to his inheritance (vs 8–9), the city of God (v 10), the heavenly destination (v 16). That is so true for us as well, isn't it? We are 'aliens and strangers'[2] and our 'citizenship is in heaven'.[3] It is this that enables us not to regard material prosperity, health, security and other earthbound values as the aims of life.

Trusting the purposes of God is most tested when things seem to go against all we expect, as here with the promise of an heir (vs 11–12), the command to offer Isaac on the altar (vs 17–19), and the act of trickery on the aged Isaac (v 20).

When things are not as we thought they would be, trust! Be like Joseph who, to the end of his life, still trusted (with his command for his bones, v 22) in the purposes of God.

1 James 2:23
2 1 Pet 2:11
3 Phil 3:20

Try to find some time to spend with God today. Let the dust settle. Then be freshly open to discern and submit gladly to his purposes for you – and keep your eye on heaven!

Daring to put Christ first

Day 158

Let the Holy Spirit help you run a test on the way you are living for Christ. Are there areas of your life which need closer examination?

 *Hebrews 11:23–31*

Moses 'chose' (v 25). Everything in this passage springs from that choice. The same principle is true for us too. We are the children of God by grace but surrendering our lives to his service is our choice. What a choice it was for Moses – power or slavery, luxury or ill-treatment. He could only make such a choice because of his deep faith in God and firm conviction about where true value lies (v 26). Our Lord similarly challenged us as to whether our treasure is laid up on earth or in heaven.[1]

We need to ask ourselves what values we live by, yet once the choice is made, the cost can be great. So our Lord emphasised that denying oneself and taking up the cross is consequential to following him.[2] For Moses' parents and himself (vs 23,27) there was the threat of reprisals. For young people today the consequence is often to face peer pressure and ridicule. For many others across the years it has meant early death or persecution. But they have pressed on, like Moses, 'for the sake of Christ' (v 26).

The choice was once and for ever for Moses. He had no choice about what might be involved. Moses would face tasks and situations he would not have chosen for himself: leadership of a multitude, the challenges of the exodus, the Passover, the Red Sea and so much more. It would require a faith of action and not of standing still,[3] just as it would later for Joshua and Rahab at Jericho (vs 30–31). Moses' life is such an inspiration because, like us, he did not find obedience easy, yet his example shows us that we can only persevere by seeing 'him who is invisible' (v 27). The Lord knew him face to face.[4] Does he know us intimately too?

1 Matt 6:19–21
2 Mark 8:34
3 Exod 14:15–16
4 Deut 34:10

Moses was indeed 'faithful in all God's house' (3:2). Today, freshly resolve to be the same.

Being commended for your faith

Day 159

Pray that your spirit will be inspired and your faith stimulated through today's reading.

Hebrews 11:32–40 

The preacher is running out of time! We now have a wide-ranging summary. At first we are cheering. In verses 32–35a, the characters, in spite of their faults, courageously set forward God's kingdom. We can also discern Daniel (lions) and Shadrach and his friends (flames) but thousands of others are included. They inspire us because they were proactive. They did not try to fade into the wallpaper when there was trouble. They spoke rather than keeping quiet. They attacked rather than defended. In verse 34 we like 'strength', 'powerful', 'routed' because we want the kingdom advanced. We rightly cheer, are encouraged and long to emulate. It is only natural to feel that these ought always to be the marks of victorious living.

Then – wham! From verses 35b–38 there is no apparent 'power-success'. Most saw no deliverance. We shudder as we read of torture (the word means stretching on a wheel), flogging, prison, death, destitution. Yet is not this the greatest list? Did they not need the greatest faith? They turned tragedy into victory. So it is today when we see Christians glowing for Christ even when they are overwhelmed by suffering.

Think of the Christians who were thrown to the lions two thousand years ago, or more recently those who are being tortured in places like Cambodia, or even now suffering massacre, slavery and the torching of their churches. They are included for us in verse 38 'the world was not worthy of them' for the list goes on through history. They certainly have shown victorious living and dying. Here in Hebrews these heroes and heroines lived before Christ with such faith. How much more should we follow them, for the plan (v 40) has been revealed to us and we know Christ as Saviour and the Holy Spirit's indwelling!

Ask the Lord for greater courage to witness and act for him with a faith that shines brightly whatever happens in life.

Day 160 Running the race it s our turn

Pray that, when you reach the end of your life, you may know that you have accomplished everything God intended you to do.

 *Hebrews 12:1–13*

Therefore (v 1) – the spotlight is turned fully on us! We are the runners. Seeing the inspirational evidence of the saints in chapter 11 and, as it were, being urged on from the heavenly stands, we should not fail our Lord because we are 'weary' or 'losing heart' (v 3) or because (v 12) we are 'feeble' and 'weak-kneed'. The best way to prevent that is to keep our eyes unswervingly on Jesus, seeing what he went through and rejoicing that he is now at the right hand of the throne of God (from where he helps us, 4:16).

Yet there is more to this than courage. There is discipline. The Olympic athletes train for four years – what discipline! If we are to run the race set before us, (and not before someone else!) we need self-discipline, to keep training, to remove sinful hindrances, and to keep running (v 1). Paul had that discipline.[1] The athlete regularly checks fitness and performance. So it is for us, checking our spiritual fitness by the Word of God and having regular times alone with God to ask him whether we are still on track and performing to his requirements.

In addition, God will discipline us. Self-discipline is under our control; God's discipline is not. However, it is personal, as a father disciplines his children with love (vs 5–7). So instead of resisting or grumbling we should co-operate and learn the lesson being taught. We need to have unswerving faith, like Paul[2] that it is 'for our good' and 'to share in his holiness' (v 10). Like the athlete running well or the musician playing superbly, there will be a rightness about the outcome and an inward fulfilling peace (v 11) as Paul knew at the end of his life.[3]

1 1 Cor 9:24–27
2 2 Cor 1:9; 4:10
3 2 Tim 4:7

Be encouraged that God has a race just for you. Ask him today if you are on track and running as he wants.

A life of true worship

Day 161

Pray that the Holy Spirit will show you any inconsistency between your words of worship and your life of worship.

Hebrews 12:14–29 

Glance first at the end of this passage (vs 28–29). 'Therefore' explains the reason for what goes before: to worship God acceptably. Now go back to verse 14. Holiness of living is shown to be vital for acceptable worship. As Jesus also taught[1] we cannot 'see the Lord' without it (v 14). Our bias towards sin requires a constant fight – 'make every effort' (v 14), 'see to it' (v 15), 'see that' (v 16). Like an unchecked weed in a garden, the bitter root of verse 15 will grow and infect us and others unless it is cut back time and again. If we do not do so, godlessness overtakes us (v 16) and we miss the grace of God (v 15) and the blessing (v 17). We do all we can to ward off infection and disease in our bodies so as to remain healthy; we must have the same determination for our lives. Regular spiritual gardening is vital!

In verses 18–24 we come to the act of worship. What a thrilling passage! The scale of it is mind-blowing. Instead of the terror and fear of the old covenant[2] here is the amazing privilege and joy of the new covenant. As we meet together to worship, the walls should fade away and we will be locked into heaven. We express this thought in many Holy Communion services: 'Therefore with angels and archangels and all the company of heaven ...'. Think of all those angels and believers who are already there and with whom you are worshipping God the Judge, Jesus the Mediator. We are one with them in worship. Wow!

The final verses (25–29) balance the picture. Yes, we have this open access to God through Jesus and his shed blood, but taking his Word seriously is obligatory, as is gratitude, reverence and awe.

1 Matt 5:82
2 Exod 19:10–25

Review your own worship and that of your church. Is it acceptable to God, full of reverence as well as joy?

Love in action

Day 162

Ask the Holy Spirit to highlight which of the many possible responses he wants you to make to this passage.

 *Hebrews 13:1–16*

After the great brush strokes of the previous verses we now come to the detail. Love for God, for fellow Christians and for other people undergirds everything here. That love within the fellowship tops the list is no surprise. This was our Lord's new commandment.[1] Paul's heart aches because of it.[2] When the church cannot live as a loving family our witness is undermined. Self-giving love is essential. It is the same love that breeds a heart of hospitality. It helps to ask ourselves how we would expect to be treated if we visited another Christian's home or church. Western Christians have much to learn from Eastern customs which Abraham (the person referred to in v 2) demonstrated with bowing, feet-washing, baking bread, and selecting a special calf, curds and milk.[3] Yet an open door and a generous heart are often the door to faith and blessing (v 16).

From blessing to love in action. 'As if you yourselves were suffering' (v 3) is love reaching into a situation – prison, ill-treatment or whatever – imagining what it must be like and so giving the kind of help that is really needed. We should remember specially those who are alone and housebound. Christian marriages of self-giving love and purity are an attractive testimony to the standards God sets in verse 4. Love of money (v 5) is the very opposite to self-giving love and looks pathetic compared with the eternal security of belonging to the Lord (vs 5–6).

Leaders must inspire others with lives of self-giving love in action, springing from their faith (v 7). But leaders come and go, and all have human faults. So we must look to the unchanging Leader, Jesus Christ (v 8), and when we contemplate the outcome of his life, in its total self-giving love, we are humbled and inspired, and will gladly own the utter self-giving of his disgrace (v 12).

1 John 13:34–35
2 Phil 2:1–18
3 Gen 18:4–8

The response today has to be an overhaul of our life and actions in terms of practical self-giving.

To him be glory for ever and ever

Day 163

Come with humility to consider your role in the church. What God-given gifts should you be using to build up the body of Christ?

Hebrews 13:17–25 

Obey (v 17) seems very strong. Some leaders misuse this command to justify near-dictatorship but that would not describe the qualities of leadership found in verse 7 nor the pattern of Jesus Christ in verse 8. (The author trusts they see these qualities in his life, v 18.) Indeed, the Greek word means 'be persuaded by'.

So there is to be gracious explanation of what the watch-man-leader believes to be right. That has to be met with trust (not, as mentioned here, much independent resistance which turns into such a burden, disadvantage and preventer of joy).

It would be good for the whole church to consider these verses together, perhaps on a day away. We can hardly ascribe glory to our Lord (v 22) unless the church's life glorifies him.[1]

The great prayer in verses 20–21 is the full orchestral climax to the letter. The foundation of the atonement, the new covenant and the resurrection summarise the magnificent teaching of chapters 8:1 – 10:18 (which brought spontaneous applause to the Lord when expounded at the Keswick Convention a few years ago). Our hearts also surely leap into praise when we think of our amazing Saviour and our salvation through him. Our home must be there for ever but our bodies must act in response (as in 10:19–25). We put ourselves under the command of the Great Shepherd who 'works in us'. We long to fulfil what pleases him and seek his gifting appropriate to the tasks he has prepared for us. But do we? When we say 'God of peace' is it both in connection with salvation and our being in harmony with his will? May our lives as well as our lips ascribe to him 'glory for ever and ever'. Amen!

1 Eph 3:20–21

Are you firm on his foundation? Are you on track with his will for you? Do you truly want him to have all the glory in your life, his church and his world?

Running scared

Day 164

Fear makes us run away; faith makes us stay put, trusting in God to protect us.

 *Psalm 56*

People often project an aura of invulnerability and of courage. Many believe that through modern science we can do almost everything. For have we not plumbed the core of the earth, scoured the expanse of the seas, and reached up into outer space? And are we not attempting to make the world one global village today? What, then, are we to be afraid of?

Yet, we know this stance is mere bluffing. Deep within us lurk many fears. Was it not only recently that fear of what the 'Y2K' bug could do to computers caused a worldwide panic, driving some people to hoard food and dig bunkers? The truth is, we are a fearful lot. When our security is threatened, our integrity is questioned, or our relationships break down, we find it hard to cope.

David felt like this as he escaped from King Saul and took refuge under one whose loyalty he mistrusted.[1] In his situation, David admitted his fear. 'I am afraid', he said and named the causes of his fear (vs 2,5–6).

To confess we are afraid is not a sign of weakness, but of courage. As we admit and articulate it, like David, we begin to see the reasons for it more objectively. And we also begin to see a way out.

After David had looked inside himself and seen only fear, he looked up to God and saw only love. He was moved to declare: 'I will trust in you'. He reiterated this (vs 4,10–11) until he stopped quaking and felt God's deliverance and peace (v 13).

1 1 Sam 21:13 – 22:1

Have you felt afraid today? Face up to your fear and offer it to God. He casts out our fear, for he is love.

Praising God from the depths

Day 165

When disaster strikes, it is easy to curse our fate rather than ask God to help us.

Psalm 57 

In these days of instant praise and glib hallelujahs, I find I am wary of church meetings which begin with 'praise and worship'. In my part of the world this is usually characterised by high-powered singing and sometimes dancing as well. Drums roar, the electric guitar soars, cymbals clash and the piano skips and trills. A cacophony of human voices shout and sing to the high heavens.

Has God become deaf, I wonder. My amazement deepens, especially when, after all the excitement, I see faces returning to their original glum expressions! Praising God is not something we only do to begin Sunday morning worship, though it may help set the tone for the pastor's sermon. Rather, praise is a habit of the heart; a movement of the Spirit within our soul making us burst into songs of adoration, regardless of our everyday circumstances. Or maybe it is our deliberate resolve to exalt God *especially* in difficult times. Our praise is at its purest and most urgent when we are down in the dumps for then it has nothing to do with us but everything to do with the Lord.

David demonstrated this truth in today's psalm. Running from King Saul, he hid in a cave.[1] Terrified, David cried out to God for mercy, and when he was assured of his presence he was able to control his feelings. Then, comforted, he awoke in the morning ready to sing, to make music, to enjoy exalting the love and faithfulness of God by letting his voice reverberate across the arid desert and even 'above the heavens' (vs 5,11).

By exalting God, David was able to put his situation into proper perspective (v 2a) By resolving to praise him, David was freed from his fear.

1 1 Sam 22:1,24

'Grant me the courage to praise you, God, despite my difficulties. Amen.'

Day 166 Corruption masquerading as government

'Righteous God, let me be an instrument of your justice today.' Amen.

Psalm 58

Here is a prayer-song that grates and gnashes. Today it could well fall into the category of 'alternative music', the sort of music which deals with social and political issues and which serves as a conscience to the powers that be.

No wonder this psalm is jarring; it unsettles us. It begins by hurling an angry judgement on rulers who use their position to commit injustice and do violence to their people. The singer says they were evil from the time of their birth like cobras already deaf to the music of the snake charmer, they inject their hapless victims with venom (vs 1–5).

Such rulers today come in many guises including democratic ones. Political power-holders in many nations hold their citizens to ransom and corruption in high places abounds to such an extent that, in some parts of Asia for example, an economic collapse was brought about recently due to the actions of grasping and greedy government officials. And the poor, who are already in the majority, continue to suffer.

But more powerful still than our presidents and ministers are the international organisations that determine the fate of our world today. Globalisation, once heralded by 'experts' as the harbinger of free trade and liberalisation, has in fact only managed to increase the poverty and violence suffered by the peoples of the Two Thirds World.

Finally the songwriter turns to God, asking him to judge these wicked leaders. The suffering of the many, which provides for the ease and pleasure of the few, arouses in David a fierce righteous indignation (vs 6–8). He prays to God for their destruction – not for any personal reasons, he says, but because God has to be true to himself as the just God of his righteous but oppressed people (v 11).

1 GK Chesterton, 1874–1936

'O God of earth and altar, Bow down and hear our cry; Take not thy thunder from us, But take away our pride.'[1]

Our strength day and night

Day 167

'Lord, thank you that you are my refuge and strength, my ever-present help in trouble.'[1]

Psalm 59 

To most of us, night is sweet. It promises rest, quiet and sleep. To others, however, the night brings unwelcome visitations, real or imagined, and only fitful sleep or anxious waiting for the dawn.

This psalm describes the latter. It is a song of desperation from one whose nights are haunted by real enemies whose voices and words are within his hearing. These 'evildoers' in the city, who are shouting their taunts into the air, are intent on doing violence.

David was himself the victim of such harassment. Though he was son-in-law to King Saul, the king, in a fit of jealousy and madness, called for his destruction.[2] He had David's palace surrounded by men who are described in this psalm 'snarling like dogs' (vs 6,14).

So David's cry is urgent and desperate: 'O my Strength, I watch for you', 'You, O God, are my fortress, my loving God' (v 9).

Discovering that God is indeed his strength, David stops lamenting, and begins to sing (v 16). No longer is he preoccupied with the dangers of the night, but now looks to the morning with music on his lips. His night-time fears give way to confidence in the morning as his focus shifts from his enemies to the loving God who protects him.

We may not have enemies like the ones described here, but it is often hard to find peace of mind and rest for our spirit. Fears may lurk in some corner of our imagination. If this is so, David has shown us an example of how to face such difficulties. Calling upon the God we trust as our strength can change our desperation into deliverance. And yes, even to delight. God does indeed make a difference – day and night.

1 Ps 46:1
2 1 Sam 19:1,18–19
3 HF Lyte, 1793–1847

'Abide with me, fast falls the eventide; The darkness deepens; Lord, with me abide; When other helpers fail, and comforts flee – Help of the helpless, O abide with me.'[3]

Facing up to life s reversal

Day 168

God has not promised us that life will be plain sailing; but he does assure us of his presence and direction. Thank him today.

Psalm 60

How could sweet victory be transformed into bitter defeat? How could shouts of jubilation turn to mournful lamentation? How could a stunning success end in a crashing failure?

This passage is a national lamentation for an unexpected reversal experienced by King David in one of his military campaigns.[1] While he was winning in one area, enemies sneaked into another and wrought havoc on his men. The sudden turn of events brought public humiliation to Israel. Hence the intensity of the lament.

What can we learn from this song? We can turn defeat into prayer (vs 1–5). The psalmist does this, implying that it is God's business to lift his people out of their misery. Their defeat has drawn them closer to God rather than alienating them from him. When you experience a setback, turn to prayer. Prayer brings us into the presence of God. Prayer opens up our eyes of faith.

We can remind God of what he has promised us. The Jews believed they were God's chosen people (vs 6–12). We too, are children of promise.[2] Depending on our circumstances, all of us have received certain promises from his Word. If that is so, then let us remind God of them, especially if their fulfilment seems long overdue.

Once we claim God's promises for ourselves, we can play our part. 'Give us aid against the enemy for the help of man is worthless' (v 11). David and his army had yet to fight, but this time victory is assured with God on their side. In the same way, we don't hang back whining about our sorry predicament, rather, we take hold of ourselves and using the resources God has given us, turn to action. God is able to turn things right side up for us again.

1 2 Sam 8:3–6
2 Gal 4:28

Are you on the downside of life at the moment? Think of God's promises to you and claim them from him today.

To live in God s favour

'Lord God, create in me a deep longing for your presence. Amen.'

Psalm 61

I once saw a television programme in which a boy was asked what he dreamt of becoming. 'I'd like to be the president,' he answered with a gap-toothed smile. And why, he was asked: 'If I became president, I'd get to live in a big, big house, ride in my own aeroplane and everyone would have to obey me,' he said as he glared at the screen.

We smile. Though it is true that some people do indeed hanker for high public positions for exactly these reasons, most great leaders know that it is extremely lonely up there.

In this psalm it is clear that David felt this loneliness keenly, although he was no mean ruler even by our standards. A valiant warrior, he was extremely popular among his people. Foreign leaders kowtowed to him and were dazzled by his personal wealth as well as that of his nation. At the height of his glory, enemies trembled at the very mention of his name. What more could he ask for?

Nothing except a longing for God's companionship. The burden of leadership, the pomp and circumstance, have not only alienated him from natural human fellowship, but from God himself (v 2). Such distance sharpens his sense of his own weakness and humanity. The more faint, helpless and fragile he feels, the more he longs for God – the solid rock, the tower, the sheltering wings under which he longs to find refuge (vs 3,4). No wonder that, for all his human failures, David is described by the Scriptures as 'a man after Yahweh's own heart'.[1] God was his continuing passion.

This is true greatness. When we put God above all others, long for his continual presence and depend only on his gracious munificence, we become kingly in God's eyes, even though no crown gleams on our head or sceptre flashes in our hand. To live in God's presence is the cry of everyone who has been filled with the Holy Spirit.

1 1 Sam 13:14; 1 Kings 15:3,5; Acts 13:22,36

Think of three things you can do every day to keep in close fellowship with God.

Finding rest in a stressful world

Day 170

The world whirls by and we are caught up in the madness. Ask God to calm you down so that you can hear his voice today.

 *Psalm 62*

We see it on the faces of everyone around us, we see it when we look in the mirror – everyone is uptight. And everything has to be done on the run. We hustle and bustle with a thousand and one thoughts jostling in our minds and begin to accept the lie that the only way to have a meaningful life is to rush about looking worried.

Tension is everywhere and can explode into violence at any time – but surely war could never happen in a world peopled with individuals at peace with themselves.

So how do we achieve that? The author of this psalm appears to have found the secret. First, he affirms that he finds rest not by psychologically conditioning himself to relax, but by realising that his rest lies outside of himself in God alone (v 1).

Why so? He's helpless. He describes himself as a wall ready to collapse, a swaying fence, threatened further by enemies masquerading as friends whose delight is to see his downfall (vs 3,4). His precarious situation could not possibly allow him to find peace within his shaking self, even if he wanted to.

The author's past experience has taught him that in God alone does his rest, hope, salvation and honour come (vs 5–7). God is all these, the 'Shalom' we all need: that quietness and confidence of spirit in the midst of pressures and conflicts, an inner sense of well-being untouched by outside anxieties and cares because we know God is with us.

To rest in God alone is to trust him fully. And this is something we should share with others (v 8) for three reasons: because God is strong, because God is love and because God is just (v 12).

'Lord God, enfold me in your strong embrace so that my rest in you may bring healing and justice to others.'

Longing for home

Day 171

Some say, home is where the heart is.
Where is your heart today?

Psalm 63 

Millions of people who come from the Two Thirds World are today far from their homes. Some are in places totally different in climate, culture, and language. In many instances, they find the inhabitants, and even the environment, openly hostile to them. One example is a man from the sun-kissed Philippines, who is learning to cope with the indescribable cold in Alaska because he has to earn a living. Most of these people are overseas contract workers. Other, less fortunate ones, are the refugees of war, famine, or political or religious persecution.

Of the few that I have met, most have a tremendous longing for home. 'It's very lonely here, elder sister', a fellow Filipina said as she cried on my shoulder at our first meeting in Germany. 'If only I could go home now', a young man said wistfully. 'My child is sick, but I can't leave'. He donned his sunglasses to hide his tears.

King David, had a similar experience. He wrote this psalm while he was in the wilderness trying to escape the threats to his life (v 9). For though he was a king, he was on the run (v 11). Now, none of the pomp and circumstance of kingship attended him. No wife, children or courtiers were there to amuse him. The ease and comfort of a royal lifestyle was a thing of the past. Only the spartan life of the desert and the howling silences of wind and sand remained. And yet the intensely deep longing expressed in this psalm was not for hearth and home, nor for power and position, but for God (v 1).

Ultimately, in our loneliness and separation, our true home can only be found with God and this is what David discovered. Though far from the sanctuary of worship, there in the wilderness he could still sing praises to God, feast on his presence and claim his promises (vs 4–11).

1 Heb 12:2a,3b

Whether you are away from home or not, fix your eyes on Jesus, the author and perfecter of your faith, 'so that you will not grow weary and lose heart'.[1]

The power of words

Day 172

'Lord, you are the Word who became flesh. Give reality and substance to my words today.'

Psalm 64

We live in an age where wordsmiths dominate our culture. The economies of nations can rise and fall on the whim of banks, investment houses and seats of power. 'Read my lips', say the politicians, who then proceed to dream up empty words, instead of acting to help their people. The media, too, claim to inform but all too often misinform, and we are often unaware of the extent to which we are being manipulated by visual images and persuasive language rather than by biblical principles. Even the church has not escaped the downside of information technology.

In this psalm David cries to the Lord for protection from enemies who are experts in manipulating words (vs 2–6). They conspire together, shout inflammatory slogans in the streets and threaten violence with their venomous words. They hatch unjust conspiracies, quite certain that no one will find them out. 'This is a perfect crime', they say.

Yet, 'the Detective detects the mystery in the dark of the cellar heart,' as Peterson expresses it.[1]

God hears their life-slaying words, and their own tongues will be the cause of their downfall (v 8).

The difference between these wordsmiths and God is that God does not use words to make empty promises. He acts to save the righteous from the 'spin doctors'. Thus the fearful supplicant at the beginning of this psalm is now an exalting victor, rallying one and all to praise God.

In this age of chatter and hype, it is all too easy for those who make the most noise to frighten and entrap the powerless. We need to know when lies are being peddled. And like the psalmist, have the courage to expose them.

1 Ps 64:6c, *The Message*

'Lord, let me not live comfortably with half lies, distortions or flattery. May my words honour you, uplift my loved ones and bring healing to my neighbours today. Amen.'

A heap of harvest praise

Day 173

'Father, make me rejoice before you as one rejoicing at the harvest.'

Psalm 65 

I live in a village tucked on a hill on a two acre plot which my husband and I always refer to as a 'gift from heaven'. We grow black pepper, bananas, lime trees, ginger, pineapples and a number of huge fruit-bearing mango trees. I have discovered that one cannot live close to the land and not offer one's thanks to God every day. For despite our efforts to coax life from the earth, ultimately it is God alone who makes things grow. Also, in the handling of seeds and soil, the drama of life, death and resurrection is continually being played out before us. I suspect it is hard for a farmer to be an atheist!

No wonder this psalm explodes with praise to God in its threefold theme:

First, praise escapes the singer's lips because God is a forgiving God (v 2). Before God's abundant grace, he remembers the overwhelming sins of his people. Yet God has forgiven them all. Confession in the midst of plenty is a precious fruit of a humble lifestyle.

Secondly, God deserves praise because he is a creative and powerful God (vs 5–8). His awesome power embraces both nature and the nations. Yahweh is not like the neighbouring gods, instead he is Lord and Creator of the whole universe.

Thirdly, the psalmist sings his praises because God is a caring, providing God (vs 9–13). The land, water, and crops are his. The grasslands, hills and meadows as well. Even the human activities of 'drenching furrows' and 'levelling ridges' the psalmist attributes to God. He recognises that the very life and strength of men and women come from Almighty God. How then can we not praise him?

Take an inventory of the many 'harvests' in your life. Make this your special day of praise and thanksgiving.

Day 174

Celebrating God in our national life

'Jesus Christ, Saviour and Lord of humankind, I lift to you all the nations of the world today, including my own. May we know you and learn to worship you, the one true God.'

Psalm 66

A national deliverance is always a cause of celebration. More so, if the deliverance is attributed to the awesome, mysterious workings of God.

I remember how my husband David and I marched, sang, prayed, shouted and danced along with a huge crowd during the 'People Power Revolution' in 1986 that toppled the twenty-year rule of dictatorship in the Philippines. It was peaceful, bloodless and even festive. Since then, political analysts have attributed the sudden fall of Ferdinand Marcos to other factors. But we Christians believed it was God who toppled him. So I can fully empathise with the exuberance of this psalm. The nation of Israel is bursting with jubilant worship and joyful singing after a national deliverance. The king himself sets the mood for this celebration.

The mood is invitational. All peoples, not only the people of God, are urged to join in this happy occasion of honouring God (vs 1,4). After all, God's eyes are on all nations (v 7). This implies that God's victory in Israel has a universal application. In his own way and time, he will hold sway over all peoples and his justice and righteousness will prevail (vs 9–12).

The mood is reflective. This happy day is not the first time that God has acted in an awesome way. Israel had already experienced his mighty deeds in the past – difficult to understand, but gloriously liberating in the end.

The mood is personal (vs 13–20). Communal, even national worship of God has its own special appeal. However, it is only meaningful when the individuals involved have themselves experienced God at work in their lives. The king's behaviour here shows that he has had this kind of experience, belying the idea that the leader's personal life has nothing to do with his public duties.

Think of three recent occasions when God has intervened in the history of your country. Give him praise!

Your people will be my people

The book of Ruth is widely recognised as a masterpiece of Hebrew storytelling. It is short, vivid and dramatic. Let us consider the main themes. The book is about ordinary people facing very ordinary events. It recounts the providence of God to a family which has undergone enormous hardship through famine and bereavement, leaving Naomi, the mother, without the means of economic support and in a foreign land. This is the problem which the plot contrives to solve; but not before remarking on the bitter realities of her desperate plight. We identify with her helpless state: what has she done to deserve this? Where is God? How come such awful things happen to good people?

Ruth plays the key role in Naomi's search for economic security. She gives up her security and her homeland and pledges loyalty to her mother-in-law. This commitment is memorably expressed in practical and spiritual terms: 'Where you go, I will go, and where you stay, I will stay. Your people will be my people and your God my God…' (1:16,17; compare also 4:15). It is this devotion which provides the key to the resolution of the problem. Though both women are categorised among 'the poor' – both are widows, and Ruth is a resident alien in Judah – yet their solidarity and resourcefulness proves them 'rich' in the metaphorical sense. The two women succeed through their loyal co-operation with each other. The story honours the enterprise of these women who – while looking to God as provider and sustainer – do not sit and wait. They take advantage of those laws which protect the poor and they seize the initiative when there is an opportunity for the security of marriage.

The book of Ruth provides a glimpse of God's covenant community as it was intended to be. The book is set within the period of the judges, an unsettled period of history in which apostasy, violence, immorality and civil unrest were rife – a period in which, surely, God's people were prone to doubt God's providence. As the book of Ruth illustrates in a particularly personal way, God's covenant with his people does not preclude mishap. However, such mishap neither denies God's providence nor precludes his grace. Rather, such a mishap is seen to provide the context for God's redemption. And the keys to this redemption have already been given to Israel, in the covenant God has made with them. If they will learn to live faithfully according to this covenant, then – as we see exemplified here – the poor will be protected, the alien included and all people look forward to the fulfilment of God's promises. God's promises concern the repair of that which is broken, the renewal of that which has gone wrong, the restoration of his purposes for the world.

Seeking God's will

I have discussed the book of Ruth as a 'story', a story that is told with consummate artistic skill. For example, it contains a symmetry in the opening account of distress (1:1–5; seventy-one words in Hebrew) and the concluding account of relief and hope (4:13–17; seventy-one words in Hebrew). In between there are four episodes: Naomi and Ruth's return from Moab, Ruth's work in the fields of Boaz, Ruth's visit to Boaz at the threshing floor and Boaz's marriage to Ruth. The turning point occurs exactly halfway between these two accounts (2:20). Other features include the careful use of contrast, vocabulary, and vivid characterisation.

The story is told to bring the insight that, even during hard times and in painful personal tragedy, we may discern the hand of a God who cares, sustains and provides for his people in their everyday life. What is more, in his providence such circumstances can become the seedbed of opportunity. For there is a final twist in this tale: Ruth turns out to be the great-grandmother of King David – and thus also in the line of our Lord Jesus.

Jo Bailey Wells

Love risks all

'Where you go, I will go…' Why not reaffirm to the Lord your commitment to follow wherever he leads?

Ruth 1:1–22 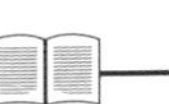

The book of Ruth is, primarily, about Naomi and her plight. Because her husband and sons have all died, Naomi is left without any secure form of economic support in a foreign land. She is embittered by the tragedy and blames God (vs 13,20–21). (This is a logical reaction for the person who looks to God as the sovereign provider of all things – the Psalms illustrate this response of dependence again and again.) Naomi is not afraid to confront God with her desperation. Yet her pain does not paralyse her faith or prevent her taking practical action. She decides to return to Judah, her homeland.

The focus becomes the question of who may go with Naomi. She encourages her widowed daughters-in-law to stay in Moab, their homeland, where they might have the opportunity for remarriage and thus for security again (vs 9,11–13). Orpah is persuaded. But Ruth refuses: she eloquently and stubbornly asserts her devotion to Naomi, even though there is no prospect for her but to share in Naomi's desolation.

Ruth's commitment to Naomi has become a classic expression of selfless devotion and unswerving loyalty. It does, eventually, lead to their prosperity. But Ruth did not choose prosperity; rather she sacrificed her own security and ambitions for Naomi's sake. What choice would you make? 'There are those who like to say "yes", and there are those who prefer to say "no". Those who say "yes" are rewarded by the adventures they have; those who say "no" are rewarded by the safety they attain'.[1] Orpah opts for safety (for which she is not condemned) while Ruth chooses adventure. It is this path of risk and faith which builds God's kingdom.

1 Keith Johnstone, director, actor, writer on improvisational theatre

God calls us to ventures of which we cannot see the ending, by paths as yet untrodden. Are you willing to step out in faith, knowing only that God's hand is leading and his love sustaining?

Day 176

Living on the (abundant) margins

'The good God always lets me long for what he wants to give me.'[1]

Ruth 2:1–23

We have here a striking example of how God's covenant society was organised to benefit the poor and powerless. These are the people who fall outside the regular means of economic subsistence – ie, those who do not own land or cannot work the land, typically the widows, the orphans and the resident aliens. The law of gleaning, for example, requires that some of the harvest be left for the poor to gather.[2] This is not a voluntary contribution, but a legal requirement on the part of the farmer. When Ruth gleans in Boaz's field, gathering the stalks of grain around the edge of the field and those left behind after the rest has been harvested, she is exercising her legal right as a resident alien (and a widow). She is, in the original sense of the expression, living on the margins.

Boaz is an unusual landowner, however. He greets his workers (v 4); he protects the women (vs 8–9); he offers Ruth his own food and *extra* gleanings (vs 14,16). He uses his position of wealth and power – as a landowner and an employer – to care for the poor and powerless, far beyond the precise call of duty. Just as Ruth acts with kindness and loyalty towards Naomi (v 11), so Boaz treats Ruth with the same caring responsibility. The Hebrew word for this is *hesed* (compare 3:10). It is just this quality of steadfast love which the Pharisees lack, according to Jesus, even while fulfilling the letter of the Law.[3] For God's covenant society to function for the benefit of all God's people, then all must interpret the legal framework with *hesed*. The alternative to *hesed* is irresponsibility and injustice, whether you are numbered among the powerful or the powerless.

1 Theresa of Lisieux 1873–97
2 Lev 19:9; 23:22; Deut 24:19
3 Matt 23:23

Do you live on the margins? Or have you been entrusted with the responsibilities of power or wealth? Pray that you may live abundantly within God's Law. Pray for *hesed*.

Female initiative

Having confidence in God's love and knowledge of his laws, we can be bold in our ambitions.

Ruth 3:1–18 

Ruth is *the* Old Testament story about women *par excellence*. The two women succeed in securing their future because they are clear in their commitment to each other, they trust each other to work co-operatively, and yet they also act with independence and initiative.

This initiative is illustrated by the gentle but unambiguous manner in which Ruth proposes marriage to Boaz (vs 6–9), following Naomi's suggestion (vs 1–4).[1] Some feminists have interpreted in this proposal a story of women resisting a patriarchal system and succeeding in spite of it. But Naomi and Ruth do not directly challenge the social norms of their time; rather, they operate faithfully and effectively within the very restricted options their society offers. They are capitalising on the responsibility of Boaz as their 'kinsman-redeemer' (v 9) to protect the interests of needy members of the extended family[2] – here, to secure the future of a widow with no son by marrying and bearing a son who could then inherit her first husband's property. Boaz is not tricked or induced to marry Ruth; rather, he is genuinely delighted at her proposal (v 10). Although Ruth appears 'forward', her moral integrity is never in doubt (v 11). Naomi's advice to Ruth is clearly for the purpose of appealing to Boaz's kinsman obligation, to which he responds willingly and openly (consulting, first, a closer relative who has a prior claim).

Today's study raises the question of how one distinguishes the *taking of initiative* (which is applauded) from *scheming* (which is condemned). There are two useful pointers. Naomi and Ruth voice their motives openly at each stage (vs 1,9), and they are determined to abide within God's ways and God's will, wherever that may lead.

1 See Ezek 16:8
2 See Deut 25:5–10; Lev 25:23–31

Is there a situation calling for you to take the initiative? Wrestle to uncover all your motives and lay them before God: 'Your will be done'.

Overwhelming fulfilment

Day 178

'Test me', says the LORD Almighty, 'and see if I will not throw open the floodgates of heaven.'[1] Have you ever been overwhelmed by blessing?

 *Ruth 4:1–22*

Yesterday was chiefly about women taking initiative; today we observe men making decisions (vs 1–12). The scene is set at the city gate, where Boaz sits with the elders who constitute the city's legal authority. There Boaz exercises his legal right, once it has been ceded him by the nearer kinsman, to redeem the land and marry the widow whose son will thus be able to inherit it. For Boaz, this marriage concerns primarily the provision of a male heir for Elimelech and Mahlon (v 10). For the people at the gate it brings rejoicing at the prospect of children for Boaz (v 11). Either way, the patrilineal descent could be secured.

These hopes are fulfilled in the birth of a son to Ruth and Boaz (v 13). Now the perspective switches to that of the women. At the naming of Obed they congratulate Naomi on the son (v 17). This is not because he is her son or even grandson in a biological sense, but because he will be the security for her old age that she thought she had lost when her own sons died. And she owes him to her 'daughter-in-law who loves you, who is more to you than seven sons' (v 15).

Thus the tension of the plot has been resolved; it seems that 'all were happy ever after'. But there is more. The book ends with an informal and a formal genealogy, explaining Obed's place within the biblical history as grandfather of King David. Read in the light of the preceding story, these point to the importance of ordinary people like Ruth, and Naomi, for the birth of David and, indeed, of our Lord Jesus.

1 Mal 3:10

Give thanks to God for the faithful devotion of Naomi and Ruth, and pray for the grace to follow their example. Who knows what significance your life may have in God's plan?

The incarnation

The Gospels are an interesting combination of history, literature and theology. The inspired authors mingle all three throughout and this is certainly true of the first two chapters of Luke, familiar probably to all of us through our Christmas celebrations. As we come to read these chapters it is worth reflecting on these three elements.

The story behind the story

Quite a lot of people today think that the birth narratives in Matthew and Luke – stories of angels, the virgin birth, prophecies, miracles – are little more than 'cleverly invented stories', nice for children at Christmas-time, but not really to be taken seriously by grown-ups. However, they have much to teach us and Luke goes to great lengths to prove their authenticity.

After a rather formal introduction with its carefully weighed statements and polished Greek, we embark upon two chapters where the language betrays considerable evidence of its Semitic origins. Maybe Luke is accurately recording what he culled from his sources – Aramaic-speaking people perhaps, like Mary, Elizabeth and the shepherds. This may be borne out by the very Jewishness of the songs, worship and prophecies of Mary, Zechariah and Simeon.

Luke, however, wants his readers to know that what he's writing about has good reason to be taken seriously as history (1:1–4). He has engaged in serious research (vs 2,3), and has sought out good sources and consulted eye-witnesses wherever possible.

Luke takes care to record when events happened (see 1:24; 2:22,38,42) and to provide evidence linking his story to world events. He identifies Herod the Great as king during the period he is describing (1:5). As Herod died in 4BC our traditional dating of Christ's birth needs some revision. Luke also offers further references in 2:1–2. He is writing about the incarnation – the moment when God himself entered definitively into history, full as it is of the joy and suffering, brilliance and squalor, friendship and hostility found in human relationships.

Series of ten stories

Church tradition has taught us to harmonise all the elements of the Christmas story in the Gospels, but Luke does not select all of the components that we are familiar with. It is a good idea to look out for clues as to why Luke may have chosen one particular story from amongst the several which he may have had at his disposal. What John's Gospel conveys in one carefully balanced theological proposition: 'The Word became flesh and made his dwelling among us', Luke conveys in a series of ten stories. Five before the birth of Jesus, then the five stories in chapter describing the events which followed after the birth of Christ.

Luke tells a good story and appreciates one too, as is shown by the number of Jesus' parables which he alone records.

Luke's theology

We don't know who 'Theophilus' was. He could be an individual, known or unknown to Luke. Quite possibly he was Luke's patron. Or he could simply be an imaginary figure for whom Luke purports to be writing. As for the kind of audience Luke might have been addressing, judging by his stress upon issues which might interest Gentiles and the comparative shortage of specifically Jewish concerns (unlike Matthew!), it seems likely that Luke was writing predominantly for Gentile Christians.

Luke has particular theological interests. He wants to demonstrate that Christianity is the natural development of Israel's history, yet he is also deeply concerned for the mission to the Gentiles, as can be seen in Acts where his emphasis is on Paul. As his stories show, Luke is concerned for the poor, the marginalised, the outcast, and he has much more to say about women and the Samaritans than any of the other three Gospel writers.

Robert Willoughby

The testing of a priest's faith

Day 179

God sometimes asks serious questions of a person's faith. Read Zechariah's story with this in mind.

Luke 1:1–25 

Luke is keen to establish his credentials as a historian. This first story is marked as occurring in King Herod's reign and concerns an elderly priest named Zechariah and his wife Elizabeth. Luke stresses Zechariah's priestly role, his and Elizabeth's blamelessness and their age (vs 5–7). As a priest Zechariah was at the centre of God's purposes. He was a guardian of the calling, worship and future hopes of God's people. His primary function was to lead them in worship and to remind Israel that they lived by God's interventions – at the Red Sea, through the plagues, in the wilderness, and so on.

It is a surprise that Zechariah should have had difficulty believing what an angel told him. Was God unable to do the extraordinary? Zechariah of all people should have known better. Moses and David before him had found that great privileges entail great responsibilities.[1] Moreover they had also prayed earnestly for a son (v 13). But Zechariah's lack of faith burst out of him spontaneously and showed how deep within his heart his scepticism had bitten (v 18). Maybe we need to ask the Lord to help us search our hearts to see if the same could be true of us.

The angel's promise included an even more surprising prediction of the baby's future role. He was to be a much-admired prophet who, like Elijah (vs 13–17), would call the people of Israel back to God in repentance.[2] He would be dedicated from birth as a Nazirite.[3] And his job would be to prepare the people for what God was about to do.

1 Num 20:1–13; 2 Sam 24:1–17
2 1 Kings 18:20–24
3 Num 6:1–2

Zechariah was struck dumb. How could an unbelieving priest minister God's Word or bless God's people? Pause to consider that God asks much from those who have received much. However, he doesn't simply discard his failing servants. As we shall see, God's discipline preceded something good.

The birth of Jesus announced

Day 180

Today's story is so well known. Pray that God will refresh in your mind something you know already, or else bring something new to your understanding.

Luke 1:26–38

Yesterday we read about Zechariah the priest. As we move to Mary, the mother-to-be, we move from Jerusalem to up-country Galilee (v 26), from an important man to an insignificant slip of a girl, from an aged patriarch to a young virgin. The contrast is great. The angel Gabriel is the dramatic common factor between the two stories. As the narrative develops, we shall see many parallels between Elizabeth's and Mary's sons.

The experience is overwhelming for Mary. After all, why should an angel visit her? And what could he mean? She is not even married. Mary's questions are no evidence of a lack of faith. She quickly resolves, 'I am the Lord's servant'. Of course she understood that pregnant girls became outcasts at best. They might be lucky to escape with their lives.[1] And what about Joseph? What a woman! What faith! It is a great pity, though perhaps not so very surprising, that so much theological bad blood has been spilt over Mary. Perhaps it is understandable that some sectors of the church have raised her almost to the level of the son she bore, whilst others have sought almost to ignore the extraordinary act of faith which we have just read about. This passage offers no justification for crowning her the Queen of Heaven. Nor any reason for ignoring her. So what do we learn from this story? First, there is the remarkable certainty of Mary's faith and of the power of God working through that same faith. Then there is her wonderful humility. God loves the poor in heart, the meek, the humble.

1 Deut 22:13–30

Tomorrow we shall read of Mary's exultant joy as she expresses her worship to God. Are these not things worth seeking to emulate in our lives?

Mary visits Elizabeth

As you read the familiar words of Mary's song, ask God to help you to use them creatively to worship him.

Luke 1:39–56 

In this story Elizabeth takes centre stage as she not only detects that Mary is pregnant but rejoices and prophesies over her. Gabriel seemed to open the way for Mary to share her story with her cousin (1:36). It is a tribute to Mary's faith that this is exactly what she does. Real faith is willing to share good news of what God is doing! As a result, Mary is further encouraged by Elizabeth's Spirit-inspired response.

Strengthened by her visit, Mary bursts out in praise. For many of the more traditional churches the Magnificat (or Song of Mary) is sung or chanted most Sunday evenings. Why worship every week in words which really belong in the Christmas season? Quite simply because, although the birth of Jesus is unique and unrepeatable, Mary says something which is eternally valid for all of God's people at all seasons! Her song is a pastiche of Old Testament references, recalling especially the song of Hannah.[1] This is exactly what you would expect of an illiterate girl from a seriously religious background. Her mind is filled with words and phrases from the Scriptures of Israel.

Mary's head could have been turned, but her song actually begins with God, rehearsing his actions and mercy. She is full of praise for her Saviour, the Mighty and Holy One (vs 46–49). Mary has no illusions despite the significance of what has happened to her. This gives her admirable perspective and balance. Despite the fact of her own special role, Mary rehearses God's repeated deeds of salvation, going back to Abraham. Our God raises up the poor and needy at the expense of the great and mighty people of this world.

1 1 Sam 2:1–10

Use Mary's words to offer praise to God. Ask God to give you a similar sense of perspective to your life.

Day 182

John the Baptist is born

Pray today for a renewed sense of wonder at what God was about to accomplish through John.

Luke 1:57–80

Luke tells us that all the neighbours and relatives came around and helped Elizabeth celebrate the birth of what was a very special child. There would have been great relief that Zechariah now had a son and heir. The action quickly moves on to the ceremony of John's circumcision and naming. Circumcision was the sign of God's covenant with his people. Normally speaking a name would be chosen which linked the child with his parents or ancestors, but that was not to be the case with John (v 61). His heritage was not important. In contrast, Jesus' lineage is later shown to be very important. But John's main description of himself was simply 'a voice' (3:4–6).

For Zechariah the naming of John is a triumphant return to obedient faith, rewarded by the return of his power of speech. Now he uses it to express praise for God rather than questioning and doubt (1:18). What follows is the second great song of praise which Luke records in these chapters.[1] Significantly, Zechariah expresses his faith in the ancient promises, the covenant and God's oath (vs 68–75). As a priest, he should have had confidence in these all along and it may be that mentioning them in his song of praise is evidence that he now realises that.

John is certainly to be 'a prophet of the Most High', who will bring Israel to repentance. But far more is to come (vs 76–77). In a reference to the Christian gospel extending to the Gentiles, Zechariah prophesies the sun rising to pour heavenly light upon 'those living in darkness', just as Simeon prophesies later on (2:32).

1 See also 1:46–55 and 229–32

Zechariah is yet another of God's failing servants to receive a second chance. Failure need never be final. Our God is the God of new beginnings. What does that say to you today?

The birth of Jesus

Day 183

Pray that God will enable you to be amazed once again at what he did that day in Bethlehem.

Luke 2:1–20 

The incarnation is about a real human life lived at a particular point in time and in a particular place. It is not a fairy story – 'once upon a time' – but the real stuff of which our lives are made.

If John's heritage was less than important, Luke takes pains to show that Jesus was descended from the right family. He is described as 'the Son of David',[1] born in Bethlehem,[2] and Luke shows how God arranges all of the secular details to ensure that God's Messiah is born where he should be.

Israelite families often lived in close proximity to their animals and at least Jesus was warm and dry. What else could be expected at a time of national upheaval caused by the census? More importantly he is one of us – sharing ordinary life with its discomforts and inconveniences, yet rising above it.

The arrival of the shepherds is highly symbolic. God is shepherd of his people.[3] His servants are shepherds of the community of faith[4] and Jesus described himself as the Shepherd *par excellence* (John 10), caring for the sheep and guiding them. The scene is dramatic once again – heaven and earth combine with choirs of angels leading ordinary working men in worship at their place of work. They are never heard of again.

The important thing is that God is worshipped in the midst of the ordinary life which he has dignified with his presence. How often do you praise God at your workplace?

1 Mark 10:47; Rom 1:3–4
2 Mic 5:3
3 Ps 23
4 Ezek 34

Mary would need the strength that these extraordinary events would give her (2:19,35). Take time, like Mary, to meditate upon some of the most amazing events which have ever happened.

Two prophecies

Day 184

God's preparation of Mary is a theme of these chapters. As you read today, pray that God will be preparing you for whatever happens in the days and weeks ahead.

Luke 2:21–40

The angel Gabriel and Elizabeth prepared Mary for the birth of God's son. Two faithful prophets now reaffirm what Mary already knew, and warn her of the pain and loss which would also be her experience.

First, we encounter Jesus' parents fulfilling the requirements of the Law both in sacrifice and in his circumcision. Luke is eager to show how the Christian gospel is directly continuous with the faith of Israel in what some scholars call 'salvation history'. Then we come to Simeon whose whole life, it appears, has been a preparation for this moment. He is a truly godly man who appreciates the honour which God has given him. In his prophecy (vs 29–32) he also has the vision to see beyond his own circumstances to the salvation of the Gentiles. He also perceives at what cost this will be achieved. Both the people Israel and Mary will be shaken by the ministry of this child. This realism was essential for Mary, following the exhilaration and joy which had accompanied the conception and birth.

The second prophecy comes from the mouth of Anna, who is described in lovingly human detail (vs 36–37). Her words are not recorded for us, but they clearly concerned 'the redemption of Jerusalem' (v 38). With such words of encouragement and warning Mary and Joseph were able to return home to everyday life again in the carpenter's shop. How many times they must have wondered at the signs and words which accompanied their son's birth!

God made good provision for Mary and Joseph, caught up in the drama of salvation history. God still cares for and prepares his people for what is to come. As you pray, be open to anything which God may wish to say to you.

Jesus in the Temple

Day 185

As we conclude this series, thank God for any insights he has given you into the earliest days of Jesus, our Lord and Saviour.

Luke 2:41–52 

The apocryphal gospels, which the church decided not to include in the canon of Holy Scripture, contain several stories from the supposed childhood of Jesus. Most of them are fairly fanciful and portray a child who is somewhat given to arbitrary displays of supernatural power. How different is this single biblical episode from the childhood of Jesus! Mary and Joseph pursue their customary Passover journey to Jerusalem. They had arranged to make the journey and celebrate the feast with relatives and friends (v 44). Nothing unusual in that. And it would be quite normal for Mary and Joseph to lose sight of their son as he enjoyed the security of those well known to him. The adults would assume a common responsibility for the children. Safety could be counted on.

When they find Jesus three days later(!) Mary and Joseph have a great shock. Perhaps this was the first time that they had had reason to reflect back upon the events of twelve years previously. In Jewish terms, Jesus was fast approaching manhood and must make a priority of preparing for the messianic task which was his calling.[1] Today's reading is a little window onto that process. Jesus has no doubts as to his destiny and makes an extraordinary reference to 'my Father's house' (v 49) – terms which even Solomon or David might have fought shy of using. But that of course is the reality for Jesus.

1 See Luke 3:21,22; 4:16–21
2 1 Cor 2:8

The story offers insights into the unique privilege and process of adaptation which Jesus' parents had to experience. The whole episode highlights that amazing process by which the Lord of Glory[2] grew in wisdom and stature (v 52). This is an aspect of the miracle of the incarnation which we rarely consider. Turn these thoughts into worship.

New and surprising

Jesus, the Son of God

In these chapters Luke treads a tightrope. He wants both to show how Jesus fulfils the Scriptures, and to make clear that he does things altogether new and surprising. He cannot be pigeon-holed! At the end of chapter 5, we meet the first parable in Luke, which is all about this surprising newness. New wine is flowing – demanding new containers, and a willingness to abandon old, familiar tastes.

Jesus alone ministers with God-like authority and power (4:14,32,36; 5:17). Only he can truly release captives (4:18), bring a tough Galilean fisherman crashing to his knees in repentance (5:8), entice a taxman out of his greed with just two words (5:27), simply speak forgiveness of sins and cleanse impurity with a touch (5:13,20) – because only he is truly the Son of God, in whom God delights (3:22).

Jesus truly understands, and rightly applies, the Scriptures. He knows how those three great verses from Deuteronomy apply to him in the wilderness, facing the devil (4:1–13). And he knows exactly how Isaiah 61:1,2 is to be fulfilled through his ministry (4:18–21).

These chapters present us with Jesus, the Son of God, and test our response to him as we see how others responded. We see him: through the eyes of John the Baptist (3:1–20); from God's perspective (3:21,22); from the perspective of world history (3:23–38); through the devil's eyes (4:1–13); in his own self-understanding (4:4,8,12,18–21); through the prejudices of his kinsfolk in Nazareth (4:22–30); through the eyes of the astonished residents of Capernaum (4:32,36), and in the responses of those whose lives he transformed – the demon-possessed man in Capernaum, Peter's mother-in-law, Peter himself, the man with a contagious skin disease, the paralytic, Levi – a series of individuals, all in different ways 'sick' and receiving the touch of the great physician (5:31).

Steve Motyer

The greatest human being

Day 186

Ask yourself how real is the second coming of Jesus? Think when you last reflected on its implications for you.

Luke 3:1–20 

With a wonderful fanfare of the names of the mighty, Luke introduces John the Baptist, the greatest human being ever born, according to Jesus (Luke 7:28). He is far greater than any of the rulers who ignored his appearance for in him – wait for the second fanfare – Isaiah's prophecy is fulfilled[1] and a voice rings out, the voice of God himself, calling his people to repentance.

People flocked to hear John, although his message was most uncomfortable to hear. He called them 'snakes',[2] enemies of God,[3] slithering out of their holes to escape the coming firestorm of God's wrath. The awful reality of God's judgement burned through John's words as he tells them that:

- They cannot rely on religious privilege or status (vs 8,9). God judges us not on our spiritual labels or reputation (church leader, successful missionary, woman of prayer), but on our 'fruit', the quality of our lives.
- They must end all selfish possessiveness (v 11). If we have more than someone else, that is God's call to share the surplus. Are we ready to hear this?
- They must renounce the use of power to get their way with others (vs 12–14). Soldiers were notoriously poorly paid, and they and tax-collectors could easily use force to get more.
- They must expect the imminent appearance of the Lord in judgement! (vs 16,17). Nothing has changed. We too await the return of the Lord as Judge and Saviour. Will we be wheat, or chaff, useless rubbish to be burned?

One of the rulers reappears with his response (vs 18–20): when forced to notice John the Baptist, Herod silences this awkward voice.

1 Isa 40:3–5
2 Ps 140:3
3 Isa 14:29; 59:5

Spiritual audit: 'Repent… bear fruit… Jesus is coming'. Pray through these words and apply them to your life.

Day 187 An even greater human being!

What do you think are the strongest temptations you face at the moment? Bring them to God today.

 *Luke 3:21 – 4:13*

If John the Baptist is the greatest, who is Jesus? We hear God's verdict (vs 21,22), Luke's comment (vs 23–38), the devil's view (4:1–13), and woven into the temptation story, Jesus' own self-understanding (vs 4,8,12). Through these three sections, a single theme runs: the Lord Jesus associates himself fully with us in our humanity.

Nothing marked Jesus as different from the crowd until the dove appeared, and the voice was heard. But both of these in fact underlined his membership of the crowd: the dove was a frequent symbol for Israel,[1] and the voice uses the words of Isaiah 42:1, where God promises to send his 'servant' to 'bring forth justice for the nations', starting with Israel. At his baptism Jesus the Servant steps right into the midst of Israel, associating himself with the people in their need, as they confess their sins. And God says 'Yes!'

Luke's long genealogy makes the same point. It lists complete unknowns (largely), and traces the line right back to 'Adam, son of God' (v 38). So Jesus is Son of God not just by direct anointing and affirmation, but also by human descent. For the rest of us, sin has destroyed divine sonship by human descent. Our humanity is incomplete. But Jesus' humanity is not!

The temptation story continues this thought. Where Adam, and Israel, failed to resist temptation, Jesus succeeds and the devil departs. Jesus quotes Scriptures which come from the story of Israel's temptation in the wilderness,[2] casting himself in the role of the people of God to which he now belongs!

These temptations are the fundamental ones that wreck our humanity: to use our gifts selfishly for ourselves (v 3), to achieve happiness by our own plans and not God's way (vs 6,7), and to use God to make others admire us (vs 9–11). But Jesus is the victor!

1 Ps 74:19; Hos 11:11
2 Deut 8:3; 6:13,16

How does your list of temptations fit with these three? Pray through them, claiming fellowship with Jesus in resisting them.

Good news ... rejected

Day 188

Think of those whose failure to believe in Jesus causes you particular pain. Pray for them before you read.

Luke 4:14–30 

This passage contains the whole gospel in a nutshell. A wonderful spiritual 'high' is greeted by the most vile reaction. Jesus proclaims who he is, why he has come, and what he will do – and his own people reject him violently. We will not read again of people trying to kill Jesus until 19:47, just before the crucifixion (apart from a passing comment about Herod in 13:31).

But doesn't Jesus actually *provoke* them? They were 'speaking well' of him (v 22) until he refused to repeat in Nazareth what he had done in Capernaum (v 23), and said that 'no prophet is accepted in his home town' (v 24). But their extremely violent reaction proves that he was right: they 'spoke well of him' because they were pleased that one of their boys had become a Galilean celebrity! Local rivalry with Capernaum is doubtless a big factor: Joseph's boy! The toast of the country!

They had fallen well and truly into the third temptation which Jesus had just resisted, and he was not going to play that game. In that state of mind, they could not recognise what he was really saying to them about Isaiah 61:1,2. Only the poor, the captives, the blind and the oppressed could truly experience what Jesus was offering them – not these self-satisfied locals who can't see further than 'Joseph's son' and do not trace his genealogy back to God, as Luke has just done.

This sets the scene for the whole Gospel. Luke has actually moved this story from its position in Mark[1] and expanded it, so that it can serve as an introduction to Jesus' mission. He will show us the poor, captive, blind and oppressed hearing the good news and being set free by Jesus – ultimately at the cost of his own life. For Jesus always provokes the anger of those who refuse to see themselves as poor and blind.

1 Mark 6:1–6

Can you share Jesus' pain at being rejected like this in his home town? Who feels similar pain today? Pray for them.

The good news of the kingdom

Day 189

Ask yourself quietly and seriously: do you love Jesus for what he gives, or for who he is? Take stock.

Luke 4:31–44

What a contrast between Nazareth and Capernaum! A crowd surges up the hill in Nazareth to throw Jesus out of the town (4:29). But in Capernaum, the crowd rushes out to stop him from leaving (4:42). And yet in Nazareth Jesus is upfront about who he is, applying Isaiah 61:1,2 to himself, while in Capernaum he veils who he is, telling the demons to be silent 'because they knew that he was the Messiah' (vs 35,41). Why does he cloak his Messiahship in Capernaum, where they respond so warmly?

The reason appears when we ask (a) why they want him to stay, and (b) why he wants to leave. They hope for more *healing*, as on the previous evening (v 40). But he wants to go on *preaching* (vs 43–44): here we meet again the terms 'preach the good news' and 'proclaim the message' from Isaiah 61:1,2.

In other words, for them the healings are an end in themselves – wonderful deliverances from handicap and disease. For him, the healings are signs of something else – the arrival of 'the year of the Lord's favour' (4:19) or, as he puts it in verse 43, 'the kingdom of God'. This is the first of no fewer than thirty-two references to 'the kingdom of God' in Luke's Gospel, all but six of them on the lips of Jesus himself. It was the heart of his message: see Luke's summaries of his teaching in 8:1 and 9:11. Jesus sees himself first and foremost as a 'proclaimer' of the kingdom: notice 'preach... proclaim... proclaim' in 4:18,19. So he will only heal if he can also explain what the 'coming of the kingdom' means – because the kingdom is where God calls us into a whole new life in fellowship with himself, through Christ. Physical healing may be part of the new life, but it's not its heart.

What is the heart of the message of the kingdom? What does Peter's mother-in-law suggest (v 39)?

The trapper trapped

Simon's boat was his pride and joy. What are your most prized possessions? When did you last offer them to Jesus?

Luke 5:1–11 

It must have been very difficult for Jesus to interest people in his teaching when there was such a terrible need for healing. But he succeeded: the crowd 'was pressing on him to hear the word of God' (v 1). Was Simon 'pressing' too? Apparently not. The nets, at this stage, were more important. But Jesus had had such a dramatic effect on his mother-in-law (4:38–39) that Simon was willing to organise his boat for Jesus, and even to throw his newly-washed net back into the sea.

What followed changed his life for ever. We must notice that the change of direction for Simon was not his initiative or decision ('I think this man deserves following!'). He wanted Jesus to go away (v 8) – the last struggles of a man who realises that, like the fish under the water, he has been steered into a net. And sure enough, the net is pulled in: 'Don't be afraid. From now on, you'll be catching people!' (v 10). He will be doing to others what Jesus has just done to him.

Is this 'calling' a special experience, just for the Simon Peters of this world? If it were, the rest of us could safely stay with our own nets, thankful that Peter, James and John – and those whose faces smile from the missionary board at church – were willing to leave theirs. But, as Luke makes very clear later in his Gospel (14:26,27; 18:18–22), giving up everything to follow Jesus is not a special calling for the few. It is the first demand made of all disciples – because disciples of Jesus are called to be there for others, to do to others what Jesus has done to them, and they cannot be there for others if their lives are devoted to cleaning nets: that is, to putting their own concerns and occupations first, while Jesus teaches further along the beach.

Go through your list of possessions again, specifically giving each of them away to the Lord. Finish by giving yourself away to him. Feel his net around you.

Day 191

A broken life repaired

Reflect: if you met Jesus today, of what would you be ashamed before him? Make a list.

Luke 5:12–16

All the stories in this part of Luke's Gospel look back to, and illustrate, Jesus' mission statement in 4:18,19. This story relates to the last line of 4:18, 'to send away the broken in release'. Recent versions prefer 'the oppressed' in their translation of this line, which in fact Jesus draws into Isaiah 61:1 from its original home in Isaiah 58:6. He clearly thought it expressed something vital about his 'anointing'. 'Broken' or 'shattered', however, is a better translation than 'oppressed'. It describes exactly the state of this poor man suffering from leprosy. His life had been shattered by the disease, which made him an outcast from his family and community, deprived him of employment and condemned him to shout 'unclean' if anyone approached – not just because people feared the infection, but because the disease made him ritually impure, so that anyone in contact with him, even indirectly, would also be rendered 'impure' and unable to participate in worship, and indeed in normal life.

How wonderful then, that Jesus' dramatic touch does not make Jesus unclean (as it should have), but works the other way, expelling the uncleanliness like snow before hot water. Thus the man's shattered life is re-made and he is 'sent away in release' to display his cleansing, as the Law required, at the Temple in Jerusalem.[1]

Jesus does it so quietly. He does not even want this man to say how his 'cleansing' occurred. This sort of thing just happens when the kingdom of God is present and the Son of God gently touches. And so it is today, when people find years of accumulated guilt and self-loathing simply soaked away by the love of Jesus; when fears melt before the sunshine of his grace, and his Spirit breathes new life into broken relationships. 'Uncleanliness' is everything that makes us unfit for fellowship with our heavenly Father, and Jesus specialises in expelling it.

1 Lev 14:1–32

Turn your list into prayer. Write 'I will be made clean' across it, and tear it up.

A sinful life restored

Here is a story about a man who was unaware of his deepest needs before God. Could the same be true of you? Reflect.

Luke 5:17–26

Yesterday's story shows Jesus dealing with impurity. Although he tells the man suffering from leprosy to go and offer the sacrifice prescribed by the Law, he actually bypasses the purity legislation and customs of the day, which were highly refined and involved frequent washings of different types in special 'water of purification'.[1] With an authoritative word, 'Be clean!' Jesus cuts through the ritual flummery.

Now Jesus deals with sin in the same way. Likewise, the prescriptions were clear: sin can be forgiven through sacrifices offered in the Temple in Jerusalem, in obedience to the Law. It is Jesus' setting-aside of the sacrificial system, replacing it with a simple 'your sins are forgiven!' which so offends the 'Pharisees and teachers of the Law' (vs 17,21). So the issue is one of authority: can Jesus have God's authority to pronounce the forgiveness of sins in this way, without reference to the legal prescriptions? Where could he get such authority? Jesus hints at the answer by referring to 'the Son of Man' (v 24). Hidden behind this innocent title is Daniel's vision of 'one like a son of man' who receives 'dominion, glory and kingship' from God himself.[2] The 'authority' to which Jesus refers is God's: he claims that God has given him authority to forgive sins, and 'proves' this by doing something else which can only be done by the power and authority of God (see verse 17!) – healing the paralysis. The healing, therefore, is a word from God affirming Jesus' claim to be able to forgive sin on his behalf.

So we see Jesus' priorities here. The biggest problem lowered through the ceiling that day was unforgiven sin. Compared to that, the paralysis was incidental. But he can deal with sin! The sin that clouds our minds, distorts our desires, removes God from our field of knowledge and ultimately kills us. Just a word is enough.

1 Mark 7:1–5; John 2:6
2 Dan 7:13,14

Turn Psalm 139:23,24 into a prayer for yourself. Watch out – God will answer it.

Day 193

A taste of new wine

Reflect on what eating together expresses and means for our relationships with each other.

Luke 5:27–39

Now we deal with the social implications of the last two stories. If Jesus can deal with impurity (5:12–16) and with sin (5:17–26) just by a word of cleansing and forgiveness, bypassing the sacrificial and purity system based on the Temple in Jerusalem, then the guardians of that system (the scribes and Pharisees) are faced with a radical challenge. Will they accept this new way? In the terms of Jesus' parable here, are they ready to provide new wineskins for Jesus' new wine? They are sure to prefer the old (v 39), but will they nonetheless be prepared to change?

What this will mean is illustrated by the call of Levi and the resulting dinner party. Jesus and his disciples find themselves rubbing shoulders with a large crowd of 'disreputables' – the kind of people whom the Pharisees, like Levi himself, never went near, because they were all 'unclean' in different ways. People who, in turn, never went near the Temple because its guardians denied them entry. But Jesus' new wine bursts the old wineskin of the Temple. Levi and his friends can enjoy table-fellowship with the Son of God himself, because he wants to call them to repentance and to speak that glorious word of cleansing to them (v 32).

But the Pharisees can only see the broken 'rules'. Jesus jumps in to protect his disciples from their carping, and when they try to drive a wedge between him and John the Baptist (who likewise offered forgiveness apart from the Temple) he agrees that there is indeed a difference: when Jesus is around, it's time to celebrate (vs 33–34)!

Rules and traditions can protect us from error, but they can also blind us to the work of the Spirit. Tradition is a great servant, but a dreadful master. Let us beware of the instinct to prefer the old, because Jesus is a purveyor of new wine!

We come as sinners into table-fellowship with the Son of God. Think of what this means for your relationship with him, and thank him.

Greater than Moses

Chapter 6 begins by showing Jesus' opposition to the old Jewish religious system. He is revealed as the new law-giver, greater than Moses, indeed 'Lord of the Sabbath' (6:5), able to give new interpretations to the old laws. Other parallels with Moses are also apparent. He spends time on the mountain alone with God before he appoints the twelve apostles, the foundational community of the restored people of God (6:12). He descends the mountain (6:17) to proclaim new rules for living (6:20–49), and all this is accompanied by evidence of God's supernatural presence (6:18,19) as with the giving of the old Law.

God's concern for the marginalised

I am preparing these notes in Nepal, a country wracked by poverty, injustice and corruption. One Sunday night a young man from a terribly deprived background told us about how he had been cured from leprosy in a mission hospital. With great emotion he declared, 'I praise God for my leprosy because through it I became a Christian'. For this brother of ours Luke's third beatitude is gloriously true – 'blessed are you who weep now, for you will laugh' (6:21).

Many characteristics typical of Luke's Gospel are evident in chapters 6 and 7. For instance, Luke's concern for the poor and the deprived is emphasised in the story of the resuscitation of the widow of Nain's son (7:15). In Luke's Gospel Jesus is proclaimed as the Saviour for all peoples, so Luke does not hesitate to show a Gentile centurion as the epitome of saving faith greater than any in Israel (7:9). Finally, Luke has a special place for women and for 'sinners' as shown in the story of the woman anointing Jesus' feet in Simon's house (7:36–50). I love the reckless abandonment of her gratitude to her Lord and Saviour, don't you?

Ross Pilkinton

Day 194 New directions for God's new people

As you read and pray today accept Jesus' invitation: 'Come with me by yourselves to a quiet place and get some rest'.[1]

Luke 6:1–26

Chapter 5 ends with Jesus showing that his teaching was a radical new way of knowing and serving God and not a patch-up job on a worn out Judaism. So chapter 6 is a record of the new things that were inaugurated with the coming of Jesus.

First, there is a new approach to Sabbath observance. The Sabbath was to be used positively for good rather than negatively for prohibition and legalism. Such a view encourages us to use our Sundays to serve God and to help people in need, but at the same time to limit our activities and our consumption on the day of rest. The Bible commentator Michael Wilcock also suggests that the Sabbath is meant to be a joyous celebration of God's 'weekend',[2] a 'visual aid' that points to the glorious messianic age to come.

Next, Jesus appoints a new leadership for the restored people of God. What is noteworthy about the twelve is how little we know about most of them, and how ordinary were the rest of them – in fact they were just like us! But they were chosen by Jesus (after he had spent a night in prayer, v 12) and appointed as apostles. The existence of the church today, which embraces a third of the world's population in almost every nation on earth, shows how well they did their job!

Finally, Jesus gives a description (vs 20–26) and an explanation of his new law of love (vs 27–42). In the West we tend to prefer Matthew's more spiritual version of the beatitudes – 'Blessed are the poor in spirit',[3] whereas the underprivileged prefer Luke's more materialistic version – 'blessed are you who are poor' (v 20). I write these notes in Nepal where the church is growing vigorously, especially amongst the poor and persecuted – a cause for great praise but also a challenge to us in the more affluent West.

1 Mark 6:31
2 Gen 2:2,3
3 Matt 5:3

How can we demonstrate the coming kingdom by the way we celebrate our day of rest? Is there any way we can include the poor, the hungry or the suffering in this blessing for our lives?

Like Father, like child

Day 195

As a treasured child, come into the presence of your heavenly Father, expecting to be nurtured and changed.

Luke 6:27–42 

The heart of this passage, indeed of the whole 'Sermon on the Plain', is in verses 35 and 36: we are to be children of the Most High God – like our heavenly Father and his Son in deeds, words and prayers.

Our actions, even to those who would harm us (our enemies), are to be uncompromisingly benevolent. Such love arises not from anything admirable in the beloved, nor because our benevolence will be reciprocated, but because we are resolutely committed to giving this kind of love – the kind that God pours out on us.[1] Like our Saviour, we are to speak well of our accusers when we are maligned,[2] and pray for them when we are mistreated.[3]

In Nepal, where national Christians and missionaries are often treated with hostility, it is common to hear heartfelt petitions for those who are persecuting the church. When this happens we are aware that the family likeness of the Son of God is being demonstrated amongst us. The examples given in verses 29,30 and 34,35 (turning the other cheek, giving without limit and lending without repayment) are hard to apply in the modern world. But the principle is clear: we are to show compassion in spite of rejection, to make our resources available to others even when they are misused, and to be generous even when our generosity cannot be reciprocated. As an example of the latter, many missionaries can praise God for receiving interest-free loans without which they could never have purchased a home for their retirement. Other characteristics of God's children are freedom from a censorious spirit (vs 37,38) and deliverance from hypocrisy (vs 41,42). To summarise: the world's morality is expected, natural; but Jesus calls us to a morality that is extraordinary, unexpected, supernatural, for then we shall be like our Father in heaven.

1 Rom 5:8,10; Matt 5:45
2 1 Pet 2:23; Rom 12:14
3 Luke 23:34
4 EM Blaiklock, 1903–83

'The whole drift … of this teaching is selfless generosity, utter self-control under persecution, absolute compassion, and Christ-like love.'[4] Pray for these qualities in your life.

Day 196

Good fruit and a good foundation

'Don't fool yourself ... letting the Word go in one ear and out the other. Act on what you hear!'[1]

Luke 6:43–49

The enemy of every New Zealand farmer is the prickly, noxious gorse bush. It spreads over all uncultivated land, inedible to animals and all but indestructible to man. I remember a children's sermon in a New Zealand rural church – delicious apples and oranges had been hung on a large prickly gorse bush. The children and their farmer parents laughed enthusiastically. It was ludicrous that such beautiful fruit should grow on such a horrible tree. Jesus' parables must have often produced a similar response (eg the speck and plank parable in yesterday's reading). Superficially the meaning is obvious but beneath the surface profound questions emerge: 'What good fruit is being produced in our lives?' 'Is it really genuine fruit or just for show?' 'How can we nurture the good and exterminate the evil fruit stored up in our hearts?' 'What do our mouths reveal of the hidden fruit in our lives?' As we examine ourselves remember that good fruit requires much patience and hard work to produce.

Both Matthew's and Luke's Gospels include Jesus' parable of the wise and foolish builders.[2] The disciples have just heard some of the most sublime words ever spoken,[3] but Jesus points out with devastating frankness that merely to hear is not enough. It is responding with obedience and action that shows true discipleship.[4] Even impassioned cries of 'Lord, Lord' (eg in worship and in prayer) count for little if there is no reformation of character and commitment to loving service.

To build on a foundation of rock requires commitment, hard work, time, discipline, self-denial – qualities not highly valued in today's world of instant success and gratification. But Jesus calls us to such commitment if we are to withstand the fierce storms in this life and the final flood of the judgement to come.

1 James 1:22, *The Message*
2 Matt 7:24–27
3 See Matt 7:28,29
4 James 2:17; 1 John 2:4

Matthew 7:21–23 is one of the most solemn passages in the whole Bible. Meditate upon it and allow the Holy Spirit to speak to you.

Amazing faith

Day 197

'Humble yourselves before the Lord, and he will lift you up.'[1]
'Lord, as we come into your presence today,
give us the grace of humility.'

Luke 7:1–10 

In his inaugural sermon in the synagogue at Nazareth Jesus reminded his hearers of Elisha's cure of a foreign army officer,[2] and Elijah's miraculous provision for a poor widow which included the restoring of her son to life.[3] These incidents are remarkably similar to the two miracles in Luke 7, so perhaps we are meant to see Jesus fulfilling the prophetic ministry he promised in Luke 4:18,19,21 – especially as it applies to the Gentiles and to the poor.

What a remarkable man this Gentile centurion was. He showed uncharacteristic compassion towards his servant. He was highly respected, had good relationships with the Jews, and shared his resources generously with them. Missionaries know the value of a comment like that in verse 5, 'he loves our nation'. If we are to reach the people of another culture (and our own), our hearts must be warm towards them. But it is the centurion's faith that particularly amazes Jesus. Only three times in the Gospels is Jesus amazed – once at the unbelief of his home town, in the same story in Matthew's Gospel, and here.

There is something very profound about the centurion's understanding of the relationship between authority, humility and faith. The person under authority knows what it is to humbly entrust themselves to a superior, so he or she can readily expect others to trust them. The person who knows no authority is a power unto themselves and finds it difficult to trust others whether they be 'above' or 'below' them. The centurion expresses his faith in Jesus to heal his servant because he had learnt to trust his superiors in the course of his military duties. For the habitually self-sufficient there is nothing so difficult as trust in God. The self-reliant rich, for example, find it difficult to trust in God while the humble poor move easily into his kingdom by faith.[4]

1 James 4:10
2 2 Kings 5:1–15
3 1 Kings 17:7–24
4 Luke 18:24; 14:24

'Lord, increase our faith. How wonderful if you were amazed at the greatness of our faith. What are you calling us to do for you today?'

Great power and deep compassion

'Lord, I come into your presence and ask that your love will transform me into your likeness.'

 *Luke 7:11–17*

A few metres from where I write these notes, a dusty lane leads down to a 'ghat' where Hindus come to cremate their dead. It is a desolate place perched on a rocky river bank. Several times each month a mournful funeral procession shuffles down the lane. Nepali horns sound, cymbals clash, the white-shrouded body on its wooden pallet is lifted high on the mourners' shoulders and behind follows a miserable stream of grieving relatives.

So it must have been in the time of Jesus (though the Jews buried their dead instead of cremating them). Imagine the drama as Jesus stepped up to the funeral procession and, to the astonishment of the pall bearers, touched the bier,[1] addressed eight brief words to the corpse (only four in the Greek, but Jesus probably spoke in Aramaic), and immediately the young man sat up and began to talk (wouldn't we love to know what he said?). This was the first biblical resuscitation from death since Elisha raised the Shunammite woman's son eight hundred years previously.[2] No wonder the mourners were filled with awe (literally – fear) and began to praise God.

This miracle shows the great power of Jesus, and equally the depths of his compassion. Verse 13 is charged with emotion. Most of Jesus' healing miracles were at the request of others, but here Jesus acts without being asked, moved by the grief and hopelessness of the woman. In the Gospels the Greek word translated here as 'his heart went out to her' is used only of Jesus.[3] It expresses his deep compassion and sympathy for those in need and here gives motivation for both his tender words and his healing action.

Two large crowds met at the gates of Nain that day (vs 11,12), one was glad, the other sad. Soon the glad overcame the sad – a wonderful picture of the power of the gospel in time and into eternity.

1 Num 19:11,16
2 2 Kings 4:27–37
3 Eg Matt 9:36; 14:14; Mark 1:41

We are surrounded by sad and lonely people. Ask God to fill your heart with compassion that leads to action today.

Living with unfulfilled expectations

'Why are you downcast, O my soul? Why so disturbed within me? Put your hope in God... .'[1]

Luke 7:18–35 

What has happened to the fiery John? Less than two years previously he had led a popular revival climaxing in the baptism of Jesus whom he confidently proclaimed to be the promised Messiah.[2] Now in prison, he seems to be wavering about Jesus' identity (v 20). Such confinement would be enough to break any man, and commentators debate whether it was John's self-confidence, his patience or his faith that was wavering. On balance it seems best to see John's uncertainty as a crisis of expectations.

One of the burdens of John's preaching had been the judgement that was coming with the Messiah as its chief agent.[3] However, Jesus had failed to meet this expectation. He had come in kindness and compassion, though not without strong warnings to the self-righteous.

Jesus' response to John's messengers is both kind and profound. He tells the disciples to report back to John the scope of his works of compassion and preaching which John would immediately identify as the fulfilment of Messianic passages from Isaiah.[4] Thus John's faith in Jesus would be restored.

There is wisdom here for us too when our expectations in God are not fulfilled. We should look for evidence of God at work in our lives and in the world, and we should look more deeply into Scripture for a more accurate interpretation of our perplexity.[5]

When the disciples had gone, how kindly Jesus speaks of John, in spite of his confusion. Of course Jesus' main intention was to place John within the totality of God's plan, but we can also take comfort that our gracious God accepts and gently corrects us when our perspective of his purposes is confused. According to verse 23 there is special blessing for those who hang on during these times of perplexity.

1 Ps 42:5
2 John 1:29–34
3 Luke 3:8–9,17
4 Isa 29:18; 35:5–6; 61:1
5 Acts 17:11

Bring to God your unfulfilled expectations. Pray also for those who are perplexed about the meaning of God's work in their lives.

Day 200

Seeing people as Jesus saw them

'Look, the Lamb of God, who takes away the sin of the world!'[1] Contemplate Jesus as the sacrifice for your sin.

 *Luke 7:36–50*

So far Luke has shown Jesus' power and authority mainly through ministry to the sick. Now he introduces another theme: 'For the Son of Man came to seek and to save what was lost'.[2] Jesus cares for the suffering but he also loves and lays down his life for sinners. Hallelujah! Like the woman in this story there must always be a place in our devotion for heartfelt, extravagant gratitude to our Lord and Saviour for the forgiveness of our sins.

The question Jesus asks Simon in verse 44 is meaningful. Simon thought he saw the woman's true character more clearly than Jesus because she was a 'sinner' (vs 37,39), probably a prostitute, and if Jesus was any sort of a prophet he would have known this. But Jesus' perception had depths that Simon knew nothing about. Jesus 'saw' the contempt for the woman in Simon's mind and also the astounding gratitude in the woman's heart that led to her extravagant, almost wanton expressions of love to Jesus.[3] He also saw into Simon's heart and exposed the inadequacy of his love through the exquisite little parable of the two debtors. Perhaps Jesus was implying that because the lesser debtor showed at least a little love there was some hope for Simon eternally. We do not know, but we do know this nameless former prostitute received salvation.

I recently worshipped in a mud-walled, thatched-roof church in rural Nepal. The church had been founded thirty years previously by five people suffering from leprosy! Ten years ago, several of the original church members had been imprisoned for their faith. In terms of this world's goods they were poor peasant farmers, but in Christian understanding I felt that I was the one who was poor.[4] We should pray often for the humility and grace to see others as God sees them.

1 John 1:29
2 Luke 19:10
3 See David in 2 Sam 6:12–15
4 1 Cor 1:26–29

'Lord, thank you, thank you so much, for the forgiveness of our sins. Help us to see others – sinners and saints alike – as you see them.'

Who is this man?

For the reader of these chapters, the question posed to the disciples in 9:20 remains fresh and urgent: 'Who do you say I am?' The surrounding narratives give information to help us answer this, as we are shown Jesus the Teacher, Healer, Liberator, Prophet and Saviour. We are also shown how to live if we recognise who Jesus really is. The true disciple is one who hears and understands, and demonstrates deep kinship with Jesus by daring to walk the same self-giving road, even if the destination is death.

Read with expectation

How, then, can we read these stories as people who do have eyes to see and ears to hear? I suggest this is best done by expecting to encounter Jesus in our reading. As we enter into the world of Luke's stories, we meet Jesus and are changed. Note what happens to each person Jesus encounters; be alert for key questions, such as 'Where is your faith?', or assertions such as 'Your faith has healed you'. Note who recognises Jesus, and what action this leads them into as a result.

As you read, imagine the scenes unfolding vividly. Feel the sun, see the colours, smell the dust, imagine the stones under your feet as you walk along the road, climb the mountain, and descend again to the rocky plain. Where do you see yourself in each scene? Are you a spectator, a disciple, or perhaps one of the people being fed or healed? Does one particular scene stand out for you, or touch your emotions deeply? If so, stay with that picture and hear what it is saying to you.

Once we have responded to Jesus' challenge, Luke expects us to make some life-changing decisions, informed by our encounters with the Jesus who walked the roads 'through cities and villages, proclaiming and bringing the good news of the kingdom of God' (8:1), and who continues to meet us as the Risen Lord in our own cities, towns and villages.

Merryl Blair

Those who have ears to hear

Day 201

Pray for an open, generous spirit as you read this passage. Spend some time meditating on one particular word or phrase.

 *Luke 8:1–21*

The parable of the sower is so well known that it can be difficult to read it with fresh eyes. This whole section is on the theme of 'listening'.

The passage ends with the rather challenging words, 'My mother and brothers are those who hear God's word and put it into practice' (v 21). This summarises, and stresses, what has come before. We note that Jesus ends the parable with the call, 'He who has ears to hear, let him hear' (v 8). He then quotes Isaiah, who was sent to prophesy to people who heard but could not understand, and who saw but never perceived and were therefore incapable of being healed.[1] The explanation of the parable (vs 11–15) repeats the word 'hear' four times, culminating in the description of the 'seed on good soil' who are those who 'by persevering produce a crop'. The lesson is further reinforced by the point made about the lamp (vs 16–18): 'Therefore consider carefully how you listen'.

If anyone has missed the reason why Luke composed the passage in this way, then verses 2 and 3 illustrate exactly what it means to 'hear God's Word and put it into practice'. The women accompanying Jesus, having heard and been cured, are now acting on the good news by sacrificially supporting Jesus and the twelve. Throughout this passage we are reminded that true family, God's family, consists of those who have encountered the kingdom of God in Jesus, and whose lives are now proclaiming the good news.

1 Isa 6:9

Which type of 'soil' do you identify with at the moment? Pray for the ongoing ability to hear and act.

Calming the storm

Day 202

Sit in silence listening to the sounds of the world (wind, traffic, voices...). Sense the love of God throughout the neighbourhood.

Luke 8:22–25 

Within only a few verses, Luke tells a story which is not only vividly described, but which highlights some interesting juxtapositions. The peacefully-sleeping Jesus contrasts with the terrified disciples. More surprisingly, the raging winds and waters appear to recognise Jesus' true identity, whereas the disciples do not.

In Hebrew cosmology water is the place of chaos, which was controlled and restrained by God at the time of the creation.[1] Various Old Testament stories show God unleashing the waters of chaos back over the land, or restraining the waters in the interests of saving his people.[2] Here, we see this saving power over the chaotic elements exerted by Jesus on behalf of the disciples. (Note that Jesus 'rebuked' the wind and the waves, as he had rebuked the demons in 4:35,41, and will again in 9:41.) The response of the disciples, 'Who is this?' (even though they had called Jesus 'Master!' earlier in v 24), shows an amazing lack of insight, compared with the instant recognition and obedience of the elements!

Hence the careful wording of Jesus' question. Unlike Matthew and Mark, who focus on the disciples' lack of faith,[3] in Luke's Gospel the emphasis is more on using that faith (v 25). Coming as it does after the parables on hearing and doing the Word of God, here faith is seen to be ineffectual when it is not acted upon.

It is easy to identify with the disciples in their fear and helplessness. The waters of chaos may look different for each of us, but Jesus' question, 'Where is your faith?' will always lead us to the underlying question, 'Who is this?' And as we allow ourselves to take on board the full implications of the answer to that question, we also open ourselves to the saving, calming power of the One who stills the waves.

1 Gen 1:1–2; Ps 29:10
2 Gen 6:17; Exod 14:21
3 Matt 8:26; Mark 4:40

Imagine Jesus' power coming to calm any storms in your life; pray for this calm to stay with you in your daily encounters.

Freedom for a prisoner

Day 203

Do you feel bound by the circumstances you find yourself in? Bring your situation before God in prayer.

Luke 8:26–39

Yesterday's reading saw Jesus' closest friends struggling to understand how this man could speak with authority over the elements. Today, that authority is shown again as Jesus demonstrates that he can calm not only the natural elements, but also the supernatural.

The demon-possessed man is one of those who is least tolerated by society: naked, living among the tombs (and therefore ritually unclean), chained, guarded, finally driven to total abandonment by society. Luke's description leaves no doubt of the social status (or rather, lack of status) of this man. Yet here is someone whom Jesus is determined to free from the power of the demons that bind him more effectively than chains (v 29).

Here is yet another example of Jesus working out the agenda introduced in chapter 4, verses 18,19. Here is a prisoner who has had freedom not only proclaimed to him, but also put into effect for him. He is found by the townsfolk 'dressed and in his right mind', and is sent back home by Jesus. His social separation has been reversed, and he is restored to community. His mandate is to 'tell how much God has done for you' (v 39). As Jesus announced earlier (v 21), the faithful disciple not only hears God's Word, but puts it into practice.

We can begin to grasp the answer to the question 'Who is this?' by watching Jesus in action, as indeed we can by listening to the demon-possessed man. 'Son of God' (v 28) is not just a title; it also announces the presence of the One who brings good news and who inaugurates 'the year of the Lord's favour'.[1]

1 Luke 4:19

We are left to grapple with the question, 'Where is your faith?'. Is it possible not to place our faith in this person who frees, heals and restores?

Healing for two daughters

Day 204

Hear the Word of God: 'Do not fear, for I am with you; do not be dismayed, for I am your God. I will strengthen you and help you; I will uphold you with my righteous right hand.'[1]

Luke 8:40–56 

This lovingly-told story ends the series of parables that illustrate the parable of the sower. The two people in need of healing appear to be quite different at first: one, a beloved only child of a person in authority; the other, an adult woman who, like the demon-possessed man, was an outcast from society by virtue of ritual impurity. They are linked in this story by the dual statements that one is 'a girl of about twelve' (v 42) and hence at the age of the onset of menstruation, and the other has been 'subject to bleeding for twelve years' (v 43). Both, in fact, have been marginal people for about the same period of time, as children (especially girls) were of little social importance, and a bleeding woman could not come into contact with any other people. Both appear to be beyond help.

But the presence of Jesus once again brings healing and restoration, and we see once more that the true follower of Jesus is known by both word and deed. The woman touches Jesus, then, when she is identified, tells of her healing 'in the presence of all the people' (v 47). Her place as 'family' of Jesus (those who hear and do)[2] is affirmed when Jesus addresses her as 'daughter' (v 48).

Even as this daughter is healed, the news arrives of the death of another daughter. Jesus' response, 'Do not be afraid; just believe' (v 50), points us back to the daughter whose faith has healed her. The little girl's parents may be astonished (v 56), but we should not be. This is, after all, the One who has promised good news, healing and release.

1 Isa 41:10
2 Luke 8:15,21

Who are the marginalised in your neighbourhood? Pray that they, as well as you, may feel Jesus' healing touch.

Day 205

Putting learning into action

Pray that God may help you to undertake your tasks today while living according to the values of the kingdom.

Luke 9:1–9

After the last chapter's teaching on the meaning of discipleship (supporting, hearing, and living the way of Jesus), the disciples are sent out to practise what they have been taught. As Jesus has demonstrated, this includes *doing* as well as *speaking* – 'to *preach* the kingdom of God and to *heal* the sick' (v 2).

For Luke, and for many other biblical writers, discipleship is a journey that is resourced only by God. Jesus makes plain to the twelve that there can be no stagnation for the true follower. Rather, the call is to travel lightly, depending on God's grace for strength and power, and on the welcome of those who have the insight to hear and recognise the gospel. The order to take nothing on the journey is a rather terrifying idea, but also very liberating! What is to prevent anyone from launching into this life? Certainly not lack of what we usually consider adequate resources.

The key question 'Who is this?' is asked again in verse 9. This question, in previous encounters with Jesus, has led to faith. Here Herod, who comes to no conclusion at this stage, anticipates Jesus' questioning of the disciples (v 18). We may see Herod as a potential disciple – 'he tried to see Jesus' (v 9) – who serves as a contrast to the real disciples who do see Jesus, recognise him, and choose to follow him. All through the Gospel of Luke, we are presented with contrasting pictures of those who dare to go on the journey of faith, and those who either have never seen the path, or who see it and yet fail to commit themselves to it. This leaves the reader with a stark choice: having heard, where to from here?

Think about your own journey of faith. Pray for insight into where it has become cluttered and held back. Think about what nourishes you and give thanks for the love and warmth you have encountered along the way.

'You give them something to eat!'

Day 206

Take some time to sit quietly. Cup your hands in your lap, and imagine the love of God filling your hands until they are overflowing.

Luke 9:10–17 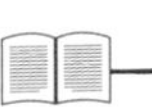

The feeding of the five thousand is a central story in Luke's Gospel, summing up in one image what discipleship is all about. On returning from their mission, the disciples are naturally eager to tell Jesus about their experiences, and he takes them away for a period of reflection. However, mission and ministry never conform to office hours, and the group appears to be besieged immediately by crowds of needy people.

Jesus' response is an example of how God wants us to respond to such need: welcoming, telling the good news about the kingdom of God, and healing (v 11). As we have seen in other stories leading up to this point, ministry according to Jesus' model requires attention to all aspects of a person's being. The welcoming is an invitation into a community, the 'family' of those who hear and follow. Telling about the kingdom of God enables people who are bound by particular ways of living to be liberated into God's way and where those who are of little importance in the world's eyes gain a special importance. The repeated emphasis on healing throughout Luke's Gospel is there to continually remind us that Jesus' mandate for ministry is wholeness, in all senses of the word. Even the disciples, who were excited by their own achievements in mission, still had much to learn by watching Jesus.

The second part of this story calls for self-examination on the part of all readers. The disciples see and identify need without any effort – and expect Jesus to fix it equally effortlessly. The response 'You give them something to eat!' makes us all think of our own meagre resources. But the story is there to tell us that we don't know what we can do until we try. God can take our little and turn it into more than enough so long as we are brave enough to assume responsibility.

How are you already feeding others? Pray for God's continued enabling for your ministry, wherever it may be.

Peter's confession of faith

Day 207

'Whoever loses his life for me will save it.'[1] Perhaps these words will have a special resonance for you today.

Luke 9:18–22

Now we come to the climax: all the previous stories have been leading to this point, and all roads of discipleship lead away from it.

In case we've missed the various questions and responses in previous passages, Luke has Jesus summarise them all for us, by asking who 'the crowds' say he is. The range of answers shows an awareness of the special nature of Jesus, but don't quite get to the point. Besides which, asking what others say is only skirting around the central concern for a disciple, 'Who do *you* say I am?' The reader can almost hear the world holding its breath as it waits for the answer to this most vital question. For once, Peter gets it wonderfully, gloriously right, with his response, 'The Christ (Anointed One) of God' (v 20). Only long association with, and careful attention to, Jesus has led him to this conclusion. He has watched Jesus live out the kingdom of God through preaching, healing, welcoming, feeding, and changing lives; he can come to no other conclusion.

The answer cannot be left there, however. Simply to recognise Jesus is not enough. Jesus goes on to explain exactly what it means to be the Christ: he knows he must suffer, be killed and wait three days before resurrection. Was this what Peter had in mind when he made his confession of faith? One suspects not. On the whole, we prefer our heroes to be powerful and victorious, or at least to make us feel good.

With Peter and the other disciples, we are left at the end of this passage wondering just what it means to follow One whose road leads to suffering and death. Even resurrection only comes after a period of waiting in the dark of despair. Who is this man, that he can ask such a journey of his followers?

1 Luke 9:24

Think back over your own experience of Jesus. Why have you chosen to follow him? Where is he now, on your journey?

The reality of discipleship

Day 208

Pray with the psalmist, 'Create in me a pure heart, O God, and renew a steadfast spirit within me'.[1]

Luke 9:23–27 

Now we reach the heart of Luke's message to his community and to us. What does it really mean to be a disciple?

The truth is this: if the Christ is defined by suffering and death, then discipleship can be no different. Throughout Luke's Gospel we have been presented with images taken straight from life. We have seen Jesus in conversation with the demented, the sick and the paralysed, social outcasts, misfits, people with leprosy, malcontents, sinners and the hopeless. All have been treated with compassion and dignity. Jesus has freely given time and energy to the needs of others, listening and teaching, feeding and healing.

Any follower of Jesus will need to offer a similar expenditure of self. Luke is the only Gospel writer who adds the word 'daily' to the idea of taking up one's cross. This is the reality of discipleship. Once undertaken, it must consume one's entire life. This is not to lose one's sense of self; rather, it is to seek self-definition in Christlikeness, not worldly possessions, position, race or gender. The paradox of discipleship is that freedom comes from this redefinition, in which the disciple is given to service through love of God. Asaph, the writer of Psalm 73, struggling with the issues of self-identity and worldly definitions, comes to this conclusion: 'Whom have I in heaven but you? And earth has nothing I desire besides you'.[2] If the task of discipleship seems too daunting, we may return to the stories preceding this passage, and know that we are fed, welcomed, healed and taught as we follow along the way – but remember, there is no turning back for Jesus' followers: 'If anyone is ashamed of me and my words, the Son of Man will be ashamed of him when he comes in his glory … ' (v 26).

1 Ps 51:10
2 Ps 73:25

'God is hiding in the world and our task is to let the divine emerge from our deeds' (Abraham Heschel, 1907–72).

Day 209

On the mountain top

Think back to your earliest experiences of God's love and praise him for those times.

Luke 9:28–36

Disciples must never stop learning! Peter, who got it so wonderfully right only a short while ago,[1] now completely misses the point of who Jesus is.

Up on the mountain top, a transfiguration occurs. Jesus, 'his clothes ... as bright as a flash of lightning' (v 29) is joined by two great figures from Israel's past, Moses and Elijah, who represent the Law and the Prophets, and who foreshadowed the coming Messiah.

Peter's response to this amazing experience was to try to hold on to it in some way. When he suggested building shelters he may have been thinking of the Festival of Booths,[2] which commemorated God's leading and nourishment of the Israelites during the exodus. The irony is that Peter wants to build a memorial, using the symbol of an earlier journey, to an event that is also a journey of faith – Jesus' 'departure' (v 31), that is, his coming death. In other words, Peter is trying to stop the journey at that particular moment, to capture and retain the 'high' of the mountain top.

What Peter saw on the mountain was the brightness and glory. What he failed to see was Jesus' deliberate journey toward death. Like most of us, he wanted to hold on to that moment of glory, enshrining it as the essence of 'Christ-likeness'. Once again, though, he is reminded, as we are too, that discipleship is not about glory, or about staying in one place. Rather we are called to step out each day and to take up the cross. The voice from the cloud (v 35) recalls the voice heard at Jesus' baptism.[3] I once heard a reflection on baptism that suggested that, instead of seeing it as a gateway to an ongoing journey, we often treat it like a revolving door: trying to repeat the same experience for the rest of our life. This passage continues to challenge us not to hold on to one experience, but to keep travelling.

1 Luke 9:20
2 Lev 23:42; Deut 16:13–17
3 Luke 3:22

Where have your 'mountain tops' been?

Back down on the plain

Day 210

'Yet this I call to mind, and therefore I have hope: because of the Lord's great love we are not consumed, for his compassions never fail. They are new every morning; great is your faithfulness.'[1]

Luke 9:37–45 

God's glory, and the work of God, are not only present on the mountain. Reality demands that the disciple descends to the plain where life goes on. As this passage shows, real life is often a matter of frustration, failure and twisted sanity. The spiritual 'highs' are confronted immediately by the tough task of ministry, in which the disciples are called upon to intervene in crises for which they feel quite inadequate (v 40).

This story takes us back to the lessons of the previous chapter. There, we read of the healing of an only daughter.[2] Now it is an only son who requires the touch of the kingdom's grace. The disciples are unable to provide that touch. Why? Only recently they were given 'the power and authority to drive out all demons and to cure diseases' (v 1). So where has that power and authority gone?

This story cuts painfully close to home for all of us who go through periods of emptiness and impotence. However it is also a story that brings great reassurance, first of all by simply showing that discipleship is like that! There will be times of failure, but despite these we are still called to be faithful followers. Secondly, the presence of Jesus is the source of power for our ministry, and that presence is always with us.

The Christian must get used to living in a paradox. On one hand, we are given the resources to minister to a sick and troubled world. On the other hand, we are not the focus of that ministry: the true focus must always be the Crucified One. Power and authority come from giving and losing, from following him.

1 Lam 3:21–23
2 Luke 8:42

Consider times when you have felt empty and ineffective. Where have you seen God at work at those times?

Day 211

Going 'resolutely' to Jerusalem

Reflect on where you have seen the presence of God in your week so far.

Luke 9:46–62

Here we have another turning point in Luke's Gospel: Jesus resolutely sets out for Jerusalem (v 51). The description of that journey occupies half of the Gospel, and includes intensive teaching on the nature of discipleship, and finally the ultimate example, namely Jesus' death.

Before they start on the journey, however, the disciples begin an argument which reveals just how little they have understood of the nature of Jesus' mission. After all they have learnt in the previous weeks, they are still arguing about position and jealously guarding their 'special' status as followers of Jesus (v 49). Once again, Jesus patiently reminds them that the kingdom of God is inclusive and democratic, unlike worldly kingdoms. But the angry response of the disciples to the villagers' hostility (v 53) still betrays their worldly view of justice and punishment. Jesus, on the other hand, remains consistent in his response: God's kingdom insists on different responses based on grace.

Once he has turned toward Jerusalem, we sense the intensification of Jesus' teaching. An earlier comment comes to mind: 'A student is not above his teacher, but everyone who is fully trained will be like his teacher'.[1] As Jesus resolutely sets out to complete his journey, so a disciple needs absolute, resolute commitment to the journey, no matter where it may lead.

Whereas Jesus journeyed with those who didn't really understand (v 45), the true disciple is accompanied and supported by the One who has already made the journey, and who knows both its cost and the joy gained from 'service in the kingdom of God' (v 62).

1 Luke 6:40

Pray for continued 'resolute' commitment to living the kingdom of God.

The theology of growth

The main actions in these chapters occur at the beginning (Jesus sending out thirty-six missionary teams) and at the end (Jesus denouncing the hypocrisy of the religious leaders). They highlight the two central themes of these readings: ministry growth and ministry opposition.

As we examine Jesus' approach to ministry growth, we will find at least three principles that apply to us today.

First, *God's sovereignty is the foundation for ministry growth.* Knowing that God is ultimately responsible for the harvest gives a whole different focus to our outreach efforts. What we do and how we do it is important, but the results are dependent on God.

Secondly, as the parable of the Good Samaritan reminds us, *having a special concern for those on the margin of society is the ethos of ministry growth.* If our outreach strategies gravitate towards the rich and famous but leave out the poor and powerless, they are not in step with our Father's priorities.

Finally, *prayer is the method for ministry growth.* Certainly there are other methods that God uses. But they all are empowered by fervent prayer, as Jesus taught and demonstrated in his life.

How should we respond to those who oppose the growth of the gospel? Our readings offer three insights.

First, we must understand that *the real enemy is Satan.* Jesus knew that the efforts of his followers were part of a much bigger struggle (Luke 10:18). The only way to overcome such opposition is to rely on God's power.

Secondly, like Jesus *we should boldly speak and live the truth.* Ministry growth that comes at the expense of truth is merely a public relations success, not the increase of God's kingdom.

Finally, *truth must not be separated from love.* If we want our ministry efforts to grow, and if we want to respond effectively to the opposition it will stir up, we must have the courage to love as Jesus did. There is no force on earth more powerful than that.

Whitney Kuniholm

Effective ministry

Day 212

When have you felt that your ministry efforts were most effective? What were the reasons?

 *Luke 10:1–16*

Perhaps Jesus had in mind Jethro's advice to Moses at this point,[1] but clearly he understands that expanding the scope of his ministry will mean giving responsibility to more people. Earlier he sent out the twelve disciples;[2] now he sends out seventy-two more followers with a twofold mission: healing and preaching (v 9).

One of the most important and difficult tasks of a Christian leader is preparing and empowering new leaders. According to J Robert Clinton: 'Leadership is a dynamic process in which a man or woman with God-given capacity influences a specific group of God's people towards his purposes for the group'.[3] The best way for a leader to have a lasting influence is to leave the work in capable hands.

But the work of the kingdom will not expand unless Jesus' followers get serious about their mission. So Jesus spells out for them and us what effective ministry is all about. The foundation is to remember who is ultimately responsible: God owns the harvest (v 2) and Jesus is the one who directs and empowers (v 3). Human effort is vital, but only God can produce fruit that will last.[4] Forgetting this can cause well-intentioned ministry efforts to produce pressure, manipulation and burn-out.

But ministry is not just the leader's responsibility. It also depends on a faithful community to provide for practical needs (vs 7,8). This not only encourages Christian workers and makes outreach possible; it also exposes more people to the life-changing power of the gospel. Finally, effective ministry has a clear message: 'the kingdom of God is near you' (vs 9,11). Jesus' followers are called to help others make a decision about him. Ultimately that's the point of effective ministry.

1 Exod 18:1–27
2 Luke 9:1–9
3 *The Making of a Leader,* Navpress
4 John 15:16

Think of some younger Christians you know. How could you encourage them to develop and use their abilities more effectively for the Lord's work?

The joy of success

Day 213

Being sure that Jesus has sent us is a key to real success. What is Jesus sending you to do today?

Luke 10:17–24 

This was a moment to savour. The seventy-two 'missionaries' have returned with reports of surprisingly effective ministry (v 17). They are filled with joy (v 17) and, interestingly, so is Jesus (v 21). It is instructive to examine the source of that joy.

The missionaries were experiencing the elation produced by success. Because they had followed Jesus' directions, they had seen results. One key to effective ministry is to follow Jesus' instructions. This requires that we regularly and prayerfully read God's Word. Very often it also requires a season of waiting on the Lord, by seeking the counsel of others and by not taking action until we gain a sense of holy peace about moving forward.

But Jesus' joy is more fervent ('through the Holy Spirit', v 21) because he sees the deeper reality to effective ministry. Satan, the real enemy, is defeated (v 18) and God's self-revelation is more clear and understandable, even to the most unlikely people (v 21). All of this confirmed Jesus' message and mission. His time had finally come (vs 23,24).[1]

However, Jesus knows his followers will face difficulties, so he explains two important truths. First, no matter what happens, whether our ministry is successful or not, we are to keep our eyes on the goal (v 20). Even in the church, our strategies for ministry and growth can lead us astray if they become ends in themselves. Jesus reminds us to 'live with the kingdom goal in mind'. That's the standard which should set our priorities.

But secondly, we are also to keep the 'big picture' in mind. It is God who has been at work for a long time (vs 23,24) drawing people to himself, and he will continue to do so. Our main responsibility is not to achieve success for God, but to remain faithful to him. When we do, he will accomplish far more than we could ever imagine.

1 See also Gal 4:4,5

Pray for missionaries and others in full-time Christian service that God would encourage them and empower their ministries.

The uncommon deed

Day 214

'Preach the gospel at all times. When necessary, use words.'[1]

Luke 10:25–37

This passage has special significance to me since my home church is called Church of the Good Samaritan. In the narthex (western entrance) we have a life-size, contemporary stone statue of one person helping another stand up, poignantly symbolising this parable and our church's mission statement: 'doing the uncommon deed in the name of Jesus Christ'.

On the surface, this man asked a thoughtful question about the next life (v 25). Not completely satisfied with Jesus' answer, he presses for a guarantee (v 29). At times, we too would wish to reduce God's *agape* love to a mere formula. But it doesn't work that way. If your relationship with God is too heavily defined by a list of 'dos' and 'don'ts' you'll have trouble being passionate in your love for God or joyful in your service to others. Jesus doesn't seem too interested in the man's 'perceived need' either. Instead, he zeros in on the real need using the well known parable, from which we notice at least two principles.

First, the outcast was the hero. No one liked or respected Samaritans, but Jesus is saying that the outcast is able to understand and express God's love better than anyone else, including the religious experts. Christian faith is not about being an expert or being perfect all the time. It's about being willing to receive God's love and forgiveness and then being able to express those realities to those around us.

The second principle, as well as the punchline of the story, is that true neighbours are those who show mercy. The word 'mercy' carries with it both the idea of a feeling of empathy and compassion, and taking action on behalf of those who are helpless. A Christian who has all the right answers but who does not show mercy is not an effective witness for God.[2]

1 Attributed to Francis of Assisi, 1182–1226
2 Luke 6:36

Who do you know who is in need of mercy? What could you do to express it to them today?

Only one thing

What is the one thing at the centre of your life? Can other people tell by how you act?

Luke 10:38–42

Why did Luke record this detail from Jesus' life? There must have been hundreds of stories not included. What makes this encounter with Jesus so significant?

We can identify with how Martha felt. She was prosperous (she owned a home, v 38), purposeful and willing to serve. No wonder she was offended at the unfairness of the situation. Perhaps her frustration (v 40) was fuelled by jealousy: 'I'm doing all the work while she's just trying to attract your attention. You know everything, Lord; can't you at least see that?'

Jesus does not criticise Martha's willingness to work hard. In fact, he emphasised the importance of humble service later in his ministry.[1] Christians should not look down on those who organise or serve as if tending to 'the details' is less important than other more visible roles. The apostle Paul affirmed that serving and encouraging were just as necessary to the health of the church as leadership and teaching.[2]

Luke identifies the real problem in a singe word: 'distracted' (v 40). Martha's well-meaning service distracted her from devotion to the Lord. What distractions have you encountered in the last week? Our enemy knows that we'll probably be on guard against the obvious ones like materialism, immorality or dishonesty. But he can create just as much damage to the church by prodding us to develop a 'martyr complex', which then turns our Christian service into a source of bitterness and resentment.

The only solution when we feel this way is to repent. Imagine if Martha had responded to Jesus' tender reminder (vs 41,42) by saying, 'I'm sorry, Lord. I just got overwhelmed. May I sit with you also?' Jesus is the 'one thing' (v 42) we need. That's what makes this encounter so significant.

1 John 13:1–17
2 Rom 12:3–8

'Lord God, sometimes it is so hard to serve you as I should. Please help me to serve others with a joy that comes from you today.'

Prayer lifestyle

Day 216

For Jesus, prayer wasn't a formula, it was a lifestyle. 'Lord, help this to be increasingly true of me.'

Luke 11:1–5

If someone asked you to help them develop a deeper prayer life (v 1), how would you respond? By explaining your prayer habits, by sharing a book on the subject, or perhaps by suggesting a helpful tape or seminar? Jesus begins his response by simply praying. If you want to get better at praying, he seems to say, don't spend too much time studying it. Just pray.

The Lord's Prayer[1] is undoubtedly the most famous and most repeated prayer in history. Over the centuries, many of the church's best minds have analysed this prayer. But for our purposes we can note that effective prayer involves two perspectives. First, in prayer we must look beyond ourselves to God, his nature, his holiness, his kingdom and his will (v 2). But secondly, we should not hesitate to focus on our day-to-day needs – food, forgiveness, and strength to avoid temptation (vs 3,4). At the very least, prayer involves adoration and supplication. Without this balance, our prayers will become lopsided and eventually less effective.

But Jesus' most powerful teaching on prayer may not have been with *a* prayer, rather it was his *lifestyle* of prayer. Notice what triggered the disciples to make their request in the first place (v 1a). As we read the Gospels we find frequent references to Jesus' pattern of prayer.[2] If you sometimes feel guilty because you can't pray for long, try praying more often throughout the day. You may find yourself feeling less guilty and more excited about your dialogue with God. And that's what prayer is all about.

Because Jesus' mind and heart were always focused on doing his Father's will, he was always praying. Too often we have to make time for prayer in our busy lives. For Jesus, interacting with his heavenly Father was the central task of his entire life. He made time for everything else.

1 See also Matt 6:9–15
2 Mark 1:35; Luke 6:12; Matt 14:23; 26:36

Experiment with a different approach to prayer today: pray aloud, or try a different posture, or go outside and look at the sky as you pray.

Perspectives on prayer

Day 217

Close your eyes and imagine that the Lord is sitting with you in the room. Which chair does he choose? How do you feel? What are you thinking? Now, what would you like to say to him?

Luke 11:5–13

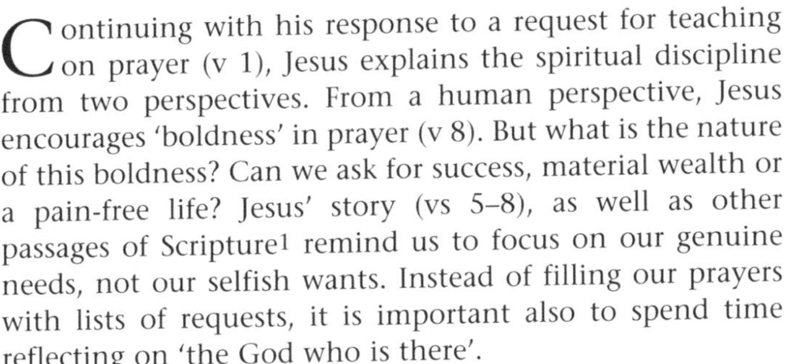

Continuing with his response to a request for teaching on prayer (v 1), Jesus explains the spiritual discipline from two perspectives. From a human perspective, Jesus encourages 'boldness' in prayer (v 8). But what is the nature of this boldness? Can we ask for success, material wealth or a pain-free life? Jesus' story (vs 5–8), as well as other passages of Scripture[1] remind us to focus on our genuine needs, not our selfish wants. Instead of filling our prayers with lists of requests, it is important also to spend time reflecting on 'the God who is there'.

The boldness Jesus encourages, however, is not related to the value or even the perceived possibility of receiving the request. Jesus himself said, 'What is impossible with men is possible with God'.[2] Rather, it is related to the intensity and persistence of the requester (vs 9,10), as well as the conviction that God is able to meet any genuine need. God will honour that kind of boldness. Merely praying for our selfish desires is not bold; it is audacious.

Jesus also reflects on prayer from God's perspective (vs 11–13), using the image of a loving father caring for a needy child. God really loves us and knows what is best for us. Even if we ask for something good, God may not give it to us because he has something even better in mind. God wants to give us good gifts – like the Holy Spirit (v 13). Our mistake is we sometimes want to determine too narrowly what the 'good gift' must be. It would be much better for our prayer lives if we spent more time simply reflecting on God's all-embracing love and asking for an understanding and acceptance of his will in any situation. Jesus assures us that faith in our loving heavenly Father, combined with a bold persistence in prayer, will get incredible results.[3]

1 Matt 6:8; 26:42; Phil 4:19
2 Luke 18:27
3 Matt 17:20

Is there something in your life that needs bold, persistent prayer? Should you stop asking for a solution and start asking for understanding?

Miracles and discipleship

Day 218

Which is a bigger challenge: to remain open to God's miraculous intervention in your life, or to remain eager to read and live out his Word?

 ***Luke 11:14–28***

Sometimes the people who are the most religious are the most resistant to a genuine work of God. That's what we see in these verses. After witnessing a miraculous exorcism and healing (v 14), the religious leaders respond with doubt. We sometimes see this same dynamic in churches that are experiencing renewal today.

What causes good people to resist God's work? Sometimes it is fear of the unknown or a legitimate desire to avoid being misled. In this case, Jesus knew the real motivations of these leaders (v 17a) and he had no problem exposing their flawed logic (vs 17–20). It is important to check the authenticity of the miraculous events we sometimes witness or experience against the plumbline of God's Word.[1] But we should be careful if we feel a resistance to new things just because they do not fit our traditions or long-held beliefs. Sometimes the most honest thing we can say is, 'This is outside my experience but I'm open to whatever God wants to do'.[2] Such trusting honesty may be the key that unlocks the door to a deeper experience of God in our lives.

Jesus also highlights the vital link between miraculous events and ongoing discipleship. God can and does miraculously remove the influences of the enemy from our lives, whether they are alcoholism, sexual addiction, greed, pride or anything else. But the important next step is then to 'fill the house' (vs 24–26) with new furniture, like the fruit of the Spirit.[3] Otherwise the devil can set up shop all over again. Jesus was so intent on making this point that even when the 'friendly heckler' tried to interrupt his train of thought (v 27), without missing a beat, he uses the woman's odd comments to suggest the best way to 'fill the house', that is, to 'hear the word of God and obey' (v 28). That's the challenge all of us face.

1 Amos 7:7–9; 1 John 4:1–3
2 Acts 5:38–39
3 Gal 5:22–23

What can you do this week to 'fill your house' with things that please God?

Motivational speaker

Day 219

What have been the biggest motivators in your life? What is the strongest motivation you have experienced in the last week?

Luke 11:29–36 

Crowds didn't impress Jesus. In fact, he often chose the times when his popularity was the greatest to say the most difficult things.[1] Why? Perhaps because he knew how easily people are motivated to do good things for the wrong reasons. What motivates you and those around you to participate in church life? Is it the benefits of Christian fellowship, tradition and culture, even a set of shared beliefs and values? These are all good.

But Jesus bluntly states that the central motivation must be a heartfelt repentance and a sincere desire to follow him. That's what the sign of Jonah was all about (vs 29–30). We must be careful not to become so sophisticated in our Christian walk that we allow other motivations to become more important.

The two analogies Jesus refers to next (vs 33–36) may at first seem out of context. But both a lamp and our eyes have the effect of bringing clear focus on the central issues. In particular, our eyes have a two-way function. They take in information, which can produce either positive or negative effects in our lives. But our eyes also give out information revealing the motivations in our hearts. What do your eyes indicate about the state of your heart today? I've often thought that it would make a tremendous impact if Christians simply looked directly into the eyes of everyone they met with the thought, 'This is a person God loves'. Why not try it today?

It's so easy to be swayed by the competing motivations we confront. But our central motivation must always be Jesus. Maybe you could take some time today to shine his light around your heart. What motivations fill your heart? Do people see an excitement about your walk with the Lord when they look into your eyes? Is Jesus really at the centre?

1 John 6:60,66

'Lord, sometimes my light is barely visible to others, mostly because I hide it. Give me the courage to shine brightly for you today.'

Who is my enemy?

Day 220

It's exhausting trying to 'look good'. It's exhilarating to be forgiven. Spend some time in prayer, especially focusing on confession.

 ***Luke 11:37–54***

As it turned out, Jesus wasn't a very pleasant dinner guest. Imagine the stunned silence after he finished his 'six woes'. Why was Jesus so angry?

For one thing, the religious leaders had been pestering him with trick questions and verbal traps and they had compounded this by mounting a smear campaign against him. Jesus had upstaged them and they were jealous. But echoing the themes first articulated by his cousin, John the Baptist,[1] Jesus forcefully identified the real problems and they were far more serious: hypocrisy and greed (v 39), neglecting love and justice (v 42), all of which put these leaders in direct opposition to God's messengers and God's Word (vs 47–49).

That's what sin can do to us. Tendencies we may excuse ('that's just the way I am'), or even justify ('at least he means well'), are often connected to a deeper root on the enemy's agenda. It's not easy or pleasant to talk about sin. And we should remember that the starting place is with our own.[2] Once we recognise sin for what it is, there are only two reactions. We can either reject Jesus' work in our lives, as these leaders did or we can repent and follow Jesus to a new level of obedience. Both reactions have long-lasting consequences.

But angry as Jesus was, we should not overlook the fact that he did accept the invitation of the Pharisee. Would you go to the home of someone who disagreed with you or who actively opposed your work? Earlier, Jesus was asked, 'Who is my neighbour?'[3] Given his example here, we may also want to ask, 'Who is my enemy?' Making peace with irritating church members or reconciling with a spouse or loved one who has offended us, may be more difficult than reaching out to those who oppose the gospel. But it is just as important to the authenticity of our witness.

1 Luke 3:7–14
2 Matt 7:3–5
3 Luke 10:29

Think of one person with whom you have a strained relationship. What could you do to facilitate reconciliation?

Return from exile

The return from exile was a key period in Jewish history. For Israel the exile had been a shattering blow. It called into question their status as the people of God. It marked the end of the Davidic monarchy and thus cast doubts on the nature of God's promise. It was accompanied by the destruction of the Temple with all that it represented in terms of the presence of God among his people. It left a disorientated, disillusioned, disappointed group of people struggling to come to terms with what this meant for national and religious life. The pain was compounded by the message from the prophets that all this had come about because of the failure of the people to obey God. So we can add a sense of failure and guilt to the emotional mix.

This forms the background to the return from exile. The first exiles returned in 538 BC and the major task was the rebuilding of the Temple. The story is told in Ezra chapters 1–6 and in the books of Haggai and Zechariah, prophets who actively encouraged the work. In 458 BC Ezra returned and in 445 BC, Nehemiah. (Much scholarly ink has been spilt over the date of Ezra's return – readers are referred to the commentaries.) This was a key period in rebuilding the shattered people. It appears not to have been an easy process, moving in fits and starts and needing much encouragement and sound leadership. By the end of the process, we have a renewed and reformulated Israel, the deal of the Davidic king projected forward into the hope of a future Messiah, the Law more important, the worship of God centre stage but no longer so heavily dependent on the Temple and the priesthood.

Nehemiah was a practical and active leader, ably complimenting the more studious and thoughtful Ezra. He had the talents to rise to a position of some prominence in the Persian capital before his visit to Jerusalem, and he used those talents to great effect. Uncompromising, always energetic, with a passion for God, he demonstrates many of the qualities of leadership.

Lessons we can learn

The significance of the book for us lies in several things:

- The story of rebuilding and restoration, not only of the city but of the people, reminding us that God is in the business of restoring waste places, be they communities or individuals. There are principles here that we can apply in our work of building the kingdom.
- The stress on the character of God, as revealed in the Law with the consequent necessity of holiness, a distinctive way of living among his people, distinguishing them from those around.
- The importance of prayer behind any significant and ongoing work of God.
- The need for repentance as part of living in relationship with God, repentance that is specific and that recognises the true nature of sin.
- The ultimate victory of God despite opposition and the inevitability of his plans coming to fulfilment. These plans continually move us forward to the coming of his Son.

Along the way there are many other things that we can learn. Nehemiah can be looked at for lessons in leadership. Much of the material in Nehemiah is written in the first person – Nehemiah's own diaries or memoirs. The remainder is written in the third person, but the material from Nehemiah's own pen is full of life and colour, giving personal insights into the man behind the activity. He is not perfect, but he remains a man of prayer, courage, faith and vision – all essential leadership qualities. There are many delightful cameo pictures of individuals who feature in God's plans. There are depictions of the joyous worship of God's people. There is a powerful testimony to the effectiveness and power of God's Word.

John Grayston

The person God uses

Day 221

Think about your own relationship with God. As you meet Nehemiah in today's reading, prepare to learn from his example.

Nehemiah 1:1–11 

First, Nehemiah is deeply sensitive; his sensitivity comes from a passionate concern for the glory and the honour of God. Seeing Jerusalem in ruins moves him deeply not simply out of love for his home, but out of love for his God. Until we can learn to share his passion for God's reputation; until we know what it is to weep for a world damaged by sin and failure, we can have no ministry.[1]

Secondly, he understands the character of God. His prayer demonstrates a sense of the holiness, awe, and majesty of God, but also a sense of the commitment of God to his purposes. Prayer can degenerate into a self-centred, self-indulgent reflection of our desires. The antidote is to keep our thoughts centred on the nature of God. When Jesus tells us to pray in his name,[2] he is encouraging us to make our request in line with the character and purpose of God as he has revealed it.

Thirdly, he is committed to prayer. His first reaction is to turn to God; all the evidence suggests that this is the prayer of a man who knows God and meets with him on a regular basis. It is a blend of intimacy, respect and urgency. All ministry has its root in prayer[3] and Nehemiah's prayers throughout the book are excellent models for us. It might be a good idea to have a pencil and notebook at hand as you read to record some of the lessons for yourself.

1 Luke 19:41
2 John 14:13,14
3 Luke 10:2,3; Eph 6:18–20

Reflect on the world in which we live. Ask God to lead you to some situation of concern. Then take Nehemiah's prayer and use it as the basis for your own prayer.

God's gracious hand

Day 222

Pause to thank God for all the times you have seen him at work in your life.

Nehemiah 2:1–20

A key phrase occurs in this reading. The gracious hand of God was upon Nehemiah (vs 8,18, see v 20). He knows that nothing that has happened has happened by chance. God has been in it all.

This introduces us to a further mark of Nehemiah – his faith. Clearly a man of action and determination, it would have been easy enough for him to have taken the credit for himself, but, like John the Baptist years later,[1] he knows that there is one greater than himself at work.

God's ultimate plans for Israel had suffered during the exile but now they move forward again. Nehemiah is a key figure; God in his grace uses us to fulfil his purposes, but it remains a work of his grace and not of our intelligence, skill, or energy. All that we achieve we achieve through the grace of God (v 20).

When the odds are stacked against us, we can draw strength from this. The work ahead of us may seem quite impossible but God can give the strength.[2] We receive that by faith, looking to him rather than our own resources. Nehemiah could encourage his friends and face his enemies in the knowledge that this was God's work, not his. The moment we assume that somehow it is ours we are in danger not only of missing the central truth but also of losing the only resource that will enable us to carry it through. This is, however, no excuse for inaction. God's grace will work through us, but this may mean the equivalent of a night reconnaissance and will demand courage, energy, time and sacrifice.

1 Matt 3:11,12
2 2 Cor 12:9; Phil 4:13

Review your diary for the next few days. Pray that you may see God's gracious hand at work in your activities.

A role for all

Day 223

This chapter may seem uninviting – a list of names and locations from a distant place and time. Pray that God helps you see beyond the details to things that will be of value to you.

Nehemiah 3:1–32 

Uninviting it may seem, but this chapter is full of fascinating insights. Why is it here?

It gives us a *sense of reality*. The work was undertaken by a diverse and interesting group of real people whose lives were in many ways similar to our own.

It gives us a *sense of history*. These people have personal, family and national histories. Insignificant though they may appear, each is important in the web of interconnected people and activity which forms the history of the covenant community. These events are rooted within the ongoing purpose of God.

It gives us a *sense of humanity*. These people shared our weaknesses and yet form a key part of God's purpose. Nobles refuse to get stuck in (v 5), while priests are happy to get involved in physical work as well as spiritual (vs 1,22,28). Goldsmiths and perfumers are willing to become stonemasons (vs 8,32), although it lay outside their area of expertise. Sometimes God will ask us to do things which are strange or unexpected,[1] things for which we may not feel qualified or gifted. That is not the time to stop and initiate a debate. It is the time to give ourselves wholeheartedly to the task. Some built near their homes, others built away from their homes – this was a community activity, not an exercise in self-interest. Nor was it a 'men only' activity – there was a place for the daughters of Shallum (v 12).

1 Exod 4:10–13; Jer 1:6–8

When God sets about restoring his people there is a role for all. Who, or what, might he be wanting to restore through you today?

Day 224

Facing opposition

Thank God for the privilege of working with him. Lay before him any work which you are undertaking at the moment, looking for his help and encouragement.

Nehemiah 4:1–23

Given the nature of a fallen world, the work of God will face opposition.[1] In Nehemiah's case there are strong vested interests which are threatened by the rebuilding of the wall. Opposition takes the form of ridicule and direct attack; there are positive attempts to dishearten those who are involved in the work. For those of us who struggle against the odds, who are wearied by the pressures of the work, the threat of losing heart is ever-present.

This means that the nature of our response to opposition is crucial. The first step is to turn the problem over to God. Any work which we undertake is God's work, not ours, and we can afford to let him fight the battles.[2] Nehemiah turns to God for he is the ultimate source of strength.[3] Prayer, however, is never an excuse not to plan and take practical steps – so he posts a guard. When there is trouble the people are to gather – and then God will fight for them (v 20).

We have a tendency either to pray or to act. We need to cultivate the ability to respond in both ways. Action without prayer leaves us vulnerable to the attacks of the enemy. Prayer without action is a form of escapism. Ultimately, however, the division is an artificial one; to act is to pray, and to pray is to act. They form a joint response to the needs, problems and dangers of the world. Prayer gives us the right perspective on things; action ensures that the work goes forward.

1 Matt 10:22
2 1 Sam 17:47; Rom 8:31
3 Isa 30:15

We can act without praying, although that is never wise, but we cannot pray honestly without being prepared for action.

Servant leader

Day 225

We all have some blind spots. Pray that as you read today God will enable you to see clearly.

Nehemiah 5:1–19 

One of the major causes of the exile was the exploitation of the poor by the rich.[1] If it seems strange that nothing has changed we have only to look at ourselves and our slowness to learn.

Nehemiah, like the prophets before him, cares deeply about the injustice. God's people are intended to make provision for the poor 'not to rip them off'.[2] Self-interest, however, takes over – as we see from the early days of the Israelite monarchy,[3] through the Corinthian church[4] to our own day. It denies our relationship to one another as God's people, it undermines our witness to the world and, above all, it brings dishonour to God's name.

Nehemiah, however, goes beyond justice. Reflecting the character of the God he serves, he is marked by a spirit of generosity. He is prepared to lend without interest (v 10), and to use his own resources to provide for the needs of others (vs 17,18). In this he is a contrast to the self-serving governors who had preceded him. It is a denial of kingdom values when leadership among the people of God becomes self-seeking rather than being marked by servanthood.[5]

What are we to make of the plea of the final verse? Nehemiah knows that God's covenant depends on grace. If there is an element of personal insecurity or his understanding is incomplete, it is encouraging to know that God can use those who do not always have it totally together. Perhaps, on the other hand, there is nothing wrong in recognising that we have done a good job and looking to God for his approval.

1 Amos 8:3,4
2 Lev 23:22
3 1 Sam 8:11–18
4 1 Cor 11:20,21
5 Mark 10:45

Think for a moment about your church, about your community. Where do you see injustice and one group using its power to deprive another of its rights? What should you do about it?

Facing opposition

Day 226

Reflect on times when you have faced opposition. Ask for a fresh sense of courage and purpose as you read.

Nehemiah 6:1–14

As the walls grow, so does the opposition. It is not an infallible mark of a true work of God that it is opposed – sometimes we invite opposition by our own foolish or thoughtless behaviour – but it is true that when we are doing God's work there will almost certainly be opposition. We have seen Nehemiah's initial response, now we see others'.

It comes from *outside*; it is persistent and marked by deception. Nehemiah confronts it head on and with characteristic bluntness. There are times when there is little value in beating around the bush. Attempts to be gentle and compassionate can end up as compromise.

It comes from *within*. Tobiah was a member of the covenant community (paradoxically his name means 'Yahweh [Jehovah] is good'), and this would have been painful enough, but the pressure from Noadiah and the rest of the prophets must have been almost unbearable. Leaders – from Moses,[1] through the prophets[2] to Jesus himself[3] – have always had to face the challenge of those who felt that they knew better and who claimed to understand God's ways better. There are few harder challenges. Religious faith becomes a way of gaining our ends rather than serving God's – something which can happen to the best and most committed of us. In the face of this, Nehemiah does all that can be done. Rather than arguing his case and justifying himself – a temptation we all face when under threat – he carries on with the work and offers the situation to God.

1 Num 12:2
2 Jer 28:15
3 John 8:48

Ultimately it is God's work and his responsibility to sort out those who oppose it. Ours is to carry on doing that to which he has called us.

Building godliness

Day 227

Prepare to be challenged about some of your priorities. Pray for the strength to face these challenges.

Nehemiah 6:15 – 7:3 

Two of the repeating themes of Nehemiah emerge again. The wall has been rebuilt with God's help, in a relatively short time. This has the effect at one level of silencing the opposition (6:15,16), although at another it remains unchanged (vs 17–19). There is danger in both the easy triumphalism that assumes that when God is at work nothing can go wrong, and the fear which comes from always looking at the opposition.

The opposition provides the second of the recurring themes. There is an important element to note here, which illuminates some of Nehemiah's later actions, and which can be instructive for us. At the heart of the opposition were some confused family relationships and loyalties. Mixed marriages later become a major issue for Nehemiah (10:30). When Jesus made the point that his followers were to place loyalty to him above family ties[1] he was not undermining the family, but recognising that it is very easy for family loyalties to get in the way of following God. Our aim should be to build relationships that will move us towards God rather than away from him – and while that does not mean exclusively Christian friendships it inevitably raises questions about the level of attachment to those who do not share our faith.

Hidden here is a marvellous cameo picture of the otherwise unknown Hananiah (7:2). There can be few more desirable testimonials than this. Integrity, a value which others can see, emerges from revering and honouring God in the hidden places of our lives. Our world looks for quick fixes and instant solutions – godliness is built slowly and steadily by giving time to God.

1 Matt 10:37–39

Pray that your relationship with God may have the same qualities as Hananiah's.

Day 228

The bigger picture

Pray for a renewed sense of your place in God's plans.

 *Nehemiah 7:4–7,66–73a*

Clearly progress had been slow in the nearly one hundred years since the first exiles had returned. Haggai may have had to rebuke the people for building their own houses in preference to the Temple,[1] but the work on houses seems to have been sporadic and incomplete. God's honour would not be vindicated by a rebuilt city with no inhabitants. In our world of rapidly growing cities, it is worth remembering how often the Bible sees the city as a place of life, energy and creativity, a place where God is to be found. To neglect ministry to the cities, often difficult places for Christian witness, is to miss something of God's heart.

The rest of the chapter looks back to the returning exiles. It repeats Ezra chapter 2 almost word for word. If we follow our inclination to pass over this as being of little interest, we shall miss something of importance. This group needed to see themselves in their historical context. They were part of the ongoing purpose of God, and this brought both privileges and responsibilities. Every generation, every community, every individual has a significant place in God's plans for the restoration of the world. People and events are connected in a way which our world with its concentration on the small, local, personal picture loses sight of. There is a bigger story, the story of God's redeeming work in the world, which passes from generation to generation and of which we too are part.

1 Hag 1:2,4

Think about the place which you and your Christian community have in the broader purposes of God. Where do you see the kingdom moving forward? Where are you conscious of links to others which show that God is at work? What have you received? What will you pass on?

Responding to the Word

Day 229

Thank God for the way he speaks through the Bible. Pray that you may be open to its message today.

Nehemiah 7:73b – 8:18 

This is a crucial incident in the rebuilding of the people. The early emphasis had been on the rebuilding of the Temple and the restoration of the worship followed by the rebuilding of the city. Now the time comes to remind the people of the centre of their faith – the revelation of God.

Nehemiah and Ezra know that unless the life of the community is firmly based on the Word of God, there is little hope of a successful long-term rebuilding. There needs to be a commitment to reading, understanding and living by the words of God.

There are many things that we could note with profit. The *commitment of the people* who stood for a long time listening to the reading (8:3). The *involvement of all ages* (8:2), which must have implications for our church life today, where the youngest and the oldest so often find themselves excluded. The *necessity of interpretation and application* (8:8) – preaching and teaching can be overrated as ways of learning but they can also be undervalued. Whatever means we use, the church has a responsibility to ensure that people of all ages have a good grounding in the Bible. The *response of the people* (8:9) to a Word which is living and active – here it brings conviction, as it often will. In it we see ourselves as in a mirror,[1] and we also see a holy God and his requirements. The gap is massive and pain will inevitably result (is there enough grief over sin in today's church?), but that is not the final word. Because that sorrow for sin leads to repentance and restored relationship with God there is a place for joy and celebration.

1 James 1:23

Spend some time celebrating the goodness and love of God.

Grace and holiness

Day 230

Pick up where you left off yesterday, praising God for his goodness.

 *Nehemiah 9:1–37*

Rejoicing in the goodness and the grace of God, has a reverse side. The initial response to the reading of the Law (8:9,10) was a correct one, but it needed to be set in a different context. The feasting and celebration of Tabernacles speak of God's redeeming love. Without that the activity we read of today would have been negative, self-condemnatory and destructive. Against the background of God's redeeming love, it becomes healing and restorative. It would be a profitable exercise to go through this chapter meditating on the character of God and its implications for our lives.

It is difficult to see exactly what happens in verses 5 and 6; the Levites' encouragement to praise suddenly moves into prayer, but whose? The Levites? Ezra (see NRSV, following the Septuagint)? Nehemiah (given the similarities with chapter 1)? It does not matter a great deal. The important feature is that the people recognise and acknowledge their failure which led to the exile. Everything is grounded in the character of God, a holy God who requires that his people live in certain ways and who will go to great lengths, in this case the exile, to bring about obedience. This should not be seen as harsh, but as the evidence of his love. In an age which has little time for authority, and when the standards by which Christians live are often indistinguishable from those of the world, we need to recognise both the grace and the holiness of God. Structure is not the mark of harsh authoritarianism – it is the inevitable result of loving concern. When we go wrong repentance is always the way back. It should never be heavy and depressing, but liberating and renewing.

Are there things in your life which displease God? Confess them now and seek his forgiveness.

Distinctive people

Day 231

As you prepare today, ask God to give you the grace and courage to respond to him.

Nehemiah 9:38; 10:28–39 

Conviction, based on a right understanding of God leads to repentance and confession which in turn leads to change. The key phrase is 'we assume responsibility' (vs 32,35). Confronted with the need for obedience, we tend to think of duty. But duty is imposed externally; responsibility is voluntarily accepted. The emphasis lies on the people's desire to respond. Any response which does not flow from a willing acceptance of God's call will fail.

The sound leadership of Ezra and Nehemiah is demonstrated in the way in which they simply lay before the people the Word of God and the character of God and then look for a response. Preaching which lays heavy demands on the listeners is rarely going to be productive, while that which opens possibilities and leaves God to do his work is more likely to produce lasting results.

Three key issues re-emerge: separation from the surrounding nations, Sabbath observance and social justice. Some of this may seem unimportant, but the significance is that the re-emerging Israel must remain distinct. All the pressures are towards conformity, as they are for us. If we are to be the witness that God wants to the standards and values of the kingdom, we have to maintain a distinctive lifestyle.[1]

The resolve of the people is costly. Unfortunately, it did not last, but there is every indication that they took it seriously (9:38; 10:29). Perhaps they didn't adequately assess the cost; more probably their failure illustrates the importance of the new covenant Jeremiah had prophesied a century and a half earlier.[2] Human resolve, however genuine, is not enough. We need the indwelling Spirit to make the difference.[3]

1 1 Pet 1:15
2 Jer 31:31–33
3 Rom 8:5–8

Pray that your church or fellowship may demonstrate a distinctive way of living.

Day 232 God-centred worship

Think back to the earlier chapters of Nehemiah. Thank God for the changes you have read about and the lessons you have learned.

 *Nehemiah 12:27–47*

People who were afraid, disillusioned and with little hope (2:17) can now rejoice in such a way that the sound is heard far away (v 43). This is the difference that pursuing a vision, with determination and purpose, can make. Nehemiah's own vision, sense of purpose and relationship with God have been fundamental to this change, but he has achieved it by winning the support of the people all the way along – all leaders please note!

This is one the great worship experiences of the Bible. Two large groups walking the newly-constructed walls, their sole object is to praise God. The culmination of worship at the Temple would have made for a thrilling experience. It was also a powerful witness to those who had earlier opposed the work. When God's people unite in thankfulness and praise directed towards the glory of God, others are bound to take notice. When our worship becomes self-indulgent and directed towards our needs rather than the glory of God, it becomes divisive rather than uniting. As we argue over forms of worship, the benefits of hymns or songs, the way we pray, the merits of guitar and organ – none of which presumably matter greatly to God who delights not in forms but in the praises of his people[1] – a bemused world looks on and marvels not at the greatness of our God but at the smallness of our minds. These verses show us what happens when the focus remains on God and what he has done; this way the people of God are united and the unbelievers challenged.

1 Ps 149:3,4

In the light of this reading think about your attitude to worship and that of your church or fellowship.

Changed people?

Day 233

Reflect on aspects of your life where you long to see change.

Nehemiah 13:1–31

My first experience of the pain of leadership came in my teens. We were on holiday in Devon when the word came through that one of the youth group had decided to relinquish her faith. After a brief family discussion my father, the pastor, headed back to Kent. Leadership, as Nehemiah discovered, is full of such pain. If we care about the lives of others, their failure will hurt.

The reality is that the chapter has a depressingly familiar ring. After the weeping of chapter 8; and the confession and dedication of chapter 9 we would hope for better things. No sooner does Nehemiah leave Jerusalem than the old patterns of behaviour emerge.

We should not be surprised. We, too, struggle to live godly lives in a sinful world and know that the path is not one of steady forward progress. The challenge for all is to keep the goal constantly in mind and, with the support of the Christian community[1] and the help of the indwelling Spirit,[2] to live in a disciplined manner. The special challenge for leaders is lovingly but determinedly to keep the goal before others. (We may feel that Nehemiah shows more determination than love!) What is the goal? In both Old Testament and New Testament terms it is to 'be holy because I ... am holy'.[3] As Christians with a New Testament perspective, it is to become like Jesus.[4] The God who used Nehemiah to rebuild a city and restore a people is in the same business today. We may sometimes feel that our lives or the lives of those we love are beyond any hope of restoration. This book, with its reminder that God is in the restoration business should encourage us.

1 1 Thess 5:11
2 Rom 8:12–17
3 Lev 19:2; 1 Pet 1:15,16
4 Rom 8:29

Give to God those things you want to change. Allow him to use your reading in Nehemiah to encourage you.

Privileges and responsibilities

For a good part of my working life I have been the pastor of a local church, speaking to people I knew. More recently, however, I have been a visiting speaker, addressing people I mostly do not know. This has its problems. What do you say to people when you do not know the joys and sorrows of individuals or the opportunities and problems facing the church? The conclusion I came to was that, while I might not know much about the congregation, since they were baptised Christians I could speak of the great hope to which God has called them and urge them to live lives worthy of this hope – exactly as Paul does in Ephesians!

Paul did not know the people to whom he wrote this letter. He had heard of their faith (1:15) and they had heard of his ministry (3:2), but he did not know them as he knew the Corinthians. Many scholars have seen Ephesians as more of a baptismal sermon in which 'we' who have been Christians some time welcome 'you' who have recently been saved into the privileges and responsibilities of the Christian family. I think the best way for us to 'hear' this letter is to return in imagination to the day of our baptism (or confirmation) and to imagine we are being addressed by a saintly old pastor (or bishop).

Summary of the letter

Paul begins with a solemn prayer of praise to God for all the benefits he has bestowed on us in Christ, from our election, through the forgiveness of our sins, to our final salvation of which the Holy Spirit and our baptism are the pledges. He extols God for his plan to bring healing and harmony to the whole universe in Christ (1:3–14). Then he tells us how he prays that we may know the hope to which we have been called and how it has been guaranteed to us by the resurrection and ascension of Christ (1:15–23), by the way we ourselves have been brought from death to life (2:1–10), and incorporated into the worldwide family of God

(2:11–22). He reminds us that the gospel is something that has been handed down to us by those who were Christians before us, often at the cost of imprisonment and even death (3:1–13), and he prays that we ourselves will take our place in that great company, fully confirmed in all the love of God (3:14–21).

As this part of the address reaches its climax we feel ourselves lifted up above the vicissitudes of everyday life and actually seated with Christ in heaven, able to see the world from his point of view, 'ransomed, healed, restored, forgiven'.

The second part of the address brings us firmly down to earth again. If that is our hope, how then shall we live? The old saint reminds us that as a church we are here to be a showcase of God's plan to reconcile the whole universe to himself and put an end to every proud division, and that through our ministers God has given us the grace we need to fulfil it (4:1–16). Getting very practical, he tells us that new life means a new lifestyle (4:17–32), and calls us away from society's obsession with sex and greed to live together as children of the light (5:1–20). The Christian life is not just for living at church but at home, and not in ideal homes but the homes we actually have (5:21–33). This is where many of our sinful divisions are nurtured, and this is where they are to be overcome in family relationships that demonstrate the character of Christ (6:1–9). Finally, like those newly baptised, we are sent out into the world 'to fight valiantly under his banner against sin, the world, and the devil', together with all Christ's faithful soldiers and servants (6:10–20).

Quieten your heart and let this uplifting letter reawaken your excitement at being a Christian.

Alastair Campbell

Day 234

Count your blessings

***'Thanks be to you, my Lord Jesus Christ, for all the benefits you have won for me'.*[1]**

 *Ephesians 1:1–14*

Ephesians begins with a majestic prayer of praise. Paul praises God for every spiritual blessing and then proceeds to list six of them. God has chosen us in Christ from all eternity (v 4); he has loved us and adopted us as his children (vs 5,6); he has redeemed and forgiven us (vs 7,8); he has let us into the secret of how he intends to bring healing to the whole universe (vs 9,10); he has made us his heirs, with great expectations for the future (vs 11,12, NIV marginal note); and he has sealed us with his Holy Spirit, to give us assurance now (vs 13,14).

This is not meant as a checklist of Christian doctrine but an act of worship, and the best way to let it have its way with us is to join in and pray it ourselves. Why not turn it into a responsive prayer with verse 3 as the repeated response? Begin by reading that verse aloud: 'Blessed be the God...' Then read out the first two blessings: 'He chose us...' (v 4), 'He predestined us...' (vs 5,6), and recite verse 3 again: 'Blessed be the God and Father...' Then move to the next two blessings: 'We have redemption...' (vs 7,8), 'He has made known to us the mystery...' (vs 9,10), and return again to the response, 'Blessed be the God...' Then the third pair (vs 11–14), and finish by reciting verse 3.

The phrase 'in the heavenly realms'[2] is not a reference to heaven as the place of God's dwelling, but to the 'unseen world of spiritual reality' (John Stott). The people of Paul's day were afraid of being influenced by unseen powers. Paul's use of the expression assures them and us that there is no place outside of Christ's rule and no power that can hurt us if we are united by faith with him.

1 Richard of Chichester, 1197–1253
2 Compare Eph 1:20; 2:6; 3:10; 6:12
3 Rom 8:31

'What, then, shall we say in response to this? If God is for us, who can be against us?'[3]

The secret of Christian obedience

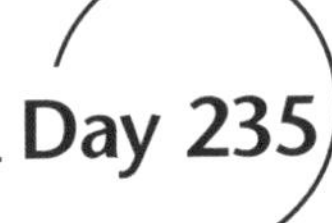

'Lord, open our eyes, that we may know how great is our inheritance, and how rich and privileged we are!'

Ephesians 1:15–23 

The best thing we can pray for Christians today is that they would know the hope to which God has called us all. This hope is vastly greater than personal immortality, and Paul is referring back to something for which he gave thanks in 1:9,10. God intends to 'bring all things in heaven and earth together under one head, even Christ'. When he does, there will be no grief, no war, no ethnic cleansing, no racial hatred. Men and women will live in harmony with each other and with Christ as Lord. The created universe will be set free from its bondage to decay.[1] The powers of sin and death will be finally defeated, and we shall be raised to life in a new heaven and a new earth, the home of righteousness.[2] This is not just wishful thinking but a hope grounded in the resurrection of Christ from the dead, an event that declares not just that Jesus is alive but that he has defeated every hostile power in the universe (vs 19–21).

The final verse of the chapter is hard to understand, but I take it that God is the one who 'fills everything in every way', or rather who is in the process of bringing the whole universe to completion. Christ is then the fullness of God, the one in whom God's love and power have been perfectly displayed (rather than the church being the fullness of Christ, as the NIV translators think). The church is, then, the body of Christ, charged with the task of making him visible to the world and working to bring about the reconciliation Jesus died to achieve. This is the calling which challenges us all, and the motivating power which tells us that the Christian hope makes everything possible and worthwhile.

1 Rom 8:21
2 2 Pet 3:13

Do you know any new Christians who need to grow? Or any old Christians who need encouragement? Pray that they may know the hope to which they have been called.

Sharing in Christ's victory

Day 236

'Hear what comfortable words our Saviour Christ says to all who truly turn to him.'[1]

Ephesians 2:1–10

The story comes from the darkest days of the kingdom of Judah.[2] Things were just about as bad as they could be: the city was in ruins, the Temple desecrated, the people in exile and their king had been in prison for thirty-seven years. Suddenly there is a gleam of light. The King of Babylon released Jehoiachin, spoke kindly to him, and gave him a seat of honour at his table. The old chronicler saw it as a sign that God had not finished with his people and that no situation is beyond the reach of his grace.

Paul says that God has treated us like that. He has released us from prison – from 'death row' in fact (vs 1–3). He has spoken 'comfortable words' to us and seated us at his table as a sign of our forgiveness and acceptance in Christ. Just as Jesus received sinners and ate with them, so the Lord's table still offers the peace of Christ to sinful men and women. But there is more. Paul says he has 'seated us with him in the heavenly realms', referring to our spiritual status as those who share in Christ's victory and authority. People in ancient times felt themselves to be insignificant beneath the mighty heavens and oppressed by the spiritual powers that dwelt in them. People today have similar feelings, even if we understand the universe differently. But Paul says that God has raised Jesus and seated him at his right hand far above every power (1:20,21). Whatever you imagine the universe to be like, Christ is its Lord. Whatever you think of evil, Christ has defeated it, and now he shares his victory with his people. Not that this victory is fully visible yet, but its effects are already enjoyed by God's people and one day will be evident to all. What a security and what an expectation are ours!

1 Book of Common Prayer
2 2 Kings 25:27–30

Celebrating the Lord's supper again, wonder afresh at how radically your status and prospects have changed.

Remember!

'Give us that due sense of all thy mercies, that our hearts may be unfeignedly thankful.'[1]

Ephesians 2:11–22

One of the disturbing characteristics of our time is that many people no longer have a strong sense of belonging to anything, whether it is a movement, a nation or the church of Jesus Christ. When combined with an 'evangelical' stress on personal religion this easily produces a consumer mentality even in Christians, who may then join in only when they feel like it and drift away when the responsibilities of membership become irksome. Paul, like a wise pastor, knows that this attitude stems from a failure of memory and the cure is to remind people who they are and tell the story of how they came to be.

Remember what you were (vs 11–13). You were rank outsiders and no-hopers, excluded from the people of God both by your own fault and through cultural and spiritual forces over which you had no control (vs 1–3).

Remember what God has done (vs 14–18). Through the cross Jesus has broken not only the barrier of sin which keeps us from a holy God, but also the barriers of all religious systems that separate us from one another. Religious traditions serve a good purpose if they nurture faith and identity, in which case they form a protective hedge around believers, but the hedge easily becomes a 'Berlin Wall' dividing people from one another and nurturing pride and suspicion.

Remember what you now are (vs 19–22). We are members of his family and also stones in his new temple. The first speaks of our belonging to him and to one another. The second makes clear that when we work together in mutual acceptance and practical sharing other people can see where God is to be found today.

1 Book of Common Prayer

What can we do to instill in new Christians a proper pride in belonging to God's people?

Day 238

God's multicoloured wisdom

'Lord, speak to me, that I may speak in living echoes of your tone.' [1]

 *Ephesians 3:1–13*

After the exposition of the gospel we have had in the last few days it comes as a surprise to find Paul talking about himself. Is he part of the gospel? In a sense he is, and so is any Christian leader. Whether we like it or not, pastors are called to flesh out Christian commitment for the whole church, and the story of our call and Christian experience is part of the reason people come to faith and stay in it (v 13). This will be part of the answer to the question we ended with yesterday.

Paul of course had a unique role in leading the whole church into being the inclusive community God wanted it to be (v 4) and a demonstration to all the powers in the universe of his plan to bring everything into unity in Christ (1:9–10). How does the church witness to the powers (v 10)? Not by shouting slogans in the streets[2] (since the powers are neither deaf nor afraid of noise!), but by its existence as an inclusive community. The evil powers are active in dividing the world along ethnic, religious and nationalist lines. Their power is seen in hatred, division, war and bigotry, and in rulers who promote such evils. Paul preaches the gospel, the unsearchable riches of Christ (v 8). People of every race believe and are welcomed into the church to form 'one great fellowship of love throughout the whole wide earth' according to the hymn writer J Oxenham. When the powers see this they know that their rule is at an end, just as in CS Lewis's *The Lion, the Witch and the Wardrobe*, the White Witch knows that her reign is ended when she sees the people partying together and celebrating Christmas.

1 Francis Ridley Havergal, 1836–79
2 Isa 42:2

What can you do to help make your church a more inclusive community?

A 'masterclass' in prayer

Day 239

'Lord, teach us to pray, as Paul prayed for his disciples.'

Ephesians 3:14–21

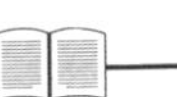

Some things are better caught than taught, and prayer is one of them. We may learn a lot about praying by joining a saint on their knees, and Paul invites us to follow him into the heavenly throne room. We learn:

To whom prayer is made. To the Father, who is to be sure my own dear Father, but who is also the Father of the whole universe. He hears the prayers and feels the groans of all creation and every order of being within it. As such he is able to do 'immeasurably more than all we ask or imagine' (v 20). We pray to a big God.

With whom prayer is made. Mention of the whole family in heaven and on earth reminds us that we do not pray alone. With the NIV, I take this to be a reference to the church triumphant in heaven and militant on earth, but it could also be referring to 'angels and archangels and all the company of heaven'. Either way, we are invited to join the orchestra and play along with 'all the saints' (v 18).

For what prayer is made. Our prayers for one another are often either vague requests for 'blessing' or specific requests for fairly trivial things. Paul asks for love and power, 'deep roots and firm foundations' (v 17 in the Revised English Bible). As Christ dwells in them, they will know his love. This in turn will give them strength to resist all the enticements and assaults of the surrounding culture. In this way they will stand firm as Christians and gradually be filled with all the fullness of God, and God himself will be glorified in his people.

Write out the prayer Paul would have prayed: 'Father, please strengthen my friend through your Spirit in his/her inner being. May s/he know your love' and so on. Then say this prayer for someone you know.

Day 240

A God-given people

'Lord, let my faith soar to see you on your throne; and then let it come down to earth to see you in your church.'

 *Ephesians 4:1–16*

In the first half of the letter Paul's concern was that we might 'know the hope to which he has called' us (1:18). Now he urges us to lead a life worthy of that calling (v 1). As the body of Christ (v 16) we are called to model the unity that is God's purpose for his whole creation (vs 4–6) through the exercise of humility, patience and love (vs 2–3), so that we can tell out God's truth in love to all men and women (v 15). That is the calling of the whole church and every member of it, and God has provided the church with the help she needs to fulfil her calling.

Christ has ascended, proclaiming his victory over all the powers of the universe, but he has not left his church orphaned or destitute. Rather, he has also descended through the Holy Spirit with gifts for his church. Where the Jews at Pentecost read Psalm 68 as the story of Moses going up to Sinai and returning with the Law, Paul reads it as a prophecy of Jesus ascending into heaven and returning through the Spirit to strengthen and equip his church. The church is to know that the gifts and graces she enjoys are the gifts of her risen and ascended Lord and no one else. Every Christian has a gift and calling (v 7), but Paul's focus here is not on the giftedness of the individual believer but the giftedness of the church. Christ has given certain people to his church who will help explain the Word of God and so equip other believers for their ministries and build up the whole body of Christ. The passage is a classic theological defence of the pre-eminence of the ministry of the Word.

Can you identify those in your church to whom Christ has given these gifts? Pray for grace to value them more and to allow their ministry of the Word to equip you for service.

Dressing as a Christian

Day 241

Reflect on the difference Christ has made to you and thank him for the work he has done in your life.

Ephesians 4:17–32 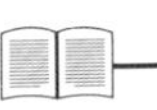

Paul addresses us as those who have been baptised, sealed with the Spirit (v 30), and tells us to 'dress' in garments appropriate to our new life. 'Put on the new self' (v 24). The word translated as 'self' does not refer to a new heart or a new spirit. It is not inward and spiritual; it is outward and behavioural. It is the person you are in relation to others, the role you play and the life you lead.

Only God can change the heart, but it is our responsibility to change our behaviour. Clothes, after all, are outward and visible things, and so are the things Paul calls us to put off and put on. We are to put off lying, anger, stealing and unwholesome talk, and we are to put on talk that is true and helpful to others. We are to be kind, compassionate and forgiving. Clothes are put on daily and by decision.

Most of us have some choice as to what we wear, and the same is true of how we behave. We can choose to lie or to speak the truth. We can choose to nurse our anger or give it up. We can choose to live for ourselves at the expense of others, or put ourselves out in the service of others. At some time or other most of us long to be better people, but we are mistaken if we think it is all down to God.

A new nature will show itself in new behaviour. But the reverse is also true. The way you behave shapes the person you become. The way to become a loving person is to do loving things. The way to become a truthful person is to practise telling the truth. The clothes we put on determine the person we present to the world. On Monday I dress for work and this helps me to fulfil my calling. On Saturday I put on casual clothes and spend the day feeling thoroughly lazy!

Spend some time examining your present attitudes and relationships, using the checklist provided by verses 25–32.

From lust to light

Day 242

'Lord, may the light of your love bring home to me my sin and point me to a way to overcome it.'

 *Ephesians 5:1–20*

We sometimes think that we are living in days of unprecedented immorality, but the smallest acquaintance with the wall paintings uncovered in the ruins of Pompeii will tell us that the explicit depiction of sexual activity and the lifestyle it encourages are nothing new. Equally, Paul's call to Christians to have nothing to do with fornication or pornography is as relevant today as it was when he wrote it, and sexual immorality exercises as big an attraction for Christians today as it did then.

It is worth noting the strategy Paul adopts in seeking to guard Christians from being led astray. He threatens them with the wrath of God and exclusion from his kingdom (vs 5,6), a neglected note in contemporary Christian preaching.[1] He challenges them to live up to their calling as children of the light (vs 8–14), perhaps using a line of a well-known baptismal hymn (v 14). Before that he reminds them of the love of Christ (vs 1,2), which does more to break down our stubborn hearts than any number of threats and challenges. Finally he offers them a practical alternative to a life of secret sin: the enjoyment of Christian fellowship (vs 19,20). Just as solitariness often leads to self-indulgence, so meetings where Christians tell one another the gospel story and take part in joyful thanksgiving are the occasion for the Holy Spirit to be poured into our hearts and make us want to lead a better life. The wise pastor will make use of all these approaches, warning, exhorting, reminding and providing a positive counterweight.

1 Rom 8:13; 1 Cor 6:9–10; Gal 5:21

In today's world, acceptance of sexual permissiveness is a 'wind of teaching' (4:14) that can easily blow Christians onto the rocks. Check your position and, if necessary, prepare to alter course!

With Christ in the real world

Day 243

'Christ be with me, Christ within me, Christ behind me, Christ before me, Christ beside me, Christ to win me, Christ to comfort and restore me.'[1]

Ephesians 5:21–33 

There are two ways to abuse this passage. One is to lay it on people as a one-size-fits-all handbook of married life and God's last word on marital relationships. The other is to discard it as a relic of first-century patriarchal society now happily (or hopefully?) left behind, at least in the Western world. It is of course a product of its time, but that is its strength, not its weakness.

On the one hand, it reflects a society where women were generally expected to take second place to men, especially their husbands, and men were expected to manage their households, including their wives. It never suggests that this is the perfect will of God, and gives us no warrant to seek to preserve or recreate such a society. On the other hand, it tells us to live out the way of Christ, not just at church but at home, and not in ideal homes, but in the homes we actually have, with all their tensions and imperfections arising from our culture or our own flawed personalities.

Paul sent his newly-baptised converts (v 26) back to their homes to live out their expected roles as husband or wife, but now with Christ's example before their eyes and his love in their hearts.[2] Many believers today struggle to live out their faith in less than ideal circumstances with rules they did not choose and partners they cannot change. Paul shows us how to find the resources in Christ to live for Christ in the place where we are.

1 St Patrick, c390–461
2 Mark 10:45

'Lord, give me the serenity to accept the things I cannot change, the courage to change the things I can, and the wisdom to know the difference' (Reinhold Niebuhr, 1892–1971).

Work out your salvation

Day 244

Recall God's purpose to reconcile all things in Christ and give thanks for every sign of this today.

Ephesians 6:1–9

People in Paul's day regarded a man's household as a mini-community consisting of himself, his wife, his children and his slaves, and believed that the well-being of the state as a whole depended on his proper conduct as husband, father and master. This way of thinking is reflected here and elsewhere in the New Testament[1] even if it is considerably modified under the influence of Christ in the direction of a greater mutuality.[2] But what is Paul's motive for adopting this household pattern at all?

Is he concerned about the personal fulfilment of the parties concerned, ie how to have a happy family? That might be our modern assumption, but there is little evidence to support that interpretation. Is he concerned for the preservation of the church's good name in society – that Christians are not seen as a threat to social order? That is the disappointed conclusion of many who read this passage and who see no sign that Paul seeks the emancipation of slaves: the church is settling down and wishes to live in peace with its neighbours. There may be an element of that, but perhaps there is an altogether higher motive.

God's purpose is to reconcile all things in Christ (1:10), and the church gives visible expression to this in the reconciliation of Jew and Gentile (3:6). In the same way, the Christian household, though structurally similar to those of its neighbours, can be the place where other ancient divisions are broken down: the gender gap (5:22–33), the generation gap (vs 1–4) and the division between social classes (vs 5–9). This will be achieved, not through a revolution, but by all parties living out their role with the example of Christ before their eyes.[3]

1 Col 3:18 – 4:1;1; Pet 2:18 – 3:7
2 Eph 5:2
3 1 Pet 2:19

Think how this might apply to other divisions in our society, such as that between married people and singles.

The body of Christ in full armour

Day 245

Take as your prayer the old hymn, 'Be thou my vision ...'.

Ephesians 6:10–24 

This passage, the climax of the letter, has often been misunderstood. We have been told either that it is about moral conflict or that it is about exorcism, whereas in fact it is about the whole mission of the church. Paul says to us:

Know your enemy! Not human rulers or hostile neighbours but the devil himself (v 11), and we see his handiwork in religious systems that keep millions ignorant of Christ and in the all-prevailing secularism of modern and postmodern society.

Know your orders! God is in a battle for the minds of men and women, and his chosen instrument to defeat the powers of evil is the church (3:10). The way we make the devil feel the power of the gospel is by preaching it to the people in his grip and demonstrating its power in our life together. As people see and believe, the powers lose ground, and the wounds we inflict are the souls we save and the communities of love we build.

Know your weapons! Despite a long tradition to the contrary, the armour of God does not consist of moral qualities so much as the gospel itself: the message of truth, righteousness, peace, faith and salvation. We are to clothe ourselves with it, know it, trust it and speak it out, wearing it like a shield and wielding it like a sword. This is addressed not just to the individual, but to the whole body of Christ. We are to stand together and pray for one another (v 18), and especially for those on the front lines. For Paul writes not from the sidelines but from the thick of the battle, despite his being in prison. Twice he requests prayer for courage to share the good news 'fearlessly' (vs 19,20).

Pray today for those you know who are in the forefront of the battle. Ask that their minds will be clothed with the gospel and their lives be an expression of it.

Day 246

'All the ends of the earth will fear him'

Let us 'lift up Christ before the world, and live so closely in him that others may see that there really is such a person as Jesus because some human being proves it by being like him'.[1]

Psalm 67

This psalm begins with the familiar words of the Aaronic blessing.[2] The writer knew the Scriptures and how to use them to enhance prayer and worship. What follows is a request for God to bless his people, but the perspective is a broader one – the reason for asking for God's blessing is so that God's name will be exalted, not just in Israel, but in all the nations of the world. For this to happen, the surrounding nations had to recognise God's greatness through the way he dealt with his people. Then they would see how he works in the world, and would begin to understand his salvation. Twice in the psalm we read, 'May all the peoples praise you' (vs 3,5), and once 'all the ends of the earth will fear him' (v 7). When they see his greatness, his justice, and his compassionate generosity, they too will be drawn to him in praise and reverent fear. Although the Israelites were God's own people, his concern for the world did not end there. He always longed for others beyond Israel to come to him.

How often do we meet in church, and enjoy praising and worshipping God together, asking him to bless us, without giving a thought to the people living around us who know nothing of our heavenly Father? How insular we are! God delights to bless his people, perhaps he expects more of us. Our experience of God is one of the ways he uses to reveal himself to those who know little about him, or who are simply not interested. If God cares so much about the non-Christian world, how can we afford to ignore it?

1 Betty Stam, CIM missionary, martyred 1935
2 Num 6:24–26

How about this for a goal? Showing love in an age of loneliness, giving witness in an age lacking standards and speaking simply of a wonderful Lord in an age that lacks a master.

Caring and compassionate

'What comes into our minds when we think about God is the most important thing about us.'[1]

Psalm 68 

This psalm is a celebration of God's greatness, power and majesty, probably written to be sung during a royal procession (vs 24–27). It enthuses that God has overcome his enemies, and no human can stand against him. God is all-powerful, he strikes fear into his enemies and scatters kings. There is a lovely picture of rugged mountains looking in envy at the mountains where God dwells. This God has thousands and thousands of chariots. The whole psalm is a declaration that God is almighty and all-victorious, and to be feared by all his enemies.

I find it easy enough to praise and worship such a wonderful God, but I find it more difficult to relate to him. In fact, he can seem quite intimidating, even frightening. So it is a relief to go back through the psalm and draw together some other strands of God's character.

After such a glorious introduction to a God who rides on the clouds (v 4), we read that God is a father to the fatherless and a defender of widows (v 5). He puts lonely people into families, and releases those who have been imprisoned (v 6). He refreshes his weary people, he provides for the poor (v 10), and he bears our burdens (v 19). And notice in that lovely description of the procession (vs 24–27) that it is the little tribe of Benjamin that leads all the singers, musicians and worshippers. Now I begin to see a God who cares about me, and with whom I can be in a loving relationship.

Perhaps too often we allow ourselves to see only one aspect of God, and forget the need to see the bigger picture. This psalm challenges me to remember God's greatness together with his compassion and care.

1 AW Tozer 1897–1963

Tell God about areas of weakness or need you are aware of in your life, and allow him to comfort you.

The Lord hears the needy

Day 248

Are you struggling with a difficult situation? Like David, tell God exactly how you feel.

 *Psalm 69*

As you read through this psalm, make a mental note of the feelings David expresses. You could start with despair, fear, helplessness... and so on throughout the psalm. David is in a particularly difficult and painful situation, and the only way he knows how to cope with it is to pour out all his feelings to God. In his intense distress, he doesn't pause to edit it, or to replace some of the strong words he uses – the words just tumble out. We too can pour out our distress to God when we feel overwhelmed by circumstances and, like David, by the injustice of it all. Because of his loyalty to God David has been shamed and feels totally isolated from his family and friends; rejected by those closest to him. The sheer injustice of it is summed up in verse 9: he is in trouble because of his zeal for God.

David knows where to look for help, however, even if it seems very slow in coming, so he asks God to deliver him, to pull him up out of the pit. And he can give good reasons why God should respond to him – he knows it is not because of his importance or status, but because of the goodness of God's love, and his great mercy (v 16). David knows that God is aware of his predicament, so he can now begin to relax in the certainty that God will act on his behalf. By the end of his prayer, although we do not know if David's circumstances have changed, his perspective has been so thoroughly turned round that he can praise God and thank him.

If you identify with David's struggles, do what he did. Pour out your heart to God, and your perspective may change too in quite unexpected ways.

Hurry up, Lord!

Day 249

'When the calm listing of requests and the courteous giving of proper thanks takes the place of the burdened prayer ... we should beware.'[1]

Psalm 70 

One of the things that draws me back to the psalms again and again is the honesty of the writers. They do not pretend to be anything other than who they really are. When addressing God, they simply pour out their hurting hearts. Surely we can take that as an invitation to do the same. Time and again, David and the other psalmists tell God about their despair, their fear, their grief and confusion, and they are not afraid of telling him what they think he should be doing about it.

Here in Psalm 70 David asks God to hurry up and do something! Hardly the appropriate way for a human being, albeit a king, to address the Almighty God, you might think.

The exact reason for David's urgency in this psalm is not known, but clearly he is in distress. Experience has taught him that there is only one thing to do in such situations and he is not afraid to tell God exactly what he wants him to do. He asks God to frustrate and overthrow the enemies who want to harm him, or kill him, or who mock his faithfulness to God. In contrast, he commends those who love God, who seek him and rejoice in him, and who want to see him exalted.

The hopelessness of his situation affects David deeply: he describes himself, a wealthy and powerful king, as 'poor and needy' (v 5). Yet his writings show that, however many times David felt bewildered and inadequate, he always knew that his help and deliverance came not from his wealth and influence, nor his army, but from his God.

1 AW Tozer 1897–1963

Tell God exactly how you feel. Be honest, and be yourself, and believe that he hears and cares.

Don't leave me now I'm old

Day 250

Are your current circumstances difficult to bear? Pray that God will help you to trust him today and always.

Psalm 71

This psalm is another prayer for help. Once again, we are allowed to enter the troubled heart and mind of someone who is in distress.

It seems that the writer is an older person, for there are several references to old age and grey hair (vs 9,18). He is concerned that he might be forgotten now that he no longer feels young, energetic and productive.

But he recognises some of the advantages of being older and more mature in his relationship with God. For example, there are more years to look back over now and see how faithful God has been (vs 5,6); more reasons to praise him (vs 17,22); and more experience to pass on to the next generation (v 18). Job also comments: 'Is not wisdom found among the aged? Does not long life bring understanding?'[1] In the psalm as a whole, the struggles and anxieties, real though they are, are outweighed by a strong sense of confidence in God (vs 14,20,21), and a desire to praise him (vs 17,22–24). This is not an unwillingness to face the facts – two sections of the psalm (vs 1–4,9–13) demonstrate the writer's anxiety and confusion – rather it is an honest recognition that even though God has allowed him to go through painful experiences (v 20), he will not leave him in distress, but will restore him again.

And here is another advantage of being more mature in his faith: the experience of how God has worked in his life over the years reassures him that he will not be abandoned now.

1 Job 12:12

As you reflect on your life, think of experiences in which God has been there for you. Then thank him.

God save the king!

Think of the qualities you would like to see in your national leader. How would he/she react to this psalm?

Psalm 72 

This prayer paints a very idealistic picture of a king and his reign, apparently a time of great peace, stability and contentment. Wouldn't it be good to live under leadership like this?

It is interesting to note what the writer considers to be the most significant features of such a perfect reign. High on his list are righteousness and justice, particularly for the poor, the needy and the oppressed. We know from experience that this is not how many of the world's most powerful leaders think today! From God's perspective, the poor, the oppressed and the needy must always be cared for and protected. The people should always expect justice from their leaders.

But the writer does not stop with concern for the poor. He also prays that the king will have a long and secure reign; in fact, he expresses it as an unending reign, where peace and prosperity go on for ever. The word used for 'prosperity' (vs 3,7) is *shalom*, meaning well-being and wholeness. This is much more than mere absence of war. His reign will extend over vast distances, taking in other, lesser kingdoms – not to dominate and exploit them, but for their own good! These people, too, will benefit from the 'shalom' of God. The king will be compassionate (vs 12–14), and he will have great wealth (vs 15–17), which will benefit all his people. What responsibility do the people have in this? They are to pray for the king (v 15).

Appropriately, the psalm ends with praise to the God who 'does marvellous deeds' (v 18). Great though the king may be, it is God who gives him wisdom, and allows him and his people to reign in peace and prosperity.

Spend a few minutes praying for the leaders of your country.

Day 252

When things get out of perspective

Reflect for a few minutes on ways in which God shows his love and care for you. Thank him again.

Psalm 73

Have you ever come to the point where everything seems to be the wrong way round? We live in a world where people who have no interest in God and who live life without moral values seem to be happy, wealthy and successful. They do not appear to have any worries or troubles. They defy God – yet nothing happens to them! So what is the point of trying to live as a Christian? Why don't we just give it all up and get a life!

If you have ever thought like that, you are not the first, as this psalm shows. It is easy to lose sight of the really important things in life, and allow ourselves to be envious of people who seem to have everything. Looking back to a time when he felt like that, the psalmist wisely begins by reminding himself of the truth: God is good to those who are pure in heart (v 1). Then he describes how his thoughts had run away with him and he had begun to doubt the value of living for God.

What turned his thinking around again? It was going into God's sanctuary and getting the bigger picture. Yes, these people seem to be doing very well now, but ultimately they will experience God's judgement. To live in relationship with God now and for all eternity, is infinitely better than a life of wealth, success or fame without God.

When you find yourself struggling like this, the psalmist's example is a good one to follow. Spend time in God's presence, and let him realign your thoughts and sort out your perspective. The last part of the psalm (vs 23–28) is a vivid contrast to the earlier struggles (vs 3–14). Now the writer understands the truth, and his confidence in God has been restored.

Use verses 23–26 as the basis for your own prayer of confidence in God.

Father, your name will endure for ever

Day 253

The Temple lies in ruins, but God our Father has not forgotten his people. Read this psalm when God seems silent, and remember that he does indeed love us.

Psalm 74 

What a sad, despairing opening sentence to this psalm: 'Why have you rejected us for ever, O God?' God's people had good reason to feel such despair, for everything had gone wrong. Enemies had attacked Jerusalem and had destroyed the Temple. The holy place, symbolic of God's presence, had been burned and smashed in an act of defiance against God. The people were devastated. How could God allow this to happen without doing anything about it? Why was God so angry with his people? Perhaps the hardest part was that God seemed to be silent. There were no prophets to explain God's actions. Everything seemed hopeless, yet God did nothing. Could he have forgotten, or even rejected, his chosen people? It was unthinkable, but was it true?

Have you ever felt like this? Maybe you have been in a difficult situation where you felt confused and hurt, and even though you tried to pray, God was silent. You wondered if he was angry with you, and you felt unable to change the situation.

Sometimes it helps to look back at what God has done in the past. In this psalm the writer turns away from the current disaster, and remembers how God redeemed his people, overcame their enemies, and cared for them (vs 12–17). Then he goes back to the present crisis, but with a different attitude. He still pleads for God's help, but 'Why?' is no longer such an urgent question. It doesn't sound so hopeless. The situation has not changed, but his attitude has. God no longer seems absent or silent, and it feels as if trust is being restored.

Think back over your life, and thank God for the different ways he has helped you in difficult situations.

God is in control!

Day 254

When you watch the news or read the newspapers, do you ever wonder whether God really is in control? Never doubt his promises.

Psalm 75

When we watch the news these days, it may seem that everything is out of control. We see violence against the vulnerable; cruel wars and brutal crimes, and perpetrators who seem (literally) to get away with murder. Sometimes we ask ourselves where we might find God in all this. Psalm 75 is a response to just such a question, and encourages us to see world events from God's perspective.

The psalm was probably a formal liturgy used in worship to remind the people that God is the one who rules over everything that happens. So, appropriately, the psalm begins with thanks and recognition of God's wonderful deeds in the past. We then hear God's voice reminding us that he is the one who orders the world and its events and who gives fair and just judgement. When it seems that everything we know is being shaken and challenged, God holds it firmly, and prevents it from collapsing. He warns the arrogant not to boast, and the wicked not to be defiant towards his rule, for they are powerless against him. Only God can allow anyone to rise in status and power: he can just as easily bring down those who think they are important. God will bring judgement, pictured here as the cup of his anger which the wicked have no option but to drink in its entirety. No wonder the writer responds with praise and states his intention to go on declaring this truth.

We may still be left with questions about why God does not act more quickly and decisively in certain situations, but the central and fundamental truth revealed in this psalm is that God is the one who has ultimate control of all that happens in this world.

Pray about a situation that is currently being highlighted in the news, remembering God's ultimate control over it.

God will judge all world powers

Day 255

Think of a national or international situation in which God's power has been evident. Praise him.

Psalm 76 

Imagine a huge, powerful army surrounding your city, intending to attack and destroy. Everyone in the city is terrified, fearing the worst. The army attacks, and, against all the odds, is soundly defeated. Everyone knows that the city could not have been saved without the help of God. That is the context in which this psalm was written. God had delivered them from their enemy, and now the people are full of praise. Jerusalem was God's stronghold, and weapons are useless against him. No one can defeat a city if God is protecting it.

Then we are given a broader perspective. Yes, God is the protector of Jerusalem, but he is much more than that. Many who raised their hands against him learned how ineffective they were against such a majestic God. He is the one who can control and judge great world powers, who protects the oppressed and stops the oppressor. He strikes fear into the hearts of evil rulers, and they hold back, in awe of God. The nations around Israel bring tribute to 'the One to be feared', whose power and greatness they affirm.

Perhaps, like me, you find it difficult to believe that this can be true in our world today. In 1989, I sat in Manila listening to the BBC World Service, and heard the incredible news that the Berlin Wall was being broken down. I was deeply moved. I had prayed for this for years, but I had not really believed it could happen. Sometimes we have to make a choice to believe, even in the face of what seems to be evidence against it, that God is the judge of all the nations, and he acts decisively in his time.

Pray for God to bring justice for the oppressed in a nation about which you are concerned – and believe that he can!

Where are you, God?

Day 256

Do you ever doubt your faith? Where do you turn for help?

 *Psalm 77*

There are times in our Christian experience when God seems far away. He does not respond to our prayers; our distress does not appear to move him, and we even begin to wonder if we are losing our faith. This is not a new phenomenon, and this psalm expresses it very poignantly. You may be familiar with these symptoms too: sleepless nights, emotional pain, and doubt about whether God loves you any more. The low point comes when we find ourselves asking the questions of verses 7–9. Has God rejected his people? Has his love for us ended? Has he forgotten what he promised? With the benefit of objectivity we know that unfailing love cannot fail, and God does not break his promises, but in the pain and distress of doubt, objectivity is a rare luxury. To feel that God has turned his back on us is a most painful experience for a Christian.

Is there a solution? There is rarely a 'quick fix', though that is what most of us would like. Simplistic answers are no help, however well meaning. The writer's solution was to remind himself of what God had done for his people over the years. Maybe that would restore his perspective and ease his pain.

Tantalisingly, the psalm ends without any resolution to the problem. We are not told whether he found an answer to his struggle. Perhaps that is to remind us that there is no standard solution: each of us needs to spend time alone with God to hear how he will speak into our particular situation. We may have to wait, however impatiently, for God may want to teach us patience and trust. And we will probably find the support and encouragement of a trusted Christian friend invaluable.

Are there painful areas of doubt in your life? Ask for God's help to work through them.

Learning from the past

Day 257

'Those who cannot remember the past are condemned to repeat it.'[1] Pray for wisdom.

Psalm 78 

History was the subject I disliked most at school, and I gave it up at the first opportunity. Only later did I understand what a foolish decision I had made. However unimaginatively it may be taught, the study of history is indispensable if we are to understand the present in the context of the past, and learn from mistakes that have been made.

This psalm makes it very clear that the Israelites did not learn from their history, and it is a challenge to them to look at how their forefathers had behaved and choose not to follow the same destructive patterns. Over and over again, they had rebelled against their loving and caring God, and had been deliberately disobedient. God punished them, and then forgave them and showed them his love again. But again they rebelled... and so it went on. Generation after generation suffered God's judgement because they did not learn the lessons that the psalm sets out so clearly.

We might say that they were 'slow learners', but before we are too critical, we need to be willing to ask questions about our own Christian lives. The philosopher Socrates, living five centuries before Christ, said, 'The unexamined life is not worth living', so the idea is not a new one. As busy Christians, how often do we take time to reflect quietly in God's presence, asking him to show us where he has been at work, or where we have acted unwisely? Without regular times of reflection, we miss seeing so much of what God is doing in our lives and in our world, and we may go on making mistakes that could have been avoided.

1 George Santayana, 1863–1952

Spend a few minutes in silence, reflecting on the day, or the week. Ask God to show you what he wants you to learn.

Day 258 God, how could you let this happen?

God disciplines his people, but he does so for our ultimate good. Talk to him about any discipline you are experiencing at present.

Psalm 79

In 587 BC the armies of Nebuchadnezzar attacked Jerusalem and overcame it. In a horrific battle many people were killed, others were taken into exile, and the rest were left in Jerusalem to live surrounded by constant reminders of their humiliation. Their beautiful city was ruined. They had lost family and friends to death or to exile. The Temple of God had been defiled. How could God have allowed this to happen? They pour out to God, with total honesty, their heartfelt despair at the brutality and destruction they have seen.

None of this should have come as a shock to them, for prophets like Jeremiah had been warning them for years about the danger of their complacency.[1] They had refused to listen, even mocking the prophets for their pessimistic message. Now, too late, they understand that this is God's judgement, and they plead for forgiveness. In spite of what has happened, they still cling to God: they are still his chosen people. They can even look forward to praising God again in the future, when he will act for them. In spite of it all, they choose to trust God.

God did not judge his people on a whim. Perhaps it was the only way he could get their attention and turn them back to love and serve him. Paradoxically, it was because he loved them that he punished them so severely. After all, he could have just given up on them.

In the New Testament we are reminded that God's discipline is a sign of his love.[2] He wants us to take seriously his call to obedience and holy living, to become more like Christ. There is no better way to live.

1 Eg Jer 18:11–12; Amos 9:8–10
2 Heb 12:5–11; Rev 3:19

Is there anything that God has been saying to you recently that you have not been taking seriously? What action do you need to take?

'Restore us, O Lord God Almighty'

Day 259

***'The raw, desperate cry of honesty penetrates the heavens immediately; the answer definitely will come – it is just the mode of transport which is not guaranteed.*[1]**

Psalm 80 

Once again God's people have found themselves in severe difficulty. Defeat has left them defenceless against their enemies, who mock them in their vulnerability. This has caused them great grief and sorrow – 'tears by the bowlful' (v 5). They know their history: they know how God protected and cared for his people in the past, but now he seems to have abandoned them. This is the worst thing that could possibly happen. Prayer is little comfort, for the only response to their prayers seems to be God's smouldering anger. All they can do is cry out to God for help. Three times they pray virtually the same prayer (vs 3,7,19), differing only in the increasing intensity with which they address God. The prayer is for God to restore them, and to show them his favour once again. The restoration for which they are pleading is not just for the physical damage: it is also spiritual restoration. They long for God to bring them back to himself. Maybe their experience of God's anger made them afraid to come back to him, or maybe they simply felt unable to turn to him in their own strength. They knew they needed his help. Without him life was very different from the old days when they were so aware of his presence.

We all go through phases in our Christian lives when God seems far away, and when we feel that we have lost the spiritual vitality we once had. Maybe we feel afraid that God is angry with us, or we may simply not know what to do. But God longs for us to turn back to him, and ask to be restored in his love. Then, in love, he runs to embrace us, as the waiting father welcomed home the prodigal son.[2]

1 Rachel Hickson, evangelist and speaker
2 Luke 15:20–24

Do you need God's restoration? Take some time to tell him what you long for.

Looking for answers

After a period of high-profile ministry and controversy, Jesus' aim now is to help his disciples to understand more deeply some of the issues lying behind the controversies they had just witnessed, and learn some lessons which would help them in the future direction of their ministry.

Perhaps we come to our daily readings a bit bruised and battered from personal experience of controversy. Or we may be incensed at something that has happened in the world around us which we have read about or seen in the media.

One of the first things we need to learn is that nothing is ever as black or white as it may at first appear, and we should beware of taking sides or jumping to conclusions with undue haste. Something we would do well to emulate is Jesus' frequent (and very Jewish) practice of asking questions, and even answering a question with a question – see for example 12:41,42. This both encourages further thought to prevent premature conclusions, and helps to clarify the inner motives that sometimes lie behind the original question. Hebraic spirituality is often worked out and expressed in this way. Christian spirituality is often fearful of questions, seeing them as a sign of doubt rather than faith.

In his book *Celebrating Life*, Chief Rabbi Jonathan Sacks recounts the following conversation between the Nobel prize-winning physicist Isidore Rabi and his mother: 'My mother made me a scientist without ever knowing it. Every other child would come back from school and be asked, "What did you learn today?" But my mother used to ask a different question. "Izzy", she always said, "did you ask a good question today?" That made the difference. Asking good questions made me a scientist'. Sacks continues, 'The greatest prophets asked questions of God ... Faith is not opposed to doubt. What it is opposed to is the shallow certainty that what we understand is all there is'.

John Fieldsend

Transparent living

Day 260

'What we are is plain to God, and I hope it is also plain to your conscience'.[1] 'Lord, I pray that I may learn to live this way more and more. Amen.'

Luke 12:1–12 

Some of the important issues being debated in our time are all about open government. They concern freedom of information and the exposure of sleaze. We fear that information about ourselves, ranging from our credit-worthiness to our political persuasions, is being stored on some remote computer to which we have no access. We don't know what is being said about us or what might be held against us. But what about our own 'secret computers'? What about those unworthy thoughts, those snide criticisms, those selfish ambitions, those censored pictures we store away in our own minds? They are, of course, open to God[2] and we can just about cope with that, but what if they were 'to be proclaimed from the rooftops'?[3] Yet even though they are not, they do in fact influence our own personal development; they do affect our ability to relate to others, and they do affect the quality of our discipleship.[4]

When we realise how much God loves us and how greatly he values us, our greatest desire will be that his Holy Spirit may do his refining work in our lives.

1 2 Cor 5:11
2 John 2:25
2 Matt 10:27
3 Matt 15:19
4 Ps 19:14

'May the words of my mouth and the meditation of my heart be pleasing in your sight, O Lord, my Rock and my Redeemer.'[4]

The heart of the matter

Day 261

'Freely you have received, freely give.'[1] 'Lord, prepare my heart that this may be true of me.'

 *Luke 12:13–21*

How would Jesus have told this parable today? Would he have spoken about European wheat and butter mountains and wine lakes? Or might he have told of selling our unprofitable shares and buying more profitable savings options, or opening bigger and better Internet bank accounts? Of course responsible stewardship is not the real issue. After all, in Egypt Joseph was praised and promoted for his well-planned grain storage programme! As so often in life, the 'why' is more important than the 'what'.

So what lay behind Jesus' response to this man's request? Matters of justice feature strongly in the Scriptures. But Jesus could see that beyond a genuine desire for a just settlement lay a greedy heart, and it was to this that Jesus addressed his parable. Jesus could easily have settled this dispute with a wisdom greater even than that of Solomon's when he was faced with a seemingly intractable conflict. Yet he knew that this would not have dealt with this man's deeper need for a change of heart.

All too easily we evangelicals can be needlessly guilt-ridden by success in material things because we make a false distinction between what we think is 'spiritual' and what is 'material'. This man's bumper harvest obviously needed wise stewardship, which rightly would have included best business practice. It was not for this that Jesus called him a fool, but for his self-centredness ('and I'll say to myself') and for his greed ('eat, drink and be merry').[2] In this sense he epitomised the well-worn description of the 'self-made man who worshipped his creator'. A good way towards a balanced understanding of this parable is to read it alongside another 'business-based' parable, that of the servants who were commended for wise financial stewardship of resources entrusted to them.[3]

1 Matt 10:8
2 1 Cor 15:32
3 Luke 19:12–22
4 1 Tim 6:18

'Lord, thank you for your overwhelming goodness. Help me to do good, to be rich in good deeds, to be generous and willing to share.'[4]

The antidote to worry

Day 262

'Father, show me the difference between right concern and paralysing anxiety.'

Luke 12:22–34 

I remember a poster caption that used to be popular a few years ago. It read, 'If you are not worried, it just proves that you don't realise how bad things really are!'.

But is a 'head-in-the-sand' attitude the only alternative to worry? Nowhere are we promised a life that is free from times of testing and difficulty. In yesterday's reading we saw that only a fool would think he could plan a life of constant ease, drinking and merriment. A bit of stocktaking and inventory-checking might well ease the worries in our lives.

After meditating on this passage for a while, make a list of your major possessions, important desires, aims and objectives in your life. Then ask about each item: 'Why do I possess this? Why do I desire that? Does it bring me peace or is it a source of anxiety? Does it help me focus on a 'kingdom lifestyle' or does it draw my focus away from Jesus?

Don't be too 'super-spiritual' about this exercise. If Jesus taught us to pray that his kingdom might come on earth, then he is not against material possessions. In this passage he counsels us to be more spiritually-minded, but to look around the created order and see there the evidences of his fatherly care and provision.

Perhaps the real issue is not so much our possessions and desires but our attitude towards them. If we see them as 'our treasures' they will become a source of anxiety. But if they can become 'tools for building the kingdom' then we can safely place our hearts where our real treasure lies.

'Not for ever by still waters would we idly rest and stay, but would smite the living fountains from the rocks along our way' (L M Willis and others).

Service in the kingdom

Day 263

'Lord, I want to open myself to you to learn more about being a true servant of yours.'

 *Luke 12:35–48*

Our meditations over the past two days will have prepared us for service. Two days ago we stripped off the mirage of complacency and self-gratification and yesterday the agony of destructive and paralysing anxiety. Now, hopefully, we are better prepared for a creative servant-lifestyle. But the 'God of surprises' so often turns the tables on us. Just when we are prepared to serve the Lord, we find that in fact he is serving us. That should not surprise us, because servanthood, as well as kingship, is his very nature.[1] He is the servant-king *par excellence*. In another act of service, after Jesus had washed his disciples' feet he told them that this was an example that they should follow.[2]

Servanthood is at the heart of the gospel. Paul saw his evangelism as a servant ministry for which he continually gave thanks,[3] and the Macedonian churches pleaded with him that they might have a share in the service of giving.[4]

How may we deal with our hurt when an act of service on our part is seemingly ignored, and not met with the appreciation and gratitude we might have expected? One way might be to thank God for the opportunity to serve and count it a privilege to have done so, and to rest in the assurance that God has not let it slip by unnoticed. He will reward us in his own inimitable way, which is to provide for us even greater opportunities of service!

1 Mark 10:45; Isa 42:1
2 John 13:15
3 1 Thess 1:2; 2:13
4 2 Cor 8:4
5 David Winter, *What's in a word?*, BRF

'We are called to serve – to serve others in their need ... Our example is the one who came "not to be served but to serve". And like his, our service will be costly'.[5]

Counting the cost

Day 264

'Lord, even though I do not know what this day will hold, prepare me to follow you into the unknown future.'

Luke 12:49–59 

Earlier (12:22–34) we were encouraged not to worry about the details of our daily living. In his goodness God withholds from us the knowledge of what the future may bring. But Jesus did not have this protection. He knew from early times why he had come, what his life was for and what his end would be. Though daily he had the inner resources to live his life fully for others,[1] even for him there were times of great foreboding and deep agony.[2]

That we may better understand this passage we need to realise that in Hebraic idiom the immediate result of an action is often expressed as though this was its original intention. This is especially seen to be true of God, for if it were less, it would seem that his omnipotence was being called into question.[3] However, the Hebraic mind is not afraid of seeing the truth in terms of holding opposites in a constructive tension.[4] Gospel presentation can lead to division, even though its ultimate aim is one of reconciliation.

Jesus experienced his share of rejection and became the focus of division within his own family,[5] and we must not think that we can escape it. However, we can sometimes all too easily use this to justify our own insensitivity or inconsistency in the way we witness and relate to those closest to us. We should not court conflict, or even assume that it is inevitable. In fact Paul counsels Timothy that Christians, and especially their leaders, should, as far as possible, live lives that gain the respect of their unbelieving neighbours.[6]

1 John 13:3
2 Luke 22:44
3 Matt 13:14
4 Luke 1:17
5 John 7:3–9
6 1 Tim 3:7

'Thank you, Lord, that my true life is now in Christ. Help me day by day to know the reality of what that means.'

Day 265

Daily repentance

'Well done is better than well said.'[1]

Luke 13:1–9

Many of us love to engage in a good theological discussion and enter into the finer points of biblical interpretation. Even within our own evangelical community, where we basically agree on the inspiration of Scripture, we allow our differences of interpretation to lead to lively and sometimes heated debates. If our search for greater understanding of the Scriptures leads us to a fuller response to God's hand upon us, that is good, but all too easily we put ourselves up as arbiters over Scripture rather than putting our lives under its searching call to continual repentance and new life.

Repentance, as a continual change of heart and mind, leading to continuing realignment of our lives under the guidance of the Holy Spirit, must be central to our lifestyle. We know that repentance does not end with our conversion. We may be prepared for and expect God's hand of discipline when we stray from his path.[2] But if we are really sensitive to our condition, then even in the midst of gratitude for God's overwhelming blessings, heartfelt repentance will not be far away.[3] How would you have responded, if you had been in Peter's place, when the Lord gave him that superabundant catch of fish? I think I would have been overwhelmed with gratitude. I would have made sure that Jesus had a permanent invitation for a place in my crew. But would it have led me, as it obviously led Peter, to an overbearing sense of my sinfulness? For Peter that new appreciation of who Jesus really was led him also to a new realisation of who he was, a sinner unworthy of the least of God's mercies, becoming the recipient of the richest of his blessings.

1 Benjamin Franklin, 1706–90
2 Heb 12:8
3 Rom 2:4

'Lord, thank you that you haven't finished with me yet. Help me to believe that day by day I am being transformed into the likeness of Jesus Christ. Amen.'

Sabbath was made for man

Day 266

'Lord, renew my mind that I may be able to test and approve your good, pleasing and perfect will.'[1]

Luke 13:10–17 

Correct Sabbath observance was a constant source of friction between Jesus and the religious authorities of his day, and that conflict has seldom been far below the surface in either church or synagogue throughout the succeeding centuries. In our own time it has been the source of often heated debate. Frequently, even when we agree on principles, we argue over their application. As regards the Sabbath the principle was not in dispute.[2]

But what constitutes work? The Jewish leadership had its own agreed priorities and exceptions.[3] Jesus wanted to get beyond these minutiae in order to develop the real principle.[4] He was so radical about this that in John 5:17 he appeared to be questioning the very root of the principle. What lay behind this? In the Genesis account God had finished his work of creation. It was perfect: there was nothing to be added or taken away. Hence God rested. However in his acts of healing Jesus is concerned to work out his Father's loving purpose for the re-creation, and restoration of a fallen world. Nowhere is it suggested that either God or we take time off from doing acts of mercy, loving kindness or evangelistic witness.

We have just read that the people were delighted with the wonderful things Jesus was doing, and later in this Gospel we shall read that the people 'hung on his words' (19:48). Can this help us toward living lives of positive and creative witness that point others to see God in a new way?

1 Rom 12:2
2 Exod 20:8
3 John 7:22; Matt 12:11
4 Mark 2:27
5 Matt 5:16

'Let your light shine before men, that they may see your good deeds and praise your Father in heaven.'[5]

What will I say to the King?

Day 267

'Lord, prepare my heart, that every day I may wonder at your gift of new life in your kingdom.'

 *Luke 13:18–30*

The two kingdom parables speak about the quiet growth of the kingdom as it permeates society, and as such Luke uses it to introduce Jesus' challenge regarding entry into that kingdom. Jesus takes what seems to be a rather arid and academic question about salvation and turns it into an urgent challenge about the eternal destiny of his hearers.

We should never allow biblical exposition to degenerate into mere philosophical speculation. Good exposition always has a sharp cutting edge of practical application.

'Make every effort ...'. But isn't salvation a gift of grace? Is it not true that Jesus has done it all and there is nothing we can or need to add to his saving work? Yes, but the repentance and faith-gate by which we enter is not a matter of mere intellectual and doctrinal assent but a total life-changing experience which involves hard-working co-operation with the Holy Spirit. We need to bear in mind the three tenses of salvation, 'I have been saved, I am being saved, I will be saved.'[1]

Rather than enter into the sometimes speculative 'once saved – always saved' debate, we can rejoice in the wonder of assurance which the Scriptures teach.[2] However, we should not be complacent. We must seriously heed those Scriptures that warn us against allowing God's wonderful gift of assurance of eternal life to degenerate into mere complacency about the way we live.[3]

1 Eph 2:5,8; 1 Cor 1:18; Matt 24:13
2 Eg John 10:28
3 Eg Heb 12:14
4 Isa 6:5

'Woe to me!' I cried. 'I am ruined! For I am a man of unclean lips, and I live among a people of unclean lips, my eyes have seen the King, the Lord Almighty.'[4]

Steadfast in purpose

Day 268

'God of all grace, thank you that you have called me to your eternal glory in Christ. Please make me ever strong, firm and steadfast in my calling.'[1]

Luke 13:31–35 

It is not uncommon for the opponents of God's people to try to discredit them, either by making them look cowardly in the face of opposition or by diverting their energies in ways other than for God's purposes.[2] On the other hand, we are not called to make martyrs of ourselves for no purpose, and to 'live to fight another day' may not necessarily be wrong.[3] Jesus knew that he was to offer up his life in Jerusalem and he set his face to fulfil that purpose.

Jesus would have been well-versed in the book of Lamentations, and he may well have had this in mind as he wept over the city. But we should not read this as a blanket condemnation. 'Jerusalem' here is used as a shorthand term for Israel's corporate leadership, in very much the same way as we might hear on the radio or television news broadcasts 'London says' or 'Washington says' when referring to an official government statement. However, the awesome truth is that when any leadership fails to live up to its calling, the whole body suffers,[4] and Jerusalem was about to face utter destruction at the hands of the Roman legions.

Let us pray daily for the peace of Jerusalem, and eagerly look forward to the day when all Israel shall truly say, 'Blessed is he who comes in the name of the Lord'.

1 1 Pet 5:10
2 Neh 6:2,10–12
3 Matt 10:23
4 Ezek 34:1–6
5 Rev 22:20,21

'He who testifies to these things says, "Yes, I am coming soon." Amen. Come, Lord Jesus. The grace of the Lord Jesus be with God's people. Amen.'[5]

What sort of man is this?

Imagine your feelings if you were one of Jesus' disciples. You never quite knew what he would say. His remarks were usually unpredictable and often confrontational. He could tell wonderful stories but he could also point out his host's discourtesy. He might deliberately pick an argument, particularly about the Sabbath. On the other hand someone might unexpectedly appear through a hole in the roof. Life was rarely dull but it could be embarrassing. The Master could say something that might mean leaving town in a hurry. Sometimes you might hear the same story several times, but on other occasions a chance remark could produce something startlingly new. Worst of all, he might say something so outrageous that you felt like giving up the very idea of being a disciple.

In these chapters we also see overwhelming tenderness in the stories about the waiting father and the generous host who compels the inhabitants of the highways and byways to enjoy his feast. The Jesus who seems to alternate between the stern and the tender is not fickle: both aspects of his ministry stream from a single, burning source of holy love.

Responding to God's grace

The overwhelming theme of this part of Luke is the grace of God and the difficulty we have in responding to it. God graciously gives the Sabbath yet people turn it into a minefield of prohibition. God gives a lavish banquet, yet we will not enjoy it. Ten men with leprosy are healed and only one is grateful. In each story the grace of God gets strangled and perverted. Either we are blind to God's grace or we keep it to ourselves. To all this Jesus says, 'Freely you have received, freely give'. At the end of our readings is a warning that God's judgement cannot be indefinitely delayed. The future will break in upon us without warning, so Jesus encourages us to live now in the light of the future.

Peter Kimber

Sabbath observance

Day 269

Prepare to be disturbed. Ask God to shake you out of your rut.

Luke 14:1–14 

Do you enjoy Sundays? No, tell the truth: do you eagerly look forward to them and look back on their passing with regret? God intended that the Sabbath would be a delight[1] yet it was often a matter for argument about nit-picking trivialities and criticism of others. It was also a source of pride for those who devoutly observed the rules. Once legalism sets in there is no end to the hair-splitting that establishes orthodoxy. Jesus' Sabbath observance became the test of his acceptability – not the intrinsic truth of his teaching nor the miracles he performed. His critics were poised to condemn but were unwilling to debate: Jesus, on the other hand, was more concerned to meet human need than to conform to a false convention.

Why does Jesus bother about so trivial a matter as where people like to sit at a banquet? Does it really matter? Yes, because the second part of our passage leads directly from the first. People who are meticulous about their orthodoxy are usually intensely proud of it – in a humble sort of way. They expect to be recognised as leaders of the faithful and to enjoy the peculiar privileges of sanctity. Organisers of big Christian events often have trouble with those who want a seat on the platform – and for their spouses as well! But Jesus won't have it. Let others be the judge of our worth. They can see it more clearly than we can. The moral is either be humble or be humiliated.

While he is on the subject of meals and status, Jesus has a searching word about hospitality. Do we choose dinner guests for our sake or for theirs? To massage our egos or to feed the hungry? Let hospitality reflect the open-handed grace of God which demands no recompense. Jesus was interested only in hungry, needy people.[2]

1 Isa 58:13–14
2 Luke 1:53
3 DA Carson, speaking at the Christian conference Word Alive in 2000

'There is no pride more deadly than that which finds its roots in great learning, great external piety or a showy defence of orthodoxy'.[3]

Hungry for God?

Day 270

The riches of heaven are ours for the asking. Ask God to increase your spiritual appetite.

 *Luke 14:15–24*

There is a great deal of feasting in the Bible, starting with Abraham's celebrations when Isaac was weaned and ending with the great marriage supper of the Lamb. God does enjoy a good celebration.[1]

One of the guests at the dinner Jesus attended made a pious interjection, presumably expecting that his place at the messianic banquet was secure. Jesus warned his critics not to assume that their virtues would qualify them for that privilege. Those who appeared to be first in virtue might well be last – or might be excluded entirely.

Jewish invitations usually had two stages – a preliminary notification and then an immediate one when the preparations were complete. In the parable the excuses are presumably at the second stage and are so absurd as to be positively insulting. Buying draft animals without previously testing them is ridiculous and although marriage exempted a young man from military service[2] it never prevented him from going to a dinner. The poor, the crippled, the blind and the lame, who are subsequently asked to the feast, find the invitation so improbable that they have to be 'compelled' or persuaded to come in. The respectable farmers and merchants who use such pathetic excuses are very different. They don't want to enjoy the banquet. Why?

I think it was the Native American Kwakiutl tribe whose chiefs once competed with each other in giving more and more lavish gifts in order to establish their high status and prestige. Receiving someone's hospitality, on the other hand, can make us seem small. In social life we correct this feeling of inferiority by returning the hospitality. Then we are equals. But we can't do that with God. Grace is free, although people often resent it.

1 Gen 21:8; Rev 19:9
2 Deut 24:5

It requires humility to believe and accept the gospel of God's grace. How are you responding to God's party invitation?

Count the cost

Day 271

Today's passage is not for the fainthearted. Ask God for the courage to take it seriously.

Luke 14:25–35 

Reading today's passage is daunting. Jesus seemed to spend more time dissuading people from being his disciples than encouraging them to follow him. By contrast when did you last hear an evangelist urge his congregation to think very carefully before committing themselves to Christ? In Britain the church has been in sharp decline for decades. Even believing Christians allow their church attendance to lapse, out of boredom more than anything else. Few if any demands are made of Christian converts, yet outsiders have high expectations of what it means to be a Christian.

One young man considering full-time Christian service was disinclined to enter the ministry because he felt he could not live up to the standards he would expect of himself in such a position and Jesus gives him good grounds for thinking so. The point of this passage is that Jesus wants no half-hearted followers.[1] The two examples of common prudence are as applicable to Christian commitment as to commerce or warfare.

Is Jesus exaggerating for effect? Are Christians really called to 'hate father and mother ...' in order to be disciples? Is this a sort of 'potential' requirement, meaning 'if necessary' we must be prepared to make any sacrifice for Christ – while fervently hoping that it won't be necessary? Looking at what happened to the disciples it is clear that Jesus meant precisely what he said. Paul's record[2] shows that he at least shared the working conditions that Jesus predicted. Converts in Muslim countries know how accurate Jesus' warning was. The record of Christians since Jesus' day suggests that the more seriously we take his word the more true we find it to be and the more rewarding our Christian life is. Risk nothing and you get nothing: risk everything and there is nothing God will withhold from us.

1 Compare Deut 20:2–9
2 2 Cor 11:21–33

'Lord, help me to take your Word to heart, and not to complain when it turns out to be as tough as you warned us it might be.'

Lost property

Day 272

Tax collectors and sinners clustered round Jesus while the Pharisees stood apart. In which group would you have felt most at ease?

 *Luke 15:1–10*

Before becoming a Christian, did you have any sense that God was pursuing you? Francis Thompson's poem *The Hound of Heaven* is full of that haunting sense that God will not let us go, and many Christians have been similarly conscious of God's pursuit like a jealous lover. These two simple stories tell similar truths but in one case the object sought is passive while in the other it is active. The coin could not help being lost but the sheep, through typical ovine stupidity, had separated itself from security. Both pictures describe the human condition: we are lost because we are human and can't help it, but we are also lost by our own fault. Fortunately God in each case is determined to find us and in each case he wants to rejoice and have a party (presumably not with roast lamb!).

But what about the nine coins and the ninety-nine sheep? Do they represent those boring but virtuous people who dutifully fill pews without sufficient initiative to rebel? Is it only the troublesome people whom God loves?

A mother was once asked which of her three daughters she loved best and said, 'The one who is sick'. We cannot make God love us more by being either bad or good. In either case his concern is simply that we are safe with the flock. His grace is sufficient.

These parables were told to warn the 'righteous' that God's special concern is for the lost rather than the 'found'. Repentant sinners create particular rejoicing in heaven, so the righteous are warned not to turn up their spiritual noses at the morally disreputable. Rather they need to see that they are equally in need of God's grace.

When did you last celebrate the return of a repentant sinner?

The pious and the prodigal

Be prepared to see yourself in this story. Ask God to open your eyes in new ways to its message.

Luke 15:11–32 

It is difficult for readers in a Western culture to appreciate the enormity of the younger son's rebellion against the social norms of Jesus' time. By requiring his share of the property during his father's lifetime he was impoverishing the whole family, including his own descendants, and bringing disgrace on the family name. Several aspects of the father's behaviour are extraordinary.

First, he appears to accede to his son's demands without demur. He apparently allows events to take their course without exercising his paternal rights to control his son.[1]

Secondly, he does not actively seek for the son as the shepherd did for his sheep: he merely waits with eager anticipation. Why? There is something frightening about the freedom God gives us. He merely tells us the truth and leaves us to make of it what we will because truth is self-justifying. There is no place for persuasion because the truth simply is. So too the father in this story has to let the son discover truth for himself and that had to be found in the pigsty. For modern parents whose children are in 'the far country' it is an agonising experience yet for them also there is no alternative but to wait – ready to give a similar welcome.

These three parables present us with a problem. Does God actively pursue us, as the first two suggest, or does he passively wait for us to return? Are both true? What does your experience suggest? These simple stories say something profound about predestination and human responsibility.

I often wonder what happened after the welcome home party. Was the prodigal genuinely repentant or did he relapse? Was he permanently grateful for his home, and how did he get on with the older brother? Did the older brother go on sulking? In similar circumstances we have our own choices to make.

1 Deut 1:18–21

With whom do you most closely identify in the story: the prodigal, the older brother, or the father?

Managing your investments

Day 274

Ask God to make you truly wise as you plan for the future.

 *Luke 16:1–18*

This is a notoriously difficult parable to understand, but a little background information helps. Jews were forbidden to exact usury (high interest) on loans, but of course there were ways of adhering to the letter of the law while undermining its spirit. Instead of stipulating a rate of interest on a business loan, the capital would be increased from the outset, so, for example, a loan of one hundred pounds at ten per cent interest to be repaid over two years would be agreed as being for one hundred and twenty pounds.

Probably something of this nature is happening here. The steward knew all the details of the original loans but agreed with the debtors that the outstanding amount would revert to its original figure, namely one hundred pounds in our example. The master couldn't complain because to do so would reveal that he had broken the law by inflating the loan. Thus the steward had made a friend, the debtor was happy and owed the steward a favour, and the master got no more than he deserved.

The parable therefore is about planning ahead. Crises do occur despite the tendency to believe that the future will be like the present. The flood struck the people of Noah's day,[1] the rich fool was struck down in his prime[2] and God's judgement overtakes us when we least expect it.

Jesus' solemn warning to his critics who loved money had a particular poignancy. Hanging over the heads of his contemporaries was the utter destruction of Jerusalem in AD70. The Temple and all its massive wealth was burnt until molten silver ran in the streets; those who did not die of starvation were massacred by Roman soldiers and the wealth which the Pharisees loved became worthless. We kid ourselves if we think that our own wealth is any more secure.

1 Gen 7:21–23
2 Luke 12:20

Where do your investments – and your real love – lie? Do you believe Jesus sufficiently to act accordingly?

The great divide

Day 275

Many of Jesus' most telling stories concern our attitude to money. Ask God for the grace to escape its destructive power.

Luke 16:19–31 

All over medieval Europe almshouses and chapels were built in response to this parable. Men who made money during their lives saw an ominous warning in the fate of the rich man in this story and hoped that endowing a chantry (donating money to a chapel or altar where prayers might be said for their souls), would mitigate their punishment. But conversely it also dissuaded them from helping the poor in this life since, it was argued, the poor would get their reward in heaven.

Neither of these conclusions follows from the parable. Lazarus was not blest *because* he was poor, nor was the rich man punished *simply* for being rich. In each case it was the attitude of mind and heart arising from their situations which decided their fate. All rich people are tempted to say, 'I have plenty stacked away. I will take it easy and have a good time'.[1] It is astonishing how easily we stifle our compassionate impulses. Even the dogs were more charitable than the rich man. The poor are more likely to 'know their need of God' and respond to him accordingly.[2] This parable was aimed at the Pharisees 'who loved money'. We in Western societies need to take serious heed of that warning.

The last verse of the chapter has a terrible irony. Miracles of themselves do not convince or convict sinners; hence Jesus' refusal to cast himself down from the Temple[3] or to produce 'signs' that would confirm his messianic claims.[4]

It is hard to know how far Jesus meant the details of this parable to be a description of the afterlife, but it is horribly clear that decisions made in this life are not reversible in the next. God respects the use we make of our freedom.

1 See Luke 12:19; 1 Cor 15:32
2 Matt 5:3, NEB
3 Matt 4:6
4 Luke 11:29

'Men's actions are determined not by what they believe but by what they love' (Augustine of Hippo, 354–430). What do you love most?

Sin and the need for forgiveness

Day 276

Three short sayings remind us about daily disciplines: forgiveness, faith and duty. Ask for grace to please God today.

Luke 17:1–10

The abuse of innocence is a terrible thing. The first four verses of our passage put side by side the severity of God's judgement against sin and the absolute necessity for forgiven people to forgive others. I suppose most of us find it easy to believe that God forgives us, though we probably expect him to be pretty severe toward those who sin against us. But *'forgiven-ness'* and *'forgive-ness'* are inseparable. As Martin Luther King Junior said, 'Forgiveness is not an occasional act; it is a permanent attitude'.

Jesus' statement on faith illustrates the difficulty of understanding the style of his discourse. To the best of my knowledge no one has ever prayed a mulberry tree into the sea and it is hard to imagine why they might want to, so presumably Jesus is exaggerating to make a point. On the other hand most Christians will have their own testimonies to how God has answered prayer in remarkable ways so that 'mountainous' obstacles to God's work have been removed. Jesus seems to mean that faith is not something to be quantified: it either exists or it doesn't. Josiah Spiers started the first SU beach mission in 1868, a tiny seed of faith in telling children something of God's love, yet that act of obedience has grown into the Scripture Union movement of today, far beyond any conception he might have had about the importance of what he did.

Jesus often says things at different times which appear to be contradictory. Here it is implied that there are no rewards for any service we might offer to God, since we are doing no more than we jolly well should. Yet elsewhere Jesus makes it clear that he offers rewards for service.[1] The issue is our attitude of mind. Whatever acts of service we might offer to God are no more than his due. Yet it is in the nature of his grace that he rewards us for them.

1 Eg Matt 6:6; 10:42; Luke 6:35

Do you instinctively expect something in return when you do some act of service for God? Instead, offer it as a gift of gratitude to him.

Dear God, save me from myself

Paul calls us to be 'overflowing with thankfulness'.[1] Spend some time thanking God for blessings you have recently experienced.

Luke 17:11–19 

When Jesus speaks of Samaritans it is usually in favourable terms.[2] When his contemporaries referred to them it was almost always unfavourably,[3] 'for Jews do not associate with Samaritans'.[4] Yet adversity drew Jews and Samaritans together when leprosy struck with all its hideous physical and social effects. Their common humanity united them, and Jesus responded to their despairing cry for help. They cried out to God for mercy, and obeyed Jesus' directions, however improbable they seemed.

Why is gratitude so difficult? It is extraordinary that nine men could be transformed from social outcasts to accepted members of their families and yet could not return to thank their benefactor. It is extraordinary yet it is so common. Gratitude is not an everyday event, least of all to God. People who are eager to condemn God when suffering comes never think to be thankful when they enjoy health. But does God exist only when he allows pain to touch us? Does he disappear when we no longer want to curse him?

Ten men with leprosy were healed; one was grateful. Ten experienced God's grace; one was grateful. Nine people were locked into their personal concern; one was liberated from himself and turned outward to praise God. That sounds about average.

Jesus' recurrent emphasis on virtuous Samaritans must have been very galling to his critics. In modern Belfast he would certainly hold up Catholics for praise to Protestants and vice versa. To all of us Jesus would point out the virtues of those outside our own faith community. No wonder Jesus' contemporaries hated him, yet they would not accept the implied criticism. Are we so very different? What did Jesus' contemporaries make of his ministry? The poor heard it with gladness and the rich went empty away – to kill him.

1 Col 2:7
2 Luke 10:33; 17:16
3 John 8:48
4 John 4:9

'Dear God, liberate me from myself so that I can praise you from a thankful heart.'

Remember Lot's wife

What place does the future play in your thoughts and ambitions? Spend time looking forward to when you will meet Jesus face to face.

Luke 17:20–37

This passage hovers on the boundary between time and eternity. As creatures trapped in time we understand how the past permeates the present through memory and the guilt it brings, but when Jesus spoke, the future invaded the present. The kingdom of God is present 'among you' but he also looks forward (or back?) to when 'the Son of Man in his day' would burst upon the world with all the immediacy of Noah's flood or the destruction of Sodom. So God's presence will bring both disaster and glory, separating friends and relations, depending on their relationship to him. But Jesus wants his people to live in the light of the future. The past has been covered; guilt is forgiven and cleansed, so we are free to look forward in hope of his return. But all that lay on the far side of the cross (v 25).

For us, the reality of the present, the ordinariness of daily routine, the cycle of birth, growth and death, seem unalterable. Jesus, by contrast, makes specific the Old Testament expectation that things will not always go on as at present. Modern cosmology sees a universe that is immeasurably old and vast, but the cosmos is only an artefact. God's timeless reality may burst upon it without warning. Human wickedness demands God's intervention in the world which sin has defaced and his coming will mean both judgement and salvation.

How can we give proper attention to the demands of daily life while still seeing how temporary these 'realities' are? Lord Shaftesbury, the great nineteenth-century reformer, lived every day knowing that he would answer to God for how he used it. His was not a morbid preoccupation with death but a realistic assessment of what lay ahead. What future hope governs my actions?

'Lord, help me live the present in the light of the future so that I shall not be ashamed at your coming.'

All about the kingdom

It has been well said that it is almost as if Jesus crept in at the window and swapped all the price tags, so that what was of great value is now of little value, and what was of little value is now of great value. Here we have a picture of an upside-down kingdom with radical demands.

First, we see the *values of the kingdom*. The kind of people whom Jesus seeks out are entirely unexpected. We will read of his concern for the widow, for the children, for the poor, even for those who are despised within society like tax men.

Secondly, we see *the qualifications for entering the kingdom*. Linked with its values, we will discover that entering the kingdom has nothing to do with religious performance, with social or economic status, with personal achievement.

Thirdly, we discover *the 'now and not yet' of the kingdom*. We will learn what Jesus has to say about what to do during the waiting time, as we anticipate Jesus' final return and live with the tensions associated with the fact that Jesus' rule has begun but has not yet been fully acknowledged.

Fourthly, we see *the costs of the kingdom*. Jesus' journey has a clear destination, as Jesus makes clear in his frequent references to his suffering and ultimate rejection in Jerusalem. And as Jesus explains, there are inevitable costs for all who choose to follow him.

Finally, we will encounter *the King himself*. Luke reveals a wonderful portrait of Jesus' authority. At times it is expressed in his confrontation with religious leaders; elsewhere it is an authority expressed in his compassionate mercy towards those in need. We also see Jesus' centrality to God's purposes, as Luke frequently quotes from messianic texts in the Old Testament to reveal Jesus as God's Son, the Sent One, the Judge and King who will fulfil God's ultimate purposes. It is a profound portrait which introduces us to the authority and grace of this unique and universal King.

Jonathan Lamb

Where wrath and mercy meet

Ask God to open your heart and mind to a fresh insight into these parables, so that your relationship with him will be genuinely renewed.

Luke 18:1–14

The waiting times in our lives are often the most testing. Uncertainty can paralyse our faith. But they are also moments of opportunity as we learn to depend on God more fully.

Luke records two parables which revolve around the fundamental issue of our approach to God. Both are set in the context of the return of Jesus.[1]

The parable of the persistent widow reminds us that God is a just God, who the wicked and acts in faithfulness for his 'chosen ones' (v 7). The unjust judge refuses to do anything in response to the widow's appeal for justice but finally acts because of her persistence.

In contrast, God responds willingly to the cry of his people. For every waiting period in our lives – shorter periods when we long for God to act, or longer waiting as we anticipate Jesus' return – our attitude must be one of dependent faith. God is not slow to act with compassionate concern and absolute justice for those who persist in faith. Don't give up trusting him. Don't give up praying.

The parable of the Pharisee and the tax collector is a stark reminder of the reason for our certainty. Jesus' return will signal the day of God's justice, and our only hope then will be that we have already met the God of mercy. The familiarity of the story should not imply that we have nothing in common with the Pharisee, for we are the religious people of today, tempted to trust in our own righteousness and to look down on others with the same spirit of self-congratulation. The only foundation for our prayer and for our confidence on the day of Jesus' return will be an appeal to God's mercy. These two parables remind us to be determined in prayer, recognising our total dependence on God.

1 Luke 17:22–37

As we grow older as Christians, let's pray that we will not lose our utter dependence on God's mercy, which is the foundation of our life in him both now and in the future.

Seek first his kingdom

What are the fundamental priorities that shape your decisions and ambitions? Pray for honesty as you read today's passage.

Luke 18:15–30 

Having spoken of the return of the King, the next few readings introduce us to what it means to enter the kingdom. We will see how counter-cultural Jesus was, and how the disciples failed to grasp the radical implications of his teaching.

Just as in the first century, we still tend to measure a person's importance by a range of social conventions – position, economic resources, gender, influence and much else. The Pharisees, looking for the coming kingdom, expected it to be revealed in power through a glorious king, surrounded by the trappings of royalty. But Jesus' kingdom values are quite the opposite of our expectations.

As he illustrates from the two encounters in this passage, access to his kingdom is denied to the proud, the self-sufficient, or those who are concerned with wealth and social status. Entry into his kingdom will only be possible through the humble trust typical of a young child. I am glad to see that for students today, educated to be independent and surrounded by expectations of career success, Jesus' kingdom values, once embraced, provide a deeply fulfilling alternative to the way of this world.

The encounter with a rich ruler presses the point home starkly. Somewhat disconcertingly, Luke frequently demonstrates that attitudes to wealth are a measure of spirituality. An apparently well-intentioned young man is confronted with the question of allegiance. What matters most to him: entering the kingdom or retaining his grasp on his possessions?

We might imagine the choice would be simple until we reflect on those things – a relationship, a position, an aspiration – which we hold dear and would never wish to surrender. Even now Jesus pinpoints similar priorities in our lives, and calls us too to seek first his kingdom.

In God's presence, try to identify those things which take first place in your lives, and surrender them anew to him.

Day 281

Unseeing eyes

'Open my eyes that I may see wonderful things in your law.'[1]

Luke 18:31–43

It is a tragedy to go through life with unseeing eyes. But the greatest handicap is not physical blindness, but to journey through life without being able to see the realities of God's good purposes. This is an affliction unnecessarily endured by many people; it is a tragedy when Christians suffer from it too.

Luke here records two incidents of blindness. First, he highlights the paradox of the spiritual blindness of those closest to Jesus (v 34). This is not the first time Jesus has made reference to the coming events in Jerusalem.

From our side of the cross we can't imagine Jesus being more specific when he predicts his death and resurrection. But whether they imagined Jesus to be speaking metaphorically, or simply refused to believe what they were told, or were prevented from understanding Jesus' prediction, Luke tells us that the disciples didn't know what he was talking about.

In the second incident we hear the blind man persistently appeal to Jesus for mercy, which was then articulated as a longing to have his sight restored. Luke constructs the account to demonstrate that both the privileged rich (18:18–23) and the poor beggar need salvation. And entry into the kingdom comes through the sense of desperate helplessness which the blind man exemplified. ('He shouted' could be translated 'he screamed'.)

The truth is that only Jesus opens blind eyes, whether physical or spiritual, and he only does so when we turn to him with a humble determination to receive his merciful gifts. There are many things in our lives which blind us to the realities of his purposes and, like Paul, we should pray frequently that the eyes of our heart may be enlightened so that we may know him better and understand our Christian calling more clearly.

1 Ps 119:18

Take the words of Paul's prayer in Ephesians 1:17–19 and make them your own.

Faith that works

Day 282

Is your faith in Jesus genuine? How will others recognise that characteristic in you today?

Luke 19:1–10 

Known and loved as a story for children, today's passage has a radical message for people of all ages. It is a beautiful illustration both of the compassion of Jesus who receives this unlikely character into his kingdom, and of the profound change which an encounter with Jesus provokes.

Zacchaeus was hardly the most obvious candidate for God's blessing. But as Jesus has already shown, those most qualified to enter the kingdom are usually the outsiders – the widow, the child, the blind beggar, and now Zacchaeus, the hated tax collector (v 8). These are the ones whom the world would expect to be excluded from God's goodness, yet paradoxically they are the ones whom Jesus seeks out and welcomes. Surrounded by the crowd and journeying towards his goal, Jesus took time to stop and seek out this despised little man.

The story is a vivid picture of the life-transforming impact of meeting Jesus. Zacchaeus is convicted of his sinfulness and places all that he has at Jesus' disposal. He demonstrates the reality of his faith by his actions. Zacchaeus went well beyond what the law demanded as he responded to God's grace with a determined generosity (v 8).

We should not miss the fact that the fundamental change of heart that came from meeting with Jesus produced a wholehearted commitment to practical action. In this account Luke reinforces the fact that the coming of God's kingdom results in radical change, expressed first at a personal level in allegiance to Jesus, and then in its impact on value systems, lifestyle, behaviour and social relationships. The kingdom will always be about personal change, but it will also have its social, relational and political impact as changed lives express kingdom values.[1] That is the kind of Christian conversion we should be experiencing day by day.

1 Compare Luke 3:8–14

Has God placed his finger on something in your life that needs to change?

The best investment

Day 283

Thank God for the good gifts he has given you, then think how he may be asking you to serve him differently today.

Luke 19:11–27

Martin Luther once said that we should be ready as if Jesus were coming today, but be working as if he were not coming for a thousand years. Whilst waiting expectantly for the King, keep active in extending the kingdom.

In today's passage Luke signals that, as Jesus came close to Jerusalem, people began to expect the kingdom to be revealed (v 11). So Jesus told a parable about how they should behave while waiting for the kingdom to come.

Each servant is given the same resource which he is to deploy responsibly until his master returns. Jesus includes a reference in the parable to the attitude of the king's subjects, who hated him and refused to accept his rule (v 14), prophetic in its anticipation of the rejection he was soon to encounter in Jerusalem.

The three servants each report to the king on his return – an accountability to which we too will be called.[1] Two of the servants had acted as faithful stewards, using their resources effectively to extend the kingdom. Their reward was still further responsibility. But the third servant, believing the king to be harsh and severe, had done nothing. So his resources were taken away and given to the one who had shown himself a good steward.

In verse 26 Jesus states a principle of the Christian life. We cannot stand still: either we use our time and resources in order to advance God's kingdom, or we experience a form of spiritual paralysis, in danger of losing the good gifts with which we have been endowed. To emphasise the seriousness of rejecting Jesus the King, the parable concludes with a devastating assertion that those who oppose him face no other expectation than final judgement (v 27).

We are called to live our lives fully for Jesus Christ, using all of our God-given resources wisely and joyfully for the cause of his kingdom.

1 2 Cor 5:10

Renew your commitment to use God's gifts creatively and effectively as you serve him today.

Joy and sorrow in Jerusalem

Day 284

How do we feel about the fact that the majority around us have rejected the King? Concerned? Apathetic? Broken-hearted?

Luke 19:28–44 

Today's passage includes two diverse emotions: the joyful praise of the disciples and the weeping of Jesus. In these outbursts we reach a climax as the journey approaches its end.

The incident is full of drama. This is no discreet entry to Jerusalem, even though Jesus was a marked man with his life under threat. His final arrival in the city was an overt declaration of his identity as King, riding on a colt in fulfilment of a messianic prophecy[1] and welcomed by the disciples as they declared his coming rule in their song of praise (adding the word 'king' to the original psalm).[2]

Were they heralding the King of Peace who was to die for them, or hoping for a warrior king who would win them a military victory? Whatever their motivation in declaring his praise, the Pharisees were keen to stop the singing! Jesus acknowledged that such praise was inevitable and unstoppable (v 40). One day the whole of creation will declare his greatness and submit to his rule.[3]

But then alongside the disciples' joy we also find the dramatic record of Jesus bursting into tears as he anticipates what will happen to Jerusalem. The complete collapse which he foresees will occur because of the city's rejection of the King who now weeps at her gates. With deep emotion he sees that the peace which the disciples declared in their song of praise (v 38) cannot be experienced in Jerusalem because of their blindness to his identity and mission (v 42).

Luke's Gospel declares that Jesus is the Saviour of the whole world, not the king of one nation alone, and his universal rule will eventually be acknowledged by all. There is cause for weeping that so many reject him, but cause for great joy as we worship the King who will restore all things on that great day of his return.[4]

1 Zech 9:9
2 Ps 118:26
3 Rom 8:19–21; Phil 2:10,11
4 Acts 3:21

Spend a moment in prayer for someone you will meet today who has not yet bowed the knee to King Jesus.

Day 285

Religion at its worst

Before criticising the religious leaders of Jesus' day, let's open our hearts and allow God to expose any hypocrisy of which we may be guilty.

Luke 19:45 – 20:8

Jesus has arrived at the Temple. Today's passage bristles with the religious authorities' hostility and highlights some ugly features of religion.

First, the religious leaders are compromised. Jesus condemns the injustice and exploitation that characterised the trading in the Temple area (v 45) and drives out those who were deliberately victimising the poor pilgrims visiting the Temple. Exploiting those who came to worship in God's house was an outrageous insult to a holy God and Jesus would have no truck with it. Regardless of the potential consequences of such high profile behaviour, Jesus is uncompromising in his condemnation, quoting Old Testament support.[1]

Secondly, the religious leaders were scheming to kill Jesus (v 47). But it would be difficult to do this without incurring the wrath of the people, for Luke records that 'all the people hung on his words' (v 48).

So, thirdly, they attempted to discredit Jesus by questioning his authority. Would he please present his official accreditation (20:2)?

By asking them about John's baptism, Jesus presented the religious leaders with a dilemma. What was John's spiritual authority? To have accepted John's baptism would have been an acknowledgement of their own hypocrisy, for they had not been baptised nor had they accepted the One to whom John pointed. To have rejected it would have been to invite the crowd's hostility.

What a dreadful thing that those charged with the moral and spiritual leadership of the nation were spiritually blind. We should note that Jesus is not universally welcomed by religious people, and we should ask if it is possible that we too are more interested in church politics, position and power, than in the authority of Jesus over our lives.

1 Isa 56:7; Jer 7:11

Pray today for your Christian leaders that they will live their lives under the authority of Christ.

A royal welcome?

Day 286

'He came to that which was his own, but his own did not receive him. Yet to all who received him ... he gave the right to become children of God.'[1]

Luke 20:9–26 

The religious leaders knew Jesus had spoken the parable against them (v 19). They could hardly have missed the point. Using an Old Testament metaphor,[2] Jesus describes a vineyard (the people), its owner (God), and the tenants in charge (the religious leaders). When the tenants attack his messengers, the owner decides to send his own son. But the tenants throw him out and kill him, so the owner is justified in executing the tenants and giving the vineyard to others (v 16).

The religious leaders had failed to fulfil their responsibility to care for God's people. They had also ignored the prophets and, finally, rejected God's Son. Here Jesus was responding directly to their earlier question (20:2) as to who had given him authority. He was the Son and heir who had been sent by God. Quoting a messianic psalm,[3] Jesus accused the religious authorities of rejecting the cornerstone (v 17), the one who made sense of the whole building. Like the tenants in the story, they must face the consequences of God's wrath (v 18).

Not only was Jesus pinpointing the failure of Israel's leadership, but he was affirming his own centrality in God's purposes. First, he is the Son and heir. The parable shows how patient God has been in sending his messengers, but how inevitable his judgement will be if we reject his Son.

Secondly, he is the focal point of the new community of God's people. A physical Temple in Jerusalem might have been the place for worship for Israel. But now Jesus himself is the cornerstone of a spiritual temple, made up of men and women who worship him from every corner of the globe. By our thoughts and actions today we should not reject the One whom God sends, but renew our devotion to him.

1 John 1:11,12
2 Isa 5:1–7
3 Ps 118:22

Our thoughts, words and actions indicate how we treat Jesus. Pray for the Spirit's help to live consistently for Jesus today.

Living in the light of eternity

Day 287

If heaven is your eventual home, how often do you feel homesick?

Luke 20:27–40

The onslaught against Jesus continues, this time with a question from the Sadducees which probed his authority to teach the Scriptures. Their question also touched on a fundamental theme of Jesus' own teaching – the issue of the resurrection. Not believing in resurrection, the Sadducees set up an elaborate story to demonstrate how ludicrous this idea really was.

Jesus' reply contains two significant themes. First, heaven will be very different from this present life. It will be a new order of existence, and all of those in heaven will, by definition, be children of the resurrection and will not die. In such an environment there will be no need for marriage, no need for procreation, for there will be eternal life for God's children and a relational harmony and depth that we have never experienced on earth.

Secondly, Jesus' reply includes a reference to Moses (v 37). It is possible that the Sadducees only recognised the authority of the first five books of the Old Testament, and so Jesus argues on their ground when he asserts that even these Scriptures proclaim the resurrection. If Moses refers to God as 'the God of Abraham, Isaac and Jacob', and if God is the God of the living, then the biblical texts which the Sadducees professed to believe also suggest the reality of the resurrection.

Paul elaborates on the significance of the resurrection[1] and we do well to consider more frequently the realities of the age to come to which both Jesus and Paul point. It was said of the Puritan pastor Richard Sibbes[2] that 'heaven was in him before he was in heaven'. The certainties of the Christian's living hope can make a profound difference in a culture like ours, where death is the embodiment of uncertainty and hope is a commodity in short supply.

1 1 Cor 15:35–49
2 1577–1635

Pray for those facing bereavement that the reality of the resurrection will transform their emotions and fill them – and you – with hope.

Pride comes before a fall

Day 288

Pray for God's grace today as you evaluate your motives and your commitment to the Lord.

Luke 20:41 – 21:4 

Perhaps the most obscene sin of all is the sin of pride. For pride seeks to snatch the glory that belongs to God alone. Its ugliness is nowhere more evident than when it sports religious clothing.

Jesus unleashes a devastating attack on all such behaviour and on the teachers of the Law whose ostentatious swaggering was expressed in their special clothing and favoured seating in the synagogue. Such was their concern to appear important, that they completely ignored the more serious question of how God saw them. Alongside their cultivated image, they exploited the most vulnerable and sustained counterfeit piety with their lengthy prayers. Religious hypocrites like that, Jesus said, will face severe punishment (20:47). Pride inevitably leads to destruction.[1] By contrast, Jesus points to the example of a widow giving to the Temple treasury (21:2). He saw that, despite her poverty, she gave all she had. There were no grand gestures, no religious show, no public honour. Yet she outdid everyone else by her quiet, sacrificial generosity.

These stories are placed immediately after Jesus' theological question about his identity (20:41). As he replies to the earlier question about authority (20:2) he asserts his divine calling. He is the Lord. So the context for his teaching about the danger of religious pride is the affirmation of his Lordship.

Pride in our achievements or religious credentials cannot sit alongside our commitment to honour the Lord wholeheartedly. For to do so would be to keep for ourselves the glory which properly belongs to him. He is Lord of our lives and Lord of the universe, and if we are truly to acknowledge him as such, then our attitude will have to be like that of the widow. We will give him all we have.

1 Prov 16:18

Jesus' teaching extends to the whole of life, but in a time of reflective prayer, review especially the question of your use of money.

Back to the future

Day 289

What emotions do you experience as you think about the future?

 *Luke 21:5–38*

There is a Chinese proverb which says: 'to prophesy is extremely difficult, especially with regard to the future'. Nevertheless there is no shortage of people trying to do so, including Christians seeking to outline the timetable leading to Christ's return! But here Jesus tries to encourage an attitude of prayerful watchfulness rather than elaborate calculation.

Today's passage needs to be understood on several different levels. In part it refers to the fall of Jerusalem. It also refers to the events surrounding Jesus' second coming and to the general conditions which will prevail in the period between Jesus' first advent and his return. There is little value in trying to guess when Jesus will return. Rather, a passage like this encourages us to cultivate some important characteristics. First, *thankfulness*. We should rejoice that history has a purpose, that God has planned the future and that its climax will be when Jesus returns. It will be a day of judgement, as the passage makes clear, but also a day of restoration when everything will find its unity and completion in Jesus.[1]

Secondly, *realism*. Jesus reminds his followers that they must be prepared for suffering (vs 12–19). Those who name the name of Christ in a world which has rejected him should expect hostility.

Thirdly, *watchfulness*. We are called to live our lives now in the light of the future, ready for Jesus' return and not fearful of its consequences. Jesus calls us to a disciplined life (v 34) of prayerful expectation (v 36).

Finally, *confidence*. Whatever the uncertainties that surround this world, whatever disruption and shaking the cosmos might endure, Jesus' words have ultimate authority and abiding significance (v 33). Trusting Jesus and his words will enable us to stand firm (vs 19,36).

1 Eph 1:10

In what ways would your life be different if you were more aware of Jesus' promises regarding the future?

Why suffering is necessary

Throughout the Gospel, there have been warnings and foreshadowings of the rejection and suffering which are to be Jesus' lot in Jerusalem. One reason why it is necessary for Jesus to suffer and die is because he is a prophet, and rejection and even death are par for the course for prophets. Jesus especially attracts opposition because of his willingness to mix with and welcome sinners, and his lack of respect for legal shibboleths, which threaten those who have influence in society. A deeper reason is because this is the plan of God (24:26; compare Acts 2:23). It is through his identification with sinners on the cross that he will be qualified to offer them forgiveness following his exaltation. Barabbas can go free because Jesus has taken his place (23:25).

Throughout Luke's Gospel there is a pattern of reversal. It all comes to a head in these chapters where Jesus is portrayed both as the Righteous One of the Psalms (eg Psalm 22) and the Suffering Servant of the Isaianic songs (see Luke 22:37, quoting Isaiah 53:12, and Luke 23:35, where the title 'Chosen One' alludes to Isaiah 42:1). God vindicates Jesus because he is innocent (a major theme in Luke 23), and because he has obediently walked the path of the servant. Jesus is truly a king, but his kingship is entered into through humble service not, as with the kings of this world, through lording it over others (22:24–27).

How is all of this relevant to us? We see here a pattern for all who would follow Jesus. We also see that suffering is not the last word. The fact of the resurrection brings great joy to Jesus' disciples (24:52), joy which is a foretaste of what believers will one day experience at the heavenly banquet. So if the path seems hard for you now, take heart! The best is yet to be, and faithfulness will certainly be rewarded.

Andrew Clark

Handed over

Day 290

Thank God that he is in control, even when everything seems to be going wrong.

Luke 22:1–23

It is sometimes said that Luke has no clear teaching about the atonement, but this is refuted by a careful study of this passage. Luke deliberately uses the word 'Passover' six times in fifteen verses, emphasising the symbolic importance of what is happening. Central to the narrative is the reference to the sacrifice of the Passover lamb (v 7). During the meal the fact that his body and blood are given 'for you' (ie for the disciples) is stressed (vs 19,20). The sacrifice of Jesus as our Passover lamb[1] brings about the new covenant prophesied by Jeremiah.[2] Luke makes it clear for those willing to meditate on the significance of events that Jesus' death is central to God's purpose to bring in his kingdom (vs 16,18).

In this passage we also see a classic example of the common biblical tension between God's sovereignty and man's responsibility. On the one hand Jesus is in control, as even the detail about the disciples finding things 'just as Jesus had told them' (v 13) underlines. Jesus goes 'as it has been decreed' in God's perfect plan. But none of this negates the responsibility of Judas the betrayer (vs 21,22) or the guilt of the chief priests (vs 2,4). The battle between good and evil that is taking place is emphasised by Luke's statement that 'Satan entered Judas' (v 3). The delight of the chief priests at his willingness to betray Jesus (v 5) contrasts ironically with the previous delight of the crowds at the miraculous works of Jesus.[3] The leaders are afraid of the crowd (vs 2,6) and end up handing Jesus over to Pilate as Judas has handed him over to them. But the deepest truth is that God handed over Jesus 'for us all'.[4]

1 1 Cor 5:7
2 Jer 31:31; 1 Cor 11:25
3 Eg 8:13
4 Rom 8:32

'Bearing shame and scoffing rude, In my place condemned he stood; Sealed my pardon with his blood: Hallelujah! What a Saviour!' (Philipp Bliss, 1838–76).

Final words

Day 291

Imagine a close friend is about to leave and you don't know when you'll see each other again. What might you want to say to each other?

Luke 22:24–38 

The disciples are, as ever, slow to learn. It must have been profoundly discouraging for Jesus that, at such a time and after all his teaching, they should still have been so preoccupied with personal status (v 24). But Jesus continues patiently to teach them. The benefactor/client relationship was central to Greek culture, the point being that the honour given was a repayment for gifts made. But Jesus insists that all lording it over others and all delight in titles and all name-dropping (who you know, where you studied etc) are inappropriate for his disciples. Since Jesus is among them as 'one who serves',[1] they must behave in a similar way.

Isn't it discouraging when people don't show appreciation for what you've done? The Lord Jesus is not like this. He not only tells his disciples how much their faithfulness means to him, he also tells them of a reward coming their way seemingly out of all proportion to their service (v 30). In Acts Luke shows the first stage of the fulfilment of the promise as the disciples become the *de facto* leaders of the people.[2]

Jesus is aware of the fierce temptation about to come on all the disciples (v 31). He prays especially for Simon (his old name here symbolising his human weakness). It must have been tremendously reassuring for Peter after his fall to remember that Jesus not only knew what was to happen, but still had a crucial ministry for Peter once he had repented. Is he calling you too to strengthen your Christian brothers?

In verses 35–38 Jesus warns his disciples that the climax of his ministry has arrived. Significantly, he interprets events in the light of Isaiah 53 (v 37),[3] which speaks prophetically of the suffering of the Servant of the Lord. Nothing was happening by accident. It had all been foreseen long ago.

1 John 13:2–17
2 Acts 4:18–22; 5:12–26
3 Isa 53:12

If Jesus turned up at a gathering of you and your friends, what issues do you think he would want to raise with you?

Failing the test

Day 292

Thank the Lord that he doesn't write us off when we make a mess of things.

 *Luke 22:39–62*

Can you remember having to sit an exam for which you hadn't prepared properly? The grim knowledge that failure is inevitable and the deep regret at a missed opportunity are not pleasant. Here Jesus warns the disciples to pray that they do not 'give in to temptation' (v 40, *The Message*).

After agonising in prayer he returns, only to find them 'asleep, exhausted from sorrow' (v 45). He warns them again with the same words. A major test is coming and they need to prepare for it. However, by now it's already too late.

The test begins, and the disciples get off to a bad start. One disciple[1] uses his sword, but he is laughably ineffective, as Christians tend to be when we try to use worldly weapons to accomplish spiritual goals. Even though this is a time 'when darkness reigns' (v 53), Jesus is able to remedy the damage done by healing the man. Maybe we need to ask the Lord to put right damage we have done by some careless word or deed.

Peter now goes on to fail in a yet more spectacular fashion. He follows 'at a distance' (v 54), he joins the Lord's enemies at the fireside. The person who challenges him is only a girl – but this means that Peter has to contend with his male pride as well as his latent fear. Peter previously said he was willing to go with the Lord 'to prison and to death' (v 33), but now he doesn't even want to admit he knows him. The second and third denials quickly follow. Jesus comes out of the house and looks 'straight at Peter' (v 61). Have you ever wondered what sort of look this was? It was certainly enough to make Peter 'weep bitterly'. How good to know that this terrible failure wasn't the end for Jesus' disciple.

The Lord had been praying for him (v 32), as he does for us too in all our failures and betrayals.[2]

1 John 18:10 tells us it was Peter

2 Rom 8:34; Heb 7:25

'Lord, grant me tears of true repentance.'

Rejected

Day 293

How easy it is to be interested in Jesus mainly for what we can get from him. 'Lord, open our eyes and change our hearts as we read.'

Luke 22:63 – 23:25 

In this passage we see different groups attacking Jesus. The soldiers play degrading games with him; the Jewish council encourage him to incriminate himself, and then make false accusations against him; Herod interrogates him while the teachers of the Law stand by accusing him; the rulers and the crowd together call for his blood; Pilate weakly gives in to their insistent shouts.

What is it that the different groups want? The Temple soldiers want fun; the council want security and the maintenance of their privileges; Herod wants a show; the crowds want Barabbas, their hero; Pilate wants peace and a quiet life. It makes you think, doesn't it, whether things have really changed much in two thousand years? Plenty of TV shows are full of cheap laughs at Jesus and the Christian faith; religious leaders still persecute radicals who want to do things God's way; many still try to fleece Christians for all they can get from them; for millions what happens to pop music or football stars (or even soap opera characters) is in danger of dominating their lives; and most of the rest of us settle for being undisturbed rather than being willing to get our hands dirty standing up for justice in our world.

Just as Jesus did not defend himself when here on earth, so he allows us to mock him, blame him or ignore him now. But the choices of rebellious people will, if they are not careful, have eternal consequences for them; God will not be mocked for ever.[1]

1 Gal 6:7,8
2 John Knox, 1900–91

'Repentance is not a merely verbal act which we occasionally perform; if real it is an act in which our whole selves, through the whole course of our lives, are strenuously involved. It is not a casual "sorry" any more than God's forgiveness is a casual "not at all".'[2]

People around the cross

Day 294

***'More and more am I jealous lest any views upon prophecy, church government, politics or even systematic theology, should withdraw ... us from glorying in the cross of Christ.'*[1]**

 *Luke 23:26–46*

Many different people were around at the time of Jesus' crucifixion, and Luke introduces us to various individuals and groups. I wonder with whom you find it easiest to identify?

Simon of Cyrene (in modern Libya) was suddenly caught up in events. The mention of his sons by name in Mark's Gospel[2] implies that both he and his sons later became believers in Jesus. The carrying of the cross behind Jesus (v 26) is certainly for Luke an image of discipleship.[3]

The crowd, including the women, are deeply concerned about Jesus, but feel helpless. Jesus, however, wants them to understand the deeper significance of the drama taking place and warns them of the coming judgement on Jerusalem – which took place forty years later (vs 28–31). Following Jesus is not enough if all it leads to is passive acquiescence in evil. Like the people in this story, we all too often do no more than stand and watch.

The rulers and the soldiers unite in jeering at Jesus. Helpless and hopeless, all his claims about himself seem to be proved false. Jesus' prayer for his crucifiers (v 34) does nothing to move them. And so it is today – many sneer at the Lord when he and his followers appear weak and powerless.

Of the two criminals crucified with Jesus, one does no more than echo the insults of others (v 39). But the second acknowledges certain key truths: the reality of God's judgement, his own guilt, Jesus' innocence and kingship. He reaches out to Jesus as best he can, and receives a wonderful response.

Are you, like him, rebuking the mockers (v 40) and appealing to Jesus for mercy? Because of the darkness Jesus endured for us on the cross, there is a way to God as Father for those who come humbly in faith.

1 CH Spurgeon, 1834–92
2 Mark 15:21
3 Luke 9:23; 14:27

'Lord, I kneel again at the foot of your cross. I lay down my pride and my sin. Please remember me.'

Waiting times

Day 295

'Copies of God's perfect timetable are not available in advance' (Mary Wang). Pray for the ability not to give up even when you have no idea of how things could possibly turn out well.

Luke 23:47–56 

The Roman centurion articulates the truth that must have been obvious to any objective observer. This was a good man, innocent of any crime. But the fact was that he was now dead. The people with the power had triumphed over the man who dared to speak out, as it seems they always do. How sad everyone felt, as they sorrowfully made their way home. For his followers, who stood watching, it must have been not just sad but truly heartbreaking. All their hopes had come crashing to the ground like a house torn apart in an earthquake.

In this context, it's remarkable that Joseph should have acted so courageously and decisively. In John's Gospel we learn that up till now he had been a secret disciple, fearing the Jewish leaders' anger.[1] But now, when we might think he'd see no reason at all to risk his neck, he goes to ask Pilate for Jesus' corpse. Maybe as a 'good and upright man' (v 50) he was so sickened by the appalling miscarriage of justice that he could stand it no more. Maybe as one 'waiting for the kingdom of God' (v 51) he somehow had faith that God would act to vindicate his name.

The narrative emphasises that there was no danger of confusion about the placing of Jesus' body in the tomb. Since this was a new tomb, the corpse couldn't be mistaken for that of someone else. Since the women visited the tomb, and saw how Jesus' body was laid, they would know where to come to anoint the body once the Sabbath was over.

1 John 19:38

John of the Cross (1542–91) wrote of 'the dark night of the soul'. If this is your experience at present, remember that courageous and loving actions even in the dark will have their reward.

He has risen!

Day 296

'All Christian thinking, speaking, and organising must be born anew out of … prayer and action.'[1] May our faith be born anew today!

Luke 24:1–12

It must have been a really scary experience for the women, going to a tomb in the half-light of early morning only to find that nothing was as they'd left it. Then two angels, filled with light, suddenly appear: they never thought this would happen!

'Why are you looking for the living one in a cemetery?' (v 5, *The Message*), ask the angels. It's all too easy for us to make the same mistake, isn't it? Maybe we seek the Lord in places where the gospel is not known and loved. Or maybe we go further afield, and investigate other ideas. But if we search for spiritual reality without any real expectation that we're going to experience the real Jesus, what's the point? Maybe we need to visit some group who really are experiencing the presence of the risen Lord among them so that we can be transformed afresh and have a testimony to share.

The women share their story with the other disciples, only to be met with unbelief and cynicism. In first century Judaism the evidence of women was not valid in court, and their witness here is dismissed as superstition. Peter, always the unconventional outsider, is the only one who feels able to go and investigate for himself. Later he is privileged with an appearance by the risen Lord (v 34), who doubtless knew that after his earlier denial he needed this personal reaffirmation. The good news is that because of Easter there is always hope. The risen Lord is able and willing to restore all who turn back to him, and he is incredibly patient with his disciples even when we are slow to believe others' testimony to what he is doing today.

1 Dietrich Bonhoeffer, 1906–45

'One morning you will see in the newspapers "Moody is dead". Don't believe it! I shall never be so alive as I will be that morning' (DL Moody, 1837–99). Thank God that for Easter people like us death is not the end, but the beginning.

Transformed emotions

Day 297

'Lord Jesus, please join me on my journey today.'

Luke 24:13–35 

Can you remember a time when you experienced a real roller coaster of emotions within a short space of time? It was certainly like this for Cleopas and his fellow disciple. We can imagine the heavy and slow tread with which they walked away from Jerusalem – a journey symbolic of all the hopes and dreams they were having to give up. When Jesus joins them and asks what they are discussing, they stand still, faces downcast (v 17). They are totally dispirited. Can you recall a time when you felt similarly depressed because your hopes were dashed?

The deep disappointment felt by the disciples comes across clearly in their answer to Jesus' question. How poignant are the words 'we had hoped' (v 21)! After three days nothing has changed. The report of the women (who they didn't feel they could trust) was only partly confirmed by the men, and obviously did nothing to reassure them.

I'm sure Jesus must have had a twinkle in his eye as he lovingly told the disciples off for their lack of faith (v 25). Then he gives them the most wonderful Bible exposition they've ever experienced. No wonder their hearts burn (v 32) and they long to hear more (v 29)! In our day with so many recordings of gifted Bible teachers readily available, there's no reason why we shouldn't seek the same means to warm our cold hearts.

The welcoming of Jesus into their home results in sudden recognition of who he really is, followed by wonderful joy and renewed energy. I'm sure the journey back to Jerusalem took half the time the outward one had taken, despite the twilight hour! They had such wonderful news to share they just couldn't wait!

In this story we see various means of grace through which we may experience the presence of the risen Lord: talking together, the opening of the Scriptures, the breaking of bread, testimony. Are you missing out at all?

Reassured and commissioned

Day 298

'The Old Testament is the crib in which the Lord Jesus Christ was laid.'[1] Pray for a new appreciation of its role in helping us understand our Lord's significance.

 *Luke 24:36–53*

It's always reassuring to realise how like us the disciples were. When Jesus suddenly appears among them, they are scared out of their wits! Jesus acts quickly to reassure them. 'It really is me!' he says. 'Surely you can recognise me?' Then he eats some fish to prove he has a real body and isn't a ghost (vs 42,43).

Sometimes with us too, Jesus can appear in our lives in very surprising and disturbing ways, upsetting all our routines and expectations. We need to be open to this, knowing that if it is he who is responsible for the shock, he'll move quickly to reassure us too.

Jesus then gives them a Bible study which must have been similar to the one he gave on the Emmaus road. It covered the three main divisions of the Hebrew Scriptures: the Law, the Prophets (which included the historical books from Joshua to 2 Kings) and the Psalms (the longest book in the section collectively known as the Writings). For us it's a reminder that we must not neglect the Old Testament, since it is full of Christ. When did you last study the types (that is, the prefiguring of Christ in people, events and institutions) and prophecies of Christ in these books?

Finally, we consider the commission the disciples are given. Its call to proclaim repentance and forgiveness of sins to all nations (v 47) remains as valid for us today as it was for them. And like them, we need the empowering of the Holy Spirit (v 49) if we are to be effective witnesses to our risen and ascended Lord.

1 Martin Luther, 1483–1546

How familiar are you with the evidence for the resurrection? Powerful arguments for its validity combined with a fresh personal testimony to the reality of the risen Lord's work in your life will make a powerful combination!

Isaiah's importance

The book of Isaiah is one of the most important books in the Bible. It is also one of the most commonly quoted books in the New Testament, comparable with Psalms, with sixty-six quotations and three hundred and forty-eight allusions noted in the latest edition of the UBS Greek New Testament. More important than mere statistics is the fact that Isaiah is above all others 'the evangelical prophet' who magnifies the holiness of God, the awfulness of human sin, and the wonder of God's grace in salvation, giving hope to the penitent through the promise of the coming Messianic King.

Isaiah, whose name means 'Yahweh is salvation', exercised his ministry in and around Jerusalem in the period c745–687 BC (see 1:1). Whether or not he was of noble blood, he certainly had ready access to successive kings of Judah, and could count at least one priest as a friend (8:2). It appears that normally he wore sackcloth and sandals, though for one three year period, at the Lord's command, he went around stripped and barefoot as a sign of coming judgement (20:1–4). During Isaiah's lifetime, in 722 BC, the northern kingdom of Israel fell to the Assyrians. Isaiah warned that the southern kingdom of Judah was heading for a similar fate due to its moral, social and religious sins.

Isaiah's call is often regarded as coming to him in the year King Uzziah died, 740 BC (6:1). But since he is said to have prophesied during Uzziah's reign (1:1), it is likely that the events recorded in chapter 6 came as a confirmation and clarification of an earlier call. Certainly his experience in the Temple was pivotal for Isaiah's ministry, involving a new consecration to a hugely difficult task.

Literary features

From a literary point of view, his book is undoubtedly a masterpiece, with a magnificent use of imagery and plays on words. His style is frequently poetic, with great rhetorical force. This literary skill is used as a vehicle to get across the messages he has received from God. Apart from the book in his name which we have, there is also evidence that he wrote about Hezekiah, the last king to whom he brought God's Word (2 Chron 32:32).

Within the chapters we are to read there is material of very different kinds. Some oracles are communicated in specific literary forms, such as the trial scene in 1:1–20, the woes of 5:8–23, the four stanza poem of 9:8 – 10:4 and the psalm in 12:1–6. The love song of 5:1–7 stands out as a gem. Elsewhere Isaiah's writing is not so poetic (at least in the original Hebrew), as for example in 4:2–6, but no less beautiful and telling. Apart from the account of his commissioning in chapter 6, the record of his confrontation with King Ahaz in chapter 7 stands out in terms of its dramatic impact.

The coming King

As for the themes in these chapters, it is worth underlining the wonderful prophecies which they contain about the coming King who will save his people from their sins, many of which are familiar to us through Handel's *Messiah*. The Davidic kings of Isaiah's day fell far short of what they should have been. Isaiah looks forward in faith to the coming of One whose reign will be characterised by righteousness and peace, and whose kingdom will have no end. As we face uncertainties on the international stage, it is healthy for us to remind ourselves that the Lord Almighty is working out his eternal plan, and that we need not be afraid amid social disintegration and political chaos. Our concern should be to allow ourselves to be purged from all that is evil, to 'walk in the light of the LORD' (2:5), that we may be found among that godly remnant who 'truly rely on the LORD, the Holy One of Israel' (10:20), and who can therefore rejoice at the wonderful prospect of fully enjoying the Messiah's reign.

Andrew Clark

True worship

Day 299

If you were God, what would please you most?

Isaiah 1:1–20

The break-up of a family is always a tragic and heart-rending experience. In verses 2–4 we have an insight into the pain in the father-heart of God because his children have turned their backs on him, and forgotten all that he ever taught them.[1]

Sometimes God has to shock us to bring us to our senses, and this seems to be the point of the accusation that Jerusalem is to God like Sodom and Gomorrah (vs 9,10). As he judged those cities long ago,[2] so he will judge the citizens of Jerusalem if they do not repent (v 20). As far as God is concerned, all the people's religious activity is 'meaningless' (v 13), or, worse still, 'a burden' (v 14). God won't listen to their prayers. Why? Because the hands they stretch out in prayer are 'full of blood' (v 15). And hence the staccato demands for righteousness, justice, and care for the oppressed and the needy (vs 16,17); these are the things God is concerned about, not impressive religious services. In our day of exuberant celebrations, this is a timely reminder.

The invitation that follows is pure gospel. The Lord calls on his people to 'reason together' with him, but actually this is a message of grace, for it is not at all reasonable for God to offer such an amazing amnesty. He will wash away the irremovable stain. There is a choice to be made by the people, however, and that choice is stark (vs 19,20).[3] To choose life will involve serious soul-searching.

1 Exod 4:22,23; Hos 11:1
2 Gen 19:24,25
3 Deut 30:19,20

Have I and my church been concerned for the homeless, for the unemployed, for immigrants, or have we ignored their calls for justice and mercy?

Purged or broken?

Day 300

How do you respond to economic crises and personal disappointments? Ask God to teach you his way as you read.

Isaiah 1:21–31

It is always sad when someone who was once an example to others slips into sin and ends up disgraced. No one respects a prostitute, and this is what Jerusalem, once 'the faithful city' (v 21), has become. God will not tolerate such a change. The Holy One of Israel (v 4) is also the Mighty One of Israel (v 24), the God who will not be mocked.[1] But his judgement is not for the purpose of destroying, but rather of purging away the evil with a view to restoration of the original faithful living (v 26). What lengths has the sovereign Lord gone to in your life to turn you from greed to godliness?

Shame and disgrace is going to be the destiny of all who follow other gods ('oaks' and 'gardens' in v 29 hint of worship of fertility gods; today's stress on sex and 'nature' is not at all new!). It will become increasingly clear that these things cannot satisfy (v 30). Similarly, all who trust in human might and achievement will find that their technological advances prove to be merely a means for their undoing (v 31). This is a lesson writ large on the pages of the history of the twentieth – or twenty-first – century.

Are you, am I, one of the penitent ones redeemed in such a way that God's righteousness was not ignored but rather more fully displayed (v 27)?[2] If so, let us continue to 'seek justice', 'rebuke the oppressor' (v 17, NIV margin), and defend the cause of the needy, knowing that this is the conduct that pleases God.

1 Gal 6:7,8
2 Rom 3:21–26

'The fatherless and widow' (vs 17,23) stand for all who, because of their lack of a powerful protector, are liable to be exploited. Ask God to show you some people you know who are in this category, and how you can help them in practical ways today.

Judgement on the proud

Day 301

What sin do you think God hates most? Why?

Isaiah 2:1–22 

The opening verses of this chapter portray beautifully a vision of how Jerusalem was to be the centre of the world, the place to which the nations came to learn about God's ways, the source of world peace. It is possible that this section about 'the city on the hill'[1] was a popular hymn. If so, verse 5 is a challenge to complacency. As Alec Motyer puts it, 'If others are ever going to say "Come let us go up to the mountain of the LORD" Judah must heed the call "Come, let us walk in the light of the LORD"'.[2] For us the challenge remains. If others are to be attracted to the light of Christ, then we must pay serious attention to the sincerity of our devotion, the depth of our teaching and the quality of our caring.

The present state of the people is dire indeed. It is very disturbing how many echoes of modern life are mentioned in verses 6 to 9: superstitions and occult practices (despite all our technological sophistication), wealth and armaments accompanied by pervasive idolatry. Such a people God must humble.

In the rest of the chapter there is a threefold reference to 'the dread of the Lord and the splendour of his majesty' (vs 10,19,21). The day of the Lord will bring judgement on all humankind's arrogance and pride (vs 15,16). All idols are to disappear, and the Lord alone will be exalted in that day (vs 17,18). How guilty are we of priding ourselves on our beautiful churches, our many activities, our sound doctrine, when God is more concerned about whether we rely on him in everything and give all the glory back to him?

1 Matt 5:14
2 *The Prophecy of Isaiah*, IVP

'What comes into our minds when we think about God is the most important thing about us' (A W Tozer, 1897–1963). How great is your God?

Social collapse

Day 302

'O come, refresher of those who languish and faint, Come, star and guide of those who fail on the tempestuous sea of the world, only haven of the tossed and shipwrecked.'[1]

 *Isaiah 3:1 – 4:1*

The focus now moves from Jerusalem's religious condition to its social condition. We are presented here with a vivid picture of society's collapse. Disintegration is portrayed in terms of 'the pressure of scarcity on a people without ideals' (Derek Kidner). All resources, whether in terms of the necessities of life (vs 1,7) or of leadership (vs 2–4), will be removed. Imagine the disintegration of society in a worldwide recession – what would we rely on when all the normal props were removed? Already in many Western societies we see 'dog-eat-dog' competition when each looks after himself, and it is not the truly worthy who are respected (v 5). Our leaders are unwise and are far more concerned with their own continuance in power than with the real needs of the people (vs 12–15). If it is already like this now, how will it be when disaster truly strikes?

In verses 3:16 – 4:1 judgement is pronounced on the women in society for their pride and obsession with fashion. Their concern is with the outward appearance, while the Lord looks at the heart.[2] All of us would do well to examine our particular trivial pursuits, asking how they will appear when the time for judgement arrives. Have we been concerned for true riches,[3] or for temporal wealth and comfort? For outward or inward beauty?[4]

1 Augustine of Hippo, 354–430
2 1 Sam 16:7
3 1 Tim 6:18; James 2:5; Rev 2:9
4 1 Pet 3:3–5

'All that is not eternal is eternally out of date' (C S Lewis, 1898–1963).

Saved and secure

Day 303

'Jesus, master carpenter ... wield well thy tools ... that we who come rough-hewn may be fashioned to a truer beauty by thy hand.'

Isaiah 4:2–6 

In these verses we find a beautiful picture of a world where sin no longer plays any role. The 'Branch of the Lord' (v 2) is a messianic title,[1] referring to the coming king as descendant of David.

But who will enjoy this paradise? In these verses we see certain of their characteristics. Each one is holy, and their names are written in the book of life.[2] As we consider the certainty of future judgement to come, let us determine to allow the Lord to be to us a 'refiner's fire'[3] now, so that we may not be devastated by the 'consuming fire' of God's holiness[4] on that day. Is there any area of your life about which the Holy Spirit is convicting you? However painful it may be, allow him to have his way today. To do so will certainly be less fearsome than to face the Lord's judgement later! For the survivors of God's wrath, a wonderful prospect comes into view (vs 5,6). The word 'canopy' is a term used for the place where the marriage of bride and groom is consummated. The mutual love of the Lord and his people expressed in the greatest possible intimacy and tenderness will be the supreme and overriding reality of the new world. In every circumstance of life the Lord's loving presence will provide protection from any possible danger or harm.

1 Isa 53:2; Jer 23:5
2 Mal 3:16; Rev 20:12–15
3 Mal 3:2
4 Heb 12:29

Commenting on Revelation 3:20, Alister McGrath remarks, 'Some Christians are too busy to hear that knocking. With a grim relentlessness they keep on being passionately busy for Christ, unaware that the same Christ who they are trying to serve is just as passionately trying to refresh and renew them'. Allow him to purify your heart and draw you close to him today.

No justice, no prosperity

Day 304

'God wants spiritual fruits, not religious nuts' says the evangelist J John. Pray that, as you read, you may come to a new understanding of what God requires of you.

Isaiah 5:1–7

Poetry and music can often move our hearts in a way that prose cannot. In this passage the prophet sings a love song which he hopes will help the people to understand the longings of God's heart. We learn that these longings are twofold.

First of all, God longs to bless his people. He longs to provide them richly with all they need (v 2).[1] When we think of what unsearchable riches the Father has given us in Christ,[2] how can our hearts not be filled with gratitude and a desire to please him?

The second longing of God's heart is that his people might yield fruit pleasing to him. But this longing is continually frustrated (vs 2b,4b). What fruit does God desire? Justice and righteousness (v 7). For those of us brought up in churches which stress individual sanctification and church fellowship as the highest goals, this may well come as a salutary reminder. When we think of our relationship with 'the world', we often think above all of evangelism. But here we learn that the God who has made all people in his image demands of us that we venerate that image by showing respect and fairness to all. If we would be in the right with God, we need to be in the right with others too in the practical details of our everyday lives.

1 1 Tim 6:17; John 10:10; James 2:5
2 Eph 3:8
3 Author, Roger Page

'Many poor and needy found their way to Jesus. Few come into our evangelical churches today. We defend ourselves in many ways from really engaging with people … Who will address the deep needs … when pain, depression, disillusionment or aloneness strip away the defences?'[3]

Woe to the comfortable!

Ask God to help you to be truly open to the convicting voice of the Spirit as you read.

Isaiah 5:8–30 

This passage contains six different 'woes' to those on whom God's judgement is about to fall. The lifestyle of these people appears to be of a kind to which many aspire. Property, parties, clever dealing – the essence of the good life, surely? At first sight we might be tempted to envy rather than pity them. But God's perspective is different, as Jesus also reminded us.[1]

Scarcity (v 10), hunger and thirst (v 13), death (v 14), destruction (vs 24,25) – what a prospect! At the root of divine judgement lie many sins. The people have no respect for what God has done for them (v 12). They are guilty of arrogance in their attitudes and actions (vs 15,16). How clever they think they are in their scoffing at God and overturning of 'traditional values'! But they have rejected God's Word (v 24), which required them to show justice to the innocent (v 23), and so God will reject them.

God is slow to get angry,[2] but heaven help those against whom his anger is aroused. His fury leads to 'darkness and distress' (v 30) for those who a short time previously thought they'd never had it so good.

Greed out of control, property speculation, a glorying in a playboy lifestyle, an arrogant scepticism about God, a reversal of proper moral values – it sounds all too familiar, doesn't it? 'Champions at mixing drinks' beware! You are tottering at the edge of a precipice!

1 Luke 6:24–26
2 Exod 34:6

'Many churches today need to hear the sermon on the "amount"' (J John). Does yours?

Holy is the Lord

Day 306

'If we invoke the Holy Spirit, we must be ready for the glorious pain of being caught by his power out of our petty orbit into the eternal purposes of the Almighty.'[1]

Isaiah 6:1–13

After a long and prosperous reign King Uzziah died a leper, having been guilty in his pride of wanting to offer sacrifices in the Temple.[2] His experience must have brought home to Isaiah the reality of God's judgement on sin. His vision of the heavenly King is clearly a devastating experience for him. The seraphs or 'burning ones' continually proclaim God's holiness (v 3). In Hebrew, repetition is used to indicate superlative quality, but only here in the Bible is a threefold repetition employed. The holiness of the King, the Lord of hosts, is the ultimate reality, and his vision of the Lord's glory overwhelms Isaiah.

Isaiah is filled with a consciousness of his sin, and knows he deserves to die. But then the unexpected happens. The live coal brought from the altar touches Isaiah at the point of his felt need, his lips. The altar is of course the place where God's anger against sin is propitiated by the blood sacrifice of a substitute. Isaiah's guilt and sin are removed and his lips will from this point on be filled with messages from the Lord.

Isaiah's response to the wonder of atonement is to make himself available for God's purposes. But he probably didn't bargain for the commission he received! His clear and persistent preaching will only further harden the hearts of those who have always refused to listen to God. Only when terrifying judgement has taken its course will the ground be cleared for new growth (v 13).

1 William Temple, 1881–1944
2 2 Chron 26:16–21

The task God has for you today may not be an easy one. Knowing that your sin has been covered at incredible cost, are you willing to volunteer for service as Isaiah did?

Fear or faith?

Day 307

When danger threatens, it's all too easy to make plans based on fear rather than on faith. Pray for God's help to resist this temptation today.

Isaiah 7:1–25 

The prospect of facing a joint invasion force fills Ahaz with dread. God's message to him through Isaiah is that he doesn't need to be afraid of these two smouldering fag ends (v 4). He should refuse the temptation to play the political game and put his trust in God's promise. We too may be tempted today to engage in power politics or to enter into compromising alliances because of the need we perceive to protect our position. But once we start on that slippery slope, the end is inevitable: 'If you do not stand firm in your faith, you will not stand at all' (v 9).

Ahaz's refusal to respond to God's request to ask him for a sign reveals the hardness of his heart. He 'shrouds his unwillingness to face the spiritual realities of the situation in a veil of piety,' says the commentator Alec Motyer. We too can be quite good at doing this.

The sign which God gives anyway is relevant to the contemporary situation. Judgement in the form of an invasion by the Assyrians, notorious for their fierce cruelty, will soon come not only on Samaria but also on Judah. The graphic images in verses 18–20 emphasise its severity, and the vivid vignettes in verses 21–25 its devastating effects. But the sign of Immanuel does of course also look forward to the distant future, and the meaning of the name ('God with us') gave a promise of hope. How wonderful that hope was to be would only become clear when Jesus, born of a virgin, came from God to save us from our sins.

Meditate on this message from the Lord when you are tempted to give in to fear today: 'Be careful, keep calm and don't be afraid' (v 4).

A stone or a sanctuary?

Day 308

As you come into God's presence, ask the Lord to give you a renewed desire to reverence him, to trust in him, to enquire of him.

Isaiah 8:1–22

It can't have been easy being the son of a prophet! Isaiah's children had to put up with having weird names which had symbolic significance. His first son, Shear-Jashub, had a name which meant 'A remnant shall return'. The concept of a minority within Judah who, unlike the majority, would respond to God's Word with faith and obedience, was very important in God's Word through Isaiah. In today's passage we see a picture of this remnant in the description of those who truly fear the Lord, and experience his protecting presence (vs 10,13,14). The name of the second son, Maher-Shalal-Hash-Baz, meant 'Quick-pickings-easy prey' according to the translator JB Phillips. Like his brother's, this name had symbolic significance, in this case of the easy victory Assyria would soon gain over Judah (v 18).

While the Lord will be a sanctuary for the remnant, to the rest he will prove to be 'a stone that causes men to stumble' (v 14). This verse is quoted in the New Testament with reference to those who are unbelieving and disobedient to the word.[1] Just as in Isaiah's time, so there are many today who would rather consult mediums or spiritists rather than God's own testimony to his nature and will (vs 19,20). And today too, such turning from the living God to the power of the evil one results in 'distress and darkness and fearful gloom' (v 22). If we will not fear the Lord, we will soon be prey to all sorts of other fears.

1 Rom 9:32; 1 Pet 2:8

Lift before the Lord those known to you who have chosen to consult mediums or engage in some other way with the occult. Pray that they may come to their senses before it is too late.

A new kingdom dawns

Day 309

'Make us of quick and tender conscience, O Lord, that understanding, we may obey every word of thine, and discerning, may follow every suggestion of thine indwelling Spirit.'[1]

Isaiah 9:1–7

The familiar words of this passage help us yet again to appreciate the wonder of both the person and the work of our Saviour.

- *Wonderful Counsellor*. How important that the ruler of a kingdom should be wise! This king's wise counsel is vastly superior to mere human reasoning and, as the song says, he is 'only a prayer away', ever ready to guide us if we will only turn to him.
- *Mighty God*. This divine warrior is more than able to rescue us from our oppressors (compare vs 4,5). Bring to him today any yoke that is burdening you. No problem is too difficult for him to deal with.
- *Everlasting Father*. Kidner (NBCR) comments that the term 'Father' 'signifies the paternal benevolence of the perfect ruler over a people whom he loves as his children'. He will love us and look after us for ever!
- *Prince of Peace*. This king brings us *shalom* in all its aspects, well-being, freedom from anxiety, harmony, and enjoyment of the favour of God.

The kingdom over which this Son of David reigns is one marked by righteousness and justice (v 7). As we praise the one born for our salvation, let us ask him to show us any ways in which we have not been doing what is right and fair. And let us rejoice in the fact that 'the zeal of the Lord Almighty' is at work to ensure that there will be no end to the increase of his government and of peace (v 7).

1 Christina Rossetti, 1830–94

Pray that somehow, amid all the business of life, you will be able to bring an offering to the child born to be king that will bring him pleasure.

Everyone is ungodly

Day 310

***'Give me, O Lord, a steadfast heart, which no unworthy affection may drag downwards; an upright heart, which no unworthy purpose may tempt aside.'*[1]**

 ***Isaiah 9:8 – 10:4***

The repeated refrain (vs 12b,17b, 21b;10:4b) makes it clear that we have here a poem giving four reasons for the coming judgement.

- *Bravado*. The pride and arrogance of the people of the northern kingdom reveals itself in their misplaced confidence in their ability not only to repair the damage they have suffered, but to make something even better out of the ruins (v 10).
- *Bad leadership*. Those who might have been expected to encourage the people to seek the Lord's face in repentance, have rather led them astray (vs 13–16). So the Lord will not show compassion on the people, for they are totally ungodly, especially in their speech (v 17).
- *Selfishness*. In this society it is very much 'every man for himself', for no one spares his brother (v 19), or even his child (v 20b). Divided, this people fall. Never satisfied (v 20), they gorge on each other in vain.
- *Injustice*. Law-makers and civil servants alike are concerned merely to feather their own nest, not to protect the weak and vulnerable. The commentator Derek Kidner says that 'the haunting question of verse 3 could undermine the exploits of a lifetime, all of them within the law of the land'.

1 Thomas Aquinas, 1224–74

The description of this society is far too close to our own for comfort: 'If one of Paul's servants (Demas) ... was afterwards drawn away, let none of us rely too much on our own zeal lasting even one year, but remembering how much of the journey still lies ahead, let us ask God for steadfastness' (John Calvin, 1509–64).

Just the rod of his anger

Day 311

Pride goes before a fall. Ask the Lord to reveal to you any hidden pride lurking in your own heart.

Isaiah 10:5–19 

God is using the Assyrians to be the rod by which he will punish his people. But they plan not only to punish, but to destroy, as they have done to many other nations. The Assyrians do not realise that, though the people of Samaria and Jerusalem are worshipping idols, they are actually the people of the sovereign Lord of all the earth.

So when the Assyrians have done all that he has intended to use them to do, the time comes for him to judge them for their pride. Like them, it is all too easy for us to have confidence in our own strength and wisdom (v 12), forgetting that God holds in his hand our life and all our ways,[1] and that we have nothing which we did not first receive from him.[2]

Whoever else the Assyrians may be able to terrify, they pose no threat to the Lord Almighty (v 15). It is all too easy for him to bring them down to earth with a vengeance, as the twin images of a wasting disease,[3] and a consuming fire make clear. All their splendour will vanish overnight. God cannot be mocked.

Is there anyone you are bullying without fully realising it? It may be your child, your spouse, your colleague at work. Remember that there is nothing which God does not see and remember, and that his time to judge you will come sooner or later if you are unwilling to change. Are you being bullied? Remember that your oppressor is on a leash. He or she can go no further than the Lord allows.

1 Dan 5:23
2 1 Cor 4:7
3 Compare 2 Kings 19:35
4 Jer 13:17

'But if you do not listen, I will weep in secret because of your pride'.[4] Weep awhile for the coming destruction of those who in their pride are rushing headlong towards disaster.

The burden will be lifted

Day 312

'Though outwardly we are wasting away, yet inwardly we are being renewed day by day.'[1] Pray that the Lord will encourage you through this passage to stand firm and not lose heart.

Isaiah 10:20–34

The theme of the righteous remnant comes to the fore in this passage. They are marked by repentance, a decision to 'return to the Mighty God', and a true reliance on him (vs 20,21). They have suffered along with the rest of God's people as his devastating judgement has come upon them through the Assyrians. But now the Lord seeks to encourage them. 'Very soon' (v 25) his anger against them will pass, and will be directed at the Assyrians instead. Just as he trounced the Midianites and the Egyptians who oppressed his people, so the Lord will annihilate the Assyrians and lift the heavy burden from his people's shoulders (v 27).

Often like the Psalmist we cry, 'How long, O Lord?',[2] when there seems to be no end to the troubles we have to put up with. We know that God disciplines us for our good,[3] but often our trials seem endless. But this passage reminds us that there really is light at the end of the tunnel. 'The yoke will be broken' (though the reason the NIV gives, 'because you have grown so fat', doesn't make much sense!). And so we are called not to be afraid of those who oppress us (v 24), and who shake their fists at the godly (v 32). For in God's good time he will bring down the proud, and lift up the humble.[4]

1 2 Cor 4:16
2 Ps 6:3; 13:1; 89:46
3 Heb 12:5–11
4 Luke 2:52

'Lord, grant that your love may so fill our lives that we may count nothing too small to do for you, nothing too much to give, and nothing too hard to bear' (Ignatius of Loyola, 1491–1556).

A branch will bear fruit

Day 313

Pray that this vision of the delights of the world to come will so enthral you that you will be filled with joy and peace in believing.

Isaiah 11:1–16 

Comparing this passage with Isaiah 65:17–25, which speaks in very similar terms of the new heavens and new earth which God will create,[1] leads to the conclusion that it too refers to the world to come. What a picture it is! First, there is a wonderful portrayal of he who is both the shoot (v 1, ie the descendant) and the root (v 10) of Jesse, David's father. The key to his qualification to rule will be that the Spirit of God will rest upon him.[2] His wisdom and understanding, undergirded by his reverence for God, will enable him to judge the world with justice and faithfulness, supporting the rights of the oppressed and judging their enemies (vs 3–5). The knowledge that such a government is coming to this earth soon should encourage us to stand up for the needy even now.

The new world will be marked by total security and a complete absence of anything which might harm or destroy. The pictures of domestic and wild animals living in harmony, and of a young child playing happily with both animals and snakes speaks powerfully of the ending of the curse on the created world which has brought ruin and disharmony ever since.[3] The key to this *shalom* is the universal knowledge of the Lord (v 9). All the world's peoples will find their rest in him (v 11).

Since we have such a hope, let us determine to root out of our lives all jealousy and strife, and learn to serve one another in love.

1 Compare 65:25
2 Luke 3:21,22; John 1:33; Acts 10:38
3 Gen 3:15–17

'Lord, forgive our foolish ways. Help us even now to live the life of heaven on earth.'

Give thanks to the Lord

Day 314

'O Lord, I fling myself with all my weakness and misery into thy ever-open arms. Pour the life-giving balm of thy love into my heart … May I be thine, wholly thine, at all costs thine.'[1]

Isaiah 12:1–6

What a beautiful song with which to praise the Lord at the end of this series of readings. Its two stanzas speak of the Lord's saving power shown to the individual (vs 1–3) and to all the world (vs 4,5).

What a joy to know that God's righteous anger against our sins has been turned away from us because of our trust in Christ, and that now we experience his comfort! This knowledge should lead us to trust him rather than be suffocated by our fears, and to praise him rather than being disheartened by our weaknesses (v 2). In verse 3 the 'you' is plural; the prophet calls on the community of the redeemed to draw out water from the wells of salvation God has provided. In other words, we should make the promises of God our own and experience their reality through the exercise of our faith, remembering that 'no matter how many promises God has made, they are 'Yes' in Christ'.[2]

The salvation God has accomplished through his Son is not just for our own enjoyment, however. The call to 'make known among the nations what he has done' (v 4) should be forever ringing in our minds and hearts. For there are still so many people groups on earth who have never heard the good news. What a day it will be when our wonderful Lord comes again in power and glory. Till that day let us determine to 'speed its coming' by calling all people to repentance and by living holy and godly lives.[3]

1 Père Besson, Catholic priest and artist, died 1861
2 2 Cor 1:20
3 2 Pet 3:9–12

'Let the song go round the earth – Jesus Christ is Lord! Sound his praises, tell his worth, Be his name adored! Every clime and every tongue, Join the grand, the glorious song!' (Sarah Stock, 1838–98).

A song of love

For many of us, the Song of Songs is an enigma. We don't know what to make of its explicit endorsement of human beauty and sexuality, and quickly apply it to our relationship with God. Snatches have found their way into our song books and wedding ceremonies. We may even have wallowed in its poetry when we were young and in love for the first time; now, however, we wonder why the book would have been read aloud at the Jewish Passover.

But today we need the Song of Songs more than ever. Society is devaluing marriage and making sex an idol; people long for the stability of commitment but find it hard to promise it themselves; personal independence has become more important than mutuality and trust.

Sing a song of love transcendent

The church has often reacted to a sex-soaked culture by not speaking positively about sex. But here in the Song is a wonderful endorsement of human love, beauty, commitment, security – all in the context of personal faithfulness and community support. It can give us the concepts, if not the colloquial language, with which to present positively what others cheapen. And it sets us on the path, however tentatively, towards an exploration of the connection between spirituality and sexuality.

It is possible to read the Song as allegory without any reference to historical context; or as typology, comparing its characters with New Testament teaching; or as a drama, intended to be acted or sung at a royal wedding pageant. But in these notes a natural interpretation is followed, starting with what the text tells us about what it means to be human as God intended.

Of course, the relationship between the two lovers can also illustrate the relationship between Christ and the believer, or Christ and the church. But if we are to overcome our reluctance to address the issue of sexuality in our day, we must first hear the poems speak to us as people made in the image of God. They amplify the creation pronouncement on male-female relationships and marriage (Gen 2:23,24).

Issues of interpretation

The Song itself is a collection of poems divided by verse markers and changes in tone into six cycles. Our seven readings follow these divisions. In each of the cycles we find yearnings for love, tension or frustration, affirmations of praise and beauty, and movements towards intimacy.

Within this pattern, dialogues are loosely organised; the literary focus is the end of the third cycle (5:1), the consummation of marriage. Using the gender of the pronouns and other indictors, translators attribute most of the dialogues to either the male or female speaker, and a few to the chorus. In the NIV these are labelled 'lover', 'beloved' and 'friends'. However, we will use 'man' and 'woman'.

The Song has many more words in the mouth of the woman than the man. She takes the initiative in their relationship as much as he. The reciprocity of their relationship, its ups and downs, its progression over time, together with the call to faithfulness, is the theme of these poems.

'Solomon' appears in the Song at the beginning, and in chapters 3 and 8, but the way his name is used varies and is not easy to interpret. As a much-married and wealthy king of Israel, he can be interpreted allegorically or perhaps he is the focus of a wedding pageant. But in a natural interpretation focusing on the God-given aspects of love and marriage this is more difficult. Scenarios which have him taking the young woman into his harem away from her shepherd lover hardly fit a book in which the whole tenor is faithfulness and keeping oneself for one's lover. For the most part, therefore, we have interpreted 'Solomon' as an expression of an idealised groom – a king to the one who loves him.

Jennifer Turner

Hello, young lovers!

Pray that God will stir love afresh in your heart – for him, for others, perhaps for that one special person.

Song of Songs 1:1 – 2:7

There is a gentle movement through this first song cycle. It focuses on the young lovers but at the same time gives us much to ponder, whether we have only recently found the great love of our life, or are simply resting in God's companionship because one special human love is not ours at this time. Themes to be explored – sexuality, marriage, beauty, the wonder of the human body – are introduced one by one in this love story.

Already the woman is breathless with anticipation (v 4), yet conscious of her Cinderella-like status at the hands of her brothers (v 6). She wants to seek out her lover but is wary of appearing so forward she is mistaken for a prostitute (v 7). He, for his part, begins one of his many recitations of her beauty (vs 9–11), likening her sex appeal to that of a mare let loose among the stallions of Pharaoh's chariots!

What pictures this conjures up for us! Better than prime time television or a blockbuster movie! Yet the subtle interplay of the lovers' delight in each other (1:15 – 2:3) also emphasises the mutuality of their growing relationship. According to the commentator Tom Gledhill, this reciprocity 'is something that shines out from the Song, something of a protest against male domination and macho-masculinity which sin brought into the world'. We know that in Christ the effects of sinful exploitation of one by another[1] can be reversed, but Paul still found it necessary to remind the Corinthians to show each other mutual respect.[2]

But if mutual longing and belonging is endorsed by God's Word, there is still a caution in the refrain that ends this cycle[3] – do not try to hurry love for it must grow slowly within proper bounds.

Can we similarly speak of a mutual relationship with God? Yes, but he is the one who takes the initiative. Our response is an answer to his love for he delights in us as we in him.[4]

1 Gen 3:16
2 1 Cor 7:4,5
3 Also 3:5; 8:4
4 Ps 149:4

Use the words of 2:4 to luxuriate in God's love for you.

Day 316

Springtime rhapsody

God often brings to us a 'season of singing'. Pray that you will recognise when he is doing this in your life.

Song of Songs 2:8 – 3:5

Spring has long been used poetically to evoke freshness, a bursting forth of potential, the time to move out of the past from barrenness to fruitfulness. All is promise of good things to come. Love can do that too. It can transform the landscape, reinterpreting even a tedious task into something exhilarating.

This 'spring' cycle begins poetically with mountains, gazelle and stag, capturing the woman's anticipation of her lover's approach. 'Look! Here he comes!' (2:8). She repeats words he has said to her in the past (2:10–13) then switches to the present tense to describe her feelings as she daydreams (2:14). This is still young love. The walls, window, lattice keep are a barrier (emotional as well as physical) to be overcome before they can be truly united. As the God-given mandate for marriage makes clear[1] there is no permanent cleaving to another until the safety found in family and home is left behind. Such a huge risk should only be entered into carefully.

Verse 15, like some others in the Song, is obscure. But something of the teasing nature of the man's invitation comes through to us. Adoration, retreat, invitation, reticence, teasing, playful banter, imagination (3:1,2) are all part of the progression of love. Which of us does not look back in wonder at our naivety or presumption about another? Perhaps we need God's forgiveness for actions in the past, or better understanding of another generation who are now enjoying young love? A cautionary note in 3:5 reminds us not to arouse love too quickly.

God knows how to perfectly pace the growth of our love for him – when to draw us out, when to lighten the script, when to comfort us. The biggest impediment is our reticence to accept his love. Do we really believe he has only the best in store for us?

1 Gen 2:24
2 Ps 37:4

'Delight yourself in the Lord and he will give you the desires of your heart.'[2]

All the world loves a wedding

Day 317

Reflect on the effect of Jesus' presence at the wedding in Cana and his replenishment of the supply of wine.

Song of Songs 3:6 – 5:1 

The verse (5:1a) describing the willing consummation of the lovers' marriage is the pivot around which the whole Song revolves. To our lineal minds it comes too early, but this kind of literary structure is often used in Scripture to draw attention to the most significant concept. A wedding full of hopes and dreams makes a very good focus.

It is preceded by the procession of the idealised groom (3:6–11). Although twenty-first century readers may find some of the pictures conjured up by the similes odd,[1] we can all appreciate sensual beauty and celebrate it with the bride and groom. We might also assert that physical beauty is only one element of the man/woman relationship, but a wedding is a socially acceptable occasion for the public glorying of a couple in their love (5:1b) as they invite others to endorse and share their happiness. In fact, if there wasn't that frisson of expectation, that wonder at how God has blessed them in each other, we would rightly fear they didn't fully appreciate the joy of intimacy God intends for them.

The Creator made us for relationship: in the image of the Father–Son–Spirit relationship. In Eden, the first couple revelled in their complementarity and partnership and they were 'naked and not ashamed'.[2] Only after the entry of sin did nakedness come to represent and provoke shame. But in the grace of God, a progressive unveiling of ourselves physically and emotionally to our spouses builds a deeper relationship.

But what of those who do not have this form of physical intimacy? For them, as for all of us, physical beauty, sensuality, exquisite friendships are still gifts from God to be savoured. They mirror his relationship with us. The God who took on human flesh, by his redemptive actions creates and re-creates a world that is good.

1 For example 4:3
2 Gen 2:25

God is always leading you gently to greater openness with himself and with those you love. Thank him in anticipation.

Day 318

Lost and found

Pray that God will enable you to see the good he brings out of loss in your life.

 *Song of Songs 5:2–16*

The path of true love never did run smooth. Is this temporary lapse in the relationship post-wedding, or is it remembered from an earlier time? It doesn't really matter. We know that every relationship has its ups and downs. How we handle them is what counts. It may be the woman's petulance that caused the rift (v 3) or perhaps it was just innocent teasing, but she is soon acknowledging her loss. The search motif (vs 6–8) echoes her earlier foray (real or imagined) into the city streets (3:1–4) but with disastrous results this time.

Loss – of dreams but especially of unrealistic expectations of the other – is an unavoidable part of a growing relationship. We learn in the pain a little more about ourselves as well as the other. And where this can be gently communicated and mutual responsibility acknowledged, good comes out of it. So now, beyond the physical attraction – and our young lover expresses that eloquently enough (6:1) to get the observers on her side – she adds the telling word, 'friend' (v 16). What a wealth of meaning in that description! That is what she has lost in driving him away, and she wants it back.

Jesus calls us friends.[1] Even in the 'dark night of the soul' when our sense of loss is acute and we have no explanation for what is happening to us, we can assume by faith rather than feeling that he is with us.[2] We may cry with the psalmist, 'My God, why have you forsaken me?' but our very cry acknowledges God's interest in us, and reinforces our strong sense that he will never forsake us.

What is God teaching us in a time of loss? Most likely he is asking us to relinquish something we are holding on to, something we have put in his place. In the long run, it is the relationship with him alone that matters.

1 John 15:14
2 Matt 28:20b
3 Richard Foster, *Prayers from the Heart*

'Today, O Lord, I yield myself to you. May your will be my delight today … May your love be the pattern of my living.'[3]

'You are beautiful, my darling!'

Day 319

Why not reflect on the impact beauty has had on your life and thank God for it.

Song of Songs 6:1–13 

Beauty is a recurring theme. Whether awesome or exquisite, fleeting or etched into ancient rocks, beauty is a gift from the Creator. Praise expresses our appreciation. 'You are beautiful, my darling' (v 4) would delight any woman's heart. But would she be equally pleased with a comparison to two cities? A modern young woman might appreciate her personal beauty (Tirzah) being complemented by awesome strength (Jerusalem). Do we receive compliments with humility and thankfulness? Do we allow them, in the appropriate setting, to arouse love? These lovers did. Praise and receptiveness overcame the blockage in their relationship.

Unfortunately, appreciation of beauty is often put in the place of God-centred spirituality. But finally beauty is not satisfying. Only God is. 'If I find in myself a desire which no experience in this world can satisfy, the most probable explanation is that I was made for another world'.[1]

'Garden' and 'fruit' are not symbols of fertility but of contentment and lush provision of delights. Walled and protected from intruders, the garden is a place of pleasure; it also represents the innermost sanctum, locked until this moment (4:12), into which the woman invites the man (4:16) to consummate their marriage (5:1). It is a natural setting in which she waters and gives him succour – a mutual possession in which they taste the sweetness of each other's fruit (2:3).

Does 'garden' suggest a wistful glance back to Eden? No – Scripture points us forward to the New Jerusalem,[2] to paradise redeemed. Although the first city was an attempt to defy him,[3] God takes the symbol and remakes it into a place with a bride where beauty is displayed and relationships are fully restored by the blood of the Lamb.[4]

1 CS Lewis, *Mere Christianity*
2 Rev 21:1–5
3 Gen 11:1–8
4 Rev 5:6–14

What symbol best speaks to you of the beauty of restored relationships?

God thought of sex first

Day 320

Give God thanks with the writer of Psalm 139 that you are 'fearfully and wonderfully made'.

Song of Songs 7:1 – 8:4

What passion! Verse 8 reveals the urgency of the man's desire. And she is willing (vs 9b,10). She knows that his frank admiration (7:1–9) is very different from public leering at a scantily-clad dancer (6:13b). The whole of nature in the spring-time will resonate with their love (7:11–13). Now is the time to awaken what has been kept for this season.

If we followed all the allusions in the passionate speeches of these lovers, we would uncover many a double entendre and sexual reference. There is a time and place for such explicit love talk, but even at weddings with their public blessing of sexual love, only select verses of the Song are suitable to be read. Yet we cannot shut our eyes to the clear endorsement of human sexuality and specifically, love-making, that the Song gives. The context is always a committed relationship. Frustrations are acknowledged. Privacy constraints are honoured. But the clear implication is that God-given sexual desire is theirs to enjoy.

Sexual delight is not just for young lovers, however. Lifelong relationships call for lifelong exploration. To fully appreciate God's gift requires laughter as well as seriousness, give and take, a recognition of the ebb and flow of libido, gentle communication, and most of all, hope in difficult times that God makes all things new.

Finally, it must be acknowledged that here is a strong affirmation of the human body created 'good' by God.[1] Rejection of the physical as if that would advance the spiritual is not God's way. Nor is the tendency of modern Western society to deny the spiritual because sexuality is all there is to life. We are body-persons whom God redeems and we remain both spiritual and sexual beings in relationship with him and with others.

1 Gen 1:26

Reflect on the connection between spirituality and sexuality in your own experience. Bring to God your pain and your delight.

Many waters cannot quench love

Day 321

Pray that your heart will be open to the kind of love that bridges great gulfs in human relationships.

Song of Songs 8:5–14 

Like a curtain call concluding a performance, all the main characters – companions, mother, brothers, the two lovers – make their appearance in this final cycle which serves as an expression of public approval of the union, an affirmation of love which cannot be bought or sold (vs 11,12). Will the young couple live happily ever after? The final verses suggest that there will always be an ebb and flow, a hide and seek, new depths of appreciation of each other.

And while this has clearly been a love match, we cannot take from it a simple endorsement of the Western view of romantic love as if that is all there is to love. Those who 'fall in love' can just as easily fall out of it, and secular wedding ceremonies with vows that apply 'as long as love shall last', merely give feelings the final say. Forgotten is the mutual care and commitment and trust needed in sickness as well as in health.

There is an enormous gulf of selfishness to overcome in any relationship, made worse by modern society's quest for independence and autonomy for the individual. It is doubly so in marriage. As a friend once observed, we think that it is a good thing to give our children separate bedrooms, but when they marry they not only have to share a room but a bed! They are ill-prepared for the mutual interdependence marriage requires.

Yet we only find our true selves in relationship with others and with God, and that requires self-surrender.[1] If falling in love helps us initially overcome our essential separateness, well and good. It also adds spice to the marriage relationship. But the greatest expression of love, the love to which we are all called, will ask much more of us.[2] We can only rise to that challenge with God's help.

1 1 John 4:8
2 1 Cor 13
3 Rom 5:5

Ask God to make the love he is pouring into your heart through his Spirit overflow to others.[3]

Sage and prophet

I have grown to value James for his deep wisdom and practical application of faith. All of us need to stand back at times and assess our spiritual progress. A journey with James is especially appropriate when we feel the need for reflection on the state of our lives, for he writes a letter full of practical wisdom.

In writing to the Jewish churches, James has plundered at least three traditions or genres in the process of composing his letter. It is not just passages directly concerned with wisdom (1:2–8; 3:13–18) that have echoes of the Old Testament wisdom tradition; rather, the whole book is filled with the pithy, practical wisdom for living that is one of the characteristics of the Wisdom literature. Then again, he has the fiery passion of a prophet, condemning the indifference and luxury of the rich like some latter-day Amos or Isaiah (2:1–13; 4:13 – 5:6). Thirdly, he is an interpreter of the teachings of Jesus, with echoes of the Sermon on the Mount in particular. It is as if, travelling through this landscape of the letter of James, we are reminded of other, vast landscapes in the territories of the Old Testament and Gospels.

Who is James?

Who is this James? He is sufficiently well-known among the fledgling Jewish church to be simply known as 'James'. There have been three main contenders in the discussion of his identity, James son of Alphaeus, James the son of Zebedee and James the brother of Jesus. Tradition has favoured the latter, and since we know James the son of Zebedee died before we believe this letter was written, there is only one James who, sufficiently well-known, could simply sign off as 'James': the leader of the Jerusalem church and the son of Mary and Joseph.

While not one of the first disciples, and possibly not a follower of Jesus until after the resurrection, he knew Jesus for longer than any of the Twelve, and we have in this letter, with its mix of traditions and links with Matthew, a perceptive insight into some of the perennial themes in the teachings of Jesus.

Key themes

The first theme is the one which Luther, with his devotion to Paul's doctrine of justification by faith, took exception to, calling this letter 'a right strawy epistle'. But deeds which point to the authenticity of faith in Christ are a necessary counterpart to faith itself. In partnership they lead to the perfection of the believer. These deeds are similar to Jewish 'works of kindness', but instead of acts which justify the believer, for James, like Paul, they are pointers to the genuine character of the believer's faith, and are best seen as examples of the acts of mercy whose presence distinguishes the sheep from the goats.

A second theme in James is the importance of our words confirming our faith. Those who say one thing but do another, or who hear the Word of God but do not obey it (1:22), or whose praise is contaminated by cursing (3:6–12) all cast doubt upon the genuineness of faith. In this theme we hear clearly the heart of Jesus that our life should be transparent and consistent.

Thirdly, James is concerned that we should follow the way of wisdom from above, the gift of God who is generous and dependable (1:5). Such wisdom endures the trials of life, and follows a path of humility and peace – indispensable virtues for these Christians who seem at odds with one another. There is a deep pastoral concern which runs throughout the letter, coupled with practical teaching which gives the letter its enduring and immediate value.

So, join me on this journey of discovery: both of the meaning of this letter, and of ourselves and our relationship with God.

Paul Goodliff

Day 322 A joyful perspective on suffering

God is generous and gives us all we need to meet with him today through his Word and Spirit: simply ask him.

James 1:1–12

James' perspective on suffering is profoundly out of step with the Western world. Today we value ease of life and comfort, and avoid trials. This is the information age, but wisdom often seems in very short supply. His values are at odds with those of our new millennium, partly because he writes to the *Diaspora*, the scattered people of God who are not 'at ease' in the world, but mainly because he writes as God's servant.

Trials, whatever their character (v 2), have value in developing the spiritual backbone of endurance and test the quality of faith. In the development stages, new products are often exposed to extremes of heat and humidity so that the manufacturer can be confident of their quality and reliability. Trials test the reliability of faith and shape it to expect God's deliverance from an eternal perspective.

The theme of testing linked to the acquisition of practical wisdom is common in the Wisdom tradition. We need the wisdom that comes from heaven (3:17) that gives us a divine perspective on life's difficulties and prevents the unstable vacillation which robs us of reliability of purpose and peace of mind. This wisdom comes from a growing relationship of trust in God,[1] so that we develop the mind of Christ and see reality through his eyes.

Whatever those trials are like for you today you need God's wisdom to endure even when you may find them difficult to understand. A steady faith that survives the scorching heat of suffering seeks such wisdom without doubting God's generous faithfulness.

1 Prov 1:7

'Lord, give me the wisdom to understand life's trials from the perspective of your loving grace, so that my faith may grow to be mature. Amen.'

A life and death situation

Day 323

Every good gift has its origins in God. Today we rejoice in the gifts of life, the Spirit and the Scriptures as we turn prayerfully to Christ.

James 1:13–18 

The theme of 'trial' continues, and James considers its outcome and origin. Facing ill health, for instance, or misfortune, many blame God and ask the question 'why is God punishing me?' James, however, is quick to emphasise that it is never God who tempts us to evil (v 13), but rather he is the source of every good and perfect gift. Similarly, popular superstition attributes the chances of life to the stars and planets, but James refutes this astrological world view. It is the Father of the heavenly lights, whose purposes drive the pattern of history.

Such a God does not suffer from mood swings. He is the faithful one who can be trusted: 'There is no shadow of turning with Thee' to quote the hymn-writer Thomas Chisholm's majestic prose. He blesses those who endure the test with the crown of life, the gift of salvation. Here is no glib promise of deliverance from the testing of our faith in the present, but rather the confidence in God's faithfulness to save those who endure, having first brought faith to birth by the truth of the gospel (v 18).

Here lies the contrast that James is highlighting. Naturally we are tempted by our own, old sinful nature and desires. What Paul calls 'the flesh' is that bias towards sin, found in our old nature, and that desire gives birth to sin and results in death. By contrast, the work of God is not to tempt and deceive (v 16) but to strengthen us to endure. We are not victims of the stars, nor yet of a capricious deity, but have been chosen by the faithful God to be the first expression of his new creation.

'Lord, help me to stand when tested today, strong in your grace.'

The blessings of obedience

Day 324

As you approach today's reading pray for a clarity of self-knowledge, and an obedient heart to walk humbly with your God.

James 1:19–27

Yesterday we read of the word of truth as the seed which gives birth to life (v 18) and today James likens the Word of God to that which, once implanted, can save us. However, this is no automatic process, for the gestation of that saving Word needs to be nourished by practical obedience. We should respond to that word, found in the Scriptures, by being quick to listen (v 19) and ready to do what it says (v 22).

It is easy to get angry with the Scriptures and their uncompromising standards. 'What has that got to do with life today?' Read any newspaper or popular magazine and sooner or later you will encounter a writer who is passionately angry with the God revealed in Scripture. Perhaps the anger comes from an unwillingness to live a life free from the 'moral filth ... that is so prevalent' (v 21). Anger with God will also inevitably reveal itself in unhelpful anger against other people.

That is not to be the pattern for those who desire to live the righteous life God wants. There is a constant battle with our shabby old nature. No sinless perfection in this life for James, so rooted in the real world. There is, however, a constant attention to ourselves as mirrored in Scripture, and therein lies the secret of true freedom (v 25), what Eugene Peterson calls 'a long obedience in the same direction'.

There are signs to substantiate this way of blessing: a disciplined tongue and compassionate caring for those in need (vs 26,27) together with purity.

'Father, help me to see myself truly in the mirror of your Word, and save me from worthless religion.'

Glory in Christ, or in wealth

Day 325

Teaching about wealth can be extremely hard for rich, Western Christians to hear. Pray for a fresh understanding and commitment to this controversial message.

James 2:1–13 

James addresses a perennial problem in church life – favouritism. At its core is the judging of others on some other basis than who they are in Christ. The circumstances of James' illustration are two strangers to the church meeting. While the wealthy man is shown a seat of honour, the shabby person is made to stand at the back. The church is not immune from the cult of the celebrity or the fawning over powerful or wealthy individuals. This is, however, sinful, says James, because it looks on the outward appearance, while God looks on the heart, often seeing a level of faithful trust among the poor that the rich can find elusive (v 5).

Of course, there are certain times when individuals are rightly honoured. For example, reserving seats for specially invited guests or the young giving up their seats for the old is commendable. To institutionalise favouritism to the well connected, however, is wrong and directly contrary to the teaching of Jesus.[1] In Luke's 'sermon on the plain' it is simply 'the poor' who will inherit the kingdom of God.[2]

The issue concerns glory. In verse 1, the phrase 'our glorious Lord Jesus Christ' is notoriously difficult to translate. It is clumsy Greek, and generally James uses rather elegant prose, so there is a purpose behind its phraseology. The Christian faith is centred upon the glorious Christ, who nonetheless became poor[3] and who will return in his glory to be our judge (vs 12,13).

1 Luke 14:7–14
2 Luke 6:20
3 2 Cor 8:9

'If you, the Lord of Glory, became a servant of all, far be it from me to favour the rich and despise the poor. I am often blind to the location of true glory – faith in you. Help me to treat everyone with the same grace as you did.'

Day 326

Saving faith is never alone

Today's Scripture calls for action. Pray for a quiet attentiveness, not quietism but an expectant listening that issues in changed behaviour.

 *James 2:14–26*

Is it *sola fide*, faith alone, that saves, or are there works to be added, so that 'a person is justified by what he does and not by faith alone' (v 24)?

In reality there is little to choose between Paul and James. Both are writing polemically to address serious problems, and both exercise a preacher's licence to emphasise certain points. For Paul, the issue is whether works of the Law are necessary for salvation, to which he gives an emphatic 'no', for faith in Christ has superseded the old covenant.[1] Yet Paul often explores the practical outworking of such faith in care and concern for others, not as an optional extra, but as the very essence of what it means to live for Christ.[2] On the other hand, for James, the issue is one of people claiming to have faith, but demonstrating little by way of lifestyle to vindicate their claim. They are 'all mouth' and no action, and as we shall see tomorrow, what comes out of their mouths further undermines their claim to faith.

It is easy to cheapen saving faith and reduce it to 'the prayer of commitment'. The hallmarks of cheap faith are superficial good wishes (v 16) which actually do nothing, or a cold, cerebral assent to the existence of God, an intellectualisation of the faith, which is the mark of a religious dabbler (v 19).

Neither produce the blazing fire of compassion and action which changes the world. There needs to be faith and action together, for both the work of God's Spirit in a person's life and his response are equally inseparable.

1 Rom 3:28–31; Gal 3:21–24
2 Gal 5:6; 1 Thess 1:3
3 Rom 13:8–10

'Father, save me from a cheap, weak faith that turns away from human need with cold indifference. Rather, help me to love my neighbour as myself, and so fulfil Christ's law.'[3]

Praising or cursing?

Day 327

As I listen, Lord, I pray: 'Master speak to me today!'

James 3:1–12 

There is a great danger in the unrestrained words of religious teachers to whom special respect is due by virtue their position, but whose words may in fact be contrary to the Word of God. No wonder James has this warning to those, like myself, who 'presume to be teachers' (v 1) for our words can so easily lead God's people astray.

James has especially in mind speech in the public assembly, where faithfulness to God's truth is especially important. Both the bit in a horse's bridle and the rudder of a ship to govern the direction of a journey. The point is that these small implements of control seem insignificant. Our words may not seem much, but in church life it is just about all there is to control and govern its direction, and when the leader's words become 'unbridled' he is but a small step from becoming a false leader and sparking a flame that is destructive to many.

In case we excuse ourselves from the demands of this passage, remind yourself that wherever you are, whoever you are, you are proclaiming something by your words. People are quick to see the hypocrisy of claiming to worship God and then gossiping or bad-mouthing others (v 10) (See 1:19). Above all, let us remember the focus of James' message: 'It is an appeal to all who in the name of professed religion – whether Jewish, Christian or Islamic – measure the strength of their zeal for God by the intensity of their hatred of their fellow human beings on the West Bank or in Northern Ireland or in Beirut or in Tehran'.[1]

1 R P Martin, *James*, Word Biblical Commentary

'Lord, "Take my lips and let them be filled with messages from Thee"' (Frances Ridley Havergal, 1838–79).

Wisdom from above

Day 328

Pray that today's passage may act as a 'mirror' for your life.[1]

 *James 3:13–18*

Yesterday James warned against an unwise desire to be religious teachers (3:1). If wisdom, a common Old Testament theme, is the application of a relationship with God to the experiences of everyday life, then 'understanding' is more closely linked to the knowledge of what we might call 'an expert'. What should the person who has learnt how to live wisely and is skilled in understanding the world and the Scriptures do? We might be tempted to say 'look for opportunities to teach', but James is more circumspect. It is in the quality of daily life that wisdom and understanding is demonstrated (v 13). If earlier James has warned against being hearers of the Word only, here he warns against being proclaimers, but not doers, of it.

Perhaps he has in mind those who always want to be prominent, failing to admit that their true motivation is not concern for the truth, but envy of other's abilities, an ambition to be 'top dog' in the church. It will come as no surprise to learn that Christian leaders and preachers can be as envious and vain as anyone else, indeed, some would say these are one of the chief sins of the full-time Christian worker. The result in the church, as in their own life, will be anarchy (James uses the same root word as in 1:8, 'unstable') and a party spirit that arises from unchecked tongues, unbridled ambition and misdirected passion.[2]

By contrast, wise leaders will be transparent in life, conciliatory in the inevitable disagreements that arise, and kind. Above all they will be amongst those peacemakers whom Jesus says are blessed sons of God,[3] the fruit of whose ministry is conduct pleasing to God.

1 1:23–25
2 1 Cor 3:3–9; 14:33
3 Matt 5:9

Pray for those who lead the church, that the results of their ministry as peacemakers may be a harvest of right living.

The cure for quarrelling

Day 329

Allow God to search the innermost motives behind your attitudes towards others as you draw near to him today.

James 4:1–12 

In a previous reading we were contrasting two kinds of wisdom, and the two opposing sources; 'above' and 'below' are explored further now. Ranged on the side of earthly wisdom (3:15) are our own sinful cravings, the world of human society at enmity with God (v 4) and, behind that, the spiritual power of rebellion, the devil (v 7). But the wisdom that comes from heaven is from God himself, and begins with a humble, submissive and repentant heart (vs 7–10).

The description of the conflicts in these churches is graphic and violent. Is this just rhetoric, or were there actual murders being committed (v 2)? Whichever may be the case, it is clear that these churches were infected with a destructive spirit, and in the name of 'faith' people had suffered, not through cruel persecution, but through internal strife. The history of the church, even in our own day, is marred by such disturbing stories, and James points to the true source of such behaviour, where a misguided faith is worn to cloak an unsanctified heart (vs 3,8). Such believers are described as sinners and double-minded, like the doubters in 1:8.

It is easy to allow zeal for the truth to overwhelm compassion for others, especially those with whom we disagree strongly. The craving to be right, to impose our will or views on others, to have our own way, is contrary to the wisdom that comes from heaven, which is peace-loving (3:17). It is from just such a desire that we need to be cleansed (v 8) in case we slander our brothers and sisters, or worse. The first step towards our hearts being made pure is being honest, and humbling ourselves before God (vs 8,9).

Pray for a pure and compassionate heart towards everyone.

Your life in God's hand

Day 330

Open your plans for today to God's searching gaze.

James 4:13–17

In this passage we are presented with more strong language from James, who exhorts people whose arrogance is betrayed by their throwaway comments (v 13). As busy with their plans as the man in Jesus' parable who builds a bigger barn, not knowing that he would not live to see its use,[1] they fail to grasp how slender is the thread upon which their lives hang (v 14). Caught up by the sheer speed of life, are we ever like them?

This kind of planning can sometimes betray contempt for others and God. There is a tendency, due to arrogance, for the moneymaker to get rich at the expense of others. (How often a poorer congregation will be much more generous than a richer one.) The goodness of the generous giver is lacking, and all that is likely is the well meant wish (2:16), which is in fact contemptuous of God because it reveals no awareness of providence.

Instead there should be the attitude of heart which relies upon God's will (v 15) and is an expression of the wisdom that comes from heaven. An earlier generation of Christians often tried to avoid James' accusation regarding forward planning by placing the two letters DV (standing for *Deo valente*, 'God willing') after the announcement of a service or meeting. There can be an overemphasis on the attitude behind 'DV' – a Christian fatalism that is not ready to challenge injustice, or even encourage a healthy sense of ambition by which we seek to fulfil our potential as members of the human race, making good use of our gifts, abilities and opportunities. It is selfish ambition that James opposes, and that too readily finds a boastful arrogance its proud companion.

1 Luke 12:16–21

'Lord, give me your perspective on my gifts and potential, and by your gracious will develop them for your glory.'

The evil of exploitation

Day 331

The handling of wealth continues to be a blind spot for rich Christians. If that is you, pray that today you might hear the Word with fresh clarity and a ready obedience.

James 5:1–6 

Liberation theology developed in Latin America against the backdrop of a system of rural land ownership, *fazendas*, that concentrates wealth in the hands of a few powerful landowners, and keeps millions of people in poverty. A similar process was current in the Roman Empire in the first century when Seneca protested against the adding of 'estate to estate' by rapacious landowners in Italy, and throughout the Empire the poor were oppressed.

Taking the Old Testament prophets as his model, James denounces those rich farmers who refuse to pay adequate wages (v 4), among them the Jewish Sadducees. Their ears may be deaf to the cries of injustice, but God has heard them, and in the coming kingdom, it will be the poor who will be vindicated. Blind to their obligations to the poor, these rich people are probably not part of the Christian community.

Jesus identified himself with the poor, and James probably has his teaching from the Sermon on the Mount specially in mind.[1] The love of riches turns possessions into idols, to be tended and hoarded, insured and protected until they assume the place of worship that belongs to God alone. Where God is replaced by some 'other' all too soon the impact is felt socially in exploitation and, says James, ultimately in murder (v 6). Archbishop Oscar Romero, a courageous advocate for the poor of San Salvador, was murdered in his own cathedral, and his blood is testimony to the enduring truth of James' denunciation.

On whose side are we? In the West we have institutionalised the injustice of the global economy in our indifference to the poor. I wonder if James' words are not addressed to those of us who live in comparative luxury and pleasure?

1 Matt 6:19–34

'Lord, give me a heart like yours that cares for the poor.'

Wait patiently for his coming

Day 332

Meditate on this saying of Augustine of Hippo: 'Patience is the companion of wisdom'.

James 5:7–12

We live in a 'now' culture. Unwilling to wait until money has been saved before purchasing this or that, we buy on credit, run up debts or increase the bank overdraft. Earlier generations often regarded debt with horror. Today's attitude is linked to the postmodern shrinkage of time, with both the future's uncertainties and the past's memories condensed into the present moment.

For James, however, the present moment, with all its difficulties, is informed by both the past and the future. If we wish to take an example of how to keep going through the trials of life, look to the prophets (v 10) and specifically, Job (v 11) who suffered so much with patient endurance. In response to the question that so often cries for an answer in the midst of suffering, 'how long, O Lord, how long?', the answer is, 'until the coming of the Lord'. The horizon against which all suffering must be viewed is the *parousia*, the technical term that New Testament writers use for the second coming. The Lord will not be long (v 8b); stand firm no matter what! People in the world may quickly reach for the valium, engage the psychotherapist, write to the agony aunt. In contrast, the Christian is to face suffering with a courageous and gutsy patience, knowing that the Lord is both a Judge, coming to right wrongs (v 9), and a Saviour who will be merciful towards us (v 11).

It is not clear whether there is much continuity between verses 7 to 11 and 12. It is best to let the verse stand alone, and simply draw attention to the parallel teaching given by Jesus.[1] If our words are honest, oaths become superfluous, and James returns to his familiar theme of the abuse of words.

1 Matt 5:34–37

'Lord, put your strength into my heart, that whatever the present or future holds, I may persevere until the end.'

Ordinary people, powerful prayer

Day 333

Begin today by praising God and confessing your sin.

James 5:13–20 

The context in which the New Testament writers consider suffering is most frequently that of adversity arising from Christian witness in an alien world. So here, the 'trouble' of verse 13 is adversity, not to be directly equated with the sickness of verse 14. The response to both conditions is prayer. The general principle is that prayer should be offered for 'one another', even as sins should be confessed, and so addresses both the physical and spiritual health of the community.

It is not uncommon for the members of my church to call for the elders to pray for them when they face serious illness. I always approach those opportunities by reading verses 13 to 18, spending some time listening to the sick person, then to God in prayer and finally anointing with oil on the palms and forehead. There is some scholarly dispute over the significance of using oil. In the ancient world, oil was deemed to have medicinal value, but I think the emphasis here is upon prayer, not the application of the oil. Rather, it seems to have a sacramental significance, vividly reminding the person of the presence and grace of the Holy Spirit, the Lord and giver of life. It is through his power that health replaces sickness, through doctor's skill or surgeon's knife, or simply the gift of healing.

The emphasis is upon the One to whom prayer is offered, 'The Lord will raise him up' (v 15) rather than the special character of the one who prays: even mighty Elijah was human like us (vs 17,18). Here is James the pastor at his most concerned to see the sick healed, the wanderer restored (vs 19,20), and the happy praising God (v 13).

Spend some time praying for those you know who are sick or seem to have wandered from a strong faith in Jesus Christ.

Ten messages

For forty years Isaiah was a king's advisor, walking quietly in the corridors of power, and challenging knock-kneed or scheming monarchs and their courtiers to trust the Lord. He was called to his work at the time when a famous Assyrian king was building his empire into the largest and cruellest that western Asia had ever seen.

Chapters 13–27 of Isaiah form an interlude between Isaiah's prediction of the Assyrian crisis in chapters 1–12 and its onset, described in chapters 28–39. In chapters 13–23, ten messages, beginning with Babylon (13:1 – 14:27) and ending with Jerusalem and Tyre (chapters 22,23), spell out the meaning of God's worldwide sovereignty asserted in 11:1–16.

No doubt the world powers of the time thought of the Jewish god as just another puny, tribal deity – not much use against their infantry and cavalry! But Isaiah said the boot was on the other foot: the Lord had chosen Zion, and he would establish his kingdom there (14:32; 24:23; 25:6–8; 27:13).

Chapters 24–27 are a cantata of hope in which certain historical allusions decrease. It is as if Isaiah is lifted up very high to a point where he can see the whole world and the end of history. Through a series of saving judgements God destroys evil powers, heavenly and earthly, establishes his kingdom, swallows death the greatest enemy, gathers in his guests and begins his coronation banquet.

The twentieth century was the century of martyrs: more were killed for their faith than in any preceding century. It was also a century of titanic and ever more horrible wars. It is not always easy to believe that God is on the throne. But through the study of these chapters we can see that the perfect peace which Isaiah promises to the trusting person (26:3) does not indicate an absence of troubles. Rather, tempered in the fires of hardship and doubt, the believer's character becomes as strong as steel.

Howard Peskett

Babylon overthrown

Day 334

Wait quietly before the Lord for a few moments, even minutes, allowing all your senses to awake.

Isaiah 13:1–22 

First, focus your mind on a name (of a person, place or group) which, because of its notoriety, arouses in your heart terror and revulsion (eg Hitler; Stalin; Pol Pot). These are the reverberations of the word 'Babylon' in many Old Testament passages.

Now, allow your eyes to travel over the scenes of devastation depicted in this chapter: the bare hilltop (v 2); faces aflame with recognition and embarrassment (v 8); desolation such that human beings are like rare, Ophir gold (v 12); ruins so complete even a passing shepherd finds no use for them (v 20). Open your ears to the sounds you hear: uproar, wailing, the hyena's howl and the owl's hoot.

How can such a cruel day be described as the 'day of the LORD' (v 9)? What associations do the words 'overthrown like Sodom and Gomorrah' bring to mind (v 19)?

Isaiah sees a day when the Babylonian empire will be overwhelmed by a Medo-Persian one more powerful than itself. But his oracle is not aggravated jingoism. It is not human nationality that provokes divine judgement but sin, evil, arrogance, ruthlessness (vs 9–11).

Does your heart long for the day when wrongs will be made right? Do you feel heartsick at the judgement this justice entails? Elsewhere in the Old Testament, the psalmist calls the sky to sing, the sea to roar, the fields to dance and the woods to sing at the prospect of the Lord coming to judge the world.[1] If this idea seems strange to you, could it be because you are accustomed to the idea of having your rights protected and receiving justice, whereas in much of the world, for much of history, getting justice has been almost impossible?

1 Ps 96:11–13

Pause on the words 'Thy kingdom come' as you say the Lord's Prayer.

Swept into oblivion

Day 335

Hold in your heart, for some moments, a refugee community about whom you know something.

 *Isaiah 14:1–23*

At the centre of this Babylon oracle (13:1 – 14:23) is God's compassionate purposes for his people Israel (14:1,2). Their exile, suffering, turmoil and cruel bondage (v 3) will come to an end and the tables will be turned on their oppressors. This is because God will never give up his purposes for his people: his gifts and call are irrevocable.[1]

The identity of the particular king of Babylon in view is unimportant because the 'taunt-song' widens like a huge river estuary to include within its sweep all the world's and history's heaven-defying, human-hating aggressors. What happens to Babylon becomes a byword for what will happen to all those who defiantly resist the Almighty Lord.

Like many of the world's famous tales, the theme of this chapter is the reversal of fortunes. What pictures about the fate of this king who wanted to be a 'star' strike you most forcibly? Lebanon's trees celebrating the felling of predatory loggers (v 8)? The king's new bed – maggots for a mattress, worms for a duvet (v 11)? Buried under corpses, in an unmarked grave, unlamented, forgotten, childless (vs 14–21)? Swept into oblivion, like Babylon today (v 23)?

This passage nourishes the unquenchable hope in the human heart for justice; the cherished belief that one day, before or after death, wrongs will be righted, tyrants will receive their comeuppance, and the kingdoms of this world will become the kingdoms of our Lord who will reign for ever and ever.

1 Rom 11:29
2 2 Tim 1:10; Heb 2:14,15

Give thanks to him who, by dying, has destroyed the power of death, and freed us for ever from the fear of dying.[2]

Carpe diem: seize the day!

Day 336

Reflect on what, today, may most hinder your decision and your determination to trust in the Almighty Lord.

Isaiah 22:1–25 

The main theme of Isaiah's forty-year ministry was trusting God in troubled times.[1] His main disappointment was his people's repeated failure to do so. Amid the swirling currents and counter-currents of international events reflected in these chapters (13–23) the people's attitude is memorably summarised in verse 13b, in a saying which has become proverbial. 'You only live once,' said the singer Frank Sinatra 'and the way I live, once is enough'.

The city of Jerusalem was busy with rooftop parties (vs 1,2). Weapons, water and walls seemed more significant resources to them than having faith in God (vs 8–11)! (Hezekiah's tunnel from Gihon spring was a technological marvel of the time.[2]) Shebna, the royal major-domo, is preoccupied with his chariots and grand mausoleum (vs 15–19). Eliakim is a trusted royal official with robe, sash and key. Without him the royal tent would collapse (vs 21–24). Unfortunately he has become another sort of peg–loaded with all sorts of hangers-on! Finally the peg gives way (v 25).

The final horizon of these verses is well below Isaiah's horizon and ours. The day of the Lord (v 5), repeatedly foreshadowed in historical disasters, is still approaching, a day for final assessment, without partiality, of our lives and lifestyle. Am I just living it up? Am I preoccupied with my own grandiose projects? Are hangers-on distracting me from fulfilling the stewardship given to me by my Master? Am I just preoccupied with the here and now, with the busyness of life, with fulfilling people's expectations, with making the best of life's opportunities? What will the 'valley of vision' (v 5) reveal about my priorities?

1 Isa 7:9; 26:2; 30:15
2 2 Kings 20:20

There is a real sense in which we are to seize current opportunities and live life to the full. How do you distinguish this from selfish, God-ignoring hedonism?

Tired of Tyre

Day 337

Think for a moment what would you feel like if you went to your local supermarket and could find in it only goods produced in your own country.

Isaiah 23:1–18

Picture the commercial centre of a modern, world-famous city; here in their gravity-defying skyscrapers, surrounded by global communications systems, sit the leaders of multinational companies. Here, each day, decisions are made which affect the lives of millions of people. It is understandable why such centres are not hotbeds of humility. Tyre was a famous port, a centre for international trade (v 3). Isaiah pictures the story of Tyre's fall sending ripples to Cyprus, Egypt and farthest Spain. Deprived of Tyre's huge Tarshish ships, the Mediterranean is like a childless mother (v 4). The city's revelries are stilled; its ancient wealth and influence, extending even to king-making (v 8) have gone.

Historically, Tyre has been repeatedly subjugated: by Babylonians, Greeks, Saracens and Crusaders. Isaiah highlights the root cause: 'Who planned this?' (v 8) 'The Lord Almighty.' Why? Because of their pride in their glory and renown (v 9). Think about the roots of pride in your own heart. Ever since the Garden of Eden the tempter has subtly insinuated the thought, 'Abandon your creaturely dependence! You will be like God!'[1] Isaiah's lifelong message was not to trust in commercial and political alliances. 'Even in Cyprus you will find no rest,' he says (v 12). Where is rest to be found? In repentance and trust in the Almighty Lord.[2]

There is a surprising twist at the end of this story: the old prostitute will be completely transformed! All her earnings will be dedicated to the Lord; there will be a new spirit of generosity, and a new allegiance to the Lord's people (vs 15–18). It is a prospect which keeps all of us hopeful, trusting, persevering, even as we travel off to another day of business.[3]

1 Gen 3:4,5
2 Isa 30:15
3 See Rev 21:24–26

'Lord, have mercy on all of us who work in the marketplaces of the nations. Fill us with your truth and grace.'

A withered, waiting world

Day 338

What aspect of global pollution disturbs you most? What can be done about it?

Isaiah 24:1–23 

Kuwait's oilfields on fire. Boats stranded miles from the shore as the Aral Sea shrinks. Drought, smog, El Niño. We are gradually becoming more aware of how all the intricate systems of our planet interact and how we are the planet's most dangerous animals: predatory, greedy, territorial.

Chapters 24–27 of Isaiah cohere and we need to stand back and see the whole picture in which the glory of the Lord's mountain rises above a ruined world.[1] In your mind's eye, gather together the words in this chapter which describe a ruined world, 'globicide'. Isaiah's picture is a collage of images – is it war? Is it flood? Is it drought? Yes, all of these and more. No one will escape (v 2). The pubs will close, the lights will go out; 'all joy has reached its eventide' (v 11, NRSV).

Why is this so? Previous chapters have spelt out the indictment; here Isaiah briefly mentions indifference to truth, disobedience to God's laws, a broken covenant, in short, treachery (v 16) and rebellion (v 20). Behind the alcoholic revelry and indifferent pleasure-seeking loom spiritual powers (v 21) and, worst of all, divine judgement. In the face of our ecological crisis, we learn, we sing, we pray. What further responsibilities do we have for action?

The chapter's first word is 'Look!' and its last word is '... glory.' Where is the glory? We glimpse it from the sound of singing from east and west (vs 14–16). In the end evil powers, heavenly and earthly, will be imprisoned, and the Lord will begin his reign; the brightness of his glory will be such that the sun and moon pale by comparison.[2] There's a new world coming. For this reason Christians never, ever give up hope.

1 Isa 25:6–12
2 Isa 60:19; Rev 21:23
3 *Book of Common Prayer*

Silently meditate on the awesome promise: 'He will come again with glory to judge both the living and the dead'.[3]

No more tears!

Day 339

What are the dominating emotions of someone suffering from bereavement or loss?

Isaiah 25:1–12

Picture a harsh, drab housing estate or a business environment or a situation of war, oppression and persecution where a Christian or a small group of Christians have 'their backs against the wall'. Here, as in verses 2–5, the ruthless (mentioned three times) seem unassailable. How does the Christian find resources to persevere trustingly in such a situation? The chapter pictures the energy of the Christian hope, personal (v 1) and corporate (v 9), for liberation. How does hope work? By holding on to God's absolute trustworthiness, his foresight and long-considered plans for our good, and by rejoicing in his strong, saving hand (he will never let us go) hope can sustain us.

The ruthless will be stilled (vs 2–5). Picture the strength of the opposition, visualised as a storm, heat (think of Lawrence of Arabia) and a war song. Then picture the delivering judgement of God as refuge, shelter, shade and quiet. What is the hottest you have ever been and how did you find relief?

Death, the great 'swallower', will be swallowed (vs 6–8). On his mountain, Mount Zion,[1] God is preparing his coronation banquet, a popular theme of Jesus' parables: the richest food, the finest wines and the best meats (a luxury eaten only by the rich). Notice the emphasis that all are invited. There will be deathless joy for all. This is the Christian's hope that no trial can spoil.[2]

Arrogant godlessness will be levelled to the ground. Now, for the moment, those forces seem to be very strong. Isaiah pictures Moab struggling against drowning in a manure pit. The prospect gives him no pleasure as you can see from his tears in 16:9–11. Inextinguishable joy or irreparable loss: the same alternatives end his book.[3]

1 Isa 24:23
2 Rom 5:3–5
3 Isa 66:22,24

'Lord Jesus Christ, Son of the living God, have mercy on me.'

Perfect peace

Day 340

Picture the environment and state of mind which you might describe as 'perfect peace'.

Isaiah 26:1–21 

Paul pictures the peace of God guarding our hearts,[1] and here Isaiah pictures believers, the righteous, as safe because they are surrounded by the ramparts and walls of God's salvation. Does this mean we should dispense with locks and security devices? No, but our deepest and most lasting security, what verse 3 calls 'the peace of all peaces', lies in a frame of mind that is undeviatingly fixed on the Lord of Lords, the eternal Rock.

In case we should misunderstand this as meaning that we should 'try hard to be as peaceful as we can', verses 12 and 13 show us that it is the Lord who establishes our peace. He gives us energy to do his will, and only with his help can we keep his name and character at the forefront of our thoughts. Does this mean we just sit back and 'let him do it'? No, our responsibility is to let him become greater in our thoughts and trust. Hudson Taylor, the founder of the China Inland Mission, was known as a peaceful man through many turbulent trials and bereavements. His favourite hymn was: 'Jesus, I am resting, resting in the joy of what Thou art'. His resting was the fruit of his trusting.

Let your heart dwell on the metaphors in this chapter of God at work: his bulldozing destruction of the proud (v 5); his providential ordering of our path (v 7), not smoothing everything out for us, but bringing us to our destination; his revealing of his lovely name (v 8); his hand raised in saving power (v 11); and, most wonderful of all, his raising of his dead to everlasting joy (v 19).

1 Phil 4:7
2 Ps 30:4,5; John 16:33

For a little while trials will continue: tears endure for a night, but joy comes in the morning.[2]

Day 341

Harvest home!

Read Isaiah's earlier song about a vineyard in 5:1–7, a song of love and disappointment. Why so?

 *Isaiah 27:1–13*

Verse 2 begins, 'In that day! A lovely vineyard! Sing of it!' It is an excited vintage song. The vine harvest was a moment to treasure, and here there is a good harvest. We already know from the earlier song[1] that the site was well-chosen, the soil well-turned, the stones removed and pedigree vines planted. And now the Lord himself is watching, watering, guarding the vineyard day and night. Weeds, watch out for his flamethrower!

What is the result? Root, bud, blossom, fruit (v 6) fulfil every hope and desire; God's people fulfil their purpose; the whole world is filled with their fruit – this was God's purpose in choosing Abraham, their ancestor, in the first place.[2] What a garden we would have if every weed was transformed (v 4)!

How is this return to Eden to come about? Israel will be blown out of her land by the desert wind of God's anger (v 8). But he will not deal with her as with her foes (v 7). Her idolatry will be ended and her sins atoned for (v 9). But the fortified city (unnamed, for any God-defying people is signified) will be left destroyed and deserted, food for calves and firewood for foragers.

In the New Testament the same sifting and sorting process continues. We also hear the sound of the great trumpet[3] and see the sight of the great homecoming.[4] All other assessments are provisional; only that of the great Gardener, the great Shepherd, matters in the end.

1 Isa 5:1–7
2 Gen 12:1–3
3 Matt 24:31; 1 Thess 4:16
4 Rev 7:9

Pray the first four phrases of the Lord's Prayer, and then reflect on the question, 'What am I doing to bring about the fulfilment of these requests?'

Call to faith

The book Isaiah has left us is a collection of messages that come from different situations and are addressed to a variety of needs and circumstances. So, apart from the historical continuity of chapters 36–39, which are lifted almost verbatim from 2 Kings 18:13 – 20:19, the remaining chapters can appear strangely resistant to orderly patterns.

The particular object of Isaiah's criticism is the nation's lack of faith, not least in the way they are scurrying about seeking outside help from the likes of Egypt, instead of trusting the Lord who had promised to shield Jerusalem (31:5) from the invading forces of Assyria. Chapters 28–39 build on the theme of the necessity for committed faith. The call to faith implies the renunciation of all alternative forms of reliance.

Isaiah also wrote or spoke at a time in Judah's history when great hopes were placed in the person of the reigning king. Apart from Ahaz, the other three kings he served were God-fearing men and it was not difficult to look beyond the godly monarch to the heavenly King who would one day come to fulfil all the idealised expectations of the Davidic dynasty. So from time to time there emerges in his prophecies an unveiling of the future, when the hopes and prayers of many generations will be realised and 'a king will reign in righteousness' (see 32:1; and also 33:17), the Spirit of God will be poured out (32:15) and creation will be transformed (35:1).

Main themes

To summarise then, the recurrent strands which hold together the diverse material contained in chapters 28–39, are as follows: the primacy of faith; the holiness of God which is contrasted with the unholiness of his people; the Lord as the righteous King who judges but will also protect his city, Jerusalem; the assurance that God is in control of human history and that ultimately everything is in his hands.

John B Taylor

Don't deceive yourself

Day 342

When we are in a real fix, we have a remarkable ability to hoodwink ourselves into thinking that all is well. Be prepared to see how that applied to the people of Jerusalem.

 *Isaiah 28:1–29*

This difficult chapter begins with some words to Ephraim (Israel), which was about to go under before the might of Assyria (vs 1–6), and only then turns to a Jerusalem which was facing a similar danger. The good news is that the same Lord who is powerful and strong enough to obliterate Samaria (v 2) will be a source of strength to the defenders of Jerusalem (v 6). The bad news is that the holy city is peopled with debauched religious leaders who scoff at Isaiah's simplistic message of faith in God (v 9). Instead they boast that they have worked out how to avoid disaster by making a truce with death (v 15).

Isaiah does not tell us what the source of their vain confidence was, leaving the door open for us to speculate what it might have been (a secret treaty with Egypt?). We may also meditate on the stratagems we employ to avoid facing up to the unpleasant realities of death and judgement – belief in oblivion? A nice long sleep? Seeing our friends again? By contrast, read the Lord's way of helping us to cope with potential disasters in Isaiah 43:1.

Ironically, what the arrogant organisers of their own security systems fail to realise is that their sure foundation is not somewhere else, but there on the spot in Zion, God's dwelling place. He can be trusted to be their rock and defence,[1] but only if they accept that his requirements are justice and righteousness (v 17). The closing paragraph (vs 23–29) is a reassuring reminder that just as crops are gathered in different ways, so God treats people and cities differently.

1 Ps 71:3

There is no hiding place from God, only in him.

Living in a dream world

Day 343

He may have known nothing about virtual reality, but Isaiah was well aware that people could easily confuse their dreams with the real world. Are we in danger of doing the same?

Isaiah 29:1–24

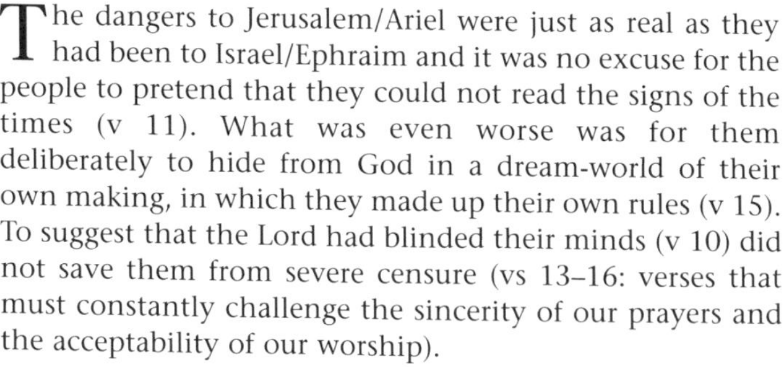

The dangers to Jerusalem/Ariel were just as real as they had been to Israel/Ephraim and it was no excuse for the people to pretend that they could not read the signs of the times (v 11). What was even worse was for them deliberately to hide from God in a dream-world of their own making, in which they made up their own rules (v 15). To suggest that the Lord had blinded their minds (v 10) did not save them from severe censure (vs 13–16: verses that must constantly challenge the sincerity of our prayers and the acceptability of our worship).

The contrast between the words we utter and what is going on in our hearts can be known only to God and to ourselves. It is much more profound than dealing simply with wandering thoughts (a difficult enough task at the best of times). It has to do with our deep-seated loyalties, our inner proximity to God. But there is hope for the deaf, the blind, the humble and the needy, if verses 18–21 are taken to heart. God is well-known for his ability to turn situations upside down (v 17), and he does it with people as well.[1]

History records that the threat to Jerusalem did in fact evaporate and that the forces of Assyria which were massed against her miraculously had to withdraw,[2] so this is no fairy tale. If God could do it then, we can be confident of his ability to do it today, and to turn certain disaster into astonishing victory.

1 Luke 1:51–53
2 Isa 37:36–38

As you pray, try to apply what you have learnt to the manner of your praying, the content of your worship and the vision you have of a God who works wonders.

Failure to consult

Day 344

The words in verse 2 'without consulting me' strike at the heart of Christian obedience. As you read today's passage, think of plans you have made and ask yourself if the cap fits.

 *Isaiah 30:1–18*

We can instinctively turn to verse 15 and cherish its words as our motto for today. They give a warm feeling of peace and security which we rightly value. But the closing phrase of the verse shows us that this is a rebuke more than a promise. Read the chapter again and pick out the criticisms, of which failure to consult the Lord before making plans is only one.

'Forming an alliance but not by my Spirit' (v 1) could relate as much to an unwise business partnership or an unequal marriage1 as to a national treaty. 'Children unwilling to listen to the LORD's instruction' (v 9) touches every aspect of Christian disobedience, including closing our eyes to the plain teaching of Scripture. Silencing the uncomfortable preachers and lionising the popular and reassuring ones (v 10) is the abiding temptation of the church that wants to be well thought of. And the plea to 'stop confronting us with the Holy One of Israel' (v 11) is the fair-weather Christian's way of wanting a religion which is strong on love (but is it really love?) but light on righteousness and holiness. That is why verse 15 includes the word 'repentance'.

But the reader is not being warned off, simply warned. The concluding verse (v 18) tells us what God longs for, that we should be the recipients of his grace and blessing. The way to that is that we wait – patiently, trustingly, eagerly – for him.

1 2 Cor 6:14

We have faced some searching questions today. Try to make time to give them further thought in case they vanish into thin air before you can address them properly.

Pictures of God

The Old Testament is rich in metaphors for God to enable its readers to pick up some clues as to his nature and character. How many pictures of God can you find in this passage?

Isaiah 30:19 – 31:9 

Although in verse 20 the Hebrew word for 'teachers' is plural, it goes with a singular verb, so commentators are divided as to whether the teachers are the prophets of Israel, coming out into the limelight and being listened to at last, or the 'Teacher-God' who will guide his people on the right path and keep them from straying. Either way, it is good news and further evidence of God's graciousness (v 18), for which we can be grateful every day of our lives. Every morning we can be sure that he has new mercies for us, and is at work in us to make us more like his Son.[1]

We are reminded in 31:4 of the old saying that God is like a lion. He does not need to be defended; just let loose! We who are often quick to spring to his defence should be reminded of his innate power. He is not fazed by the clamorous cries and insults of ancient Assyrians or modern anti-Christians.

A further beautiful simile is that of birds hovering overhead (31:5). Not menacing vultures, but rather parent birds protective of their nestlings on the ground. The use of the verb 'pass over' is a deliberate echo of the escape from Egypt, and the angel that protected those who sheltered under the blood of the Passover lamb, while at the same time he was executing judgement on the Egyptians.[2] Maybe there is a hint in 31:7 that the golden calf mentality had not entirely lost its hold on them.[3] Has it on you?

1 John 14:26; Isa 50:4
2 Exod 12:13
3 Exod 32:1-35
4 1 John 5:21

'Dear children, keep yourselves from idols.'[4]

A King will reign

Day 346

Let this chapter remind you that you are coming into the presence of the King of kings. He is supreme. You may like humbly to bow your head and your knee before him.

 *Isaiah 32:1–20*

The prophet consistently interweaves his predictions of a future messianic age with the strongest criticisms of current failings. He combines this with appeals to his hearers to change their ways and repent, which suggests that to a degree the blessings which are to come are contingent upon the people's response to his warnings. They may not simply sit back and let it happen.

The particular objects of his appeal are the fool, the scoundrel and the complacent women of Jerusalem (vs 6–13). God's judgement, directed here towards uncaring complacency, is a daunting aspect of his character to experience, as can be seen from the poetic imagery in verses 9–13. Think how complacency[1] might show up in your life.

But the focus of the chapter is on the King and his reign of righteousness and justice. Inevitably we see this in terms of the kingdom of God, heralded and brought about in the person of his Son, Jesus Christ. Human behaviour will be transformed and nobility will be the order of the day (v 8). The land too will be transformed, as the Spirit is poured out upon God's people in Pentecostal style (v 15), and they will dwell in safety and security. What is the difference between the messianic security of verse 18 and the complacent security of verse 9?

Verse 17 suggests that the righteousness of the kingdom will not be an end in itself, but a means to other beneficial ends. Meditate on the three qualities mentioned in this verse.

1 Amos 6:6
2 Matt 6:33

'… and all these things will be given to you as well …'[2]

A rich store of salvation

Day 347

Before reading this chapter, repeat verse 2 quietly as an opening prayer to prepare you for your meeting with God.

Isaiah 33:1–24 

The theme which unites the chapter is the welfare of Jerusalem, or Zion, and God's intentions for her people. An opening 'woe' upon the Assyrian invader is followed by a prayer (vs 2–4) and then a hymn of praise to the Lord (vs 5,6). From verse 10 onwards God speaks, declaring his intention to rise up and act in glory, and he calls upon Gentile and Jew 'far away' and 'near' (v 13) to acknowledge his power.

There follows what is called a 'Torah liturgy' (vs 14–16), in which the question is asked, and answered, what sort of worshippers God requires. The answer is a kind of ethical checklist, not as comprehensive as the Ten Commandments, but incorporating some rather surprising features which we would do well to take to heart. Read the similar lists to be found in the Psalms and in Micah.[1] We can also use the beatitudes[2] for this purpose, but the point to note is that any liturgy without a built-in moral requirement like this is sadly lacking. We still need these educational tools to remind us of what God looks for in those who come to him.

The promised king (v 17) is clearly more than merely human and the chapter reaches its crescendo in verses 20–22 as the Lord is acclaimed as king, judge and mighty one in what is a new Jerusalem. He will give his people a new stability and they will be enriched with a vast store of his blessings (v 6). As the heirs of the promises, we have access to these self-same benefits through Christ until the day when we too will see the King in his beauty.

1 Ps 15; 24; Micah 6:6–8
2 Matt 5:3–10

'The fear of the Lord is the key to this treasure' (v 6). In what area of your life is a greater reverence for the Lord called for?

Dark days ahead

Day 348

We come today to a chapter of unrelieved horror which most of us would prefer to leave out of our Bibles. But it is there and so we must read it with the solemnity it deserves.

 *Isaiah 34:1–17*

The theme of God's judgement runs throughout the Bible but it is usually interspersed with blue sky between the dark clouds. Here we have no such relief and our eyes have to stray to the chapters before and after to bring us a more comfortable message. It is helpful to note that:

- Judgement is a necessary consequence of justice, and a God of justice must condemn if he does not acquit or justify.
- God's actions are always marked by moral rectitude, even though the language used to describe them may all too easily be confused with the hatred and vindictiveness of human emotions.
- There is no antithesis between God's wrath and God's love, for the opposite of love is not wrath but hate.

But having said that, the context of this chapter is eschatological, presenting the outworking of human behaviour in a futuristic setting to serve as a warning to today's evildoers to change their ways before it is too late. And if that is to work, the prophets are not above using frightening language about the fate of the wicked. In order to pinpoint the reality of the message, Isaiah focuses on the age-old enemy, Edom (vs 5–15), as an illustration of what might be in the days to come.

We who are inclined to think that we are on God's side, or at least that he is on ours, could well pause and think more in the light of today's reading, of what it must be like to be on the wrong side of God. Loved, yes, but even love has to say 'no', as every parent knows.

Meditate on Psalm 90, especially verses 11 and 12.

On the journey home

Day 349

The Christian life is like a journey, but it is not a case of travelling for its own sake, pleasurable as that may be, but of making our way home to God.

Isaiah 35:1–10 

Just as Abraham was the archetypal pilgrim, going out into the unknown at the command of God, so Moses, and Joshua after him, typified the one who leads his people out of slavery and home to God. It is this latter theme on which today's reading was based. The return of the exiles to Jerusalem, the return of the Jews to their Promised Land and the Christian pilgrim's journey back to God have all drawn on this graphic symbolism.

Note the way in which Isaiah describes the landscape (v 1), the needs of the pilgrims (vs 3–6), the direction they take (v 10), and the limitations on those who travel that way (vs 8,9). To the Israelite the desert was what the earth reverted to when cultivation ceased; in another climate it could be the rainforest. For the pilgrim, God would reverse the natural order and make the barren surroundings lush and burst into bloom. Pilgrims need strength for the long walk and the encouragement of a Joshua.[1] It is not all plain sailing. But human limitations will be overcome (vs 5,6) and the body's ills will be healed (as Jesus sought specifically to do during his earthly ministry). The road however will not be for everyone (only the redeemed) – if this sounds hard it is only what Jesus said in the Sermon on the Mount.[2]

The joy of the Christian's journey is not in the scenery on the route so much as in the prospect of going home to Zion, the heavenly Jerusalem, where the One who has accompanied us on the journey will be there to welcome us into his nearer presence. That really is something to look forward to.

1 Josh 1:6–9
2 Matt 7:13,14

Every day is a day's march nearer home. Give praise for what is to come.

The voice of the serpent

Day 350

The tempter comes to us in a variety of guises, often human ones. Today, we can learn more of how to recognise some of his wiles. Pray that you will be on your guard against him.

 *Isaiah 36:1–22*

Hezekiah's chief officers seem powerless to respond to the challenges of the Assyrian Rabshakeh (AV, NRSV), a title for the field commander. He is an astute politician and deploys his arguments persuasively. They play down Hezekiah's confidence on four counts.

- Egypt has already proved a pathetic ally (v 6).
- The Lord has already seen his centres for worship denuded, and cannot be any too pleased – this would have appealed to those in Judah who were opposed to Hezekiah's centralist reforms.
- Judah did not have the manpower to mount any effective resistance even if horses were made available to them (v 8).
- In any case the Lord was on the side of the Assyrians (v 10).

No wonder the delegation tried to hush the commander's words and keep them from the people. However loyal they may have been to Hezekiah's policy of faith in the Lord's protection, these were plausible arguments. The enemy can usually find a sympathetic ear from every Adam and every Eve. 'Perhaps he has a point', we say to ourselves.

In his second speech, the enemy addressed the Jews in their own language (as he does with us) and adopted the direct approach – 'do not let … do not listen' (vs 15,16,18). The only response is equally direct – 'do not answer him' (v 21). But the attractions of peace with relocation (v 17) and the argument from recent history (vs 18–20) constitute a powerful plea to weakening resolves. The people of Jerusalem were not alone in finding that the fight of faith is one of the hardest battles that the believer has to struggle with.[1]

1 2 Cor 10:3–5; Eph 6:10–18; 1 Tim 6:12

When tempted, say nothing and go quickly to your King.

At your wit's end

Day 351

Here is an object lesson in what to do when you are in deep trouble. It is a reminder that the pathway of faith often leads to the very edges of despair.

Isaiah 37:1–20 

Hezekiah's distress was total. He had acted through intermediaries in his dealings with the Assyrian commander and he also did so with Isaiah, but the time would soon come when he had to wrestle with God alone. He had staked his all on following the words of the prophet, and now it was to Isaiah that he turned once again. He could have made up his own mind, but even kings need prophets and wise counsellors to turn to. So when you pray for rulers, pray too for those who advise them, on whom so much depends.

Isaiah focuses not on the need to maintain resolve but on the sheer blasphemy of the Assyrians' threats (v 6), which will guarantee that they receive their due reward. For a brief moment it seems as if the danger is going to recede, as the Assyrian army becomes otherwise engaged and the threat from Egypt is revived (v 8), but the uncompromising message from the Rabshakeh makes it abundantly clear what the Assyrian intentions are. Now Hezekiah has to face God himself.

Study his prayer, with its mode of address, its reverent acknowledgement of the one true creator, God, its appeal for help and its honesty as he faces what he is up against. Spreading the letter before the Lord and coming to him in complete reliance are also pointers to the way we should cope with comparable disasters.[1] Hezekiah needs more than a word from the Lord through Isaiah. He now needs that inner bolstering of the spirit which only a face to face encounter with the living God can give. There is no substitute for being alone in the Temple.

1 2 Chron 20:12

'Just as I am, ... I come, I come.'

Insolence rewarded

Day 352

It is always comforting to know that the Lord brings down the mighty and lifts up the humble and meek. Think about these words from the Magnificat while you read this chapter.[1]

Isaiah 37:21–38

Hezekiah might not have been given such an affirming word from the Lord through Isaiah, had he not laid this letter before God in the Temple and given himself to prayer and seeking the Lord. The casual and the confident miss out on God's promises, even if in other respects they are on God's side. Sennacherib on the other hand had sealed his fate with his high-handedness and arrogance which in turn had led him to blaspheme the God of Israel (vs 23,29). Supreme power carries with it dangerous temptations. We need to beware of flaunting our successes, as he did (vs 24,25). God is not impressed; after all, it is he who has allowed them to happen (v 26).

The treatment to be meted out to the Assyrian king (v 29) sounds brutal but is nothing less than the standard way in which the Assyrians dealt with their enemies. There is no evidence that Sennacherib met such a fate. The unexpected disaster that befell his army caused a sudden and most welcome lifting of the siege. An interesting confirmation of such a massive setback is attested from secular sources, in that Herodotus, the Greek historian, tells of a precipitate Assyrian withdrawal occasioned by a plague of mice! Could it have been a bubonic plague that caused the mayhem? The king's eventual death at the hands of his own sons, though happening twenty years later, was seen as the ultimate reward for his insolence.

Now contrast with this the friendly oracle to Hezekiah (vs 30–32). It has a messianic quality with its mention of a remnant and the zeal of the Lord. God's promise for his people is still security (taking root below)[2] and fruitfulness (bearing fruit above).[3]

1 Luke 1:46–55
2 Col 2:6
3 Col 1:10

'Because you have prayed to me...' (v 21).

A hero with feet of clay

Day 353

Hezekiah was undoubtedly a good king and a God-fearing man. But notice how his humanity breaks through and he lets himself down more than once. Meditate on 1 Cor 10:12.

Isaiah 38:1 – 39:8 

God is not averse to changing his mind, or apparently so, especially in response to prayer and penitence. Jonah was made to feel a fool and resented it,[1] but Isaiah takes it in his stride, concerned only with passing on his Lord's words. If God wants to rewrite history, that is his prerogative; just as he is free to transcend natural laws and work supernaturally. The miracle of the shadow on the stairway defies explanation, and that is as it should be.

After such a gracious answer to his prayers, Hezekiah's psalm (which is unique to Isaiah) has echoes of self-pity and self-centredness, but he ends up with faith and thankfulness. Verse 17 assumes that his penitence has brought him forgiveness of his sins as well as healing of his sickness, for there is often a link between the two, as Jesus indicated.[2]

There is clearly a story behind the goodwill visit of the messengers from the Babylonian king. He was not simply enquiring after Hezekiah's health, but pressing for an anti-Assyrian alliance and he was shown too much sympathy for safety. God's intention was that Israel should trust in him, not in powerful friends, and condemnation came fast. In a strange irony, it would be another king of Babylon who a hundred or more years on would be the agent for God's judgement on Hezekiah's foolish pride.

1 Jonah 4:1–5
2 Mark 2:5–10

The sheer selfishness of Hezekiah's closing words shows up the glib piety of his previous comment (39:8). Are we ever like him?

Sound the alert, celebrate grace

Day 354

'O my people … if you would but listen to me' (v 8). 'Holy Spirit of God, help me now to listen deeply to your Word.'

 *Psalm 81*

If you would but listen to me …: perhaps some of you identify with my experience of finding it hard to listen to the Lord during holidays and weekends, while from Monday to Friday it seems essential for survival! From now on perhaps it will be possible to spend some leisurely Sunday time to allow this poetry to seep deeply into us, opening us to new possibilities of living responsively to God.

Psalm 81 is probably a song for the Feast of Tabernacles, the cheerful yearly autumn camp out of the Jewish people. It takes them back in memory to the time of their precarious desert freedom from the forced labour, racism and, yes, the delicious diet of Egypt.[1] Imagine the psalm sung aloud, full orchestra and massed choirs (vs 1–3), in celebration of the exodus, God's startling, unfathomable expression of grace (v 5). But after the tents of green branches are taken down for another year, well… it's back to business as usual, to the many tangible, safer alternatives to God (vs 8,9), to dogged, joyless self-sufficiency (v 12).

We're here too in this poem. We regularly commemorate the great act of God which brought us freedom. And instead of living responsively to him (vs 8,11,13), we tone down the vast truths of Jesus' cross into something manageable, undemanding.[2] Only emergencies make us serious about the Lord (v 7).

So we mostly live skimpy, risk-free lives, without passion towards the God who covenants to give us life at its best, sustaining goodness in the hardest places (vs 10,16).

1 Exod 1:9–14; Num 11:4,5
2 Heb 12:2,3; 1 Pet 4:1,2
3 Hag 1:5,7

'Give careful thought to your ways. You have planted much, but have harvested little. You drink, but never have your fill … This is what the Lord Almighty says, "Give careful thought to your ways".'[3]

What does the Lord require of you?[1]

Day 355

'Lord, your Word is open before me. Help me, by your Spirit, to be open to you, willing for you to change me.'

Psalm 82 

I recently enjoyed a radio interview with Albie Sachs which was interspersed with his favourite music. Justice Sachs became a senior judge in South Africa. In the years of struggle against apartheid he was one of the few white members of the African National Congress (ANC). A record stretch of solitary confinement was followed by terrible injuries in a car bomb attack in Mozambique. As a legislator in the new South Africa, Sachs has chosen to renounce membership of the ANC for the sake of credible impartiality. In several trials his judgements have benefited people who formerly hated and harassed him.

Sachs is no orthodox believer. But I found his exacting commitment to the practice of justice and mercy probing my response to this poet's vision. In the court above all courts, powerful 'gods' of civil society face the charges of the Judge of all the earth (vs 1,6,8).[2] They have overseen the wholesale distortion and corruption of justice (v 2); they are indifferent to the 'non-entities' of society, those with no one to stand for them (vs 3–5).

There are many ways to 'bow before the text' (the writer Walter Brueggemann's phrase) of this psalm: in serious reflection on, and confession of, our own partialities and prejudices; in practical commitment to act against injustice and practise mercy; in informed intercession for ourselves or others as political leaders, lawmakers, those responsible for exercising justice in ever more complex situations; in indignant prayer on behalf of the weak, poor, parentless, oppressed. Be open for prayer to lead to involvement.

1 Mic 6:8
2 Amos 5:10–12; Jer 7:1–7
3 Eugene Peterson, *Earth and Altar*, IVP

'The test of our work is not ... profit ... or ... status ... but its effects in creation. Are persons impoverished? Is the land diminished? ... Is the world less or more because of my work?'[3]

Day 356

Whose are the world's pasturelands?

'Lord, truth incarnate, let thy Spirit overshadow us in reading thy Word, that learning of thee with honest hearts we may be rooted and built up in thee.'[1]

 *Psalm 83*

What can this seemingly angry, outspoken song say to us today? It's so local, so specific to one people's history (vs 5–11). Two insights may help us, one Christian, one secular.

In *Interpretation and Obedience*,[2] American scholar Walter Brueggemann reflects on what he understands as the relevance for his community today of the Old Testament theme of land and the reiterated question of its ownership: 'We are deeply enmeshed in the dispute over land, for our economy and foreign policy largely concern the cynical management of other peoples' land'.

Brueggemann's critique of his own society surely applies wherever human power structures operate autonomously, seeking to stamp out evidence of God (v 4). In the experience of Israel, the God-denying power of urban Egypt had been replaced by the God-denying Caananite confederations (vs 6,7) and the looming threat of the Assyrian superpower (v 8). While Israel's confession was 'The earth is the LORD's, and everything in it' (Ps 24:1), the surrounding nations claimed the land as theirs (v 12).[3] The Old Testament prophets record the struggle to retain among God's people an utterly distinctive understanding of God's lordship of all.[4]

Some rare people still treat the world's pasturelands as God's. Brueggemann tells of the Christian manager of a bank in a farming community who extends the mortgages, interest-free, of farmers struggling to keep going. 'The banker was practising the jubilee, though he did not call it that'. Meanwhile UK economist Will Hutton writes in the Guardian newspaper of the 'biblical proof and moral imagination of religion' as inspiration for the Jubilee 2000 campaign which seeks the cancellation of unrepayable debt by the world's poorest countries.

1 William Bright, 1824–1901
2 Augsburg Fortress, 1991
3 Gen 47:20; Ezek 29:3,9
4 Mic 2:1–5; Isa 5:8–12

'Lord, wake us to the opportunities of living "jubilee" lives that reflect your grace and generosity.'

Dwelling place, pilgrim heart

***'Prayer is not asking for what you think you want but asking to be changed in ways you can't imagine.'*[1]**

Psalm 84 

As you reflect on Kathleen Norris's definition of prayer above, you might choose to pray through this psalm before you read on.

In his thoughtful reflections on the psalms, Eugene Peterson points out that these poems constitute one half of a dialogue, that the psalms are 'answering prayer', expressing what the one who prays knows and is discovering daily about the God with whom he talks. He spreads out his experience of life in the light of what God has already said to him. 'What is essential in prayer is not that we learn to express ourselves, but that we learn to answer God. The psalms show us how to answer.'[2]

It seems to me that this psalm answers 'yes' to God's invitation to us to 'dwell' – to spend time – in his presence (anonymously, not up on the platform, v 10), experience life-bringing intimacy (vs 2,3) and learn ever-new praise (v 4).

The psalm also says 'yes' to God's invitation to walk the pilgrim road with him, trust him in the dry places and find he transforms them into oases of refreshment (vs 5–7).

The psalm says 'yes' to a paradoxical invitation: stay and dwell; get on the pilgrim road.[3] We might need to battle with our preference!

1 Kathleen Norris, *Amazing Grace*, Lion
2 *Answering God*, Harper and Row
3 Heb 11:8–10; Luke 4:42–44
4 Sheila Cassidy, *Prayer for Pilgrims*, HarperCollins

'All powerful God, look in your love upon us, your pilgrim people, as we struggle towards you. Be our food for the journey, our wine for rejoicing, our light in the darkness, and our welcome at the journey's end.'[4]

God of fidelity

Day 358

The Lord invites you as you are. Worship him, bring him your feelings and needs. Ask his Holy Spirit to help you understand and respond to what you read.

Psalm 85

I'll always remember a reading of this psalm at a conference on peacemaking and reconciliation. Men and women from Rwanda, Northern Ireland, Bosnia and Croatia described their struggles with prejudice, hatred and fear and their commitment to seeking reconciliation in their societies. One Christian leader from Belfast spoke passionately of how easily we domesticate God's requirement to love our neighbour as ourselves, how glibly we read a psalm like this, filtering out its true demands on us.

He asked four groups of people to act out the four values of verse 10: love (or mercy in some translations) and truth (or faithfulness), righteousness (or justice) and peace. If justice and truth were to take priority in any peace process (as many who had suffered violence and terror wished), how did mercy and peace feel? Conversely, justice and truth expressed their sense of betrayal if mercy and peace were to stand on equal ground with them. Participants expressed their anger and frustration, wept their pain, as they struggled to give way to a seemingly opposing value in order to reach reconciliation rooted in all the qualities God values.

'Restore us again ... revive us again' (vs 4,6), can be prayers for our community and for ourselves in relationship with God. This poem works in our imaginations to show us the possibilities of life centred on God's priorities (v 8), not a life of pragmatic balancing acts, but one in which seemingly opposing values can meet in creative resolution (v 12).[1] 'The God of fidelity continues to open what the world regards as closed.'[2]

1 Isa 42:8,9; 2 Cor 5:17; Rev 21:5
2 Walter Brueggemann *Deep Memory, Exuberant Hope*, Augsburg Fortress

'Lord, you know where and how our lives need you to open up, restore and revive. We trust you to "give what is good" (v 12); keep us from foolish ways.'

'Give me an undivided heart ...!'

Day 359

'A phrase ... heard often ... will one day come with the urgency of a telegram and the name on the envelope is no longer "Everyman" but "You".'[1]

Psalm 86 

Hear, O LORD, and answer me, for I am poor and needy' (v 1): the LORD's delight in those who are willing to be teachable (v 11) and unashamedly dependent on him (v 7), is a powerful theme in Scripture.[2] This way, it seems, lies wholeness, the coming together of our lives into harmony under God's lordship.

This psalm seems to me to be an expression of longing for true wholeness. It gives us words for our quest for authentic humility. The magnetic north of the poet's compass is not his meagre self (v 1) but the loving, merciful, joy-bringing, responsive God he is daily learning to trust (vs 2–7).

Awareness of our lack of wholeness, our divided and proud heart, comes about in different ways: an encounter with someone whose deeply attractive integrity shows up our shabby ambiguities; or some crisis (vs 13,14,16) which pushes us to take stock of our position and direction (v 11) and – perhaps – return again to the certain truth of God's nature (v 15).[3]

The French Christian thinker Paul Ricoeur has written on the transforming power of Jesus' parables that 'it is in the heart of imagination that we let the Event happen, before we may convert our heart and tighten our will'.[4] I suggest we let our imaginations work on the image of the 'undivided heart' and the dimensions of the 'Event' of wholeness to which we still need to be converted.

1 Sheila Cassidy, *Prayer for Pilgrims*, Harper Collins
2 2 Kings 5:9–15; 2 Cor 12:7–10
3 Exod 34:6,7; Luke 15:13–20
4 *The Philosophy of Paul Ricoeur*, Beacon Press
5 Gal 5:22,23

'The fruit of the Spirit is love, joy, peace, patience, kindness, goodness, faithfulness, gentleness and self-control.'[5]

Cosmopolitan Zion

Day 360

'Lord, we become dulled to your apparently familiar Word. Alert us to your surprising ways, and deal with our fears of them. Amen.'

 *Psalm 87*

I wonder how the first hearers of this psalm responded when they heard, 'The LORD loves the gates of Zion'? Or 'Glorious things are said of you, O city of God'? 'Amen! Yes, indeed! That's what we like to hear'? But how about 'Rahab ... Babylon ... Philistia ... Tyre ... Cush ... born in Zion ... born in Zion'? Indrawn breath, disapproving frowns? The ancient enemies, enslavers and marauders, now incredibly – offensively – listed among God's own people?

Scholars describe this psalm as one of the most jumbled and disordered texts in the Old Testament. Eugene Peterson suggests that this chaos is not the result of poor transmission or copying, but 'honest, awkwardly spontaneous prayer in the presence of an excess of meaning, a surplus of reality'.[1] The poet seems overwhelmed at the revelation of Zion, Jerusalem, as the place of new birth, of God's welcome, for all peoples. At its best, there was a gritty authenticity about Israel's lifestyle that drew people from the surrounding nations to worship the living God. We keep meeting them in the Bible.[2]

Perhaps some of the poet's original listeners shared his stammering delight at God's surprising ways. I'm sure others felt uneasy about these 'outsiders'. As we do today, we who are supposedly biblical Christians, as war and economic turmoil uproot distant people – from Rwanda, Bosnia, Somalia, Uganda, East Timor, Indonesia – and make them our neighbours. We find that many are passionate God-lovers, evangelists in places the Western church has given up on. But somehow God's new ways of reaching the world with his love don't suit us. They're untidy and alien, so *different*...[3]

So... will we choose to make music together, or shall we stay uneasily outside the vitality of our common life in God (v 7)?

1 Josh 2:1,8–13; Ruth 1:4,16,17; Isa 44:28; Acts 2:5–12
2 *Earth and Altar*, IVP
3 Acts 10:9–15

'Lord, help us not to prescribe the ways in which we're prepared to recognise your work.'

Song from the lowest pit

Day 361

***'O God, early in the morning I cry to you. Help me to pray and to concentrate my thoughts on you. I cannot do this alone. In me there is darkness.'*[1]**

Psalm 88 

TS Eliot once wrote (in *The Sacred Wood*), 'Poetry is not a turning loose of emotion, but an escape from emotion ... But of course only those who have ... emotions know what it means to want to escape from these things'. This anguished song expresses the darkest, minor chords of human experience. The faithful record gives words to countless people who find themselves in the dark pits of life – of bereavement, unemployment, illness, inexplicable depression, injustice, exile, loneliness, misunderstanding, exhausted old age, violence, prison, homelessness, loss of direction. For some of us today, these will be words we need to pray.

There is no mandate in Scripture for a stiff upper lip in suffering.[2] God's Word invites us to answer the God who spoke to us first of his saving activity in our lives (v 1). But – at least in the circumstances of this particular psalm – that's *all* we can be sure of, and that he listens to us, sometimes (vs 2,5).

I wonder how many of us have talked to the Lord with the raw emotional truth of this psalm. Listen again: you've forgotten me, God; *you* are responsible for this pit experience; you've overpowered, not empowered, me; you've made sure I'm abandoned; you deliberately reject me; you bring terror – and it's a long-term experience; 'darkness is my closest friend'. In many of our churches, anyone praying like this would be written off as a spiritual failure.

There are times when the *only* authentic communication with God must be a 'psalm of disorientation'. The expression to God of disorientation is itself an act of trust; it may help to bring reorientation.

1 Dietrich Bonhoeffer, 1906–45
2 Jer 15:15–18; Mark 14:33,34,36

To what extent do the authenticity and depth of our praying match the realities of our daily lives?

Claims for God, assaults on God

Day 362

'It is when we refuse to recognise and welcome tensions which are life-giving that we fall a prey to tensions which are death-dealing.'[1]

 *Psalm 89*

Yesterday we reflected on the almost unrelieved distress of Psalm 88 and recognised it as encouraging us to be real with God. Psalm 89, which closes the third book of the collection of Psalms, is a more ambiguous and tension-filled reflection on the relationship between God and us.

Up to verse 37 this hymn is a full-throated celebration of the covenant faithfulness of God to King David and his successors. The theme word in Hebrew is *hesed*: steadfast, faithful love or mercy (vs 1,2,24,28). Up to verse 37, this is a psalm Onesimus might happily have turned into praise as Philemon welcomed him back to the transformed relationship Paul proposed in yesterday's reading: 'Yes, Lord, your faithful love, your *hesed*, has indeed been with me, my Father, my God, the Rock my Saviour' (vs 24,26).

But suppose Philemon rejected Paul's proposal? The abrupt shift of verse 38 is the kind of bump in the terrain of Scripture which we often seek to smooth over. It makes us uneasy. But yes, this is an expression of deep suspicion, of complaint towards God and the promises he has made, of hurt at being abandoned (vs 50,51). This is the response to God that the exile provoked[2] and the crucifixion provoked[3] and that the 'pit' experiences of our own lives will provoke. 'It is an act of faith to enter into the suffering that gives the lie to theological triumphalism. In such a practice that does not need to protect God and does not fear to enter into the texts that voice protest, we may become more responsible … people who know about strength and weakness, about new life out of death'.[4]

1 Harry Williams, *Tensions*
2 Ruth 1:13,20,21
3 Matt 16:21–23; 1 Cor 1:18,23
4 Brueggemann *Deep Memory, Exuberant Hope*, Augsburg

'Lord, forgive us when we do not recognise your presence and activity when we experience brokenness and seeming failure.'

To gain a heart of wisdom

Day 363

'Grant to me, above all things to be desired, that my heart may find its peace in Thee. Thou art the peace of my heart – out of Thee all things are hard and unquiet.'[1]

Psalm 90 

When my mother was terminally ill, a friend sent me these words to pray for her: 'God keep you safe until the word of your life is fully spoken'. This psalm seems to me to be the prayer of a person who longs that the word of her life before God will truly be 'fully spoken'.

I suggest that we can speak this psalm again to God as a review of our lives, or of this past year – a looking back and a looking forward. Let your imagination work all the time with the idea of a 'fully spoken' life.

Verses 1 and 2 help us reflect, with joy and pain, on our 'generations', our families and their relationship with God – recent or long-standing. Whatever your story here, remember 'from everlasting to everlasting you are God'.

Verses 3–6 keep us humble about God's perspectives. I'm writing this on the first day of 2001 and this psalm tells me all the human enterprise of the past thousand years is a mere one circle of the clock to God.

Verses 7–12 alert us to the other side of this truth, the worth God gives each day[2] and the choice we face to let wisdom or foolishness shape our life.

Verses 13–17 encourage us to review our experience of God – his compassion, the fulfilment of his love, times when he has seemed inactive in our lives, has even 'afflicted' us. And what 'work of your hands' would you ask him to establish as you look forward to a new year?

1 Thomas à Kempis
2 Luke 12:6,7; Ps 139:1–4,15,16
3 Kathleen Norris, *The Cloister Walk*, Lion

'One rides the psalms like a river current, noticing in passing how alien these ancient and sophisticated texts are, and how utterly accessible.'[3]

True to experience?

Day 364

***'Father of our Lord Jesus Christ, grant us to be grounded and settled in thy truth by the coming down of the Holy Spirit into our hearts.'*[1]**

 *Psalm 91*

Philip Yancey's book *The Bible Jesus Read* contains a thoughtful chapter on the Psalms. Yancey talks of his struggle to move beyond an impoverished experience of this literature as a 'spiritual medicine cabinet' to be dipped into for biblical pills to alleviate the need of the moment. Reading like this led to boredom and cynicism. It was when he stopped trying to systematise the psalms and read them more as a spiritual journal that they began to resonate with him. A single page in my own journal would lead you to all kinds of odd conclusions about my spiritual state! Similarly, a psalm opens to us a journal page reflecting a particular mood of faith. Some psalms offer glimpses of faith hanging on by its fingernails, as we have seen.

Yancey cites Neil Plantinga's reading of Psalm 91: 'With a kind of quiet amazement, the psalmist bears witness that under the wings of God good things happen to bad people. You need another psalm or two to fill in the picture, to cry out that under those same wings bad things sometimes happen to good people'.

The Russian dissident Anatoly Shcharansky spent thirteen years in prison for his attempts to emigrate to Israel. His most treasured possession was a little book of the Psalms in Hebrew. His wife spoke of his experience: 'locked alone with the Psalms ... Anatoly found expression for his innermost feelings in the outpourings ... of thousands of years ago'. Those outpourings include both this psalm ('under his wings you will find refuge ... no harm will befall you') and Psalm 88 ('you have put me in the lowest pit').

1 St Clement of Rome, c 95 AD
2 James 1:17

'Every good and perfect gift is from above, coming down from the Father of the heavenly lights, who does not change like shifting shadows.'[2]

Songs of praise

'It is good … to proclaim your love in the morning and your faithfulness at night' (vs 1,2).

Psalm 92 

I'm always taken by surprise that the music of Christmas praise never seems to grow stale or routine. Somehow despite our familiarity with it, it is always refreshing. There's even Christmas music in today's psalm.

'Glory to God in the highest,' sang the angels soaring above the Bethlehem fields, to the terrified and then exalted shepherds. They returned to their work making music to the name of the Most High for his love and faithfulness (vs 1–3).[1]

The wise men sensed deep joy at the work of the Lord's hands – the unfailing guiding star leading them to worship in the stable (v 4; Matt 2:9–11).

Mary's quiet heart folded away the extraordinary comings and goings in the stable and pondered: 'How great are your works, O Lord, how profound your thoughts' (v 5; Luke 1:46–55; 2:19).

Foolish and fearful Herod thrashed about in a futile orgy of destruction. He passes from history, remembered mostly for his suspicions and murderous outbursts (vs 6,7; Matt 2:16–18).

Old Zechariah, speech restored, boldly spoke of imminent redemption, 'a horn of salvation', rescue from ancient enemies and a fear-free future (vs 9,11).[2]

And two more very elderly people welcomed the Saviour: 'righteous and devout' Simeon, and Anna the prophetess who 'worshipped night and day, fasting and praying'.[3] Verses 12–15 might have been written specifically about the older generation whom Luke describes with such affection and respect in the Christmas story!

1 Luke 2:13,20
2 Luke 1:67–79; compare Ps 92:9–11
3 Luke 2:25–38

'Lord, help us to enter deeply into the great love and faithfulness which sent your Son to share our humanity and be our Saviour.'